Praise for *Blood of Tyrants*

"Gripping. Relevant. Revolutionary. This page-turning historical thriller is packed with fresh factual narratives that draw the reader into the scenes to show how the United States earned its stripes. The wisdom of 1776 was never more crucial than today."

—Amy Chua, Yale Law School professor and best-selling author of *Battle Hymn of the Tiger Mother*

"A fresh and stimulating history of the American Revolution . . ."

—James McPherson, Pulitzer Prize–winning author of *Battle Cry of Freedom*

"[T]here is almost no tale told of the Revolution that does not find its way into *Blood of Tyrants*, provided it is juicy enough."

—*Wall Street Journal*

"A timely, insightful, and much-needed reminder why America does best at war when it honors rather than erodes its founding principles."

—Victor Davis Hanson, senior fellow in classics and military history at the Hoover Institution and author of *A War Like No Other*

"[A] fresh new perspective . . . . Beirne's genealogical and personal interest in history, politics and the military makes for an enjoyable read."

—*Washington Times*

"*Blood of Tyrants* strips away the fantasy and lays bare the violence and political intrigue needed for the American Revolution to succeed. Lurid, horrifying, scandalous. I could not put it down."

—William Eskridge Jr., Yale Law School professor and author of *Republic of Statutes*

T0265964

"In this fast-paced narrative, Logan Beirne vividly explains something every American should know, but which few of us really understand."

—Jack Rakove, Stanford University professor and Pulitzer Prize–winning author of *Original Meanings: Politics and Ideas in the Making of the Constitution*

"Anyone interested in the original meaning of the Constitution, or America's revolutionary struggle generally, should read this riveting and informative account."

—*Weekly Standard*

"Those who want an unvarnished account of how a great leader handled nasty and messy problems of war: prepare to be shocked, amazed, and educated."

—Hon. Michael W. McConnell, Stanford Law School professor, director of the Stanford Constitutional Law Center, and former federal judge, U.S. Court of Appeals for the Tenth Circuit

"There was more to the founders than noble sentiments and fine words—they were revolutionaries, who fought for and won America's freedom on bloody battlefields. *Blood of Tyrants* tells this gritty story smartly and compellingly —and plumbs it for practical lessons for the toughest issues of our times."

—Adam Cohen, research scholar at Yale Law School and author of *Nothing to Fear: FDR's Inner Circle and the Hundred Days That Created America*

"Beirne's narrative pulls the reader directly into the scenes, filling the void in our understanding of the presidency and our ingenious Founders' pragmatic approach to issues we still face today."

—*Huntington News*

"Future roads of national promise rest on proven paths of the past. Colby Award winner, Logan Beirne, points us on our way by strikingly using Washington's guideposts. Tomorrow is yesterday."

—John Borling, Major General (Ret.), U.S. Air Force, 6.5-year POW in Hanoi, and author of *Taps on the Walls*

BLOOD OF TYRANTS

BLOOD
of
TYRANTS

GEORGE WASHINGTON &
THE FORGING OF THE PRESIDENCY

LOGAN BEIRNE

Encounter Books New York • London

First American edition published in 2013 by Encounter Books,
an activity of Encounter for Culture and Education, Inc.,
a nonprofit, tax exempt corporation.
Encounter Books website address: www.encounterbooks.com

Manufactured in the United States and printed on
acid-free paper. The paper used in this publication meets
the minimum requirements of ANSI/NISO Z39.48-1992
(R 1997) (*Permanence of Paper*).

First paperback edition published in 2014.
Paperback edition ISBN: 978-1-59403-640-8

THE LIBRARY OF CONGRESS HAS CATALOGUED
THE HARDCOVER EDITION AS FOLLOWS:
Beirne, Logan
Blood of tyrants: George Washington & the forging of the presidency / Logan Beirne.
p. cm.
Includes bibliographical references and index.
ISBN 978-1-59403-640-8 (hbk.: alk. paper)—ISBN 978-1-59403-653-8 (ebook)
1. United States—History—Revolution, 1775-1783—Influence. 2. United States—
History—Revolution, 1775-1783—Campaigns. 3. Washington, George, 1732-1799—Influence.
4. Washington, George, 1732-1799—Military leadership. 5. Strategic culture—United States—History.
6. Civil-military relations—United States—History. 7. Presidents—United States—Biography.
8. Generals—United States—Biography. 9. United States—Politics and government—1775-1783.
10. United States—Politics and government—1783-1809. I. Title.
E209.B37 2013
973.3—dc23

2012038961

Title Page: The Battle of Princeton. Photograph of painting by John Trumbull. Springfield, Mass.: Taber-Prang Art Co., c1900. Library of Congress Prints and Photographs Division, LC-USZ62-469. *Part I*: Scene at the Signing of the Constitution of the United States. Painting by Howard Chandler Christy, 1940. Collection of the U.S. House of Representatives. *Part II*: The Battle of Bunker Hill. Copy of engraving by James Mitan after John Trumbull, 1808. National Archives, 148-GW-454 (George Washington Bicentennial Commission). *Part III*: Province of New York, 1767. Created by Bernard Ratzer. London: Jefferys & Faden, 1776. Library of Congress Geography and Map Division, G3804.N4 1767 .R3. *Part IV*: Last Moments of Major André. Copy of engraving by F. F. Walker after M. A. Wageman. New York: Virtue & Co. Publishers, 1861. Courtesy of the Author. *Part V*: The Victory Ball, 1781. Painting by Jean-Léon Gérôme Ferris, c1929. Courtesy of Virginia Historical Society. *Part VI*: Triumph of Patriotism, 1783. Copy of engraving by Alexander Hay Ritchie after Felix Octavius Carr Darley, 1853. National Archives, ARC ID 532881. *Epilogue*: The Prayer at Valley Forge. Copy of engraving by John C. McRae after Henry Brueckner. New York: John C. McRae, c1866. Library of Congress Prints and Photographs Division, LC-DIG-pga-03965. *Insert, first image*: George Washington, 1796. Gilbert Stuart, American 1755-1828. Oil on Canvas, 121.28 x 93.98 cm (47¾ x 37 in.), Museum of Fine Arts, Boston. William Francis Warden Fund, John H. and Ernestine A. Payne Fund, Commonwealth Cultural Preservation Trust, and the National Portrait Gallery, Washington D.C., 1980.1.

For Sheila and Thomas Beirne, my two favorite patriots

CONTENTS

Contents

PREFACE TO THE
PAPERBACK EDITION

"What is past is prologue." These words, penned by William Shakespeare in *The Tempest*, are inscribed into the granite of the National Archives Building in Washington, D.C. The inscription is fitting when you consider how many recent headlines could have been plucked right out of the American founding era: ASSESSING THE TRADE-OFFS BETWEEN SECURITY AND CIVIL LIBERTIES; or, HOW THE GOVERNMENT SPIED ON ME; or, POW SWAP TOOK PLACE IN A LEGAL GRAY AREA.[1] The United States has faced this all before, and our past might offer a guide for our future.

Never was a more compelling prologue written than when the founding generation forged our nation. Whether it is the NSA intercepting Americans' emails today or the Continental Congress intercepting citizens' letters during the Revolutionary War, there are parallels between the present day and the nation's humble beginnings. Technology has changed but our fundamental rights and American values need not.

I was raised in a family and a community where the patriotic spirit of the American Revolution remains very much alive. My parents constantly reminded me, "You are descended from Revolutionary War patriots. James Madison is in your family tree. These people matter!"

Yet I found the study of history to be boring. Eventually I realized that it was not the history that was uninteresting, but the way it was often presented. So I left behind the textbooks and sought out the Founders' writings to hear the story in their own words.

Soon I learned that some of George Washington's lost papers had been discovered in one of my ancestor's storage chests. Intrigued by this familial connection, I began to take a keen interest in the first president of the United States, and when I had to write a lengthy research paper to graduate from Yale Law School, it was natural to focus on Washington. Specifically, I aimed to determine what the U.S. Constitution meant when it designated the president as "Commander in Chief." To me, the answer seemed obvious: the text was referring to the powers exercised by the only commander in chief the nation had ever had at that time, General George Washington.

The subject continued to captivate me long after the school paper was graded. With controversies arising over the ways that successive presidents have invoked their power as commander in chief, I found myself looking to the past for insight into how best to assess these debates. After graduation, I continued researching the topic while practicing as an attorney at a New York law firm, and finally completed this book after I returned to Yale Law School as an Olin Scholar. My goal has always been to show that our nation's early history is neither dry nor dead. Not only is it fascinating and colorful, it is also relevant to modern concerns. This history has real legal weight that influences how the president, the Congress, and the Supreme Court interpret the powers of the presidency in our modern era.

Blood of Tyrants brings long-forgotten episodes from the Revolutionary War back to life with surprising new facts. I wanted this book to be as enjoyable to read as fiction, yet painstakingly researched and factual down to the minute details of weather, food, clothing, and personalities. But most of all, I wanted to get people discussing issues that the American Founders faced while winning independence and creating a new nation—issues that still confront us today.

In this last respect, the book has succeeded far beyond my hopes. *Blood of Tyrants* has been featured by ABC News, Fox News, the History Channel, C-SPAN, Reuters, *USA Today*, the *Wall Street Journal*, the *Washington Post*, the *New York Post*, *National Review*, and many other media outlets. It won the William E. Colby Award, and I have had the chance to speak across the country to lively audiences from Boston to San Diego, Miami to Seattle, and many points in between. I continue to do my small part in encouraging people across the United States and abroad to reflect on our nation's founding struggles and how they informed the meaning of the Constitution—especially when there are public controversies over the legitimate use of governmental power.

Too often, those disputes are colored by partisanship more than principle. When I see headlines like DANGEROUS DIVISIVENESS: POLITICS GROWS MORE PARTISAN,[2] or watch the acrimonious political morass in Washington, D.C., I cannot help but think about how George Washington denounced political faction. He called it a "fire not to be quenched . . . demand[ing] a uniform vigilance to prevent its bursting into a flame, lest, instead of warming, it should consume." Our first president urged us to use our votes and civic engagement to fight against "ill-founded jealousies" among politicians and to install principled leaders, as our Founders were.[3]

The Founders developed an ingenious political system, which Washington described as "nearer to perfection than any government hitherto instituted among men."[4] This government "by the people, for the people" empowered the citizenry to select representatives who would reconcile factions while protecting the liberties that so many had died to defend. Under this system, the United States has prospered beyond the founding generation's wildest dreams; and I wrote this book to help illuminate the constitutional principles that have enabled us to thrive.

The Constitution of the United States embodies the path on which the Founders set the nation. George Washington wrote in 1795, "the constitution is the guide, which I never will abandon."[5]

Neither should we.

INTRODUCTION

*"The tree of liberty must be refreshed from time to time
with the blood of patriots and tyrants."*

—THOMAS JEFFERSON, 1787

A bloodthirsty Congress demands revenge. The commander in chief weighs torture. Politicians clash with generals over war policy. Americans' liberties come under attack. No, this is not the post-9/11 United States. This is the side of the American Revolution you never knew.

Many hold the mistaken belief that America's Founders simply divined the answers to antiquated problems that are of little importance today. This could not be further from the truth. Instead of knowing all of the solutions, the founding generation battled the horrors of war as they struggled to define what it meant to be an American. And their definition remains relevant. While much of their correspondence involved horses and bayonets, they nevertheless confronted the same fundamental issues of leadership and government that continue to perplex us. In doing so, the Founders forged the American way. From their triumphs emerged bedrock principles that have direct applicability to contemporary debate. This book tells the story of those American ideals from our humble beginnings.

Long before he was known as the "Father of Our Country," George Washington was the "Devourer of Villages."[1] The great leader first tasted warfare two decades before the Revolutionary War when he led a peacetime act of aggression against a French diplomatic party. In doing so, he unwittingly sparked a bloody war that spanned two continents.

At the time, the territory inland from the eastern seaboard of the American colonies was a vast wilderness, dominated by the rolling hills of the Appalachians. On a wet May morning in 1754, an abundance of broadleaf trees created a thick canopy that shaded Washington and his troops from the rising sun. The smell of fresh pollen and moist earth permeated the air as the soldiers crouched behind the large, moss-covered boulders thrown haphazardly about the little glen. The natural beauty of the verdant fauna amidst the jagged rock was the least of Washington's cares, however. He and his regiment were primed for attack.

Washington's early morning trap consisted of forty haggard colonists along with thirteen semi-naked Native American allies. Ironically, Washington and his soldiers were poised in this foreign land under orders not to destroy, but to build.[2] Not yet at war, the age-old blood rivals Britain and France fiercely contested this region, since each viewed the Ohio River basin as the key to dominating the continent. And the young Washington marched headstrong into this international powder keg.

Not yet the regal image now depicted on the dollar bill, Washington was a fresh-faced surveyor-turned-warrior with long, red-brown hair atop his prominent forehead, large gray-blue eyes, long, broad nose, and rippling jaw.[3] A muscular six feet and 175 pounds, he was literally a giant among men of the time, although a bit unusually proportioned, with "[h]is shoulders narrow for his height but his hands and feet tremendous."[4] He possessed a commanding presence despite his youth, and "exuded such masculine power as frightens young women."[5] This fearsome young man ached for glory.

When the upper echelons of Virginia society sent Washington to stake Britain's claim to the Ohio Valley, the twenty-one-year-old

Washington was determined to prove himself. But dealing with the French was no easy task. During his first diplomatic attempt to drive them from the region, Washington was cordially received and invited to dine with the French officers. "The Wine, as they dosed themselves pretty plentifully with it, soon banished the[ir] Restraint," he wrote. "They Told me That it was their absolute Design to take possession of the Ohio [River basin], and by G___ they would do it."[6] Washington used this alcohol-induced intelligence to advocate that the British construct a fort in the area to establish control.

Obtaining approval to do so, the ambitious young lieutenant colonel led his militia through the spring mud of the thick virgin wilderness, lugging along the supplies necessary to construct the stronghold. But what had begun as an adventure quickly deteriorated into a perilous mess. As it turned out, the colonists enjoyed the realities of military service far less than their idealized notions of battle.

Washington struggled to hold his militia together as they grumbled about their low pay, dwindling rum, and the wet, inhospitable conditions.[7] Some deserted and many others were threatening to follow suit. Desperate to pacify his shoeless—and even shirtless—men, Washington confiscated supplies along the way.

"I doubt not that in some points I may have strained the law," he recorded, "but I hope, as my sole motive was to expedite the march, I shall be supported in it, should my authority be questioned, which at present I do not apprehend, unless some busybody intermeddles."[8] Bending the rules as his unit slowly disintegrated in the middle of the vast wilderness, Washington was not only wary of Native American attack, but above all feared disgrace before his superiors back in Virginia.[9]

It was at this increasingly desperate time that he received intelligence from his Native American ally, a shrewd Seneca warrior named Chief Tanacharison. Although not the actual ruler of the Iroquois Confederacy that dominated much of the region, Tanacharison was called the "Half King" due to his diplomatic and military leadership within the confederation. The man's very appearance provoked fear in the British and French alike: usually bare-chested except for ornamental necklaces that swung around his sinewy neck, the Half King wore large earrings in his startlingly stretched earlobes. Above a dark, weathered face and wrinkled brow, his bronzed head was bald except for long, braided hair stemming from the very back of his scalp.[10] And this menacing warrior had an ax to grind—both figuratively and literally.

The Half King harbored a seething hatred for the French, whom he accused of boiling and eating his father.[11] Tanacharison was born into a tribe described by Jesuit missionaries as "altogether barbarous, being cruel, sly, cunning, and prone to bloodshed and carnage," and his vendetta was no trivial matter.[12] He viewed the British "fools" as the lesser of two evils and was eager to fight alongside them to exact his revenge.[13] So he approached Washington with a report that a French scouting party of approximately fifty soldiers loomed nearby.[14] The Half King convinced the young Virginian that they "had bad hearts" and were "resolved to strike the first English they meet."[15]

Under strict orders from the French governor not to attack unless provoked, these French soldiers were likely to be little threat. France's explicit goal, in fact, was to "keep up that Union which exists between the [British and French] Crowns."[16] Although Washington was likewise ordered in no uncertain terms to act "on the defensive," he feared imminent attack and lusted for a glorious military victory before his enemies could strike.[17] Late that night, Washington led his small force on an eight-hour march "in small path, & heavy rain, and night as dark as it is possible to conceive," to rendezvous with the Half King's war party.[18] "They groped their way in single file, by footpaths through the woods, in a heavy rain and murky darkness, tripping occasionally and stumbling over each other, sometimes losing the track for fifteen or twenty minutes," but found the enemy camp before sunrise.[19]

Disregarding his direct order to warn all Frenchmen away before initiating hostilities, Washington was persuaded by Tanacharison to stage a joint strike. He approached with his exhausted men "in Indian fashion," stealthily setting up his ambush.[20] He and his still-soaked team peered over a small cliff at the French force, whose blue, well-tailored uniforms made them absurdly obvious targets against the muted browns and greens of the early morning forest floor.[21] Washington's hodgepodge group of young militiamen presented a stark contrast to their foes' prim color coordination. Some, like Washington, boasted decorative red uniforms complete with three-pointed black hats. Others sported the tattered remains of the earth-toned wool and linen coats and breeches that they wore on their farms back home. Whatever their dress, all had guns pointed at their French foes.

They patiently aimed between the small maples that clung to the cracks in the outcropping and waited with bated breath in anticipation of an intense firefight. Alongside Tanacharison's braves, they watched their prey wake and prepare for the day. The groggy, unsuspecting French party was surrounded.[22]

In his signature gallant fashion, Washington rose from his hiding place at seven o'clock and boomingly ordered the attack.[23] A startled French sentry attempted to sound an alarm, but to no avail, as he quickly fell to the Americans' lead. Although they were meant to serve more as a construction crew than a lethal fighting force, Washington's men proved exceedingly efficient in mowing down their targets as they took "their Arms, and fir'd briskly till [the French] were defeated."[24] After this brief, bloody firefight, a majority of the Frenchmen were killed or captured.

Washington's formal report back to his commander described the battle with detached military precision: "I there upon in conjunction with the Half King . . . formed a disposition to attack them on all sides, which we accordingly did and after an Engagement of abt 15 minutes we killed 10, wounded one and took 21 prisoners, amongst those that were killed was Monsieur De Jumonville, the Commander."[25] His diary account provided a fuller picture, albeit one that still glossed over the more gruesome details: "we killed Mr. de Jumonville—also nine others . . . . The Indians scalped the dead."[26] Washington's brevity, however, was largely self-serving. Though accounts of that day differ, it appears that Washington was actually covering up a massacre.[27]

After the firing abated, the French regiment's wounded commanding officer, Joseph Coulon de Villiers de Jumonville, attempted to negotiate a surrender.[28] He handed Washington papers showing that the party was merely on a diplomatic mission. But as Washington attempted to translate them from French, Tanacharison seized the opportunity to exact his revenge.[29] Shouting "Tu n'es pas encore mort, mon père," which translates as "You are not yet dead, my father," he split Jumonville's skull with his hatchet and plunged his hands into the Frenchman's brain.[30] "The tall Virginian who until that instant had thought himself in command did nothing while the Half King's warriors, as if on signal, set about killing the wounded," an egregious violation of European military protocol.[31] Washington, powerless, stared in horror as the helpless Frenchmen were cut down in a bloody rage. In a matter of seconds, nearly all of the injured Frenchmen were slaughtered before his eyes.[32]

Fearing French reprisal as well as damage to his own reputation, Washington astutely communicated only the most self-aggrandizing details back to Virginia. In demonstration of his bravery, he wrote, "I heard the bullets whistle, and, believe me, there is something charming in the sound."[33] But despite his best efforts, the cover-up was unsuccessful and word of the massacre quickly reached the colonial, British, and French governments. The French were incensed by the atrocity and readied their counterattack against Washington and his countrymen. In London, the debacle was derided as "a volley fired by a young Virginian in the backwoods of America [that] set the world on fire."[34] Washington's scandalous "Jumonville Affair" had sparked the global Seven Years' War.

•

This telling episode serves as a symbolic prelude to Washington's epic role in achieving the United States' independence. The life-and-death struggles were violent. They were desperate. They were messy. And above all, Washington did what he thought necessary to defend his country. In doing so, the "Founder of Our Nation" sent shockwaves throughout the world and set enduring precedents that continue to define us to this day. With so many repercussions across space and time, this real life story holds more twists than any fiction writer could invent.

History books often portray Washington as a semi-omniscient demigod who was so unlike us that he never struggled to find his way. America has lost sight of the man and replaced his memory with a distant sphinx. This is not a new phenomenon. When British novelist William Makepeace Thackeray made Washington into a character in *The Virginians* in 1857, it elicited public outcry. America was horrified at the attempt to portray Washington "like other men."[35] One critic of the book exclaimed, "Washington was not like other men; and to bring his lofty character down to the level of the vulgar passions of common life, is to give the lie to the grandest chapter in the uninspired annals of the human race."[36]

Nathaniel Hawthorne joked, "Did anyone ever see Washington nude? It is inconceivable. He had no nakedness, but I imagine he was born with his clothes on, and his hair powdered . . . ."[37] While it lacks (too much) nudity, this book unveils Washington and the other extraordinary yet very real human beings behind that great chapter of history. It honors the Revolution's leaders not by burying their humanity or enshrining them as one-dimensional figures; instead, it depicts them as actual people who faced and triumphed over seemingly insurmountable obstacles—ones remarkably similar to those that still plague us.

When Washington led the Continental Army through the Revolutionary War, he had learned from his youthful blunders of two decades earlier during that morning ambush. He drew upon his harsh experience along with his own wisdom to formulate principled approaches to dilemmas that are eerily similar to those we face today. By confronting—and eventually conquering—these challenges, he defined the American way. His epic role in leading the states to independence would forever shape the new nation.

As the United States' first and only commander in chief prior to the drafting of our Constitution, Washington personified our Founders' intent when they ratified the Constitution's precious few words proclaiming "The President shall be Commander in Chief of the Army and Navy of the United States . . . ."[38] The unquestioned choice to be the first president, he served as the model for the office at its creation. The founding generation looked to Washington's Revolutionary War leadership as their guide for designating the presidential powers in their new government. This book analyzes General Washington's specific actions and beliefs as he forged the very meaning of our Constitution amid the heat of battle for independence.

We all know how the war ended. What is surprisingly unknown are the specifics of how we achieved that grand victory. This book reveals the Revolutionary War precedents for America's modern crises.[39] It delves into some of the overlooked—and often lurid—details that are especially applicable to today's most contentious debates. To best discuss the varied episodes in America's chaotic triumph, this book organizes the chapters by topic. Rather than just providing an ordinary "play-by-play" of the war, it groups the discussions according to the topics most relevant to today: prisoner abuse, congressional interference in war policy, military tribunals, and Americans' rights.

By drawing from reams of primary source documents, this book brings to light facts that have been largely overlooked (and sometimes intentionally buried) by history. The subsequent pages hold such forgotten materials as the Founders' warnings against government debt, General Washington's letters justifying prisoner abuse to save American lives, a vivid eyewitness account of the military commission that swiftly executed a captured enemy operative, and evidence of a power struggle between Washington and Congress over war tactics. These surprising stories help fill the void in our understanding of our ingenious Founders' pragmatic approach to governing an America at war.

The book begins after the United States' victory. It traces the formation of our democratic republic, with Washington serving as the prototype for the presidency. The chapters in Part I answer the "why should we care?" question at the outset of the book: we should care about our history because the supreme law of the United States was shaped by these very events. By establishing that Washington's Revolutionary War powers were the same ones that the Framers intended for the presidency, this part encourages the reader to actively deduce the direct modern constitutional relevance of Washington's surprising precedents discussed in Parts II–V.

The subsequent parts address Washington's approach to hot-button issues of post-9/11 America: prisoner abuse (Part II), congressional war power (Part III), military tribunals (Part IV), and Americans' rights (Part V). The final part brings us full circle back to the end of the war. It discusses the founding generation's idolization of Washington and their hearty approval of his leadership chronicled in Parts II–V. This serves as a capstone, leading up to Washington's role in forming the postwar government and the practical implications of his wartime actions for our Constitution. Finally, the Epilogue discusses the modern legal significance of this forgotten history, showing the practical means by which the precedents explored in this book have a direct impact on modern law.

These pages emphasize the many colorful characters of the Revolution in order to tell the vivid stories of the war based on the people who lived them. Instead of taking a high-level approach, the book shows the personal impact of the Revolution on the human beings directly affected. To do so, it relies heavily on primary sources from both the American and British sides in order to provide rich eyewitness accounts.[40] Delving into some of these previously lost documents, this book injects incendiary new facts into the present discussion and is intended to serve as fodder for debate.

No longer is Washington "entombed in his own myth—a metaphorical Washington Monument that hides from us the lineaments of the real man."[41] The following pages depict a great human being who struggled with dilemmas similar to those we face today. With tremendous strength of character, he successfully led his countrymen through deep crises and helped found the most prosperous nation on earth. Over two centuries later, we still have more to learn from him.

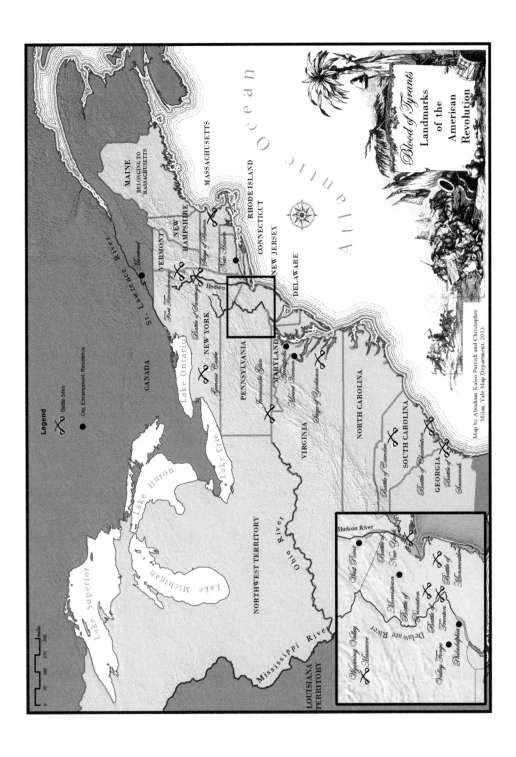

Blood of Tyrants
Landmarks
of the
American Revolution

Map by: Abraham Kaleo Parrish and Christopher Milan, Yale Map Department, 2013.

Legend

✗ Battle Sites

● City, Encampment, Residence

Atlantic Ocean

CANADA

MAINE
BELONGING TO MASSACHUSETTS

NEW HAMPSHIRE
VERMONT
MASSACHUSETTS
RHODE ISLAND
CONNECTICUT
NEW YORK
NEW JERSEY
DELAWARE
MARYLAND
PENNSYLVANIA
VIRGINIA
NORTH CAROLINA
SOUTH CAROLINA
GEORGIA

St. Lawrence River
Montreal

Lake Superior
Lake Huron
Lake Michigan
Lake Erie
Lake Ontario

Fort Ticonderoga
Battle of Saratoga
Siege of Boston
New Haven
Hudson

Genesee Castle
Johnstown Glen

Brandywine Gap
Mount Vernon
Siege of Yorktown

Battle of Camden
Battle of Charleston
Battle of
Battle of Savannah

NORTHWEST TERRITORY

Ohio River
Mississippi River

LOUISIANA TERRITORY

0   50   100   150   200
miles

Hudson River
West Point
Battle of New York
Morristown
Battle of Princeton
Battle of Trenton
Delaware River
Valley Forge
Philadelphia
Battle of Monmouth
Wyoming Valley Massacre

I

THE KING OF AMERICA

"I am free to acknowledge that His Powers are full great, and greater than I was disposed to make them. Nor, Entre Nous, do I believe they would have been so great had not many of the members cast their eyes towards General Washington as President; and shaped their Ideas of the Powers to be given to a President, by their opinions of his Virtue."[1]

—PIERCE BUTLER, REPRESENTATIVE
OF THE CONSTITUTIONAL CONVENTION, 1788

Even as the embers of war still smoldered, he found peace. Standing alongside the blue-gray waters of the Potomac River, the gentleman farmer gazed across his sprawling estate. The lush foliage of billowing weeping willows and blossoming laurel dotted the softly rolling fields, which glimmered in the fiery light of the rising sun. A silent spring breeze grazed his weathered face, sending the aromas of earth and grass into the air. Over the farmer's impressive frame, still powerfully built after fifty-five years of backbreaking use, soared his mansion's majestic white columns. They rose two stories to meet a striking red roof, topped by two large chimneys, pointed dormers, and an ornately domed cupola. Beneath this grandiose architectural crown, a white, neoclassical Georgian-style mansion provided a comfortable home for the gentleman and his beloved wife, along with her two rambunctious young grandchildren who had been orphaned during the war.

He had fought courageously for his country and had earned this peaceful life with his loved ones. And he enjoyed it immensely. But as the sun's first rays appeared to ignite the horizon, his serenity was shattered by the clacking hooves of an approaching horse. The messenger brought dire—but not unexpected—news: the gentleman farmer's nation was crumbling and it needed him. Emerging from his retirement, he would save the country. Again.

The chapters in Part I explore the creation of the United States Constitution. They examine Washington's crucial role in its formation and how his wartime precedents shaped the powers of all future American presidents.

1

The Not-So-United States

Victorious, they set the world on fire. The scrappy Americans stunned Great Britain—the mightiest empire on earth—and sparked a powder keg of political unrest across the Old World and the New. These patriots' revolutionary republican ideology and military triumph helped ignite uprisings in France, Ireland, the Netherlands, Poland, Haiti, and Latin America.[1] At home, the Americans needed to harness that revolutionary fire to forge a nation, lest it rage out of control and consume their grand experiment. For while their victory in the Revolutionary War was glorious, the aftermath was less so. Facing bankruptcy and internal strife, the United States turned once again to its father and protector: the warrior-turned-farmer, George Washington.

As commander in chief of the Continental Army during the Revolution, Washington triumphantly led a confederation of thirteen allied state governments. But following their victory, the American states were only loosely united under the governing document known as the "Articles of Confederation and Perpetual Union." Ironically, these Articles created a decentralized union that proved to be far from perpetual.

The United States *were* less a cohesive nation than thirteen independent, sovereign states loosely tethered by a weak central government—the Confederation Congress.[2] Americans of the era often referred to their nation in the plural form. They did not yet conceive of themselves as one indissoluble nation composed of thirteen parts, but rather as a voluntary confederation of independent allied states where many citizens felt greater allegiance to their own region than to any new national government.[3]

Washington had seen this firsthand back during the war. His Continental Army—sick, hungry, shivering—huddled within their makeshift winter encampment at Valley Forge, where bone-chilling winds proved far more deadly than the British could ever hope to be. With ice and bodies piling up around him, Washington feared mutiny among his troops and sought reassurance. He did not obtain it. In one of the Revolution's darkest hours, he ordered a few soldiers to swear allegiance to the United States. They shockingly refused, instead declaring, "New Jersey is our country!"[4]

Such political disunity stemmed from deeply rooted fear. Americans were wary of replicating the British system where their liberties were suppressed by a distant government that was deaf to their wishes. To avoid the reemergence of such a regime after their fight for independence erupted, the states clung fiercely to local rule. The individual states retained most of the power over their own citizenry rather than relinquish it to the new national Congress. Even though it had authority over diplomacy and military decisions, Congress was at the mercy of the states since they supplied most of the soldiers and resources to the Continental Army.[5]

Under this arrangement, rather than a single American army, Washington had led what was akin to a coalition force, supplied with food, munitions, and soldiers by separate little nation-states.[6] And despite having a common foe, the states bickered among themselves about the costs. As a result, they dangerously undersupplied Washington's army, and the weak Congress could do little but entreat them to provide more troops. Like unruly children supervised by a feeble grandmother, the states quarreled while the Congress implored them to behave.

Washington saw this as a deeply flawed system. He described the national Congress as a "half-starved government [that] limped along on crutches, tottering at every step."[7] The fragile nation did have its glue, however. The thirteen states' coalition was held together during the war in large part by the states' belief in the leadership of one man: Washington. As commander in chief, he had become "the most effective bond, as well as conspicuous symbol, of union."[8]

But the war ended and the Americans' conspicuous symbol retired. Mere weeks after the last British troops evacuated New York City following the peace treaty, Washington resigned his commission as commander in chief in order to "retire from the Great Theater of Action" and "take leave of all the employments of public life."[9] He returned to Mount Vernon, his sprawling plantation on the Potomac, where he enjoyed the life of a gentleman farmer.

When not spending time with his family, entertaining dinner guests, or partaking in his favorite leisure activity of foxhunting, Washington oversaw a diversified business that included farming tobacco and wheat, breeding mules, milling flour, and weaving cloth. He commanded hundreds of slaves, who worked from sunrise to sunset on the many tasks of his bustling estate. While he increasingly recognized the contradiction between his fight for liberty and his ownership of slaves, writing, "there is not a man living who wishes more sincerely than I do, to see a plan adopted for the abolition" of slavery, he declined to free them.[10] Eventually he would arrange for their emancipation in his will, but during his lifetime he remained far too dependent on them to tend his home, fields, and other enterprises.[11] And after years of neglect during the war, he found his estate especially in need of their hard work.

Washington's was a busy but tranquil occupation: instead of leading armies across the Delaware River to defend American liberty, he led investors in building canals so that he could better transport produce.[12] Retiring to bed by nine o'clock almost every evening, he rested well, knowing that he had liberated his country after so many years of war.

While he was far removed from the public spotlight, he was certainly not forgotten. In fact, his self-imposed exile from politics stunned the world. After the war, his popularity was at such a height and his hold on the military so ironclad that some expected him to pronounce himself king of the United States. Washington's voluntary surrender of power only further elevated his demigod status among the people. The annals of civilization were littered with triumphant generals who had helped their people throw off one tyrant only to take his place. But Washington broke from that cycle. He freed his people and then returned to his farm to leave the path open for republican self-government.

For both his inspirational leadership during the Revolution and his selfless retirement afterward, Washington was almost universally revered throughout America and beyond. A mere rumor of Washington passing through a town was enough to elicit a spontaneous parade. Even his critics were pressured into silence, since any attack against the great man was considered unpatriotic.[13]

One of the few men of the era to dislike Washington was his portraitist. Gilbert Stuart was a personable Rhode Islander whose lifelike portraits catapulted him to artistic stardom. He was a powerfully built, happy-go-lucky gentleman with an "attachment to the pleasures of the table and convivial society," which a friend attributed to his time living in Ireland.[14] Possessing "wit at will," the painter relied on his knack for conversation to keep his subjects animated and to draw forth "the inmost soul upon the surface of the countenance."[15] But when he landed the appointment as Washington's portraitist, his charm failed him.

Washington despised sitting for portraits almost as much as he disliked strangers' attempts at familiarity. In no mood for idle conversation about military tactics with some bohemian artist, he rebuffed Stuart's efforts at small talk. He was a master at masking his emotions and was not about to bare his soul. At one point during the sitting, Stuart tried to loosen up his subject by pleading, "Now, sir, you must let me forget that you are General Washington and that I am Stuart the painter." Ever advocative of proper decorum, Washington replied, "Mr. Stuart need never feel the need of forgetting who he is, or who General Washington is."[16]

Despite this resistance, Stuart perceived that beneath Washington's stern, composed exterior was a man of fiery temperament. He perceived "features in [Washington's] face totally different from what he ever observed in that of any other human being; the sockets of eyes, for instance, are larger than what he ever met with before, and the upper part of the nose broader." His unusual features were "indicative of the strongest and most ungovernable passions, and had he been born in the forests, it was [Stuart's] opinion that he would have been the fiercest man amongst the savage tribes."[17] The painter wanted to capture his subject's true "fierce and irritable disposition" in the portrait, but Washington shut him out. Stuart believed that Washington, "like Socrates," was possessed of "great self-command [that] always made him appear a man of a different cast in the eyes of the world."[18]

Stuart grumbled, "an apathy seemed to seize him, and a vacuity spread over his countenance most appalling to paint."[19] Possibly out of spite, the artist emphasized Washington's stern glance and the severe lines around his mouth that were caused by his false teeth.[20] This portrait was far from a flattering glamour shot, and Stuart never actually finished it. But Americans loved Washington so much that they nevertheless embraced the steely image that emerged from the sitting. Ironically, it was this stiff, almost annoyed-looking representation of the dynamic man that would grace the dollar bill and shape countless people's perception of him.[21]

Whatever his expression, Washington was internationally recognized as liberty's great champion and seen as "a living embodiment of all that classical republican virtue the age was eagerly striving to recover."[22] He was lauded for uniting "the intrepidity of Aristides, the patriotism of Cato, the military prudence of Caesar, and the humanity of Scipio."[23] The world marveled at "[t]he virtuous simplicity of his retirement after the consummation of his country's independence; the harmony of his public and his private life; the purity of his patriotism and the splendor of his military career, [which] formed altogether such a union of goodness and greatness in the character of one individual as was calculated to excite the warmest interest, and command the admiration of mankind."[24]

Distant admiration, however, was not what the United States needed after the war. Washington's retirement had added to the political void. No longer faced with the immediate threat of British invasion, and without a leader to unite them, the states quickly fell into discord. And Congress was ineffectual at holding them together—the quarrelling children were growing into rowdy teens and the feeble grandmother was losing control. The United States were far from united.

2

Not as Happy in Peace as They Had Been Glorious in War

These were desperate times. Besides being perilously disunited, the country was in dire straits economically. In order to fund the war, America had already spent far beyond her means, racking up $54 million in federal debt and an additional $24 million in state debt.[1] The fragile nation was deeply indebted to her French allies for their wartime monetary assistance and also owed vast sums to her own American patriots who had provided guns, rations, and blood for the war effort. These soldiers and civilian suppliers had been essential in keeping Washington and his army fighting. But now that they had won, the resultant debt threatened to crush the fledgling nation. The thirteen states were not "as happy in peace as they had been glorious in war."[2]

Thomas Jefferson expressed the view of many Americans in decrying "public debt as the greatest of dangers to be feared."[3] The nation's vast outstanding debt was reminiscent of their plight under the British monarchy. The Crown had exhausted much of its wealth during the Seven Years' War and endeavored to fund its debt by taxing the colonies—which was one of the main reasons for the Revolution in the first place. Now America had its own financial predicament, and many feared that a large national debt might pave the way back to monarchy. "We must not let our rulers load us with perpetual debt," Jefferson warned.

We must make our selection between economy and liberty or profusion and servitude. . . . This is the tendency of all human governments. A departure from principle becomes a precedent for a second; that second for a third; and so on, till the bulk of society is reduced to mere automatons of misery, to have no sensibilities left but for sinning and suffering. . . . And the fore horse of this frightful team is public debt. Taxation follows that, and in its train wretchedness and oppression.[4]

While he disagreed with Jefferson on many issues, Alexander Hamilton, the primary architect of the American financial system, likewise wrote, "Nothing can more interest the national credit and prosperity than a constant and systematic attention to husband all the means previously possessed for extinguishing the present debt, and to avoid, as much as possible, the incurring any new debt."[5] As far as many of the Founders were concerned, "Public Debt is a Public curse."[6]

Americans and the world were losing faith in the new nation's ability to meet its obligations. Veterans began to assume that they would never see their war salaries. They had been given IOUs because Congress and the states lacked the funds to pay them. But by the late 1780s, the war had been over for a few years and the veterans had lost confidence that they would ever see their hard-earned compensation. The humble veterans began selling their government's promissory notes for a fraction of their value. They needed to eat today, and gave up hope that the United States would repay them tomorrow.

The veterans certainly had good reason for concern. Some politicians believed the nation should extricate itself from its crushing burden by simply refusing to repay, thereby making the loans worthless to the nation's—irate—creditors. But while many people did not mind bilking the French, such a default would severely harm those veterans and other Americans to whom vast sums were owed.[7] Further, it would destroy the government's credibility and make borrowing in the future difficult, to say the least.

Washington had already made up his mind on this issue: he insisted that the country pay down its debt. He approached the matter as a question of honor, explaining, "the path of our duty is plain before us, honesty will be found on every experiment, to be the best and only true policy, let us then as a Nation be just, let us fulfil the public Contracts . . . with the same good faith we suppose ourselves bound to perform our private engagements."[8] Only by acting honorably and working to extinguish the debt would the new nation enjoy legitimacy and thrive.

Washington joined with those who advocated that the country repay quickly. "No pecuniary consideration is more urgent, than the regular redemption and discharge of the public debt," he believed; "on none can delay be more injurious, or an economy of time more valuable."[9] He encouraged the nation to act virtuously by "shunning occasions of expence, but by vigorous exertions in time of Peace to discharge the Debts which unavoidable wars may have occasioned, not ungenerously throwing upon posterity the burthen which we ourselves ought to bear."[10]

In the 1780s, however, it appeared that the nation would never be able to dig itself out of its financial hole—no matter how virtuously it behaved. Congress had little means of doing so, since under the Articles of Confederation it lacked the power to control the nation's spending or collect taxes.

Congress could do little more than implore the states to finance the central government with donations. Congress proposed various methods by which the states might raise revenue towards paying off the national debt, but the states, each unwilling to have its citizens bear the brunt of higher taxes, refused to implement any of these ideas. They had their own debts to handle and their own citizens to care for.

The impasse fed interstate strife. Politicians clashed over whether the states should repay separately or the national government should assume the debt as a united body. While some intellectuals like Jefferson opposed entrusting the national government with such power, other, more down-to-earth Americans criticized the measure as simply unfair—certain southern states had already made great headway in repaying their debt and decried efforts to bail out the northern ones.

The debt controversy threatened to split the United States apart. The situation became so desperate that the Congressional Board of Treasury warned that if the national government could not procure more funds from the states,[11] "nothing . . . can rescue [the United States] from Bankruptcy, or preserve the Union of the several States from Dissolution."[12]

Washington certainly had his opinions, but he largely remained on the sidelines—albeit monitoring the situation intently. Although geographically isolated out on his farm, he was kept apprised of the nation's struggles by the parade of visitors who came to pay homage. These uninvited guests showed up at his door just about every day, sometimes ten or twenty at a time. Whether they were friends, veterans, or curious strangers, Washington was ever polite. Seeing it as his public duty, he fed and visited with almost every one of them. The retired commander was so inundated, in fact, that he went for over a year-long stretch without a peaceful dinner alone with his beloved wife. In search of some respite, he resorted to posting inadequate signage to his estate, causing many prospective visitors to get lost on the snaking paths through the dark woods that hid Mount Vernon.[13]

While exhausting, these visitors kept Washington abreast of the condition of the republic. Between them, his deluge of letters, and the many newspapers he avidly read, he became "the focus of political intelligence for the new world."[14] And he was aghast to learn of the nation's looming economic collapse. But it was not his place to interfere. He was retired. He had successfully done his part to set the nation on its course and now hoped that it would find its own way forward. While Washington passively observed, however, matters only grew worse.

The United States' fiscal disarray fed rampant inflation. The national currency, called the Continental, became virtually worthless as Congress attempted to print the country's way out of debt. With so many bills in circulation, the Continentals' value plummeted and many

Americans' cash savings became worth less than the mattresses that hid them. It became common to describe something of little value as "not worth a Continental."[15] The currency was such a laughingstock that "barber-shops were papered, in jest, with the bills; and the sailors, on returning from their cruise, being paid off in bundles of this worthless money, had suits of clothes made of it, and with characteristic lightheartedness turned their loss into a frolic, by parading through the streets in decayed finery, which, in its better days had passed for thousands of dollars!"[16]

Rather than place blame where due—on the nation's massive war debt and the states' refusal to coordinate a response—citizens and leaders alike turned their wrath on merchants and creditors. Even though these shopkeepers and financiers were merely acting rationally when they refused to take payment with the worthless Continentals, they became the scapegoats for public outrage. For example, the Connecticut legislature blasted them as "evil-minded persons, inimical to the liberties of the United States of America," who had "endeavored to depreciate the bills of credit of this and the said United States."[17] Reflecting the public anger, Washington likewise lashed out against "monopolizers, forestallers, and engrossers," describing them as "pests of society" who should be "hanged upon a gallows."[18]

With the national currency crumbling, rather than work together to return to solvency, some states turned to further emissions of their own separate currencies. This drove inflation higher and fractured national unity.[19] It was an economic and political mess, as the sister states not only refused to work together, but also blamed one another like "little jealous, clashing, tumultuous commonwealths."[20] The states' bickering took on "an ominous likeness to the meetings and resolves which in the years before 1775 had heralded a state of war." Many ventured that it would not be long before "shots would have been fired and seeds of perennial hatred sown" among the peoples.[21]

Such insolvency and internal turmoil left the country perilously vulnerable to external threats. The weak young nation found itself in a world fraught with aggressors. This was an age when a renewed British assault appeared imminent. The British had already violated their peace treaty with the Americans by retaining troops on the United States' western frontier for years after the Revolution ended. Britain made it abundantly clear that she was bitterly unwilling to relinquish her interests in America's lands and many feared that she would soon come to collect her lost colonies. And Britain was not the only threat.

Reports abounded that Spain might prey upon the nation's weakness to expand her New World empire. The Spanish began aggressively asserting their military might in the region by restricting America's navigation rights on parts of the Mississippi River, thus impeding the nation's development of its western frontier. Although humiliated and outraged by these affronts, the nation was too weak to respond. Not only was Congress too broke to pay for a national army, the government could not even fashion a united military front from among the states' separate militias. Congress simply did not have the power under the Articles of Confederation to protect the nation.

Upon obtaining reports of his country's deteriorating condition, Washington derided the nation as "little more than a shadow" and Congress as a mere "nugatory body."[22] The country was increasingly helpless as the major European powers licked their lips, hungrily eyeing America's fertile territory.

3

The Shadow Government

The American "shadow" government was unable to reverse the nation's descent into anarchy. This fact was made abundantly clear to Washington and the rest of the nation by a poor farmer in the Massachusetts backcountry.

Daniel Shays, the uneducated son of an Irish indentured servant, toiled on a small farm with his wife and six children. His dark, accusatory eyes, doughy chin, pug nose, and drooping jowls made him resemble a bulldog, which was a fitting match to his personality.[1] A "smart, active" man with "much taste for the military," he was a fiery veteran of the Revolution who had courageously fought in multiple decisive battles.[2] But he had fallen on tough times after the war ended.

In a microcosm of the nation's general suffering after the grand Revolution, Shays' family was brought to the brink of financial ruin by the deep recession and rampant inflation that gripped the country. Like many other veterans, he had yet to receive his military pay and pension from the cash-strapped government and was therefore unable to pay down his debts. He lost possession of half his farmland to creditors. And he was relatively fortunate, since many of his neighbors lost everything.[3] Even worse, others were carted off to jail, since any debt above a mere five dollars was cause for imprisonment. The people of

Massachusetts—the hotbed of unrest that had started the Revolution just a few years earlier—were again rearing for a fight.

Reigniting his firebrand spirit and oratory, Shays led his fellow debtors in protest. The frustrated group started out peacefully, calling for debtor relief and government reform. But the financiers were unwilling to lose money on their loans and continued to go after the delinquent farmers' lands. Unmoved by the farmers' pleas, the Massachusetts government refused to halt the foreclosures. Instead, the state infuriated the farming communities by suggesting they exercise patience and frugality.[4] From the farmers' perspective, it was preposterous to ask them to be any more patient as their lands were confiscated. It was impossible for them to be any more frugal when they were having trouble just feeding their families.

Enraged, the protesting farmers seized local courthouses—without courts, the creditors could not foreclose on them. Meeting with success, Shays' mob grew bolder. During the dog days of summer in 1786—barely two and a half years after the official conclusion of the Revolution—Shays donned his Continental Army uniform once again and led a crowd armed with muskets, pitchforks, and clubs to the highest court in Massachusetts. A reluctant leader who yearned to preserve peace amidst the protest, Shays negotiated the peaceful surrender of the courthouse; however, such a transgression would not go unanswered by the state.

Declaring that he would "vindicate the insulted dignity of government," the governor of Massachusetts sent the state's militia to confront the insurgency.[5] Governor James Bowdoin was a stern-looking gentleman with a gently cleft chin, arched eyebrows, and a high, aristocratic brow framed by long, regally styled gray hair. A brilliant intellectual in his mid-fifties who had served in the Continental Congress as well as various political posts during the Revolution, he was no stranger to rebellion. But although he had helped to lead the people in their revolt against the British monarchy, he had little sympathy for rebellion against the new republic.

Bowdoin feared that if he did not crush the uprising quickly, the republic for which they had just fought would be lost. Unwilling to allow this "civil War" to "destroy the fair temple of American liberty,"[6] he vowed to take "vigorous measures [towards] the effectual suppression of the Insurgents."[7] Instead, he ended up fanning the flames.

Having inherited enormous wealth from his merchant father, this Harvard-educated member of the Boston elite was far more adept at writing scientific papers in Latin than at empathizing with farmers. He thus became an easy target for the rhetoric of the brewing class war. The poor farmers viewed Bowdoin as yet another wealthy Boston merchant seeking to oppress them. The firestorm spread further, and Shays was unable to mediate a peaceful resolution when Bowdoin's state militia fired on a group of rowdy protesters one hot summer day. Three farmers fell dead, while the rest scattered in terror. With blood spilled, Shays proclaimed, "The seeds of war are now sown."[8] And with that, the farmers began a new revolution. This time they sought to throw off the reins not of the British but of Massachusetts and the new American government.

Calling upon the lingering revolutionary spirit, thousands of famers—many of the very same men who had just fought the British—joined in the so-called "Shays' Rebellion." The revolt raged for almost a year, pitting Bowdoin's Massachusetts establishment army—financed by the wealthy merchants of Boston—against the "common people," whose champions "tried to make real the vision of justice and equality embodied in our revolutionary declaration of independence," as a monument to the rebellion put it. Adopting the revolutionary rallying cry, "True Liberty and Justice may require resistance to law," these class warriors' uprising led many Americans to fear that the Revolution's democratic impulse would rage unchecked, pulling the nation into perpetual anarchy.[9] Democracy was a new experiment for the Americans, and perhaps it was already a failed one.

In bloody skirmishes that pitted neighbor against neighbor, the poorly armed farmers were confronted by the booming cannons and rifles of Bowdoin's well-trained state militia. Despite Shays' fierce leadership, his hungry, ill-equipped and ill-trained men were scattered before the Massachusetts militia's firestorm. Losing battle after battle, the farmers began to return home as the bodies began to pile up in the fields. The rebellion was crushed. With ransoms on the heads of the rebel leaders, Shays fled into hiding in Vermont. He lived on the lam for many months, seeking to escape the Massachusetts gallows.

Governor Bowdoin, meanwhile, suffered politically for his harsh suppression of the rebellion. He was voted out of office and replaced with a more conciliatory administration. The incoming governor pardoned Shays as a step towards reconciliation with the farming communities. Shays was able to return to what was left of his farm and resume his humble existence. Although his rebellion in and of itself was not much of a military threat to the new country, it was significant as a symbolic one. The message of Shays' Rebellion was clear: the American republic was failing miserably.

Washington could remain on the sidelines no more. He was appalled by the country's downward spiral. "What gracious God, is man! that there should be such inconsistency and perfidiousness in his conduct?" he lamented. "It is but the other day, that we were shedding our blood to obtain the Constitutions under which we now live; Constitutions of our own choice and making; and now we are unsheathing the sword to overturn them."[10] Reflecting on the economic and political turmoil all around him, Washington bemoaned how far his nation had fallen:

> No morn ever dawned more favourably than ours did; and no day was ever more clouded than the present! . . . Without some alteration in our political creed, the superstructure we have been seven years raising at the expence of so much blood and treasure, must fall. We are fast verging to anarchy and confusion![11]

He warned, "the wheels of Government are clogged, and . . . from the high ground on which we stood, we are descending into the vale of confusion and darkness."[12]

So perilous was the situation that "even respectable characters [spoke] of a monarchical form of Government without horror." Washington exclaimed, "what a triumph for our enemies to verify their predictions! what a triumph for the advocates of despotism to find that we are incapable of governing ourselves, and that systems founded on the basis of equal liberty are merely ideal and fallacious!"[13]

Just four years after his glorious victory over America's bitter British foes, the nation's founding hero asserted in 1787, "We are either a united people under one head, and for federal purposes; or we are thirteen independent sovereignties, eternally counteracting each other."[14] Without some sort of federal power that "pervade[d] the whole Union," Washington could "not conceive" how the United States would survive.[15] The nation needed a new government.

Washington was gravely concerned about his legacy. He was intent on protecting his pedestal in history and feared risking it by coming out of retirement. He agonized over the reputational damage should he throw his support behind government reform only to have it fail. But in the end, he was a man of action and not about to sit idly by while his beloved country unraveled. He readied his trusty horse and set off from his estate to meet with other leaders in a desperate attempt to salvage the United States.

4

The Phoenix

Washington leapt back onto the public stage in grand style. On a bright Sunday afternoon in May 1787, his black carriage cut through the bustling streets of Philadelphia.[1] And this was no understated entrance. Accompanied by a ceremonious cavalry escort and a parade of top military officials, his arrival was heralded by the competing booms of celebratory cannon and gun salutes. With a population of 30,000 people, the city was the largest in the nation and throngs of these inhabitants were eager to witness the national hero's thundering arrival.

The spring air was filled with a fanfare of chiming bells and the loud cheers of citizens crowded alongside the dusty cobblestone streets.[2] As the carriage passed, admirers fawned from the ornately trimmed windows of the two- and three-story brick buildings that hugged Philadelphia's streets. Women applauded in their colorful, low-necked cotton bedgowns and white ruffled aprons; men in billowing white shirts, woolen waistcoats, dark breeches, and white stockings waved their tricorne hats in the air; children, squirming in uncomfortable miniature versions of the adults' clothing, cheered the procession. Washington was the first American superstar and known to elicit a few shrieks from young women—puritanical norms be damned!

Washington's carriage slowed to a stop in front of the finest house in the city. Here he was to be graciously hosted by its owners, who were honored by his mere presence. As the crowd roared in adulation, Washington's large, almost majestic frame emerged from the carriage. Standing up to full height, his tall powerful figure presented a simply regal appearance. With his white-powdered hair tied in black satin and his famously masculine features, he exuded the confidence and grandeur for which the nation yearned. A man of elegantly under-stated fashion, he dressed in the fineries befitting his high station, yet nevertheless carried himself with his trademark humility as a servant of his nation.[3] Although he was not a king, the eminent man sure was treated like one.

Washington was just one of Virginia's delegates to the nation's Constitutional Convention. The elected assemblies of the states had chosen representatives from among America's top political leaders to attend this convention for the purpose of fixing the nation's government.[4] These seventy men were considered by many to be the "wisest and best men in the country," and such confidence in their wisdom and character would be crucial to the public's acceptance of their plans for mending the country.[5]

Americans feared both ends of the political spectrum: a repressive government that would lead them back to monarchy or an unchecked democracy where unruly masses effectuated perpetual chaos. Further complicating matters, each state had different—and often conflicting—interests. For example, small states wanted protection from the large states' dominance in national affairs, and southern states wanted to ensure the continuation of slavery while many northern states had abolished it.

The country was so fractured, in fact, that Rhode Island refused to send delegates to the Philadelphia convention. The Rhode Islanders viewed the meeting as an illegal assembly that threatened to usurp their state's sovereignty.[6] They even threatened to use their veto power under the Articles of Confederation to quash anything the convention accomplished. In such a climate of dissention and suspicion, to say that the public was skeptical of the ability of even the nation's "best and brightest" to create a sound and agreeable government was an understatement. Everyone knew that the situation was precarious and that the delegates needed to find a delicate balance in order for the public to accept their reforms.

Washington gathered with the first-arriving delegates at the Pennsylvania State House. This two-story hall was already historic: it was colloquially called "Independence Hall" because the Declaration of Independence had been signed there eleven years earlier. With that one daring stroke during the early part of the war, America dismembered the British Empire. And in the ensuing struggle, the hall remained a meeting place for the Continental Congress and the epicenter of the American war effort. The stately brick building had black shutters and white trim, with pale masonry and ornate windows lending decorative detail to an otherwise boxy facade. The small grounds included a square courtyard that was barren except for a few freshly planted elm trees. Guarding this yard was a seven-foot wall that afforded an air of solemn secrecy.[7]

Privacy was of the utmost importance in fostering frank discussion among the delegates. To this end, the building was shielded from curious onlookers by sentries posted at all doors. To protect further against distraction, the guards spread fresh dirt on the cobblestones outside to soften the blows of powerful hooves of passing horses. High above the dampened din of the street, this sanctuary's gently slanted roof was dominated by a tall, churchlike bell tower that coaxed the delegates' eyes heavenward as they approached. This was fitting, since they faced a lofty challenge and would need all the help they could get to prevent the country from disintegrating.

The May sun's powerful rays poured through high windows as Washington entered the building. The obsessively punctual celebrity was cordially greeted by the few delegates already present.[8] Also in attendance was perhaps the second most famous American: Benjamin Franklin. This world-renowned scientist and diplomat had not only greatly advanced human understanding of electricity, but also invented the lightning rod, the Franklin stove, the odometer, and a host of other contraptions. During the Revolution, the wily gentleman had used his guile to charm the French court—particularly the female contingent. Through parties and chess games, he wore down France's resistance to involvement in the fight against the British. He masterfully persuaded the French to send aid to the American cause and eventually declare war on Britain, which proved decisive in the American victory. For these many achievements, he was internationally praised.

Now in his mid-eighties, Franklin suffered from gout, a painful form of arthritis caused by eating rich foods and imbibing large quantities of alcohol. So immobilized, he had to be carried to the hall from his nearby home.[9] Even as his frail limbs hobbled beneath his round abdomen, his aged, balding head was ever filled with ingenious ideas, and he still inspired deep reverence. His star power combined with Washington's to lend the convention an even greater air of importance.

As Washington and Franklin entered the hall's cavernous meeting room, they were greeted by its familiar dark hardwood floors and white walls adorned with ornate molding. Before them was a grand fireplace topped with a white mantle beneath a large chandelier encircled by a decorative ceiling medallion. The room was a beautiful sight.

The gentlemen present were from all walks of life—farmers, lawyers, printers, merchants, financiers—but all were patriots and the vast majority had served their country during the Revolutionary War, politically or militarily, or both.[10] These proud men took the opportunity to rekindle friendships and reestablish acquaintances with fellow alumni of the war effort. They could accomplish little else, since they had to wait for other states' less punctual delegates to arrive.

At first, Washington and the other delegates were unconcerned about the paltry attendance. The journey from far-flung states such as New Hampshire and Georgia took up to three weeks and, with bad weather hitting parts of the eastern seaboard, it was possible that some of the other delegates were merely delayed. But as the nation's leaders trickled into Philadelphia only slowly over the next two weeks, many feared that some delegates were boycotting the Constitutional Convention and that it would end before it started—they were keenly aware that many Americans opposed the convention and there was a real chance that a proper quorum of states would never be reached. And without a quorum, the convention's recommendations would lack the political weight necessary for legitimacy.

With this elephant in the room, a palpable anxiety permeated the hall despite the cordial conversation. The delegates knew that without adequate attendance, their convention would fail, and possibly the nation along with it.

Finally, they arrived. With just twenty-nine delegates from nine states in attendance, they reached a quorum and the convention was officially convened. Over the next few days, twenty-six more delegates trickled in, better late than never. In all, fifty-five of the seventy delegates originally chosen actually showed up to represent the independent states. America had sent her finest and the convention proved to be quite an eclectic assemblage of minds.

Their ages ranged from an impetuous 26-year-old veteran named Jonathan Dayton to the sickly 81-year-old sage, Franklin.[11] Like Dayton and Franklin, the vast majority of these men were held in high esteem for their contributions to the patriot cause during the war. Alexander Hamilton, for example, at only thirty years old, had already served as Washington's shrewd right-hand man and closest confidant during the war. His sharp chin and pointed nose matched his cutting criticism of the Articles and ardent advocacy of a more centralized nation. While Washington, Hamilton, and Dayton were joined by other decorated war veterans, the room was actually dominated by politicians.

About three-quarters of the delegates had served in Congress, while others had served in their state legislatures. Each was lauded for steering the United States through the perilous Revolution. One such politician was James Madison, who at age thirty-six had already proven himself a masterful consensus builder as a member of Congress during the Revolution. He was a mere five feet tall and 120 pounds, but his intellect towered over the convention even if he did not. The young gentleman was praised for blending "the profound politician, with the Scholar"[12] while adeptly "command[ing] the rich resources of his luminous and discriminating mind."[13] Such mental prowess and the "polish of his pen" were "united [with] a pure and spotless virtue."[14] The fine-featured Madison, with his white powdered hair and prominent widow's peak, arrived to the convention in his usual fastidiously prepared fashion: he had already outlined a plan for a whole new government. With this trick up his sleeve, the slight young man quietly joined the assemblage as they took their seats.

Whether military or political veterans, these august men were the nation's elite. They were property owners and professionals. In a time when few Americans attained any advanced education, 60 percent of these gentlemen had attended college, touting degrees from Yale, Harvard, Princeton, or Columbia.[15] Whatever their credentials, they were quite a colorful—and rather portly—group.

From the upper crust of society, the majority of this well-fed contingent were rather overweight, a sign of wealth during this era since it signaled access to plentiful food and minimal manual labor.[16] These men were certainly known more for their oratory than their aerobics. Because clothes were a signal of a gentleman's station, each was fashionably dressed in a painstakingly tailored waistcoat that primly hugged his torso and flowed to mid-thigh.[17] The rich greens, blues, browns, and reds of their jackets made them a more colorful group than the typical men outside. Their metal buttons, fine threading, and straight lines added to the air of dignity with which these lauded men carried themselves. Under their coats were white ruffled dress shirts crafted from fine fabrics and lace, neatly tucked into snug-fitting breeches that typically matched the colors of their waistcoats. In the fashion of the time, they wore white knee-high stockings and low-heeled leather shoes fastened with ostentatious buckles. The attire would certainly have been uncomfortable in the summer heat, but it was important to the delegates to dress properly. They were intensely aware that they were important men doing historic work.

Despite the impressive assemblage of intellect and accomplishment, Washington stood head and shoulders above the rest, both literally and figuratively.[18]

5

Wield the Sword

From the start of the Constitutional Convention, Washington was "held in awe by the delegates and already the de facto leader of the country."[1] In one of their first acts, his fellow delegates unanimously elected him president of the convention. Washington, meticulously groomed in his characteristic understatedly elegant fineries, presided from a lone desk in the front of the room. Adding to the pomp, his station was elevated by two steps above the rest. Here, he sat on a throne-like wooden chair with a high back, topped with a gilded carving of a rising sun that vaguely resembled a halo over his head.[2]

When Washington rose to speak, a reverent hush seized the delegates. This silence was not just respectful but also practical—Washington was not a powerful speaker. It would take some effort to hear his words.

Washington did not like making speeches. At parties he was "much more open and free in his behaviour," especially "in the company of ladies," but when addressing large crowds he came off as stiff and mumbling.[3] This awkwardness owed partly to his horribly uncomfortable false teeth, which continuously chafed his mouth as he labored to project his voice. He had begun losing his teeth in his twenties and they were almost all gone now. He blamed this on his penchant for cracking nuts with his teeth, but it was more likely due to the nutrition and dental hygiene typical of the time, along with the noxious substance called calomel that was used as a medicine for the many illnesses from which he suffered as a young adult. As was common practice for a man of his stature, he obtained dentures made from hippopotamus ivory and human teeth. However, in an age when dentists typically only offered teeth they purchased from white men, what was uncommon was that Washington used teeth pulled from slaves—more likely due to his frugality than egalitarianism.[4] In any case, while his language was "manly and expressive," his voice was hushed and his words indistinct.[5]

Being such a force of nature, he nevertheless commanded the room when he set forth the challenge they faced:[6]

> It is too probable that no plan we propose will be adopted. Perhaps another dreadful conflict is to be sustained. If to please the people, we offer what we ourselves disapprove, how can we afterwards defend our work? Let us raise a standard to which the wise and honest can repair. The event is in the hand of God.

After this statement, Washington remained largely silent for the rest of the convention. His silence, however, did not mean he was not heard. He was still a dominating presence, one that was crucial to keeping the delegates in check as they argued over how to salvage the nation. His glance was often enough. Even though these men were prominent in their own right, they all revered Washington to the point of trepidation.

Washington, distant and aloof as he monitored the debates, was like a stern judge before a courtroom. In fact, at one point during a lull in the discussions, Hamilton dared a fellow delegate to slap Washington on the back like a close chum and say, "My dear General, how happy I am to see you look well." Accepting Hamilton's challenge, the delegate stepped up onto Washington's platform, bowed, and carried out the dare. Washington was offended by the young man's audacity. Not taking kindly to displays of familiarity, he frigidly pulled his hand away and glared. The silence was broken only by the sounds of the other delegates squirming with embarrassment.[7]

With this intimidating man watching over them, the delegates met day in and day out, engaging in fervent debates. But they did have a way to calm their nerves—for while the state of the nation was sobering, the delegates were not. They began their mornings with light breakfasts accompanied by beer or hard cider.[8] The discussion continued during their large midday meal, consisting of pork, beef, stews and meat pies, potatoes and puddings, along with relishes and sauces.[9] All was washed down with plenty of rum, wine, ale, and hard cider, as the delegates talked on into the night by flickering candlelight.

On one particularly rambunctious night at a local tavern, 55 delegates ran up a tab showing 60 bottles of claret, 54 of Madeira, 22 of porter, 12 of beer, 8 of whiskey, 8 of hard cider, and 7 bowls of alcoholic punch "so large that, it was said, ducks could swim around in them."[10] Since that equaled three bottles of alcohol and multiple shots per delegate, it is likely they had some assistance from thirsty locals.

While Washington viewed alcohol as "the source of all evil" and partook only sparingly in such gatherings,[11] Franklin was happy to take advantage of the delegates' thirst. During the proceedings in the assembly room, he sat near the front immediately opposite Washington's "throne," peering wisely through the bifocals he invented and only occasionally making a pointed statement.[12] Franklin chose instead to conduct his important diplomacy during the after-hours parties at his nearby home.[13] He was credited with saying, "God, to relieve [man's] dryness, created the vine and revealed to him the art of making le vin. By the aid of this liquid he unveiled more and more truth."[14] With alcohol in their systems, Franklin was able to uncover his fellow delegates' candid views and use one-on-one diplomacy to make them more amenable to his "truths" for the direction of the nation.[15]

The delegates soon came to the realization that the Articles of Confederation needed to be scrapped, just as Madison had planned. Their convention had originally been intended to fix the existing government rather than scrap it, but the delegates decided it was unsalvageable. As Madison and Hamilton so ardently insisted, if the nation was to survive, they would need to "rethink leadership of the colonies from the ground up."[16] And so they began to discuss radical new ways to govern. Their goal was to craft a new kind of constitution to replace the Articles that would govern the nation effectively and according to the Revolution's principles of liberty and equality. This was easier said than done, however.

The precious few words in this new constitution would, they hoped, govern the nation for many years into the future. Washington and the Founders were quite cognizant of the need to structure a government that would function not only during their lives, but for generations to come.[17] Therefore, they needed to create a written constitution that was acceptable to the people of the present, but also flexible enough to respond to the needs of the future. This central governing document would serve as the "Supreme Law of the Land" for millions of Americans over many generations, and so the delegates agonized over what to include in it. The stakes could not be higher.

Washington and his compatriots sought to create a sweeping new system in which the failings of the British monarchy would never reemerge.[18] William Maclay, a skeletal-looking, outspoken veteran of both the Seven Years' War and the Revolution, captured the prevailing sentiment among the citizenry, writing "We have lately had a hard struggle for our liberty against kingly authority [and] everything related to that species of government is odious to the people."[19] Unsurprisingly, the office of the presidency became a hotly contested issue, since the delegates feared it would lead to a new kind of king.

The delegates spoke out fiercely against creating a presidency that could potentially serve as "the foetus of monarchy."[20] Although monarchy was a time-honored form of governance, Madison declared that creating even a "limited monarchy . . . was out of the question." He added, "The spirit of the times—the state of our affairs, forbade the experiment."[21] Washington and the vast majority of other delegates could not agree more. They "did not consider the Prerogatives of the British Monarch as a proper guide in defining the Executive powers,"[22] and worked to ensure that "America's president would wield a less threatening kind of executive power than Britain's king."[23] As the delegates debated how to accomplish this goal, the heat of their passions filled the room—quite literally, since the windows remained shut and the heavy green drapes drawn in order to maintain secrecy.

To these patriots, one of the most dangerous of the president's powers was his command of the military. After all, the Americans had just fought a bloody war against the British Crown's abuse of his military power. The Declaration of Independence, which listed their justifications for rebellion a few years earlier, clearly stated:

> [King George III] has kept among us, in times of peace, Standing Armies without the Consent of our legislatures. He has affected to render the Military independent of and superior to the Civil Power . . . : For quartering large bodies of armed troops among us: For protecting them, by a mock Trial from punishment for any Murders which they should commit on the Inhabitants of these States . . .[24]

The British monarch's use of his commander-in-chief power had led to the bloody war. And a repeat was to be avoided at all costs.[25]

At the outbreak of the Revolution in 1775, the king's example certainly had a profound impact on Americans' understanding of the term "commander in chief."[26] Many of the states had previously modeled their respective governors' military powers around British precedent, and the Founders had looked to them as a starting point of reference at the beginning of the war. But as the Revolution escalated, the king's powers—and even some of the governors'—were increasingly rejected. Americans feared that if they merely followed the British example, they would wind up having their liberties quashed all over again. The patriots sought to build their own commander from the ground up.

Luckily, by the time of the Constitutional Convention twelve years later, Americans had an intellectual antidote to the evils of the British example. To find a model for the new American commander in chief, the delegates and the citizenry at large had to look no farther than the statuesque man sitting quietly at the front of the room. "As Americans in 1787 tried to envision a republican head of state who could protect them against old King George without becoming a new King George, they did have a particular George in mind."[27]

Washington afforded the nation "an example of the national leader par excellence."[28] While America had seen other commanders in chief,[29] it was Washington who distilled these precedents into a distinctive, American version. He had overcome many of the evils of the old ways and introduced new meaning to the term commander in chief amid the bloodshed of war. Thus, when it came time to contemplate how to allocate military powers within the new government, the Americans looked to the decorated war hero whom many considered "the greatest man in the world."[30]

While the delegates originally considered spreading the command-er-in-chief powers among multiple persons, that notion changed when they appealed to their memories of the "situation during the late war."[31] The memories of Washington's actions as revolutionary commander convinced the delegates that "[f]rom the nature of the thing, the command of armies ought to be delegated to one person only. The secrecy, dispatch, and decision, which are necessary in military operations can only be expected from one person."[32]

And with Washington in mind, the delegates scrapped the idea of dividing up the commander-in-chief role. Instead they determined "that the sword ought to be put in the hands of the representatives of the people."[33] That person would be the president of the United States.

6

Supreme Law of the Land

With a vote, the delegates bestowed the full set of commander-in-chief powers on the president. But they did not elaborate on what exactly those powers were. They did not need to. When the delegates described the new presidency's military power with the amazingly few words, "The President shall be Commander in Chief of the Army and Navy of the United States," they were not being cagey. On the contrary, they needed no further description because it was so evident to the voters what they meant: the same powers that General Washington had exercised in the war to protect them.[1]

"When men spoke of the great national representative, of the guardian of the people" that the proposed president would become, "they were thinking in terms of the Father of His Country."[2] As the only American commander in chief, Washington had forged the meaning of presidential war powers in the heat of battle. He taught America "how to govern a nation at war"[3] and showed firsthand that the country needed a strong commander to survive. While his military authority was sweeping, he used it virtuously. This convinced the delegates and the broader populace that the new American commander in chief, based on Washington's precedents, could be powerful without trampling liberty.

One delegate warned, "The Executive will have great opportunitys of abusing his power; particularly in time of war when the military force, and in some respects the public money will be in his hands."[4] But Washington's example assuaged their fears. Another delegate explained that the powers allocated to the president in the Constitution were "greater than [he] was disposed to make them," and he believed those powers would not "have been so great had not many of the members cast their eyes towards General Washington . . . and shaped their Ideas of the Powers to be given to a President, by their opinions of his Virtue."[5]

The patriots were confident in knowing that their paradigm for the new presidency's military powers was the man who was pivotal to the birth of the United States. Washington had served as "the great protector of the Mass of the people," and now the president would continue that role.[6] Surely, lesser men would eventually occupy the office. But if they ever questioned what it meant to be the American commander in chief, the country needed only to look back to the righteous precedents that Washington had set during the Revolution. With this in mind, they finalized the Constitution.

After an entire summer of vigorous argument and difficult compromise, the great republic began with a sacrificial lamb. The lamb's skin was soaked in water for one day and then placed in an alkaline vat of liquor and lime. Stirred at least twice daily with a long wooden pole, the lambskin sat for about a week before it was hung to dry on a stretching frame. A craftsman painstakingly scraped the skin with a blade, turning it into a fine parchment. Once prepared, it was shipped to Philadelphia, where the fledgling nation's anxious political leaders transcribed onto it the concise words of the new Constitution.

Washington's exalted example and unfailing perseverance had guided the delegates through long cantankerous days and nights to agree on a mere four pages of parchment that would create the new American government. In addition to naming the president as commander in chief, the Constitution outlined his nonmilitary powers, as well as the powers of Congress and the Supreme Court. On September 17, 1787, the thirty-nine exhausted delegates who had not abandoned the effort signed the parchment. Few were completely satisfied with the new Constitution. Washington certainly was not, but he conceded that it was the best they could do. He wrote, "That the Government, though not absolutely perfect, is one of the best in the world, I have little doubt."[7]

After the convention, a woman asked Benjamin Franklin whether this Constitution would create a monarchy or a republic. Franklin dryly replied, "A republic, if you can keep it." Our Founders provide guidance on how we might do so.

⚜

When the Constitution went before the states for ratification, it faced a barrage of criticism. Many believed it would be rejected. The voters feared relinquishing local power to a national government. They were suspicious of the new presidency.[8] But in the end, the American people adopted the Constitution largely because of their esteem for Washington's Revolutionary War leadership. As a delegate admitted, "Be assured, his influence carried this government."[9]

That unsatisfying eighteenth-century document became the "Supreme Law of the Land" and still governs the United States to this day. The few words immortalized on that old parchment define the nation. They embody the radical ideal that every citizen has a right to "life, liberty, and the pursuit of happiness," regardless of his or her heredity.[10] Forged amidst turmoil, this document has never really escaped it. Its words not only have served as kindling for uprisings and wars but also remain at the center of contemporary debates over our nation's soul.

America's memory of General George Washington's Revolutionary War powers has faded over the past two centuries. However, the Constitution has not. The Commander in Chief clause remains unaltered. The president still derives his constitutional military power from those precious few words that the Founders wrote during that hot summer of 1787. What it means to be the "American commander in chief" may be murky now, but it was not so back then. The founding generation ratified that clause with a specific person in mind. That gentleman farmer, who saved the fledgling nation, set precedents that still define those war powers necessary to defend the United States.

II

CRUEL AND USUAL PUNISHMENT

"Justice and Policy will require recourse to be had to the Law of retaliation, however abhorrent and disagreeable to our natures in cases of Torture and capital punishment."[1]
—GENERAL GEORGE WASHINGTON, 1776

The lessons may be forgotten, but history never dies.

Early in the Revolution, an enraged General Washington wrote to Congress regarding the capture of a young woman "of easy virtue."[2] The "trollop" of a Loyalist spy, she had been instructed to transmit to British forces an encrypted letter concerning American military plans.[3] But she proved to be a bumbling conduit. Disobeying orders, this "infamous hussy"[4] gave the letter to a local baker with whom she had "shared idyllic hours of dalliance," and requested that he deliver it instead.[5] Noticing that the letter was directed to a British officer, the baker grew suspicious and turned it over to the American authorities.

Washington was outraged by the treacherous letter and dispatched his troops to capture the woman. They quickly located the not-so-sly minx and brought her back to their general. Washington notified Congress, "I immediately secured the Woman, but for a long time she was proof against every threat and perswasion to discover the Author."[6] He was desperate to find the mole among the American forces, but the "subtle, shrewd jade" obstinately refused to reveal the traitor behind the plot.[7] General Washington faced a familiar dilemma: how far are we willing to go in order to save American lives?

Through undisclosed means, "at length she was brought to a confession."[8]

The Americans captured a whopping 14,000 enemy soldiers during the Revolutionary War, and some of them became casualties in the United States' struggle to forge a nation.[9] The chapters in Part II analyze General Washington's treatment of enemy combatants.[10] Part I demonstrated that Washington served as the model for the future presidents' war powers, and this part begins delving into precisely what his Revolutionary War precedents were.

7

The Currents of War

A midst the bubbling waterfall of a sleepy New England state park lies an innocuous boulder. As the afternoon sun pours through the leaves of the maple trees that dominate the area, this curiously round stone blends into the picturesque scenery. Here, the boulder lay forgotten for hundreds of years, much like the lessons to be learned from the story behind it.

The quaint Connecticut town of East Haddam that developed around the boulder appears distinctly puritanical to this day, with friendly suburbanites painstakingly grooming their neat lawns and colonial style homes. At a small bend in the tame Connecticut River, the village is known for its stately opera house, quiet streets, and serene fall foliage. Of all places, one would never expect East Haddam to have been the site of a gruesome crime spawned from the fervor of an angry mob. But it was. That boulder's present location is a testament to the violence that once engulfed the region—it lies there as the direct result of a horrific attack on a local family.

In the lead-up to the Revolutionary War, the American colonists began to rebel against Britain's dominion in the 1760s. Following the Seven Years' War, Britain passed several measures that infuriated the colonists. British taxpayers were fed up with the enormous expense of defending the colonies from the French, the Native Americans, and other aggressors. Thus, the British government sought to force the colonists to share more of the burden for their own defense. The Americans did not take kindly to this new, stricter motherland.

First, the British forbade the colonies from expanding into the vast, fertile lands west of the eastern seaboard. Britain's objective was to appease the Native Americans by permitting them to live peacefully on these lands and thereby avoid costly battles. With the Appalachian Mountains between them, the tribes and the colonies were less likely to fight. But the Americans, having long eyed these lands for their own westward expansion, were incensed by such meddling.[1] And London was not done antagonizing them.

Next, London struck closer to home with a law commanding that the Americans quarter British troops in their houses. This Quartering Act seemed fair to the British, since they were merely requiring the colonists to house their own defenders. From the American perspective, however, their military protectors suddenly appeared more like oppressors. At any time, the Americans might face armed British soldiers bursting into their homes and demanding quarter. In light of this perceived threat to their property, family, and liberty, violent rebellion began to seem all the more justified.

But nothing enraged the Americans as much as London's encroachment on their wallets. In an effort to increase tax revenues, Parliament passed the Tea Act of 1773.[2] This law was intended to induce the Americans to switch from smuggled, untaxed Dutch tea to the British variety. Even though this infamous act reduced the price of legally imported tea, it created a tea monopoly for the British East India Company, thereby threatening to force tea smugglers and other "entrepreneurial" colonists out of business. Although the colonies were not only among the most prosperous but also among the lowest-taxed places on earth, the Americans were nevertheless outraged by the Crown's intrusion.[3] To them, the Tea Act stood "as a mark of Supremacy of [the British] Parliament."[4] In retaliation, bands of protesters throughout the colonies used force and intimidation to drive the British tea from colonial ports. The Connecticut contingent of one such group, called the "Sons of Liberty," was particularly irked by a certain East Haddam resident's penchant for British tea.[5]

Abner Beebe was a mill owner and physician who remained loyal to the British Crown even as the colonies were beginning to rebel. He was an educated, churchgoing man who gave food to the poor and contributed funds to the local paupers' cemetery. A middle-aged father, he was born in East Haddam and raised to respect his colony's mother country. Staunch in his convictions, he "spoke very freely in Favor of [the British] Government" and criticized the tea parties staged by the patriots.[6] He publicly argued that the motherland's "government had a right to make whatever laws they pleased" and refused to join the boycott on British tea.[7] The Sons of Liberty viewed Beebe's obstinacy as a grievous transgression against the patriotic cause.

Heated with patriotic passion, a mob of young men swarmed towards Beebe's home, undeterred by the bone-chilling winds of the New England winter. Inside the house on that dreary February night, the unsuspecting family labored to stay warm as they tended to a child who had fallen ill. Their quiet was shattered by a pounding at the door. Abner Beebe unlatched the door to find a mob at his step. As he spoke to them, it quickly became apparent that they were not seeking a gentlemanly political debate. They were lugging hot pitch. As his family watched in horror, Beebe "was assaulted by a Mob, stripped naked, & hot Pitch was poured upon him, which blistered his Skin."[8]

The practice of "tarring and feathering" had originated in 1189 with Richard the Lionheart during the Crusades, but was not used extensively until the colonists revived it during their revolt against Britain. It entailed stripping the victim to his waist or completely naked, and then pouring hot, hissing tar over him. This would burn his bare skin, and, if poured over his head, it would likely render him blind in one or both eyes.[9] The tar of the revolutionary era was of such a quality that it melted only at relatively high temperatures, the average being 140°F.[10] With painful third-degree burns sustained after just approximately five seconds of contact with material of that temperature, Beebe's skin was likely heavily damaged as a result of his prolonged exposure.[11]

Removing the tar was even more painful. It took hours or even days to peel the hardened tar from the victim's body, and his flesh often peeled off along with the tar. Infection typically followed, especially in a case like Beebe's, where the attackers concocted a humiliating covering more creative than feathers.[12]

As if being beaten, stripped, and burned with tar were not enough punishment for Beebe, he was then "carried to a Hog Sty & rubbed over with Hogs Dung. They threw the Hog's Dung in his Face, & rammed some of it down his Throat." To ensure public disgrace, he was "in that Condition exposed to a Company of Women." Leaving Beebe's body virtually lifeless (although he would survive the attack), the mob next turned to his home and family. "His House was attacked, his Windows broke." So traumatized, "a Child of his went into Distraction upon this Treatment." Finally, the mob ransacked Beebe's gristmill and rolled its millstone down into the stream, where for centuries the boulder has remained by the waterfall in East Haddam, largely forgotten, much like the story behind it.[13]

Attacks of this kind were rampant during the Revolution. People like Abner Beebe were viewed as a threat to the revolutionary spirit and the emergence of the new nation. For his part, Washington morally abhorred such cruelty. He wished for America to treat her enemies with dignity and humanity. But despite his moral opposition, he came to find harsh measures necessary for victory. In fact, his conversion was swift—he arrived at this conclusion soon after the outbreak of war.

After years of smoldering discord between the government of King George III and the American "rabble in arms," war erupted on April 19, 1775, at 5:00 A.M., in the small town square of Lexington, Massachusetts.[14] The British had placed neighboring Boston under martial law in an attempt to subdue the surging patriot defiance. They quartered troops in private homes and turned the freedom-loving city into an occupied zone. The Massachusetts legislature had been stripped of its political power and the people were now subjected to edicts from the royal governor and the occupying military forces.

The New Englanders were not the sort to be suppressed without a fight. Hearing the British drumbeat at sunrise on that brisk spring morning, the American militiamen emerged from a local tavern to defy the occupiers. The colonists had long relied on such groups of townsmen for defense. However, while their original purpose was to protect the towns from a Native American or perhaps French attack, the colonists now saw their former protectors as the threat.

The British troops were on their way to confiscate the rebellious Massachusetts colony's munitions, but the patriots would not stand for another such affront. As the first rays of morning light illuminated the village, Lexington's stout little wooden bell tower continued—almost pathetically—to sound the alarm while British soldiers poured into the town square.[15] They were surprised by what they found. About seventy bold American farmers and shopkeepers stood tall on the small, dewy town green, boldly facing a well-trained column of approximately one thousand British regulars.[16]

The British—derisively called "redcoats" or, more colorfully, "lobster back sons-a-bitches" by the Americans in a scornful nod to their well-tailored red uniforms—were in sour spirits. They had marched all night and waded up to their waists through a swamp that blocked their route. Enraged by the insolence of the colonists before them, the British demanded: "You damned rebels, lay down your arms!"[17] This remark was particularly offensive because the Americans did not see themselves as treasonous rebels, but as honorable men courageously defending their families and property. When the defiant colonists scoffed at the demand, the British shouted "huzza!" and raced towards the Crown's unruly subjects with sharp bayonets affixed to the end of their muskets.[18]

Terrified by the enormous mass of red and metal rapidly nearing, some of the Americans decided to go home. But suddenly, just as the Americans began to disperse, the confused scene was pierced by the boom of a gun. While each side blamed the other, reports of that fateful moment indicated that an unknown man had been secretly watching the events unfold from afar.[19] He peered down his Scottish flintlock pistol at the advancing redcoats and, pulling the trigger, unleashed a deafening thunder and spray of pungent, singeing gunpowder.[20] The explosion sent the lead ball hurling erratically through the barrel of the gun towards the startled British. And with this "shot heard round the world," all hell broke loose.

Redcoats and patriots flinched at the sound. They squeezed their trigger fingers, sending simultaneous blasts hurling in every direction. Before the British officers could regain control of their units, blood flew and men on both sides fell to the ground, yelping in pain. The British shot a volley of fire towards the startled colonists, killing ten and injuring ten others before the Americans scattered in terror.[21]

Word of the bloodbath spread like wildfire throughout New England. One patriot reported, "there was a general Uproar through the Neighboring Colonies; the Echo of which soon extended through the Continent."[22] *Rage militaire* engulfed the region as men grew impassioned in defense of their families and homes.[23] Militiamen responded to the call to arms by the thousands. The war for America had begun not with an eloquent speech or a noble declaration but with one unauthorized shot from a lone sniper.[24]

8

Exitus Acta Probat

At the outset of hostilities, America's Continental Congress met to plan a strategy for the patriotic cause. This group was composed of political and intellectual leaders from throughout the colonies, with Washington attending as a representative of Virginia. Having gained approximately twenty-five pounds of muscle since the Jumonville scandal in 1754, the matured man carried his formidable two-hundred-pound frame with the majesty of a natural-born athlete. When ordering from his tailor, he described himself as "a Man full 6 feet high & proportionably made; if any thing, rather slender than thick for a person of that highth with pretty long Arms and thighs."[1] Many history books describe him as taller, but Washington was not one to misinform his tailor—he took his appearance quite seriously.

Washington arrived at Independence Hall in 1775 looking the part of a military expert. In a not-so-subtle reminder of his previous military service during the Seven Years' War, he shrewdly wore his blue Virginia militia uniform. This was complemented by his hair, which was powdered white and tied in the back with a satin bow. Such a style was considered very masculine and militaristic, thereby serving as yet another indication of his soldier status.

Ironically, Washington had in fact been retired from military life for fifteen years. His only military experience after the Jumonville disaster had been predominantly in backwoods warfare, and he had done poorly by most standards. He had never commanded anything larger than a regiment, let alone an army, in battle. Due to his limited success, Washington had been unable to obtain a commission in the British Army and had resigned from the Virginia militia.

Despite his lackluster record, Washington still had more military experience than most Americans in 1775. To the group of military novices in the Continental Congress, he was the relative expert. And defer to him they did. When military questions arose, their natural reaction was to turn to the man in uniform standing with a militaristic posture "as straight as an Indian."[2] Although he preferred to remain silent, Washington provided thoughtful contributions if asked for his opinion. Unsurprisingly, when time came to decide who would lead the new American army, Washington catapulted to the shortlist of candidates.

The southern gentleman's impeccable manners, humble demeanor, and almost aristocratic dignity endeared him to the congressmen. Cited for his "handsome face," "graceful attitude and movements," "self command," and willingness to risk his personal fortune, he embodied the noble new "American Commander in Chief" that Congress aimed to create.[3] One delegate observed that Washington had "so much martial dignity in his deportment that you would distinguish him to be a general and a soldier from among ten thousand people."[4] On top of all these attributes, Washington humbly exuded a *je ne sais quoi* that the Revolution badly needed. And so, after much deliberation and argument, dominated by north-south tensions, the Virginian was unanimously appointed as America's first commander in chief.

In all of these deliberations, however, Congress neglected to address the matter of how to treat their foes. They passed not one resolution concerning the treatment of captured British and Loyalist fighters. Congress's first mere mention of the subject on record was in Washington's commission as commander in chief of the Continental Army:

> You shall take every method in your power consistent with prudence, to destroy or make prisoners of all persons who now are or who hereafter shall appear in Arms against the good people of the united colonies.
>
> And whereas all particulars cannot be foreseen, nor positive instructions for such emergencies so before hand given but that many things must be left to your prudent and discreet management, as occurrences may arise upon the place, or from time to time fall out, you are therefore upon all such accidents or any occasions that may happen, to *use your best circumspection and (advising with your council of war) to order and dispose of the said Army under your command as may be most advantageous for the obtaining the end for which these forces have been raised,* making it your special care in discharge of the great trust committed unto you, that the liberties of America receive no detriment.[5]

With this resolution, the Continental Congress empowered their new commander to decide whether to destroy or imprison enemies of the fledgling nation. They immediately followed this grant of authority with a further declaration leaving much to Washington's discretion, or "best circumspection," in how to deploy the Continental Army in defense of the emerging states.[6] In so doing, Congress indicated that decisions regarding prisoner treatment would be the commander's prerogative.[7]

With these powers, Washington set out for Boston. His mission was to defeat the British who were besieged within the city by enraged New Englanders. The city had been transformed into a virtual military camp as nearly 14,000 British troops poured in and the townsfolk fled. Boston's civilian population had plummeted by more than 60 percent, to a mere 6,753 American inhabitants.[8] With the town largely emptied, the redcoats had certainly made themselves at home, living in the stately brick and wooden homes of Boston, making use of its tidy shops and churches, helping themselves to its bountiful fish stocks, and patrolling the cobblestone and dirt roads for spies loyal to the patriot cause. But however comfortable the redcoats were, the fact of the matter was that they were dangerously trapped—pinned by the tens of thousands of American militiamen from Massachusetts and surrounding colonies who had joined the cause after the opening battle on Lexington's town green.

Before things escalated further, Congress attempted to negotiate peace during the summer of 1775. They presented the British with an "Olive Branch Petition" in which the colonies agreed to cease their uprising if King George III and Parliament revoked their oppressive new laws and withdrew their troops. But by August, the king had had enough insolence.

The first in a line of British kings of German descent to have actually been born in Britain, George III proudly declared, "Born and educated in this country, I glory in the name of Britain."[9] And he was certainly ready to place Britain's interests before those of the American colonies. Thirty-seven years old at the time, he had already ruled for fifteen years and had supported certain efforts to tax the colonies. This did not win him fans in America. Washington captured the sentiment of many when he said, "Great Britain hath no more right to put their hands into my pocket . . . than I have to put my hands into yours."[10] As the conflict escalated, the colonists came to vilify George III as a ruthless tyrant, who "has plundered our seas, ravaged our Coasts, burnt our towns, and destroyed the lives of our people."[11]

In reality, the king was a reserved, thoughtful man, willing to endure pains to do what he thought was right—and he expected others to do the same. For example, when his bid to marry his true love was opposed, he broke off the relationship, writing, "I am born for the happiness or misery of a great nation and consequently must often act contrary to my passions."[12] He eventually married, and even though he did not meet the bride chosen for him until their wedding day, he nevertheless enjoyed a happy marriage—and a remarkably faithful one for monarchs of the era—fathering fifteen children. But this happy twist of fate did not erase his "grin and bear it" mentality. So when the colonists rebelled against the burdens placed on them by Parliament, the king was not particularly sympathetic.

With large bulging eyes and cheeks, George III possessed a high forehead and thick, carefully groomed hair. He was so well coifed, in fact, that the arsenic used in the hair products of the time may have contributed to his bouts of insanity.[13] He was very lucid, however, when the patriots began to rebel. Infuriated by their attack against British power, he declared war on the "dangerous and ill designing" patriots.[14] Although a pious Anglican, he was not particularly forgiving and vowed to crush these "wicked and desperate persons within [his] Realm."[15] Britain scoffed at America's olive branch. The fight was on.

In summer of 1775, the war escalated and prisoner counts along with it. Reports abounded that the British were mistreating their American captives. "His Excellency," as Washington was called, raised the matter with his British Army counterpart, General Thomas Gage, a high-browed, beady-eyed aristocrat. The two men were no strangers. Ironically, the now bitter rivals had once been rather friendly. Gage had commanded Washington in the Seven Years' War and respected the young man's bravery after he organized a successful retreat that saved many of Gage's troops. In fact, the British general had sympathized with Washington when he was passed over for promotion in the British Army many years before and the two had maintained cordial relations following the war. However, after two decades, time and distance had severed their ties and their relationship had cooled, to say the least.

Washington was shocked and horrified by reports that Americans captured during the siege of Boston were left "languishing with Wounds, and Sickness; that some have been even amputated" by British troops under Gage's command.[16] He yearned for all prisoners to be treated with humanity and had ordered his men to care for the enemy combatants in their custody. But Gage was not reciprocating. To Washington, this conduct was a terrible offense, and it was very personal. Both honor and pragmatism demanded retribution.

Washington was not a detached general but one who fought alongside his men. Battle after battle, he led the charge, sometimes having multiple horses shot out from under him as he continued to fight. Although none of his several horses were actually white, popular tales often depicted him as a princely leader atop a great white horse in the thick of battle. While aloof in his mannerisms and occasionally gruff with his subordinates, he suffered alongside his troops, and it fostered mutual respect. So when his captured brethren were abused, he wanted not only to avenge them but also to protect other Americans from future harm. Using his British captives as leverage achieved both objectives.

Washington's personal motto was *Exitus acta probat*, Latin for "the outcome justifies the deed." He was an extremely principled man, but history has lost sight of his very practical side. While he earnestly endeavored to raise America's treatment of her prisoners above the barbarity of previous European wars, it became clear to him that the only way he could save his captured countrymen was to potentially mutilate the redcoats in his custody.[17] Washington was morally opposed to mistreating prisoners. But he was even more opposed to letting Americans suffer. He was a practical man and if he could use British captives to defend his countrymen, he would. When it came down to saving Americans, the outcome justified the deed.

Retribution was the primary means by which armies remedied enemy breaches of the laws of war. And so Washington warned Gage, his friend-turned-foe,

> My Duty now makes it necessary to apprize you, that for the future I shall regulate my Conduct towards those Gentlemen, who are or may be in our Possession, exactly by the Rule you shall observe towards those of ours, now in your Custody.
>
> If Severity and Hardship mark the Line of your Conduct (painful as it may be to me) your Prisoners will feel its Effects.[18]

In the broadest reading, this letter expressed the view that the enemy's actions justified amputating limbs of British prisoners. And these were not empty threats, since Washington held a number of British troops captive early in the war. While it was unlikely that he truly intended to go to that extreme in order to protect American prisoners at this stage, the British indeed complained that the American side was already mistreating British captives in other ways.

One report of abuse comes from when Washington's forces attacked the lighthouse on an island in Boston Harbor that summer of 1775. Their mission was to disrupt British night shipping by extinguishing the warning light. And so on a steamy July night, with the darkness and crashing waves masking their advance, three hundred American minutemen boarded whaleboats and stealthily made their way towards the small rocky island and its thirty-two unsuspecting British guards.[19] In a fierce 2:00 A.M. ambush, the stench of gunpowder pierced the salty sea air. The patriot muskets quickly killed a third of the redcoats and the remainder surrendered before the Americans triumphantly ignited the lighthouse into a towering inferno.[20] But the Americans' jubilance was short-lived. The tide had receded, beaching their getaway boats. Trapped on the island, the Americans watched the British gunboats race to the scene.

The tide returned just in time for the Americans to jump into their makeshift armada with their captives and get to the opposite shore before the British cannon could blow them to pieces. The infuriated British were able to hit only two Americans before the rest made it to safety. Once ashore, the Americans promptly put their new captives to work, forcing them to carry a cannon up a hill.[21] Word traveled back to the British lines that this was just the tip of the proverbial iceberg.

After Gage had received Washington's warning, he spat off an angry rejoinder. His intelligence, he said, had indicated that Americans were abusing captured redcoats, using extreme forced-work tactics and even starvation in order to compel the captured British troops to help the American side:[22]

My intelligence from your army would justify severe recrimination. I understand there are of the King's faithful subjects, taken some time since by the rebels, laboring, like negro slaves, to gain their daily subsistence, or reduced to the wretched alternative, to perish by famine or take arms against their King and country. Those who have made the treatment of the prisoners in my hands, or of your other friends in Boston, a pretence for such measures, found barbarity upon falsehood.[23]

Neither Washington's threat to General Gage nor the Americans' possible abuses were based on any congressional resolution regarding the treatment of enemy captives. Washington led the way, informing Congress of his actions only after the fact.[24] Likewise, no state legislative body instructed the commander on the matter of prisoner treatment. Instead, the Continental Army informed the Massachusetts legislature that "Gage is resolved to know no distinction of Rank among our Prisoners in his Hands, which obliges Genl. Washington (very contrary to his disposition) to observe the same Rule of Treatment to those Gentlemen, . . . which otherwise may appear harsh and cruel."[25]

Washington considered it within his powers as commander in chief to decide the treatment of enemy prisoners without any need for a congressional resolution. He determined the best course of action based on his understanding of the laws of war. And his views on the matter did not always align with those of Congress.

9

American Fortitude

In August 1775, mere days after Washington's hostile exchange with General Gage, the Americans ambushed the British transport ship HMS *Hope* as it sailed up the Delaware River.[1] The outnumbered British quickly surrendered, and the Americans captured a British officer named Major Christopher French. Approximately fifty years old, described as "small of stature" and having coarse, stern features, he was imprisoned in Hartford, Connecticut.[2] While there was little indication of serious mistreatment, the prissy Major French began complaining to Washington about the "Incivility or Contempt" with which he was treated by the townspeople.[3] They mocked and insulted him, leaving him outraged that such rabble should dare speak to a British officer in such a manner.

Like a disgruntled customer who sends a note to the corporate office about an unpleasant cashier, French dashed off several angry letters to Washington, who diligently replied to each. At first the general responded cordially, pledging that "suitable Provision shall be made for you and your Companions, and shew you every civility."[4] But as the war dragged on and the British continued to abuse their captives, his tone shifted.

Referring to the mistreatment of Americans by the British, Washington curtly told French, "I should illy support my Country's Honor,

and my own Character, if I did not shew a proper Sense of their sufferings, by making the condition of the Ministerial Officers, in some
Degree, dependant on theirs."[5] Major French escaped before Washington educated him in the sufferings of American prisoners, but the
commander's thinly veiled threats conveyed his emerging belief that
abusing British prisoners was justified.

In December 1775, over seven months after the outbreak of war,
Congress finally passed a resolution concerning prisoner treatment.
However, it was largely at odds with Washington's declared stance. As
he held the British forces in Boston, the Continental Congress resolved

> That such as are taken be treated as prisoners of war, but with
> humanity, and allowed the same rations as the troops in the
> service of the Continent; that the officers being in pay should
> supply themselves with cloaths, their bills to be taken therefor,
> that the soldiers be furnished as they now are.[6]

With this edict, Congress sought to take the high road and elevate the
nation's conduct above less-noble struggles of the past.

As a matter of principle, Washington agreed. He was morally
opposed to mistreatment, in theory, and had initially preferred to "err
on the side of mercy than that of strict Justice."[7] Experience taught him,
however, that the high standard he sought was not practical, and that
harsh measures might be necessary to save American lives. Just weeks
after Congress's decree that prisoners be treated humanely, Washington
again threatened to abuse a British captive.[8] This time, he needed to
protect a captured national hero.

Washington was enraged by reports that the British had abused the
popular American patriot Colonel Ethan Allen. Allen was a flamboyant
farmer-turned-statesman-turned-land-speculator best known as the
charismatic leader of a "merry band" of militiamen called the Green
Mountain Boys.[9] Allen was born into a relatively prosperous farming

family in the sparsely populated hills of northwestern Connecticut. But farm life was not enough for this fiery character. Like many ambitious youth at the time, he journeyed to the frontier to find his fortune and eventually made his way to the wilderness of Vermont. Not yet a state, it was a hotly disputed area over which New York landowners attempted to assert control while the squatters living there sought independent statehood. The "wild west" of New England, this region was dominated by a rambunctious lot. Allen fit right in.

With a long face, narrow-set eyes, big nose, and bushy brown hair, Allen matured into a loud man with a penchant for taking the law into his own hands. Married to an uneducated and rigidly religious woman who did not care for her husband's debaucherous streak, he faced constant criticism at home.[10] This made Allen rather eager to escape the house.

He escaped to the local taverns and town hall, where he became not only a connoisseur of cheap rum but also a raucous figure in the community. Standing over six feet tall, he was impossible to ignore as he shouted and his large face grew ruddy with passion. With his incendiary oratory, Allen had a knack for whipping his audiences into action. He soon emerged as the grandiloquent leader of the frontiersmen seeking to forcefully secure their Vermont land claims against wealthy New Yorkers. Many of these Green Mountain Boys, including Allen himself, had outstanding arrest warrants in New York for beating anyone who challenged their claims. Enjoying a good fight almost as much as a good drink, this guerilla force readily followed Allen into battle time and again.

When the Revolutionary War broke out, the unhappily married thirty-seven-year-old Allen was ready to leap into the center of the struggle. Even though most of the action was in Massachusetts, Allen led the unruly Green Mountain Boys into the backwater of upstate New York to take part in America's first offensive of the war. Their target was the formidable, granite-walled Fort Ticonderoga. Known as the "Gibraltar of North America," this imposing British fortress secured the waterway connecting Canada to New York. Overlooking Lake Champlain, Ticonderoga was in a heavily wooded and largely uninhabited area, then just beginning to enjoy the effects of spring's slow march northward.

Allen's men set out on a midnight raid on a rain-soaked May night in 1775, under orders to seize the boats of wealthy British merchants so that the American forces might use them as ferries across the lake.[11] Stumbling upon "choice liquors" in a Loyalist's cellar, however, the Vermonters took to drinking instead.[12] At three o'clock in the morning, they decided to make do with just the single boat they had secured to ferry as many men as possible before they lost the cover of darkness.

After two trips across the choppy, cold water, only ninety men were in place. Two-thirds of the American troops were still stranded on the other side of the lake, but Allen decided to attack before daybreak anyway. His force a less-than-optimal mixture of drunk and hung over, the brazen Allen and his dysfunctional militia charged the fort.

Luckily for Allen, the British had only one sentry on duty, and he was helping himself to an unauthorized catnap. Taken by complete surprise, the undermanned fort put up little resistance, as the half-naked British soldiers did not even have time to put on their pants, let alone ready their muskets.[13] In a stunning blow to the British, the fort fell to the Americans, thereby thwarting Britain's plan to invade through Montreal. Perhaps more importantly, the Americans acquired the gunpowder and artillery that Washington needed to rain hell on the British in Boston. Washington was rather pleased.

Drunk with confidence—and booze—after this triumph, Allen began lobbying Congress to expand the war, writing, "I will lay my life on it, that with fifteen hundred men, and a proper artillery, I will take Montreal."[14] Eager to spread the Revolution to the French Canadians, Congress agreed to a daring invasion of Canada. Washington, though not technically authorized by Congress to do so, was so enthusiastic about the plan that he sent up his own separate brigade.[15]

As usual, Allen was among the first to charge to the front lines of the fight. Patience not being one of his virtues, he led approximately one hundred men in a foolhardy attack on Montreal ahead of the main American force.[16] Outnumbered two to one, his rogue team fought ferociously but was quickly defeated and Allen was captured. Now wise to the plans for a larger assault, the British repelled the American invasion of Canada. Allen was trapped.

British Brigadier Prescott ordered that Allen be tightly shackled and chained within the dark hull of a prison ship moored in Montreal's harbor. Prescott was an odious character, whose large, almost serpentine eyes were suited to his oppressive disposition. He became known for his "many acts of petty tyranny," and Allen felt the brunt of his wrath.[17]

Rather than languish in defeat in his dank wooden prison, however, Allen was defiant, much to his dour captor's vexation. Choosing to "behave in a daring, soldier-like manner, that [he] might exhibit a good sample of American fortitude," the colorful Allen challenged each of his guards to a manly fistfight as they passed by.[18] While not one of them accepted his challenge, Prescott found Allen's bravado infuriating and ordered that he be treated "with much severity."[19]

The British beat Allen, deprived him of adequate water and rations, and repeatedly threatened him with hanging.[20] For weeks he was held almost naked, wearing little more than the heavy iron chains that cut his wrists and weighed him to the ground.[21] "I have suffered every thing short of death," he reported.[22] The large man withered as his health deteriorated. But the plucky Allen survived. Unsure of what to do with this defiant troublemaker, the British shipped him off to England, where he was imprisoned in a dark old castle in Cornwall.[23] Like an exhibit at the zoo, he slept in hay infested with vermin as locals bribed guards for a peek at the giant who had taken Ticonderoga.

Everyone expected that Allen would be swiftly hanged. But when word reached Washington that Allen was "thrown into Irons and suffers all the Hardships inflicted upon common Felons," the commander was incensed, to put it mildly.[24] He felt bound by his strong sense of honor to employ all means necessary to protect Allen. And Washington was prepared to go to great lengths to save an American life.

10

Necessary Evil

In a lucky twist of fate, the Americans captured Ethan Allen's tormentor, Brigadier Prescott, during a subsequent battle. Washington now had his bargaining chip. And he used it. He promptly contacted the new commanding British general, William Howe, who had assumed leadership of the British forces after Parliament recalled Thomas Gage. The British government had lost faith in Gage after he had failed to finish off the colonists' insurrection in Boston, and had transferred the reins to Howe in hopes of a speedy end to the war. Washington was now negotiating with a more sympathetic character.

General Howe was a British aristocrat who, although a capable commander, nevertheless benefitted from his family's money and connections. His grandmother had an affair with King George I, and so his family tree—more resembling a twisted bush—positioned Howe as King George III's illegitimate uncle. Having begun his military career as a teenager, Howe gradually rose through the ranks to achieve his current lofty rank. Now forty-seven years old, he was a brawny six feet tall, with a broad nose and black eyes that sparkled almost as much as his stellar reputation.[1] While fond of merriment—"a glass and a lass" in particular—Howe also had a darker side and "suffered from the Howe family fits of gloom."[2] And he was a bit gloomy about his present appointment as well.

Ironically, Howe sympathized with the American cause, and he took up arms against the colonists only because he "was ordered, and could not refuse."[3] Even as he plotted to trounce them, he nevertheless hoped for reconciliation.

Washington was not so conciliatory, however, when he warned Howe that "whatever Treatment Colonel Allen receives; whatever fate he undergoes, such exactly shall be the Treatment and Fate of Brigadier Prescott, now in our Hands. The Law of Retaliation, is not only justifiable, in the Eyes of God and Man, but absolutely a duty, which in our present circumstances we owe to our Relations, Friends and Fellow Citizens."[4] He seemed to go beyond Congress's resolution on the subject, which had merely "Ordered, That General Washington be directed to apply to General Howe on this matter, and desire [Prescott] may be exchanged" for Allen.[5]

Washington was ardent in the defense of his men. He made it clear that if the British continued to abuse Allen and carry out their plans to hang him, Prescott would suffer for it. And this more extreme stance likely saved Allen's life: although the British repeatedly threatened to hang Allen without trial, when rumors reached England that Prescott was being dreadfully abused and would likely be killed if they executed Allen, King George III took notice. He ordered that Allen be sent back for a fair trial.[6] After Allen arrived in America, Washington secured his release in exchange for a captured British colonel, and he commended Allen for his fortitude and "enthusiastic zeal."[7]

General Washington's hard-line view on the treatment of enemy captives was not reserved for captured British troops. At a time when American courts were sentencing Tories to brandings and Continental Army troops purportedly executed surrendering Loyalist soldiers, Washington also condoned at least some of this conduct.[8] After word reached New York City that the Americans' invasion of Canada had been repelled, there was a great uptick in the "bitterness of feeling already shown towards the loyalists."[9] Tensions boiled over one balmy June night when patriots hauled Tories into the streets "with candles forced to be held by them, or pushed in their faces, and their heads burned."[10] By Wednesday of that same week, the riots continued in broad daylight throughout downtown Manhattan.

Pastor Shewkirk, viewing the pandemonium from his Moravian Church, chronicled the "unhappy and shocking scenes" in his diary. He reported witnessing several Tories being made to "ride the rails," a practice in which a victim was forced to straddle a sharp metal rail that was hoisted onto patriots' shoulders. They paraded through the streets, the victim wincing as the rail cut into his legs and groin. "Some were stripped naked and dreadfully abused."[11]

Israel Putnam, a stout, burly American major general affectionately called "Old Put" by his troops, confronted one such procession. Known for his reckless courage and fighting spirit, he was nevertheless appalled by the abuse and would not stand for it. The rotund leader condemned his fellow patriots' behavior and dispersed the angry mob. Surprisingly, however, Washington reprimanded Old Put for doing so.

While the commander would not order that Loyalists be abused—they were Americans, after all—he would not necessarily stop others from doing so. Washington scolded Old Put, arguing that "to discourage such proceedings was to injure the cause of liberty in which they were engaged, and that nobody would attempt it but an enemy of his country."[12] Washington's arguments justifying abuse sharpened further as the war went on and the Americans' desperation increased.

Following the standstill at Boston, the British evacuated. In what was perhaps the most memorable Boston Saint Patrick's Day parade, the redcoats marched down the city's streets on March 17, 1776, and onto their cannon-laden ships. Howe retreated to Canada and the Americans rejoiced. Spontaneous celebrations erupted. Rum spilled into the streets of Boston to the sound of fife and drum.

But Washington knew better. He foresaw darker days ahead. Like many others, he predicted that New York City would be Howe's next target. In light of Britain's naval supremacy, the location was indefensible from the American military's perspective. "What to do with the city?" asked Washington and his officers. ". . . It is so encircled with deep navigable waters that whoever commands the sea must command the town."[13] While the British had over one hundred men-of-war in their worldwide armada, the Americans had zero. These were not good statistics for defending an island. But America and its political leaders expected a defense of the city, and the commander obliged. He marched with the Continental Army for over two hundred miles down from Boston to occupy Manhattan and Brooklyn.

Washington began to brace for the impending attack, ordering that his troops erect elaborate forts and dig trenches throughout the area. After months of toil, the Americans watched in dread as the British armada approached the city. But with his army in good health and good spirits, Washington tried to stay optimistic. Having chased the British from Boston, he hoped that he could repel their superior firepower and numbers again. He believed that the righteousness of the revolutionary cause would make the Americans formidable fighters even if they lacked experience and training. "Let us therefore animate and encourage each other," he declared, "and show the whole world that a freeman, contending for his liberty on his own ground, is superior to any slavish mercenary on earth."[14] America was drunk with confidence.

It was at this time, July 1776, that America was officially born. At the outset of hostilities in Massachusetts a year earlier, only the radicals had wanted independence while most of the colonists hoped for reunification. But after a year of fighting, reconciliation became impossible in the face of the British atrocities and America's surging patriotism. Thomas Paine, a recent immigrant from Britain, wrote a stunning essay calling for an American republic to break from the British monarchy. This bestselling pamphlet, *Common Sense*, galvanized public support for independence and convinced the colonists that "The Sun never shined on a cause of greater worth" than their revolution.[15] In response, the congressmen decided to do something of which they became rather fond: they appointed a committee.

This five-man committee was tasked with drafting a statement justifying the colonies' break from their mother country. Thomas Jefferson, a brilliant thirty-three-year-old attorney from Virginia, took the lead. He was a man of striking contrasts. Born into one of Virginia's most distinguished families, he could be rather elitist at times but nevertheless fancied himself fiercely egalitarian and even sneered at the mention of aristocratic blood.[16] He took obsessive notes, including each day's barometric pressure and the minute details of his vegetable garden, but somehow lost track of his own debts to his wine distributor. He was a rather humorless intellectual, yet one of his favorite books was *Don Quixote*.[17]

Jefferson enjoyed the privilege of a classical liberal education, studying philosophy, language, science, history, law, and the classics. He loved to learn almost any subject, although he complained while studying ethics and metaphysics.[18] After his formal schooling ended, he read ravenously throughout his life. His genius was seemingly limitless: besides being a lawyer and statesman, he was also an architect, geographer, scientist, inventor, naturalist, agriculturalist, fiddler, and philologist—to name just a few of his "hobbies."[19] Although his looks improved with age, as a youth he was described as "certainly not handsome, and in order to establish his social attractiveness, his friends f[e]ll back on 'his countenance, so highly expressive of intelligence and benevolence.'"[20] With his freckles, sandy hair, long gangly limbs, and soft-spoken demeanor, Jefferson appeared to his fellow congressmen as more of a gawky youth than a powerful politician. But whatever he lacked in public presence, he more than compensated with his mighty pen.

With only a couple of weeks and a busy schedule, Jefferson pretty much threw the Declaration of Independence together. Downplaying his masterpiece, he later wrote, "Neither aiming at originality of principle or sentiment, nor yet copied from any particular and previous writing, it was intended to be an expression of the American mind."[21] His Declaration eloquently outlined America's grievances against

King and Parliament, making a rousing case for the colonies' natural right to throw off the bonds of tyranny. But the Continental Congress decided to table it.

Fierce debate ensued, with multiple colonies initially rejecting the call for immediate independence. But Congress finally voted in favor of officially breaking from the British Empire on July 2, 1776. One delegate prophesied: "The Second Day of July 1776, will be the most memorable Epocha, in the History of America. . . . It ought to be solemnized with Pomp and Parade, with Shews, Games, Sports, Guns, Bells, Bonfires, and Illuminations from one End of this Continent to the other from this Time forward forever more."[22] But the fastidious delegates wanted to make some edits to Jefferson's draft, so they did not adopt the Declaration of Independence until two days later. And hence, even though July 2 marked the day of the official vote for independence, July 4 stuck in the national consciousness as the United States' birthday.

The nation was born into the jaws of an angry lion. The British were not as pleased with the Declaration of Independence as the Americans were. They saw it as outrageously treasonous and were determined to squash the rebellion. They invaded.

Howe's troops landed in Brooklyn in the heat of late August 1776. He faced the scattered American force, which was little more than a mob, untrained and underequipped. Most had "nothing but a wretched farmer's costume and a weapon."[23] In contrast, the British troops were well equipped and had five or six times as much military experience. Typically in their late twenties, they were about five years older on average than America's army of "beardless boys."[24] The British promptly routed the Americans, sending them recoiling back to the banks of the East River. Here, lacking a navy, the Americans were trapped with no avenue of retreat. The Revolution was nearly ended right then, as Washington's Continental Army stared in the face of annihilation.

In a fortuitous twist, the prevailing winds shifted. Unusually for August, a large storm brought strong northerly winds that made it impossible for Howe's ships to sail up the East River. But Howe was patient, perhaps overly so. The British troops in Brooklyn set up camp for the night, fully confident that they would destroy Washington's forces when the winds shifted again in the morning. The Americans hunkered down in their trenches, miserable in the pouring rain, dreading the inevitable bloodbath. Ominous booms of thunder mingled with those of British mortars in signaling the doom of the coming onslaught. Washington, with hardly any sleep in days, must have been gut-wrenchingly distressed by his army's plight, but he did not show it. He maintained his outwardly cool composure and made his rounds to assess the situation. After much deliberation, he decided he had no option but to retreat.

In a bold maneuver, Washington ordered his men to commandeer every small ship they could find for a stealthy withdrawal across the river. But his plan quickly went awry when the sailors determined that the waters were too choppy to ferry the men and equipment across. And so the stoic general waited in Brooklyn, hoping for a break in the storm. When one of Washington's officers reported that retreat would be impossible that night, all seemed lost. But in another bizarre turn of fate that many would later call divine intervention, the winds suddenly shifted at around eleven that night, allowing passage.

Washington rode his horse through the downcast camps, instructing his regiments on the clandestine mission. "All orders were given from officer to officer," one soldier explained, "and communicated to the men in whispers."[25] The soldiers, "strictly enjoined not to speak, or even cough," silently filed into the boats.[26] Washington's team of Massachusetts fishermen and sailors put their experience navigating New England's perilous waters to amazing use, as the makeshift armada silently ferried thousands of men across the rough river all night.[27] The howling winds and choppy seas masked the sounds of their escape from the unsuspecting British crouched in their trenches nearby.

But as the sun rose, Washington feared his time was up. He had left hundreds of his men at the front line so as not to alert the British to the withdrawal. These decoys had no backup nor any means of escape should the British pounce in the morning light. But in a final "peculiar providential occurrence . . . a very dense fog began to rise, and it seemed to settle in a peculiar manner over both encampments" in Brooklyn while miraculously leaving much of the river and Manhattan clear for the Americans to escape.[28] Under this cover of fog, Washington remained in Brooklyn, fearlessly rounding up the last troops onto the boats. The fog lifted and the winds shifted later that morning, allowing the British ships to complete their trap. But they were too late: their prey had escaped.

Although Washington's main force had slipped away, the British were not left empty-handed. From the Battle of Brooklyn and subsequent victories, Howe greedily collected thousands of captives. The British now had plenty of hapless American prisoners at their disposal, on whom they "took a most cruel revenge. Out of over 2600 prisoners taken on [one] day, in two months & four days 1900 were killed in the infamous sugar houses and other prisons in the city, [perishing] of hunger, cold, infection, and in some cases, actual poison."[29] This mass slaughter was overseen by a sadistic Loyalist named William Cunningham.

Howe appointed Captain Cunningham, a man "whose cruelty and wickedness [were] almost inconceivable,"[30] to serve as provost marshal in command of Britain's prisons in the area. Described as "a man of great physical powers, and of fine personal appearance,"[31] Cunningham was placed in the post as a reward for his "blatant toryism."[32]

This native of the Ninety-Six District in the backwoods of South Carolina possessed quite a vicious streak. A "scaw-banker" by trade, Cunningham had made his living by "enticing mechanics and rustics to ship to America, on promise of having their fortunes made in that country; and then by artful practices, produced their indentures as servants, in consequence of which on their arrival in America they were sold."[33] After his return from the seas, his "fiend-like disposition" only intensified. Once, upon receiving word that a man had insulted his elderly father, Cunningham walked nearly four hundred miles from Florida back home to South Carolina with a rifle on his shoulder and "his blood on fire." Arriving at the offender's house, Cunningham barged in and shot him in front of his own family. It was here that he "first tasted blood; and like the tiger, the taste created a thirst which could never be quenched." Cunningham formed a band of merciless Tory "blood-hounds" who roamed the South, massacring any patriots they could find, even torturing those who had retired to civilian life.[34]

Once he was promoted to the command of the prison camps in New York City, "Bloody Bill" Cunningham's cruelty and bloodlust knew no bounds. The tortures he inflicted on the American prisoners became infamous throughout the colonies.[35] In order to "gratify his bloodthirsty instincts,"[36] Cunningham made his captives suffer horribly. One such prisoner described finding himself "among the collection of the most wretched and disgusting looking objects that I ever beheld in human form . . . surrounded with the horrors of sickness, and death. Here thought I, must I linger . . . til death should terminate my sufferings."[37] And Cunningham was happy to assist with the dying part.

Bloody Bill openly confessed to being an accessory to thousands of murders as provost marshal, "both with and without orders from Government." He admitted that "there were more than two thousand prisoners starved . . . by stopping their rations," which he sold for his own profit.[38] He used this ill-gotten profit to pay for the "drunken orgies that usually terminated his dinners."[39] For those prisoners who were able to subsist on the meager nourishment left over after Cunningham's greed was satiated, many "fell victim to his murderous violence."[40]

Cunningham's "hatred of Americans found vent in torture by searing irons and secret scourges to those who fell under the ban of his displeasure."[41] Others "were hanged in the gloom of night without trial"[42] while their "ferocious murderer" indulged in "the pleasure of hearing their shrieks of agony at the gallows."[43] The bodies were either buried in ditches or simply dumped into the harbor.

So grotesque were the accounts that Washington commissioned a special envoy to investigate their truthfulness. When questioned,

Cunningham put his hands on his hips and "with great insolence answered every word was true."[44] Washington felt powerless to stop his countrymen's suffering, and confided to his brother, "I am wearied almost to death with the retrograde Motions of things."[45] With the American cause on the brink of defeat, Washington lashed out.

He swiftly shot off a warning to General Howe:

> I am again under the necessity of remonstrating to you upon the Treatment which our prisoners continue to receive in New York. Those, who have lately been sent out, give the most shocking Accounts of their barbarous usage, which their Miserable, emaciated Countenances confirm. . . . [I]f you are determined to make Captivity as distressing as possible, to those whose Lot it is to fall into it, let me know it, that we may be upon equal terms, for your Conduct must and shall mark mine.[46]

Washington was going to protect his compatriots, and if that meant threatening—and potentially applying—Cunningham's own gruesome tactics, so be it.

11

Fully Justifiable

The tension over prisoner treatment escalated when Washington's jealous second-in-command,[1] Major General Charles Lee, was captured by the British. Sloppy in appearance and crude in manner, Lee was reputed to have a sex life "of the transient kind."[2] And it played right into British hands: Lee was caught after leaving his army behind for an evening of "female sociability" at Widow White's Tavern in Basking Ridge, New Jersey.[3]

The eccentric Charles Lee was born into an unhappy home in Cheshire, England. The son of a British officer, he served in his father's regiment starting at the shockingly young age of eleven.[4] Although he was never properly socialized, he grew into a shrewd tactician as he fought for the British all over the world. Unlike Washington, he distinguished himself enough in the Seven Years' War to warrant promotion in the British ranks. Returning to Europe, he continued his successful military career in wars from Portugal to Poland.

Lee was a man who made enemies quickly. On one such occasion, he took umbrage at an Italian officer's comments, grabbed his gun, and challenged the offender to a duel. In the end, he lost two fingers and killed the Italian.[5] Lee's "warmth of temper" resulted in many similar encounters while he battled his way across the continent.[6]

As the colonists and Britain headed down their collision course during the early 1770s, Lee grew ever more sympathetic to the patriots' loudening calls for liberty. He left the battles of Europe behind and returned to America in 1773 to set up a farm in Virginia. But his quiet life as a farmer was short. When war broke out in 1775, Lee leapt into the fray. He was not one to shy away from a fight.

At the outbreak of war with his mother country, Lee possessed far more military experience and education than Washington, so he expected to be appointed commander in chief. But when the Continental Congress met to select the commander, Lee was in for a surprise. The Congress viewed the tall, dignified, and morally respected Washington as a better leader for the colonies' cause than the crude, pinched-faced Lee. Unlike Lee, Washington was "discreet and virtuous, no harum-scarum, ranting swearing fellow, but sober steady and calm."[7] While Washington was seen as a happily married pillar of Virginian society, the skinny, homely Lee was continuously rebuffed by women and displayed "hints . . . of homosexuality."[8] Perhaps most importantly, Washington was willing to work without pay, while Lee demanded a stipend from the cash-strapped Congress.[9] Washington won the job, but Lee remained insubordinate.

Many regarded the slovenly Lee as militarily superior to Washington. In fact, the British viewed Lee as their primary strategic foe.[10] Lee agreed. Living up to his spiteful and arrogant reputation, he showed his animosity towards Washington by writing letters to various American leaders explaining why he should replace Washington as commander. And, being the opposite of Washington, he was completely unrestrained in his angry tirades.

In fact, after spending the night with Widow White, the undressed Lee was finishing a letter denouncing Washington as "damnably incompetent" when the British dragoons appeared outside.[11] Unluckily for Lee, his sentries were busy sunning themselves when the redcoats swept in on horseback.[12] The British quickly scattered Lee's unwary guards and secured the tavern's perimeter. The pack of dogs that invariably—and bizarrely—accompanied Lee began barking, and the house erupted into a hushed frenzy. Before Lee could even get his clothes on, Widow White frantically burst into the room and attempted to hide him under her bed. But the British would not be fooled, and they fired into the tavern. The commanding British officer announced from outside, "If the general does not surrender in five minutes, I will set fire to the house." After two minutes of panicked debate, Widow White emerged from the door into the chill morning air. Screaming for mercy, she offered the general's surrender. Lee, caught with his pants down, followed.[13]

Howe was overjoyed with the capture of America's tactical genius. The British predicted that the "Coup de Main [had] put an end to the Campaign," since it would leave the Continental Army without a true military strategist.[14] British bands played victory tunes to honor the "most miraculous Event," while soldiers toasted the king until they were too inebriated to raise their cups.[15] The news raised such "great hopes . . . of an early termination of the war" that a dreadful speller in one British village speedily organized a festival:[16]

> Thursday next will be helld as a day of regoicin in com-
> memoration of the takin of General Lee, when their wil be a
> sermint preached, and other public demonstrascions of joye,
> after which will bee an nox roasted whole & everery mark of
> festivety & bell ringing imagenable, width a ball & cock fiting
> at night. [17]

The guards who had to watch over Lee were less pleased. They quickly came to despise his crude, conniving ways, and complained about having to spend any time with such an "atrocious monster."[18]

After obtaining intelligence that Lee was being abused, Washington jumped to his defense—even though he knew that Lee had been exploiting the Continental Army's recent defeats to garner support in Congress for his ouster as commander.[19] Washington warned General Howe that "any violence which you may Commit upon his Life or

Liberty will be severely retaliated upon the Lives or Liberties of British Officers, or those of their Foreign Allies at present in our hands."[20]

While Washington did "beg that some certain Rule of Conduct towards Prisoners may be settled," he reasoned that abuse was not only justified as a means of protecting Americans but required by honor.[21] Shortly thereafter, he again warned the British forces that "if their rule of Conduct towards our prisoners is not altered, we shall be obliged, however disagreeable it may be, to make retaliation," and that "any Accounts of ill Usage coming thro' them, would be so authentic, that we might safely proceed to take such measures towards their prisoners as would be fully justifiable."[22]

In expressing his position to Congress, Washington was even more candid. After learning of the "Inhuman Treatment to the whole, and Murder of part of our People after their Surrender" in New York, and now of Lee's condition, he determined that "Justice and Policy will require recourse to be had to the Law of retaliation, however abhorrent and disagreeable to our natures in cases of Torture."[23]

Despite their previous resolution directing that prisoners be treated with humanity just six months earlier, the Continental Congress came to follow Washington's lead. After waffling in the early stages of the war, they relinquished their idealistic opposition to prisoner maltreatment in light of the practical realities of battle, observing, "No fact can be clearer that interest alone (and not principles of justice or humanity) governs men."[24] Just as Washington had been doing, Congress began to convey this hardened view to the enemy. Benjamin Franklin wrote to the British saying, "the United States are not unacquainted with the barbarous treatment their people receive when they have the misfortune of being your prisoners." He warned, "if your conduct towards us is not altered, it is not unlikely that severe reprisals may be thought justifiable."[25]

Echoing Washington's position that unsavory tactics might sometimes be called for in the course of war, Congress formally resolved, that if the enemy shall put to death, torture, or otherwise ill-treat any of the hostages in their hands, or of the Canadian or other prisoners captivated by them in the service of the United Colonies, recourse must be had to retaliation as the sole means of stopping the progress of human butchery, and that for that purpose punishments of the same kind and degree be inflicted on an equal number of their subjects taken by us, till they shall be taught due respect to the violated rights of nations.[26]

With this official resolution, Congress's stance finally fell in line with their commander's actions post hoc. Congress declared that prisoner abuse was a necessary—if unseemly—tool to fight the war effectively and maintained this position for the rest of the Revolution.

Like their commander, the congressmen were outraged by the reports of the British troops' treatment of Lee. They retaliated by urging the Massachusetts Council to inflict similar treatment on Archibald Campbell, a British lieutenant colonel in their custody. Campbell, "a member of parliament and a gentleman of fortune," was one of Britain's finest leaders.[27] At thirty-six years old, he was a somewhat portly gentleman with large, bulging eyes and a double chin. Nicknamed "Archy," he not only "greatly distinguished himself by his proficiency in the various branches of erudition"[28] but also "proved himself an able and gallant officer."[29] Nevertheless, he was captured when he sailed right into an American-controlled port, due to a rather stupid error.

General Howe, in his haste to escape Boston, had failed to warn Campbell about the evacuation.[30] Believing that the city remained under British control, Campbell approached its harbor and discovered a hodgepodge American flotilla swarming around him. Though outnumbered and outgunned, Campbell resisted ferociously. Six American boats repeatedly charged Campbell's two ships, only to be repelled over and over. But as the sun began to set on the day of fighting, American reinforcements finally arrived and Campbell desperately tried to escape—by dashing deeper into the harbor, which he still believed to be in British hands. He was shocked by the thunder of shore batteries when the Americans began to fire on him. Disoriented, Campbell put up one last fierce naval firefight. But it was in vain. His ships ran out of ammunition and he reluctantly surrendered. The Americans stormed the boats and took him as their prized prisoner.[31]

Washington was bemused by the blunder and incredulous that Howe allowed it to occur. But regardless of how he captured Campbell, he was ready to use him as a bargaining chip. Congress, likewise eager to do so, resolved

> [t]hat General Washington be directed to send a flag to General Howe, and inform him, that, should the proffered exchange of General Lee . . . not be accepted, and the treatment of him, as above mentioned, be continued, that the principles of retaliation shall occasion five of the . . . field officers, together with Lieutenant Colonel Archibald Campbell, or any other officers that are, or shall be, in our possession, equivalent in number or quality, to be detained, in order that the same treatment which General Lee shall receive, may be exactly inflicted upon their persons.[32]

The Massachusetts Council responded to this resolution by placing Campbell in "severity of . . . confinement as is scarce ever inflicted upon the most atrocious Criminals."[33] He was subjected to a forced march, showered with "dirt and filth," and struck with stones. Deprived of the "very necessities of life," he had to survive on bread and water.[34] As he attempted to keep up a stoic front, his American captors held him in a small, cold, dark dungeon that was covered with excrement.[35] For a toilet, he used a bowl that was neither cleaned nor even emptied. Having a long, pale face even prior to captivity, the wretched aristocrat now undoubtedly presented a simply ghostlike appearance.[36] The British were outraged by the "cruel and savage manner" in which Campbell was treated, and they vowed revenge.[37]

Meanwhile, Washington had obtained new intelligence indicating that "General Lee, though under confinement, is comfortably lodged, has proper attendants, and a plentiful table."[38] Rather than suffering the tortures originally feared, he was being provided with a "very decent room" as well as "all necessaries that are requisite, and amongst others, a bottle of wine per diem." Although he "frequently behave[d] as if he was not in his perfect mind," he was in relatively good shape.[39] In fact, he was said to have voluntarily supplied the British with secret advice on how to defeat the American forces as he dined with the officers and drank away the days.[40]

In light of this information, Washington decided that Campbell's cruel treatment was injurious to the American cause, "for the Enemy have three hundred of our Officers, whom we have little Chance of exchanging, upon whom they may retaliate."[41] While abuse could be used to save American lives, it was a double-edged sword: unjustified cruelty could provoke the British to slaughter more Americans. And Washington's goal was to protect his men. Now denouncing Campbell's harsh treatment as "impolitic," he urged Congress to reverse its tactics.[42]

Congress rejected Washington's plea and refused to reverse its bloodthirsty stance. Even though it had originally resolved to treat Campbell in the same manner as the American prisoner Lee was being treated, it rebuffed Washington's efforts to ameliorate Campbell's cruel confinement.[43] Campbell was being treated more harshly than Lee, but "[t]here were other circumstances beside the treatment of General Lee, to produce this indignant sensibility on the part of Congress. Accounts were rife at this juncture, of the cruelties and indignities almost invariably experienced by American prisoners at New York."[44] The congressmen were also offended by Howe's conduct, including his abrasive response to their attempts to make a trade for Lee. Congress declared, in a statement originally laced with epithets, that "the conduct of General Howe alone induces Congress to treat [Campbell] in [such] a manner . . . ."[45] Digging in their heels, the congressmen had apparently broadened their justification for the severe treatment of Campbell. Washington and Congress were at odds.

Despite congressional pressure, Washington maintained that mistreating Campbell in this instance was unjustified and would not further the American cause.[46] To abuse a prisoner in false retaliation would be a tactical error, since it would erode Washington's power to use prisoner abuse as a means of improving the treatment of those American prisoners who were actually being abused.[47] As Congress and Washington wrestled over Campbell, it was unclear who should dictate such treatment.

Washington professed to Campbell, "it is as incompatible with my authority as my inclination to contravene any determination Congress may make." But he nevertheless wrote to the president of the Massachusetts Council on his own accord—effectively circumventing Congress—in order to express his "disinclination to any undue severities" and to advise against the abusive measures.[48] In response, Congress passed a resolution ordering that "General Washington be informed, that Congress cannot agree to any alteration."[49]

But in the end, it was Washington's—and not Congress's—order that was heeded. The Massachusetts Council moved Campbell to a more comfortable setting, where he was better treated.[50] Washington again wrote to Congress, which then finally backpedaled and formally directed months later that Campbell be treated humanely.[51] After their initial indecisiveness, Congress came to abide by Washington's case-by-case determinations and eventually acknowledged, "so far as regards the Treatment of Prisoners, and the Conduct of the War many public Exchanges having taken place by agreement of the [American and British] Commanders in Chief."[52] The commander decided whether to abuse or not, based on what he deemed consistent with the laws of war.

Lee was eventually freed when Washington exchanged him for Brigadier Prescott (Ethan Allen's former tormentor). By that point, his

British captors were happy to see their irksome prisoner go and even congratulated one another on being rid of him.[53] The episode was over, but not before Washington had flexed his authority on the subject.

While Washington sought better treatment for Campbell in this episode, he did not show the same mercy to all of the British captives. In fact, with reports circulating that the British were inflicting "torture by searing irons and secret scourges,"[54] his arguments for treatment in kind involved gruesome practices.[55]

12

To Defend the Nation

The British vehemently protested the "outrages committed by the American troops" against their British and Tory prisoners, and "their violations of all the humaner principles of war."[1] One British officer decried how his compatriots in captivity were "experiencing every severity, perhaps famishing for want of food, and ready to perish with cold," adding that these prisoners had "little to expect from the humanity of Americans."[2] Reports circulated that bands of Americans were "stabbing and knocking out the brains of innocent [men]."[3] Other witnesses lamented the "List of Barbarities which have been committed by Washington & his Savages."[4]

When General Howe pressed the issue, Washington responded delicately. He admitted, "'tis true, there are some who have been restricted to a closer confinement and severer treatment."[5] He did not elaborate on those severities, but confirmed that at least some of the British intelligence was accurate.

Potentially signaling the existence of barbarous practices being employed by the Continental Army, Howe learned that musket balls with nails through them had been found at abandoned American encampments. He wrote angrily to Washington, appalled that the Continental Army had evidently been employing the "infamous" practice of "the Ball."[6] Exactly how these nail-spiked musket balls were used is unclear, but one technique referred to as "the ball," originally developed in China and later adopted in Europe, involved restraining a person against a wall with ropes or even nails and then repeatedly swinging a small ball, suspended from the ceiling, into the victim's forehead. Initially this torture was psychological, but after repeated bouncing over days or even weeks it caused blood to rush to the victim's forehead and eyes, resulting in pain, blindness, and eventually death.[7] Using a ball embedded with a nail would be bloodier faster. Another possibility—perhaps more probable—is that these balls were intended as projectiles. A hurling musket ball with a nail in it would inflict maximum damage on an enemy's flesh. However the ball was used, the results would be gruesome.

Washington responded to Howe's complaint with a parry, saying, "the contrivance is highly abhorred by me, and every measure shall be taken to prevent so wicked and infamous a practice being adopted in this Army." But he did not deny that the ball had already been used.[8] And this was not the only abhorrent contrivance employed by the Americans in their efforts to survive the war.

Another documented practice was called "spicketting," in which the victim was "bound, stood with one foot on a sharpened stake and then whirled around literally screwing the stake into his foot."[9] This was typically used by angry mobs against Loyalists and often rendered the victim permanently crippled. While Washington expressed his "most earnest wish, that . . . there be every exercise of humanity, which the nature of the case will possibly admit,"[10] he indeed found cases whose nature did not permit humane treatment. Mistreatment indeed occurred—mobs forced some onto hot coals, whipped others, and even cut off some men's ears[11]—and Washington did not always express a desire to stop it.[12] In fact, behavior of this kind was at times openly condoned and even rewarded.

In one such incident, an American officer was accused by the British of "the most indecent, violent, vindictive severity" against British prisoners and of "an intentional murder."[13] Colonel David Henley, an impetuous twenty-nine-year-old patriot from Massachusetts, was a zealous defender of the revolutionary cause, known for being "warm and quick in his natural temper."[14] He turned that temper on the British, even going so far as setting his hometown aflame because it was occupied by redcoats.

After his brother was killed by the British, Henley's anger blossomed into searing hatred, which he vented on the British prisoners in his custody. British eyewitnesses alleged that Henley came upon eight prisoners conversing casually one day. Then, for some unknown reason, he purportedly went berserk, charging at them "with a drawn dagger like a maniac, and in an instant mortally wounded two of the group."[15] Another witness claimed that Henley stabbed a prisoner with a bayonet because the redcoat had defiantly declared he "would stand by King and his country, till he died."[16]

To appease the British for these alleged offenses, the Americans put Henley on trial. But it was a sham inquiry since the Americans were unwilling to condemn one of their own.[17] The tantrum-prone patriot was cleared of wrongdoing, and Washington then appointed Henley as his intelligence officer and commander of prisoners. The commander had placed Henley in charge of screening prisoners and procuring intelligence.

Washington had shown that he was willing—if absolutely necessary—to use prisoners as pawns in an effort to protect his people. In fact, British intelligence suggested that he may even have used random executions to further the American cause. One episode revolved around a gentleman affectionately known as "Old Huddy."

Captain Joseph Huddy was an ardent patriot from New Jersey.[18] The state militia had sent him to oversee the defense of Toms River, including its small yet strategic port and its salt warehouses. At the time, Toms River was a busy seaside village that had become a prominent center of activity for patriot privateers, who used small merchant ships jerry-rigged with cannon to seize the lucrative cargoes of Loyalist and

British ships. They grew to be quite a threat. One privateer sailed across the Atlantic to assault the British mainland—the first such attack in seven centuries—in the process coining the battle cry "I have not yet begun to fight!"[19] Britain was determined to eradicate the menace and encouraged Loyalist assistance in doing so.

After a privateer attacked a prominent Loyalist ship off the coast of New Jersey, the outraged Tory's "Board of Associated Loyalists" launched an offensive.[20] Their heavily armed regiment descended on Toms River in a surprise attack. Old Huddy's small defensive force was completely outgunned and outnumbered, but refused to surrender without a fight. Stationed in a wooden blockhouse—more akin to just a reinforced house than a true defensive fortification—Huddy bravely defended the town.[21] Despite his heroics, the patriots were overwhelmed. The town rendered defenseless upon Huddy's defeat, the Tories then went about pillaging, burning down the blockhouse, the salt warehouse, and all but two homes.[22] The privateer port destroyed, the Loyalists next turned their bloodlust back towards their new captive, Old Huddy. They grabbed their defenseless prisoner and "on a gallows made of mere rails he was cruelly treated and then hanged."[23]

As the shell-shocked townspeople emerged from the rubble, news of the gruesome episode began to spread rapidly throughout the countryside. The inhabitants of the surrounding region "cried out for retaliation."[24] Referring to the incident as "the most wanton, unprecedented and inhuman Murder that ever disgraced the Arms of a civilized people," Washington demanded that the Loyalist officer who ordered the execution be handed over.[25] Otherwise, he wrote, "I shall hold myself justifiable in the Eyes of God and Man, for the measure to which I shall resort."[26] When the British refused to comply, Washington called for blood.

Terrified British captives reported to their superiors, "Mr. Washington & Congress are going to commit such an act of Cruelty, and Breach of Faith that cannot be equaled in civilized Nations."[27] One

British prisoner explained that the Americans were intent on making "the Innocent suffer for the guilty" by ordering prisoners to draw lots for their lives.[28] Thirteen slips of paper were placed in a hat, "all blank except one, upon which was written the word 'unfortunate.'"[29] In protest and fear, the British prisoners refused to draw. The Americans were unrelenting, however, and simply drew slips for them. The "unfortunate lot" fell on Captain Charles Asgill, "who was immediately ordered into close Confinement . . . and [was] to be hanged" unless the British surrendered the leader of the party who murdered Old Huddy.[30]

"An amiable youth," Asgill was the twenty-year-old son of a prominent English baronet.[31] With his soft, youthful features, arched eyebrows, and pug nose, he certainly looked the part of a lamb being led to the slaughter. His noble family's only son, he had lived a privileged life, splitting his time between London and his family's scenic holiday estate along the River Thames. Washington agonized over the quandary before him. He was all too aware that the young man was an innocent victim in all this. However, not only did Huddy's murder demand retribution as a matter of principle, but to turn a blind eye could endanger future American captives. If Washington did not retaliate, the British side was liable to treat other American prisoners similarly.

Washington needed to send a strong signal to his enemies. While he suffered "anxiety and poignant distress" over the pending execution, he nevertheless remained "firm and inflexible in his determination to obtain satisfaction, or pursue a course, that will tend to deter others from a repetition of crimes so derogatory to the laws of humanity, of war, and of justice."[32] Supported by Congress and the American public, Washington did not relent. And his resolve set off an international incident.

When word of Asgill's plight reached his family estate, his mother fainted and his sister disintegrated into an emotional wreck. "The extreme grief of his mother, the sort of delirium which clouded the mind of his sister at hearing of the dreadful fate which menaced the life of her brother, interested every feeling mind."[33] Lady Sarah Asgill, determined to save her son, composed herself and quickly launched an international lobbying campaign.

The valiant woman proved to be a shrewd diplomat. Spreading word of her family's plight—albeit with the slight misinformation that Charles was only nineteen, a detail that made her "teen" son seem even more sympathetic—she successfully elicited the "attention and solicitude of almost all Europe."[34] In a time when news generally traveled slowly, this heart-wrenching story spread like wildfire as it found its way to the lips of every town gossip. The far-flung "interest which young Asgill inspired" was so great that "the first question asked of all vessels that arrived from any port in North America, was an inquiry into the fate of this young man."[35] The world watched the showdown as Britain refused to remit Huddy's killer and Washington readied the young man to be hanged in retaliation.

Pulling on Britain's heartstrings, Lady Asgill threw herself at the feet of George III and pleaded for direct intercession. The British king, eager to have this scandal behind him, ordered his commanders to remit Huddy's killer to Washington. They disobeyed—whether from shocking insubordination or simple miscommunication is unclear. Since the British proved immalleable, Lady Asgill redirected her efforts to the Americans' allies. Next, the Dutch implored the Americans to pardon young Asgill, but Washington was unrelenting.[36] Finally, the resolute Lady Asgill approached the United States' most important ally, France.

The Americans desperately needed French money and support for their cause, and Lady Asgill knew it. And luckily for Captain Asgill, she was of French Huguenot origin and held sway in the French court. She wrote a letter to France's leaders, "the eloquence of which [was] that of all people and all languages, because it derive[d] its power from the first and noblest sentiments of our nature."[37] It was "enough to move the heart of a savage," yet Washington refused to back down.[38] Only after months of negotiations and even a direct appeal from Queen Marie

Antoinette was Asgill released, but not before Washington had made America's intent to exact an eye for an eye abundantly clear.

⁂

George Washington abhorred prisoner abuse. He wanted to elevate his nascent republic's conduct to a higher moral plane than the brutal European wars of the past. And so, at the start of the war, he ordered that the British prisoners in his custody be treated with humanity. But the brutal realities of war compelled him to deviate from this lofty ideal.

The British fiercely abused their American captives. They beat them. They burned them. They starved them. They butchered them. Washington was forced to act. And so he used his captives. Abuse became a weapon by which Washington could retaliate against the British outrages and help prevent future harm to his people. It was a horrible but practical tool. It was used to obtain better treatment for American prisoners, to suppress Loyalists, and even to save lives. The commander in chief was willing to deploy this necessary evil against the enemy in order to defend the nation.

The world and circumstances certainly have changed. Brute reprisals have largely been replaced by individual punishment for violations of the laws of war. No longer are we using prisoners as leverage to save American captives—we have given up on hopes that terrorists will treat our people with humanity. Instead, we debate whether torture should be a last resort in obtaining information that will save American servicemen and civilians alike. However imperfect the analogy may be—and it certainly is imperfect—it is worth remembering Washington's precedents as today's commander in chief grapples with what must be done to defend the American people.

Washington's actions were rooted in an innate sense of right and wrong in view of his moral obligation to protect his countrymen. This fundamental principle continues to influence our thinking today.

Walking along the well-trod paths of a serene park in East Haddam, Connecticut, one could expect to pass families out for an afternoon of exploring nature. The park is known for its tranquility, as the gentle roar of a waterfall drowns out the noises of the quaint suburbia that surrounds it. The peacefulness that visitors enjoy as they stroll alongside the gushing stream's gray boulders ensures that thoughts of war and prisoner abuse are the last thing on their minds.

While times and tactics may have changed, history does not. America's past remains, bubbling just beneath the surface like Mr. Beebe's millstone.

III

DICTATOR OF AMERICA

"[T]he Congress having given up the government, confessing themselves unequal to it, and creating Mr. Washington dictator of America . . ."
—Lord George Germain, before the British House of Commons, 1776

At the heart of New York City's famous Wall Street, a majestic statue of George Washington soars above the bustling foot traffic. From atop a large marble pedestal, the towering bronze sculpture stoically gazes over the crowd towards the New York Stock Exchange. The great hero wears a flowing jacket decorated with large buttons beneath a striking cape. With his right hand extended outward, he steps forward as if to honor the proverbial right foot on which he set the nation.[1]

This tribute to the nation's father stands before the entrance to Federal Hall, which houses a museum commemorating Washington's role in founding our country. In a nod to the democratic republic's roots in classical antiquity, the hall boasts Greek revival architecture with marble columns and a relief etching inspired by the Parthenon. Complete with Washington's Greek-godlike statue in front, the scene appears to have been plucked from the Acropolis and dropped into Manhattan. Although such a grand building would rise over its surroundings in most other parts of the United States, here it is dwarfed by gleaming skyscrapers on all sides. As the fabled New York financial district has grown around it, Federal Hall has remained as a tribute to a long-ago era. The stark contrast between the sleek modern city and the stout old hall presents the appearance of a time warp—one that abruptly pulls passersby back to the nation's roots.

Washington's image stands at a symbolic crossroads of America's affluence and apprehension. Like the republic they honor, Federal Hall and its monument have not been immune from attack. The terrorist attacks of September 11, 2001 marked a turning point not only for the nation, but also for Federal Hall. The structure was so shaken when the Twin Towers fell that the trauma spread deep cracks in its walls, and many feared they might crumble. As the country has worked to mend its wounds from that infamous day, construction crews have labored to reinforce Federal Hall. But the nation has not just returned to the status quo. The national psyche has been fundamentally altered as we seek to guard against future attacks.

Vowing "never again," New York City blockaded Wall Street as a precaution against the terrorist threat. This historic street, which has borne the weight of everything from horse-drawn carriages to Model Ts to yellow hybrid taxicabs, is now accessible only on foot. Pedestrians are closely monitored by video surveillance and heavily armed New York police as they mill beneath Washington's likeness.

The statue's face glimmers with the reflections of camera flashes. Visitors from all around the world, wearing jeans and T-shirts, come to snap photographs of the area, blocking annoyed financiers, lawyers, and other professionals busily rushing by in their well-tailored dark suits. Whether the members of this motley crew of pedestrians take the time to admire historic Federal Hall and get a picture or just take it for granted as they bound to their next meeting, Washington's monument stands as a testament to the great man's critical role in creating the prosperous city and nation around it.

On Wall Street, Washington is celebrated for making America possible. He changed the course of history, and the Americans working in the skyscrapers that surround Federal Hall owe him their gratitude. Even as those buildings shook and the Twin Towers fell, the "Father of Our Country" stood firm as the stoic protector of New York City. Little do the passersby know that Washington once lobbied Congress to burn lower Manhattan to the ground. And he got his wish.

The chapters in Part III delve into how Washington exercised his war powers in relation to the authority of Congress. In so doing, they detail how the concept of the American commander in chief developed in the heat of war.

13

Scorpion on a Leash

"Had I been left to the dictates of my own judgment," General Washington confided to a relative, "New York should have been laid in Ashes."[1] He wrote these words in a moment of frustration. Congress had just overruled his military tactics. While willing to grant him broad authority over enemy prisoners, they were wary of granting any military leader sweeping control over war strategy. Instead, they kept Washington on a short leash early in the war and micromanaged his military decisions. But this leash lengthened as the war raged—and Washington became untethered once America realized that their commander needed to be a powerful one in order to protect the nation.

Washington was not always so trusted. In fact, America watched him with suspicion at the outset of the Revolution. Many feared that he might use his military power to subjugate the politicians and strangle the infant republic in its crib. One such watchdog was a fiery patriot from Massachusetts, John Adams.

At forty years old, Adams was a prominent Boston attorney who had emerged as one of the leaders of the Revolution. His ingenious head was balding on top, with a powdered mane that bushed out on the sides. Highly educated in Enlightenment republican values, he drew upon his vast erudition as his small bow mouth lobbed fierce calls for independence. Accentuating the ardor of his fiery words, his ruddy cheeks grew redder and his blue eyes blazed with his passion for the revolutionary cause.[2] Known to drink a large tankard of hard cider every morning before breakfast, Adams was not a man characterized by unfailing restraint.[3] In his unbounded zeal to oust the British, he was a strong proponent of creating an army and selecting Washington to lead it. This did not mean he had complete faith in Washington, however. "We don't choose to trust you Generals, with too much Power, for too long Time," he said.[4] Prevailing republican ideology held that a professional army was a tool of tyranny that was liable to corrupt whoever controlled it. Needless to say, Adams kept a close eye on the United States' first commander.

With this kind of mistrust permeating the nation, it was unsurprising that Washington's commission as commander in chief was careful to remind him that he was required to "observe such orders and directions, from time to time, as you shall receive from this, or a future Congress of these United Colonies, or committee of Congress."[5] Adams and other suspicious congressmen were intent on scrutinizing his war tactics, and with this directive they reserved the right to meddle incessantly. They developed committees to oversee the war effort, even sending (sometimes militarily clueless) congressmen to the warfront so that they might approve or disapprove of Washington's proposed tactics. While America saw Washington as a virtuous and principled man, they were not ready to hand over the reins completely . . . yet.

Washington was careful to earn America's trust early in the war. He assured Congress and the state legislatures that he was a reluctant general who had given up "the Enjoyments of domestic Life" in order to restore "Peace, Liberty, and Safety."[6] Keenly aware of the long history of military leaders helping to overthrow one tyrant only to take his place, Washington knew that Congress feared their commander would turn out to be the fabled scorpion hitching a ride on the frog's back across the river. And so he tried to convince the political "frogs" that it was not necessarily in a commander in chief's nature to sting them by usurping their power and trampling the Revolution's republican ideals.[7] He reminded Americans of his great devotion to liberty as a civilian, and he asked them not to perceive him differently now that he was the commander in chief. "When we assumed the Soldier," he said, "we did not lay aside the Citizen, & we shall most sincerely rejoice in that happy Hour when the establishment of American Liberty . . . shall enable us to return to our Private Stations in the bosom of a free, peaceful & happy Country."[8] And his actions reinforced his words.

The commander endeavored to shape the army into a symbol of American virtue. He wanted to show that his army was not something to be feared, but a group of upstanding fellow citizens led by a righteous commander who humbly served them.

Washington encouraged his men to attend religious services. Although raised in a pious Christian household, Washington himself was not openly religious, partaking in Anglican services only irregularly and refusing communion.[9] In keeping with his proclivity for under-statement, he chose to keep his beliefs private, shying from displays of religiosity and even direct references to Jesus Christ, preferring to instead refer to "the Divine Author of our blessed Religion."[10] While he was unwilling to shout it from the rooftops, Washington's writings reflect deep-seated faith. He repeatedly wrote of a divine "Providence" that "protected [him] beyond all human expectation" so that he might serve a higher purpose—leading his country.[11] And religion was crucial to doing so. Washington viewed it as an important part of the budding republic, and professed his ardent desire that "every officer and man, will endeavour so to live, and act, as becomes a Christian Soldier defending the dearest Rights and Liberties of his country."[12] To this end, he provided for chaplains from various denominations to accompany his army. Ecumenical in his approach, he understood religion to be crucial to fostering morality among his troops, thereby assuaging the fears of the populace they were supposed to protect.

In other attempts at imposing piety on his ranks, he actively combated his troops' vices. As his troops enjoyed all that New York

City had to offer, prostitution flourished. "The whores continue their employ which is become very lucrative," wrote a New England colonel, reassuring his wife that he only learned about it as part of his official duty.[13] An area near St. Paul's Church in lower Manhattan, ironically called the "Holy Ground," became a notorious rendezvous spot for soldiers and the "bitchfoxy jades."[14] One soldier wrote of the women, "I thought nothing could exceed them for impudence and immodesty .... To mention the Particulars of their Behavior would so pollute the Paper I write upon that I must excuse myself."[15]

The Holy Ground was not just debauched but also dangerous. Tales of murderous prostitutes gained support from discoveries of soldiers' limbs and heads at the park.[16] Washington did his best to stamp out the prostitution, sending patrols and repeatedly warning his men of the dangers of such moral failing. And prostitution was not the only vice that Washington actively combated.

Although fond of occasional gambling himself, he outlawed dice and cards, viewing them as pastimes that should be kept in check.[17] He strongly discouraged profanity and worked—often in vain—to make his army into a good neighbor to the surrounding populace. When citizens complained of soldiers skinny-dipping within eyesight of refined women, Washington strove to keep his troops clothed and in line. Frisky, naked soldiers were terrible for public relations. Despite Washington's efforts, rumors of depravity circulated—even about Washington himself.

Some gossips claimed that the great moral enforcer did not practice that which he preached. A rumor circulated that Washington was "very fond" of a Jersey girl named Mary Gibbons. A Tory spy testified at his own trial that the commander "maintained her genteelly in a house [and] came often at night in disguise" to visit her. Upon hearing the startling accusation, the patriot judges immediately halted the trial to confer with the general. After "many conferences" with Washington, the trial resumed with no further mention of the alleged affair.[18] Such accusations were very likely just vicious rumors circulated by Loyalists in an attempt to discredit Washington and the revolutionary cause along with him. If they fostered distrust in Washington and his army, the Loyalists could help end the war.

But Washington was tireless in shining his own image along with that of his army. The last thing he wanted was to stoke the citizenry's fear that the army would run out of control and trample on their liberties.

To assuage their fears, Washington consistently avoided any action that could be perceived as a power grab. As the leader of these soldiers, he knew his every action was eyed with suspicion. And so he went out of his way to demonstrate that he had no intention of wresting power from the politicians in Congress or the states. In fact, he chose to err on the side of being overly deferential.

General Howe once addressed a letter to "George Washington, Esq." But Washington refused to accept the letter. This was because Howe had failed to acknowledge his official designation as the congressionally appointed leader of the American army. After some diplomatic haggling, Howe tried presenting the letter to "George Washington, Esq., &ca, &ca.," attempting to use "&ca." as a sort of catchall to cover Washington's positions. Washington again rejected the letter. Finally, Howe addressed the letter to "His Excellency, General Washington," and Washington accepted it.[19] He was not being vain. On the contrary, he was making it clear that his position as commander of the army had been delegated to him by the civil authorities. So if Howe harbored any illusions of negotiating a separate peace with Washington, thereby leaving Congress without a military, such hopes were swiftly put to rest.[20]

Washington also tried to allay suspicion by seeking congressional authorization for his every move. Even on matters such as troop deployment and the interception of ships—matters that just about any other military commander in history would have assumed he had authority to decide—Washington asked Congress for approval.[21] When he received an answer, he followed it almost unquestioningly. Although he did not have Jefferson's erudition or Franklin's quick wit, Washington was politically brilliant, and he knew precisely how he needed to act in order to engender trust and define the role of America's first commander in chief. And so, like a child eager to please a hovering parent, he asked, "Mother, may I?" at almost every turn. And Congress was quite the helicopter mother.

The "obedient son" wrote Congress constantly, informing them of his actions. Rather than focusing all of his energies on formulating tactics, "[i]n the hours 'allotted to sleep,' [General Washington] sat in his headquarters, writing a letter, with 'blots and scratches,' which told Congress with the utmost precision and vigor just what was needed" to conduct a war.[22] In fact, he produced so much correspondence—a whopping 140,000 documents during the war—that he employed a team of scribes who lived with him for this purpose.[23] Foreseeing his letters' value to posterity, he checked virtually all of the scribes' work and held it to exacting standards. Every letter bearing his name had to be direct, grammatically correct, and free of the slightest error. Washington wanted perfection. And that was a lot to ask, considering the tremendous volume of letters he sent.

Washington also wanted each letter to display the right tone. At the beginning of the war, that tone was one of deference. Even when seeking such basic necessities as munitions or money to pay troops, he carefully worded his letters as requests rather than demands. "I am not fond of stretching my powers," he wrote tellingly; "and if the Congress will say, 'Thus far and no farther you shall go,' I will promise not to offend whilst I continue in their service."[24]

Congress did not hesitate to appoint committees to pull their commander's strings. And if Washington was frustrated with the growing bureaucracy's micromanagement, he certainly hid it well. He trod patiently as he shaped this novel role of American commander in chief. This concept was an experiment and Washington sought to define it very carefully. The concept of "the republican commander" was an evolving one, however. It was adapted as the new nation learned the necessities of war the hard way.

Washington's strict subservience to Congress waned as the war effort deteriorated, for while he was amazingly restrained and principled, it eventually became clear that this new kind of scorpion needed a more powerful sting if America was going to win. This reality became extremely apparent when Congress's meddling helped lead the nation to the brink of destruction.

The politicians in Philadelphia did not fully grasp their army's predicament in 1776. John Adams, who headed the Board of War in the Continental Congress but admitted that he knew little about warfare, urged Washington to defend New York City. "No effort to secure it ought to be omitted," he said, for the city was "a kind of key to the whole continent."[25] The congressmen were not military experts, but that would not stop them from letting their commander know their opinions. They were motivated by the political—rather than military—consideration that ceding a major city was liable to turn public opinion against the war.

And Washington hung on their words. He knew that in attempting to defend an island without a navy, he was at a tremendous disadvantage. But, after heading to Philadelphia for a strategy session with Congress, he agreed to make a stand at New York.[26] Bending to political pressure and perhaps his own inexperience, Washington attempted to fortify the city.

Washington's first attempt to defend New York had almost destroyed the new country, as we saw in Chapter 10. The British onslaught in the Battle of Brooklyn had nearly crushed Washington's army. Even after his brilliant escape across the East River, Washington was not safe yet. He found himself precariously situated in Manhattan. Like Brooklyn, the island was indefensible against Britain's overwhelmingly powerful navy coupled with its better-trained army. However extensive his fortifications, he could not count on his shaken men to stand and fight. To make matters worse, even if he could find a way to inspire courage, many of his men were not physically capable of standing. Washington's own army was in tatters, quite literally.

Adams, ever the gifted orator, described the troops' sorry condition: "Our Army . . . is an Object of Wretchedness, enough to fill a humane Mind, with Horror. Disgraced, defeated, discontented, dispirited, diseased, naked, undisciplined, eaten up with Vermin—no Cloaths, Beds, Blanketts, no Medicines, no Victuals, but Salt Pork and flour."[27] Unable to obtain funds from the cash-strapped Congress, Washington was months behind in paying this wretched lot, and he had no way to provide supplies either. At this stage in the war, the leashed American commander could do little more than plead with Congress for more supplies. And his requests went largely unfulfilled.

In an attempt to remedy their hunger, the "filthy, divided, and unruly" troops violated Washington's orders and ransacked deserted homes in search of food and clothing.[28] It made for a miserable end to the summer, as the soldiers were preoccupied merely with eating rather than such "luxuries" as cleanliness. Contrary to Washington's hygiene orders, they bathed and washed their clothes rarely, if at all. One traveler described these desperate men in rather colorful terms: "These troops stationed here are Yankee men, the nastiest devils in creation. It would be impossible for any human creature whose organs of smelling were more delicate than that of a hog to live one day under the less of this camp."[29] At this point, Washington might have been less cross if they had resumed their skinny-dipping antics.

In these conditions, infection and disease ran rampant. The Americans were so plagued by "putrid disorders" that an estimated one in four soldiers were diseased.[30] The most dreaded ailment was smallpox, a vile malady that brought rashes, burning fever, and death. Extremely contagious, it festered among Washington's men and erupted in an epidemic so dire that John Adams described it as "ten times more terrible than Britons, Canadians and Indians together."[31] Smallpox threatened to decimate Washington's army.

While the British troops had some natural tolerance to the disease from repeated exposure in their densely populated home country, the virgin American wilderness had isolated the colonists from it. Therefore, this new outbreak hit them much harder since their immune systems needed to work to develop the antibody defenses that many of their enemies' bodies already possessed. Washington himself had contracted the disease as a teen, and his face still bore the scars (it is believed that he never fathered children due to sterility caused by this bout with smallpox). His troops lacked his immunity, however.

The British sought to exploit this advantage by pioneering in germ warfare. One British officer recommended, "Dip arrows in matter of smallpox, and twang them at the American rebels [to] disband these stubborn, ignorant, enthusiastic savages."[32] There was little evidence that the British utilized arrows, but many accused them of using human conduits instead. Reports abounded that they went as far as intentionally infecting American civilians and sending them to spread the disease to the American side.[33] While it is difficult to confirm such accusations, Howe indeed dumped boatloads of sick civilians near Washington's lines. Whether these civilians were intentionally infected or Howe merely took full advantage of their preexisting illness is unclear, but the effect was the same: they spread horror and disease.

Washington was aghast and wrote, "The information I received that the Enemy intended spreading the smallpox amongst us, I could not suppose them capable of; I now must give some credit to it, as it has made its appearance."[34] Days later, he wrote with more conviction, saying, "This I apprehend is a weapon of defence, they are using against us."[35] Such germ warfare was not unprecedented—General Gage had purportedly used smallpox to wipe out some of his Native American foes during the Seven Years' War. What was new and particularly outrageous to Washington was that such dirty tactics might be used against other white men. While he could not prove that the British were doing so, he was ready to take every precaution. The viral threat was so extreme that Washington's most important military decision of the war was not a tactical one during battle. It was medical.

Many doctors and New York's legislature, called the Provincial Congress, warned against smallpox immunization, claiming that it actually exacerbated the epidemic.[36] The inoculation was a grotesque procedure that had been used in India for thousands of years but was still relatively new to the Europeans. First, the administering doctor used a pin to prick the pustule of a smallpox victim. Next, he extracted the puss and contained it in a jar. Then the doctor would scratch the skin of a healthy inoculation recipient to create an open wound. Finally, he dabbed the infected puss into the wound to spread the disease in a controlled fashion.[37] This was a far healthier way to contract smallpox than by inhalation or casual contact. The patient inoculated with the puss would normally contract just a mild case of smallpox for a few weeks and then enjoy immunity to subsequent exposure. However, there was a catch. During those weeks of illness and recovery, the patient could spread the disease to others, giving them a full-blown, deadly case. While those who contracted the disease via inoculation suffered a mere 0.9 percent mortality rate, among those who contracted it via natural means, 17 percent perished—and the others suffered horribly.

Washington had mixed feelings about inoculation. He was reasonably well acquainted with the process, since his second cousin had previously set up a smallpox inoculation hospital, and Washington had even allowed his beloved stepson Jacky to be inoculated before going away to school in Europe. Nevertheless, he feared that mass inoculation would spread the disease further if the newly inoculated patients were not properly quarantined. And even if they were, Washington ran the risk that the British might attack while many of the American troops were still weakened.

Although he had seen the efficacy of inoculation firsthand, Washington—in his typical subservient fashion—abided by the New York legislature's opposition to it. Upon receiving news that the New York authorities had arrested a doctor caught inoculating American troops, Washington presented "his Compliments to the Honorable The Provincial Congress, and General Committee" and expressed that he was "much obliged to them, for their Care, in endeavouring to prevent the spreading of the Small-pox (by Inoculation or any other way) in this City, or in the Continental Army." He then ordered that his officers "take the strictest care, to . . . prevent Inoculation" and that any soldier who allowed himself to be inoculated "must expect the severest punishment." Further, any officer who was inoculated would be "cashiered and turned out of the army, and have his name published in the News papers throughout the Continent, as an Enemy and Traitor to his Country."[38]

Washington was serious about following the New York civil authority's direction. But, with his headstrong wife's help, he came to change his mind. And in doing so, he altered the course of history.

Martha Washington was a "small plump, elegantly formed woman"[39] with hazel eyes, dark hair, and "those frank, engaging manners, so captivating in Southern women."[40] She was certainly seen as physically attractive, but people seemed to be most struck by her intelligence and her "sweet and radiant" temperament.[41] A rich widow, she had married Washington when they were both twenty-seven years old, and in doing so, catapulted his social and financial standing. You can make more in a minute than you can make in a lifetime. While their relationship was not a particularly romantic one, they nevertheless shared a deep devotion to and admiration for one another. In fact, Washington was said to wear a locket containing a miniature picture of her around his neck every day of their marriage.[42]

Loving life almost as much as she loved George, Martha saw inoculation as a way to pursue both loves: if she gained immunity, she could join her husband at his encampment without contracting the deadly version of smallpox from his soldiers. So she took matters into her own hands. Despite the fact that her husband's army threatened death to soldiers who sought inoculation, she pressed on undeterred. Washington, underestimating her tenacity, privately confided to his cousin, "Mrs. Washington . . . talks of taking the Small Pox [inoculation], but I doubt her resolution."[43] To his surprise, she underwent the procedure.[44] After several weeks, she recovered and rejoined her beloved husband without trepidation of the baneful disease.

Rumors had it that one of Martha's reasons for being inoculated was to persuade her husband of the procedure's merits.[45] And it was around this time that Washington began to tout its benefits. The Americans' efforts to combat smallpox by outlawing inoculation had failed, and Washington came to see the procedure as the only solution to the epidemic.

Despite the opposition from civil authorities in New York and elsewhere, Washington asserted his military authority and petitioned Congress to reverse course.[46] Congress agreed, and Washington ordered mass inoculations of his troops to commence. This move was unprecedented. Washington's army would become the first in history to utilize wholesale smallpox inoculation. Washington's emerging boldness as a leader in the face of civilian disagreement would help save thousands of men and probably the American army itself.

The inoculation campaign did little, however, to alleviate the near-term suffering in New York during the summer of 1776. It was too late to help the soldiers who had already contracted smallpox. They languished in the streets of Manhattan along with their comrades who suffered from other diseases such as dysentery. In all, nearly 3,800 men reported being too sick to fight.[47] And to make matters worse, even those who did not succumb to illness were ready to desert.

Thousands of American deserters filled the roads to Connecticut and New Jersey as soldiers fled to the comfort of their homes. Some were ill; others were just sick of being unpaid, inadequately supplied, and poorly led by civil authorities. One proud soldier, a devout patriot who had served the cause dutifully, wrote to his wife, "You are afraid that I shall stay in the cause of liberty till I shall make myself a slave to it. I have too much reason to fear that will be the case. I hope to come home soon and see you. Wishing you goodnight, your most kind and affectionate husband till death."[48] Suffering terribly and longing for home, he soon quit and returned to his family in Massachusetts, where he worked as a shoemaker for the rest of the war. Similar sentiments were rife in the American ranks, threatening to tear Washington's army apart.

As impotent as he was angry, Washington complained to Congress that his soldiers, "instead of calling forth their utmost efforts to a brave and manly opposition, in order to repair our Losses, are dismayed, Intractable, and Impatient to return. Great numbers of them have gone off . . . ."[49] Worse yet, many of the Americans did not merely go home, but actually defected to the British side. This was unsurprising, since the British redcoats were faring much better just across the river in Brooklyn.

14

Between a Hawk and a Buzzard

The British were far happier and healthier than their wilting foes. Rather than a weak commander and an interfering, cash-strapped civil authority, the British enjoyed a powerful, streamlined military leadership. They received regular pay from Britain's deep coffers and even gorged themselves on the plentiful food provided by Britain's all-powerful navy.

Contrary to the popular American conception of the redcoats as battle-scarred "sweepings of the London and Liverpool slums, debtors, drunks, common criminals and the like, who had been bullied and beaten into mindless obedience,"[1] they were actually demographically similar to their American counterparts. The redcoat foot soldiers were mostly young farmers and unskilled laborers who were not forced into service but instead lured by the promise of food, pay, and adventure.[2] And while the Americans thought the redcoats were street trash, the British soldiers did not think too highly of the patriots either. One Brit wrote of them:

> While every clown that tills the plain,
> Though bankrupt in estate and brains,
> By this new light transformed to traitor,
> Forsakes his plough to turn dictator.[3]

The young men on both sides of the war had a tremendous amount in common. The patriots and redcoats shared the same religion, customs, and heritage. Despite popular misconceptions, they even shared a similar accent. While one might imagine the British complaining about preparations for the coming "ha*h*d wint*uh*," denizens of the British Isles actually spoke like the Americans in lamenting the "ha*r*d winter."[4] This is because the "British accent" is actually a manufactured one that did not fully take hold until after the war.

Both the British and the Americans originally shared a rhotic accent in which they pronounced the "R's" in their words. However, around this time, something peculiar started to occur in Britain: the people began a concerted effort to change their pronunciation to non-rhotic.[5] As the Industrial Revolution catapulted individuals of low birth rank into titans of British industry, these nouveau riche Londoners sought to distinguish themselves from fellow commoners.[6] And so, they actively cultivated a non-rhotic accent to signify their new elite status. "London pronunciation became the prerogative of a new breed of specialists—orthoepists and teachers of elocution," and it was these men who "decided on correct pronunciations, compiled pronouncing dictionaries and, in private and expensive tutoring sessions, drilled enterprising citizens in fashionable articulation."[7]

Thus, while the British manufactured their posh new accent during the late eighteenth century, the Americans continued to pronounce their "R's"—only Boston and New York City followed the trend, developing their own non-rhotic accents since they remained "under the strongest influence by the British elite."[8] During this summer of 1776, however, the new accents had not yet taken hold and the British and American soldiers still largely spoke in the same rhotic manner. They were still brothers—albeit bitterly estranged ones who were prepared to kill one another.

Unlike their republican brethren, the British soldiers were proud to fight for their king. They faced harsh penalties for breaking the British military code, but those strict regulations kept them safer and healthier. For example, they were required to put on a clean shirt two or three times a week, and to ensure that their linens were washed.[9] Needless to say, Brooklyn smelled far better than Manhattan on those hot summer nights. Reasonable hygiene, adequate rations, and a natural resistance to smallpox helped keep disease in check and the redcoats prepared for their next attack.

The British discipline was far from perfect, however, and the redcoats also found time to abuse the locals. One British officer described the New York women as "fair nymphs" who were "in wonderful tribulation, as the fresh meat our men have got here has made them as riotous as satyrs." Rape had become so commonplace, he wrote, that "A girl cannot step into the bushes to pluck a rose without running the most imminent risk of being ravished, and they are so little accustomed to these vigorous methods that they don't bear them with the proper resignation."[10] A fiendish British officer made light of the situation, joking that as a result they had "most entertaining courts-martial every day" to try the attackers.[11]

One girl complained of being deflowered by a band of British grenadiers.[12] Picked from among the strongest and tallest soldiers, grenadiers had the power to hurl baseball-sized iron spheres far away from their comrades before the burning fuses ignited the gunpowder within. Apparently, some of these elite fighters also used their strength against American women. Rather than condemn the attack on the girl, the British laughed at her testimony that even in the dark she knew that her attackers were grenadiers by their size. In another case, the British troops mocked a woman who was attacked by seven men. They claimed laughingly that her real complaint was "not of their usage" but rather "of their having taken an old prayer book for which she had a particular affection."[13] Washington and his troops were powerless to stop these atrocities.

In September 1776, one British officer wrote to the chief strategist in London that the war was "pretty near over," and King George III believed his forces were close to victory.[14] His army sickly and disintegrating,

Washington was close to agreeing. At this point, General Howe could pretty much destroy the Continental Army whenever he wished. But he still hoped for a peaceful end to the rebellion and for the colonies' return to the British Empire. Viewing himself as a sort of peace negotiator, he rejected the "rash" course of "*crushing at once* a frightened, trembling enemy," and instead "he generously gave them time to recover from their panic . . . ."[15]

Washington used this time to formulate a plan. He knew that he had little hope of defending Manhattan Island against the combined power of Britain's healthy, well-trained, and well-armed army and navy. And so he decided to run—again.

The American commander made the rather obvious military observation that he should retreat. But he was not confident that he had the authority to order a full withdrawal, since his commission from Congress directed him to confer with his "council of war."[16] Washington felt bound by this language to obtain their sign-off before any major action.[17] The members of this war council were all appointed by the meddling Congress, and most were relative novices in military matters. In fact, only one, the slovenly military genius Charles Lee, was a professional soldier. Seeking to be deferential to the politicians' and officers' wishes, however, Washington dutifully brought the question of withdrawal before this group.

Washington and the war council "all agreed that the Town was not tenable if the Enemy was resolved to bombard and Cannonade it."[18] Yet a majority on the council foolishly decided against a full withdrawal. Instead, "a Course was taken between abandoning it totally and concentrating our whole strength for its defence."[19]

Why would Washington take this militarily inexcusable risk? Because he believed that the micromanaging politicians expected him to do just that. Washington and the council were "influenced in their Opinion, to whom the determination of Congress was known, against an Evacuation totally; suspecting that Congress wished it to be maintained at every hazard . . . ."[20] Further, many of the novices on the war council—and even Washington, to a degree—had the naive view that they could still defeat the British, and they did not want to hurt morale further by another retreat. Therefore, the council made a decision that was contrary to Washington's best judgment, but the commander respectfully acquiesced.[21]

Washington quickly informed Congress that he would retain forces on Manhattan Island even though it was "extremely obvious, from all Intelligence," that the British intended to encircle the Americans and "endeavour to cut this Army in pieces."[22]

Washington and his officers had bowed to civil authority, but their discontent was surfacing. With Congress and its war council peering over his shoulder at every turn, the commander in chief still lacked full command over his army.[23] His officers, feeling that Congress was forcing them to fight the war with one arm tied behind their back, began to question their political masters more openly. "The councils of the Congress seem to be dark and intricate, and very badly calculated," wrote one of Washington's officers. While the soldiers were trapped on the island, fearing for their lives and "anticipating the apprehended evil," Congress was at a safe distance in Philadelphia.[24] And when Congress did send observers to survey the army's condition, these "Philadelphia gentlemen who came over on visits, upon the first cannon shot went off in a most violent hurry."[25] Washington and his army remained on the field, almost literally staring down the barrel of a gun. Washington's assistant wrote to his wife, "We are still here in a posture somewhat awkward; we think (at least I do) that we cannot stay and yet we do not know how to go—so that we may be properly said to be between a hawk and a buzzard."[26]

Meanwhile, a comfortable eighty-two miles away in Philadelphia, Congress spent precious time debating the predicament. With the army's fate hanging in the balance, the politicians back at cozy Independence Hall finally decided to send a small delegation to meet with Howe. This group consisted of Ben Franklin, John Adams, and Edward Rutledge, a twenty-six-year-old South Carolinian who was the youngest man to sign the Declaration of Independence. The distinguished trio set off immediately by horse across New Jersey and then rowed out to Howe's base on the southernmost tip of the island.

Greeted by an intimidating row of enemy fighters, Franklin and his two young co-diplomats were escorted into Bentley Manor, a stately stone house that was being used as a barracks. It was in a filthy state, but the redcoats had cleaned up one room overlooking the bay for the meeting.[27] Once inside, the Americans drank claret and ate ham, tongue, and mutton while they awaited their British adversary.[28] The veil of civility failed to mask the dangerous situation in which they sat.

The so-called "Staten Island Peace Conference" convened on September 11, 1776. This attempt to end the war was doomed from the start, however, and both sides knew it. Howe entered the meeting room in his sharp uniform, fully aware that he had the upper hand. He informed the delegation that it was in the Americans' best interest to rescind their Declaration of Independence. While Howe attempted to be conciliatory, he could not help but act the role of a conqueror stating his terms: should they rejoin the empire, he would spare them. Howe indeed had authorization from London to pardon many of the patriots, and he was surprisingly eager to use it.

After three hours of discussion (in which Howe did most of the talking), the British general emotionally revealed that he viewed the schism between Britain and her former colonies with regret and still regarded the congressmen as his British kinsmen. He continued, "if America shall fall, I should feel for and lament it like the loss of a brother." The wily Franklin said dryly, "we will use our utmost endeavors to save your lordship that mortification." Howe, not one for dry humor, responded with a long monologue outlining his attempts at peace to the stone-faced congressmen. He explained his desire to reunite the empire by bringing the colonies—whom he viewed as his American brothers—back under the Crown. To that, Adams retorted with his typical biting eloquence: "Your lordship may consider me in what light you please . . . except that of a British subject."[29] Little did

Adams know that his name was on a secret list of patriots to whom Howe was forbidden to grant pardon should America agree to end the rebellion.[30]

Luckily for Adams, there would be no peace or pardoning that day. As Howe's secretary summarized the conference, "They met, they talked, they parted. And now nothing remains but to fight it out."[31] Although their meeting was fruitless, at least the congressmen had bought Washington a few more days of respite.

Washington met again with his war council. This time, they had intelligence that the British forces were preparing for an imminent attack, and the council agreed to a full withdrawal from Manhattan. Congress also changed tunes, deciding to allow the commander in chief to determine the timing of an evacuation.[32] Finally relinquishing the power to make such a tactical decision, Congress notified Washington that no part of the army "should remain in that city a moment longer" than he judged appropriate.[33] Washington could now do what he needed in order to save his army. He quickly pressed every available horse and wagon in the vicinity into service and commenced another mass retreat.[34] But Congress still prohibited him from acting on his more controversial wish: to set Manhattan ablaze.

Washington knew that the British forces were salivating at the thought of taking the island. With its large Loyalist population, great ports, ample housing, and plentiful sources of supplies, New York was the perfect place for them to live during the coming winter. The British troops could be healthy, well supplied, and ready to trounce the feeble American forces come spring. Further, Washington knew he had little chance of recovering the island, since such an amphibious invasion would require a navy to match mighty Britain's, and he had virtually none. So the only logical tactic was to deprive the British of the city.[35]

But Congress forbade him. They ordered Washington to do "no damage" to New York. Clueless of the military realities, they declared that they had "no doubt of being able to recover" the city if the British took it.[36] Washington grudgingly obeyed, although in private he grumbled that if he had his say, he would have "laid the city in ashes."[37] And his wish would come true.

With the British invasion looming, Washington hurriedly withdrew his army up Manhattan with the goal of escaping into the Bronx. But he was too late. Howe was not about to allow him to slip away yet again. This time, the British pounced before the Americans had the chance to run.

15

Onslaught

One Sunday morning during the dog days of summer 1776, a groggy baby-faced Connecticut private named Joseph Plumb Martin lay quietly in a defensive trench.[1] Only fifteen years old, he was too young to fight without his guardians' consent, so he had threatened to run away unless his grandparents allowed him to enlist. They gave in.

And now this headstrong youth from a wealthy family, excited to be a part of the American cause, had been enjoying a seemingly peaceful morning. "The Hills, the Woods, the River, the Town, the [British] Ships . . . all Heightened by a most clear & delightful morning, furnished the finest Landscape that either art and nature combined could draw, or the Imagination conceive."[2] With the sun little over an hour high, the day was already warm. As the menacing British warships silently passed by, Martin began amusing himself by reading some papers he found among the debris on the ground. It was the calm before the storm.

"I was demurely perusing these papers," the teenager recalled, "when all of a sudden there came such a peal of thunder from the British shipping that I thought my head would go with the sound. I made a frog's leap for the ditch, and lay as still as I could, and began to consider which part of my carcass was to go first."[3] The ground trembled along with the American soldiers as the British warships launched a fear-some barrage from seventy cannons. Just four days after the collapse of peace talks, the violent bombardment of Manhattan was underway.

One British soldier observed, "The scene was awful and grand, I might say beautiful, but for the melancholy seriousness that which must attend every circumstance where the lives of men, even the basest malefactors, are at stake."[4] The patriots did not think the scene was quite as beautiful. They were cowering in their trenches when 12,000 well-aligned British troops began to wade onto the shore in droves like a red war machine. Spotting their approach, the panicked Americans ran or surrendered. Barely any American rounds were fired, and the British forces invaded with "nothing to hinder them."[5]

Once ashore, the redcoats were welcomed by New York's Loyalists as a liberation party. To the patriots' chagrin, the Tories cheered and hoisted the British troops onto their shoulders as they celebrated like "overjoyed bedlamites." The British soldiers were equally elated: they had landed without losing a single man.[6]

Receiving no orders from their superiors, Martin and his battalion ran like hell, while "the grape shot and langrage flew merrily, which served to quicken [their] motions."[7] They made a mad dash to a nearby house, where they came upon women and small children crying amidst the mayhem. Even though it was still morning, the soldiers were in need of a stiff drink. Much to their delight, the women placed a bottle of rum on the table and the thirsty soldiers helped themselves. Forti-fied with some liquid courage, Martin and his friends then snuck out the door and ran for miles to safety.

Hearing the British bombardment, Washington leapt onto his horse and raced to the scene. When he arrived, he was not pleased with what he saw. "The demons of fear and disorder" had infected his troops, sending them scattering.[8] Even in areas where they outnumbered the British, the Americans fled, dropping their muskets, bullets, food, and even clothing to run faster.[9] In Washington's view, his soldiers were becoming a little too adept at running away. He was a man of action.

Honor required that he stand and fight. Therefore, he boldly ordered his troops to stand their ground. Almost as if he were trying to beat honor into them, he struck several officers as they disobeyed.

Washington scrambled to organize a counterattack, but the Americans were too terrified to return fire. He could take no more of such impotence. In one of the few times the remarkably stoic general lost his temper, he dashed his hat on the ground and exclaimed, "Good God, have I got such Troops as those!"[10] Mad with rage, he mounted his horse and charged at the invaders. Almost no one followed him.

The commander rode with nearly suicidal fury and virtually no backup to within a football field of the redcoats. Frustrated by his inability to stop the British and distraught over the peril to his nation, the tremendously unflappable man lost control of his faculties. And it almost cost him his life. There he was, blind with anger, singlehandedly opposing the invasion. Realizing the horror about to transpire, two of his aides frantically grabbed for his horse's reins as bullets whizzed past, kicking up the earth around them. The commander almost died in that instant. But luckily for the him—and for the Revolution—muskets were rather inaccurate weapons.

The French developed the flintlock musket in 1610. This ingenious contraption antiquated the need to ignite gunpowder with a match. Instead, the hammer used a piece of flint to cause the spark that created the (somewhat) controlled explosion that forced the lead musket ball through the gun barrel and hurling towards its target. This invention helped revolutionize warfare. The strength of these guns accounted for the prominence of the French musketeers, who were immortalized in the famous novel *The Three Musketeers*. Not to be outdone by their rivals, the British developed a similar musket and introduced it to their American colonies. Although tweaks were certainly made to the design over the next century and a half, the weapon remained largely the same. And Washington owed his life to this lack of innovation.

Violently propelled by exploding gunpowder, the musket ball rolled around the gun's barrel in an erratic spin. Like an inexperienced pitcher trying to throw a curve ball, the musket sent the ball hurling on an unpredictable path. A famous British marksman noted that "a soldier's musket, if not exceedingly ill-bored (as many of them were), will strike the figure of a man at eighty yards" or perhaps more, but at a distance much farther than that, "you may as well fire at the moon and have the same hope of hitting your object."[11] Although this clumsy musket was the preferred weapon, both sides of the conflict had varied arsenals at their disposal.

Both the Americans and the British used rifles as well. Rifles enabled far greater accuracy, but they were often "more noisy than useful" in warfare, for three main reasons.[12] First, they required a longer reload time. While a trained soldier could reload a musket in about thirty seconds, a rifle could require a multiple of that time since the powder needed to be packed more tightly. And those extra seconds could mean the difference between life and death as the enemy swarmed towards him. Second, line marksmen had little chance to make use of their rifles' accuracy: they lacked the time, and often they could not see well enough to aim amidst the smoke of battle. Finally, the rifle's third fatal flaw was that it lacked a bayonet. Muskets were often fitted with sharp metal bayonets at the end of their barrel so the gun could be used like a spear. This was crucial. Just as a schoolyard fight might start out with punches and turn into a close grappling match, a battle of armies would often progress from distant shots to messy hand-to-hand combat. These factors helped ensure that the musket remained the weapon of choice for modern armies—fortuitously for Washington.

The young Brits peered eagerly at the large enemy leader draped in his gold-trimmed blue coat astride a brawny, brown horse. Their glorious target mere yards away, they pulled their triggers, emitting a cloud of gunpowder that singed their hands and nostrils. The lead balls bounced around the chambers of their muskets, burst out haphazardly, and spun harmlessly past Washington and his horse. This gave the irate commander's aides the opportunity to usher him to safety. Thus, the clumsiness of the old musket design saved the Revolution, allowing the commander an opportunity to flee with his troops up Manhattan.

While disgraced by his troops' cowardly retreat, Washington did see one of his goals accomplished: the Americans left the British with a nasty surprise.

Downtown Manhattan erupted into a raging inferno. Although Congress had forbade Washington from destroying the city, some of his less deferential compatriots apparently took matters into their own hands. Ardent in their attachment to the revolutionary cause, some patriots declared that they "would set fire to their own houses sooner than they should be occupied by the King's troops."[13] Around midnight on September 21, 1776, a fire broke out at Fighting Cocks Tavern and simultaneously in other downtown locations.[14] How it started was never proven, but Americans and British alike believed that the patriots used "matches and combustibles that had been prepared with great art and ingenuity" to set the town ablaze.[15]

Aided by the summer evening's warm breeze, the fire quickly spread among the wooden homes and shipping wharves. The sky soon turned a smoky red as the scorching heat engulfed a quarter of the city. Because Washington had taken many of the city's church bells for smelting into cannon, the British had difficulty sounding an alarm.[16] This not only slowed the containment effort but also exacerbated the panic. Many of the sleeping townspeople were not awakened to the danger until the fire was lapping at their doors. Others did not wake at all. One aghast British soldier described the heartrending scene:

> It is impossible to conceive a scene of more horror and distress . . . . The sick, the aged, women, and children half naked were seen going they knew not where, and taking refuge . . . . The terror was increased by the horrid noise of the burning and falling houses . . . the confused voices of so many men, the shrieks and cries of the women and children, the seeing the fire break out unexpectedly in places in the distance, which

manifested a design of totally destroying the city . . . made this one of the most tremendous and affecting scenes I ever beheld.[17]

The redcoats wanted instant revenge. Mobs of British soldiers and Tories seized two suspected patriot saboteurs and threw them into the fire. The British brutally cut off the hand of another patriot suspect and hung him up by his feet.[18]

Some inevitably suspected that Washington was secretly behind the plot—especially in light of his professed desire to burn the city. "Many circumstances lead to conjecture that Mr. Washington was privy to this villainous act," it was asserted.[19] Finding "villainy even in the virtuous Washington," the British pegged the arsonists as his "emissaries."[20] It is unlikely that Washington was directly complicit in starting the fires since Congress had forbade him and he remained deferential. But that did not mean he was unhappy about the blaze. Privately he applauded the destruction since he was convinced that the congressmen's order was an imprudent one. "Providence, or some good honest fellow, has done more for us than we were disposed to do for ourselves," he wrote.[21]

While Washington would have liked to see the whole of Manhattan burn to the ground, about a quarter of it did. And the Americans were not done making the British miserable.

Desperate to stand up to the British after months of defeat, Washington eventually succeeded in organizing a counterattack. He knew that even a moral victory would do much to assure Congress that their budding faith in him was justified. At Harlem Heights, miles north of the British forces, he got his troops to stop their panicked flight and huddle in a line of trenches that stretched across the woods and buckwheat fields that dominated the area.[22] There, in the late summer heat, they lay in wait for their pursuers. His trap set, Washington patrolled on horseback, ready to ambush the rapidly advancing British forces.

When the redcoats finally arrived at Harlem Heights, they were stunned. Expecting the Americans to run away as usual, they "were never so surprised" as to see the Americans charging at them instead.[23] The patriots fought ferociously, and many lives were lost on both sides. But then an unusual thing happened. From the booming smoke of battle, a mass of red uniforms began to real backwards. For the first time in the New York campaign, the British retreated. One "mortified" British officer later wrote to a friend, "If I only had a pair of pistols, I am sure I would at least have shot a puppy of an officer I found slinking off in the heat of the action."[24]

The Americans had little time to gloat, however. British reinforcements soon arrived, and Washington prudently decided to retreat rather than pursue. Although his instinct was to fight, his level head prevailed. He knew that winning the war required him to protect his army.

Had Washington ordered a full retreat days earlier, as he had contemplated, the patriots would have had time to evacuate in an orderly fashion. But the commander had bowed to political pressure and the delays permitted the disastrous redcoat assault. Thus the evacuation was so chaotic that a large battalion became detached from Washington. Trailing behind, this 3,500-man force was marching up Manhattan away from the British invasion when it came terrifyingly close to an enemy contingent of 8,000 advancing along the same road. The British would easily have decimated the American force but for an unexpected bit of good luck named Mary Murray.

While Congress's political pressure and meddling had helped get the Continental Army into this mess, she would help get them out. An ardent patriot who lived on that road, the fifty-one-year-old Quaker still possessed the wiles to attract the British officers' attention. And work her charm she did, luring them into her home. Inside, she showered them with jokes, cakes, and generous helpings of wine.

Inexplicably, "they were induced to tarry two hours or more." As the officers lingered with Mrs. Murray and her Portuguese wine, the patriots fled to safety. "It became almost a common saying among our officers," wrote one soldier, "that Mrs. Murray saved this part of the American army."[25]

Mrs. Murray may have helped them live to fight another day, but the Americans' problems were far from over. With all the desertion and defeat, Washington's army was now mostly a ragtag group of neophytes. One redcoat described them as a band of "lads under 15, and old men. And few of them had the appearance of soldiers. Their odd figures frequently excited the laughter of our soldiers."[26] The British were shocked to discover that the American soldiers were not even all male. The revolutionary cause was so desperate for manpower that some women entered the fight.

When John Adams wrote his wife of the army's defeats, Abigail Adams confidently declared that if the men failed, the British forces would then be forced to fight "a race of Amazons in America."[27] And the British side certainly did confront some ferocious American women. The patriot ladies were particularly active on the home front, quartering soldiers, defending their homes, and hiding supplies from enemy raids. By working the fields and sewing uniforms, they fed and outfitted the troops. And as these ardent patriots played their part, God help those who opposed them.

In one comical incident, a "stingy merchant" in Boston refused to sell his coffee, a commodity that was in very short supply. His refusal was seen as unpatriotic and it brought the ire of the local populace. Fed up, a hundred or more caffeine-deprived women marched down to demand the coffee. But when they arrived, the wealthy bachelor rebuffed them—not the smartest move. As "a large concourse of men stood amazed," one of the women "seized him by his neck and tossed him into the cart." Thoroughly frightened, the merchant handed over his keys and the women seized the coffee. The miser purportedly received multiple spankings before the women finally released him.[28]

Some women even followed the men right onto the battlefield. Like many others, Mary Hays McCauley was eager to take an active role in the fight for independence. She followed her husband to the army camp, where she cooked and cared for the soldiers. But the fiery twenty-three-year-old did not stop there; she became a "pitcher," bringing water to cool the cannon that her husband manned. A strong, heavyset woman described as having a florid complexion and a love of banter, she dashed through the smoke, whizzing to and fro, helping her husband and his fellow soldiers.[29] Accounts of the battle say that when her husband was wounded, an enraged Mary grabbed a ramrod, hiked up her dress, took over the cannon and continued to fire incessantly at the approaching British. Both the Americans and their enemies were stunned. Joseph Martin described the scene in his diary:

> One little incident happened, during the heat of the cannonade, which I was eye-witness to, and which I think would be unpardonable not to mention. . . . [W]hile in the act of reaching a cartridge and having one of her feet as far before the other as she could step, a cannon shot from the enemy passed directly between her legs without doing any other damage than carrying away all the lower part of her petticoat, looking at it with apparent unconcern, she observed, that it was lucky it did not pass a little higher, for in that case it might have carried away something else, and ended her and her occupation.[30]

Even Washington was reportedly impressed. Mary and her husband survived the battle and she returned home to live a good, long life.

Mary Hays McCauley was far from the only female soldier among the patriots. Not only did other women jump to the aid of soldiers in battle, but some even enlisted.[31] In fact, "It was not an unusual circumstance to find women in the ranks disguised as men, such was their ardor for independence."[32] The Americans needed all the help they could get, and Washington certainly appreciated patriotic zeal from wherever it came.[33]

Washington's men (and women) not only faced the well-trained redcoats, but also Britain's German mercenaries—the dreaded "Hessians." In the eighteenth century, Germany was not yet a united nation but a patchwork of impoverished smaller states. These agricultural communities had little commercial activity and poor farmland but droves of excellent fighters. And so their rulers utilized this resource by selling mercenary services to other princes and nobles around Europe. The German states became the largest suppliers of soldiers in the world and charged a premium for their men's fighting prowess.[34]

Ever mindful of its coffers, England had first attempted to obtain cheaper troops. British envoys requested soldiers from Catherine the Great in Russia and Frederick the Great in Prussia, but both Greats refused. To them, lending troops to the British war machine was akin to throwing their young men to the wolves. After approaching the Netherlands and even considering the Moors in Morocco, the British finally decided that the Hessian warriors were worth their price.[35] And it was steep. In fact, the Duke of Brunswick sent just 4,300 soldiers but received 160,000 pounds (roughly equivalent to $300 million in modern U.S. dollars), while another noble used the profits from his fighters to build a new castle. Taking on this hefty expense, Britain hired 30,000 German mercenaries to crush the American rebellion.[36]

The Hessian soldiers were, by and large, castoffs of German society. Referred to as "expendable people" in their homeland, their ranks included debtors, unemployed laborers, and school dropouts. Many of them were forced into service involuntarily when they were kidnapped by wandering bands of military "recruiters."[37] Once in the "employment" of the German nobles, these ruffians were ruthlessly shaped into a lethal fighting force. Unlike Washington, their generals exercised iron-fisted control.

The common soldiers saw little of the hefty compensation paid to their nobles. Instead, many hoped to get rich from the plunder they could carry from battle.[38] As they marched, some would sing:

Be quick, brothers, to arms!
Let us go to America.
Assembled is our army.

Long live victory!
That red gold, that red gold
That comes rolling out from there
There we'll all get it, get it, there we'll all get more gold.[39]

To obtain that gold, some Hessians resorted to ransacking American towns. The Americans accused them not only of looting homes and farms, but also of slaughtering surrendering soldiers, abusing the sick and elderly, and raping women.[40] Britain had used foreign mercenaries such as these for centuries, but in America they were especially hated since they were seen as vicious interlopers in a battle between estranged brothers. And, along with his German friends, the British older brother was winning.

The Americans viewed the Hessian hordes as demonic, otherworldly creatures. The patriots described these frightening figures as having "broad shoulders, their limbs not of equal proportion, light complexion with a b[l]ueish tinge, hair cued as tight to the head as possible, sticking straight back like the handle of an iron skillet." The Hessians wore distinctive armored helmets, and blue or Jäger green uniforms with brass ornamentation that made an intimidating clanging sound as they marched.[41] Many of these seasoned mercenaries sported large bushy mustaches, which many boys fighting in the American army could not yet grow.

In his chaotic, ill-timed, ill-managed retreat, Washington had lost New York and many of his troops along with the city. It was starting to become clear to everyone that congressional meddling was not helping the cause. Americans needed a decisive military leader if they were going to stand a chance against the world's greatest military power.

But Washington would have to wait. As he watched helplessly from across the Hudson River, the last American stronghold on Manhattan, Fort Washington, fell to the combined Hessian and British force. The commander witnessed his troops fight bravely, only to be overrun. Even more heart-wrenching, many of those who surrendered were brutally slaughtered by the slashing Hessians.[42] Washington was reported to turn away from his officers and cry "with the tenderness of a child."[43] This was perhaps the lowest point in his life. He had failed his nation. He feared that the Revolution was lost. And it nearly was.

16

The Times That Try Men's Souls

By the fall of 1776, the commander had nearly run out of troops to command. Devastated by losses and desertions, Washington's force was slashed to just a couple thousand men. While he had commanded about 20,000 men prior to the British invasions of Brooklyn and New York, he now led a mere 3,500. His army was vastly outnumbered. To compound matters, more American Loyalists were joining the British side than there were patriots joining Washington. The states refused to send Washington more troops since they wanted to keep their men close to home for their own defense rather than send them away to another defeat.[1] Congress was impotent. In fact, Congress would not—and could not—even give Washington money to pay his men.

The army had many directors but little coherent direction. Washington had bent to the political pressure in defending New York and it had led to disaster. This was no way to fight a war. With Congress attempting to micromanage Washington's every move, the American war machine was less a machine than a schizophrenic squirrel that jumped from one task to another without coordination.

Washington recomposed himself and resolved to find a way to salvage the American cause. While the valiant general's propensity was to stand his ground and "fight like a man," he knew he could not win in New York. Honor gave way to reason, and Washington took the advice of his officers: the only way to give the Revolution a chance was to flee with his disintegrating army into New Jersey.

He was now on the run—and he loathed every minute of it. His confidence fading as quickly as his troops, Washington fled through the cold, muddy streets of New Jersey during the miserable autumn of 1776. They were chased by a seemingly unstoppable British and Hessian force, which ravaged the countryside as it pursued. "Indiscriminate ruin" and "horrid depredations" fell upon "every person they met with, infants, children, old men and women."[2] Rape was reportedly commonplace. In one account, a young girl "was taken from her father's house, carried to a barn about a mile, there ravished, and afterwards made use of by five more of these brutes." In another, a man's wife and ten-year-old daughter were likewise brutalized.[3] The advancing British and Hessians were seen as a demonic horde that the American commander was powerless to stop.

All Washington could do was flee. The American army retreated all the way across the state, finding a slight reprieve once they had crossed the Delaware River, whose flowing waters finally halted the destructive British advance. But with the world's mightiest navy at General Howe's disposal, this river provided Washington only temporary protection—the British could readily continue the chase. And with the weather unseasonably warm that December, the British appeared ready to do precisely that.

But before he squashed Washington's tattered force, Howe bizarrely ordered his troops to halt. As usual, he was in no hurry. Still holding out hope of reconciliation between Britain and its colonies, Howe felt no need to crush Washington's army—only to intimidate them.[4] So he stationed three Hessian regiments to harass Washington from across the river, where they taunted their prey with intermittent bouts of artillery fire. While their presence was unnerving, these Hessians were little immediate threat. Howe had decided it was winter.

A hard frost had arrived just in time to cool Howe's pursuit. As was custom during the era, the British forces would hunker down for the winter of 1776–1777. Rather than remain in the field and endure the ravages of the cold, gentlemanly armies instead withdrew from battle until spring.[5] Accordingly, leaving the Hessians in New Jersey, Howe and the bulk of his men returned to their winter quarters in their new prize: New York City. Although he should have chased Washington and crushed him with the full might of the British forces, Howe preferred to retire to his elegant New York City mansion, where he "lay warm in bed with Mrs. Loring."[6]

An attractive blonde in her mid-twenties, Elizabeth Loring was married to a Loyalist named Joshua Loring. She interpreted her marriage vows loosely, however, as did her husband. Joshua served in Howe's staff and seemed unperturbed by his wife's rather public dalliance with his boss. In fact, he acted more like her pimp than her husband as he gladly accepted generous military payments in exchange for permitting this not-so-secret affair.[7] "He fingered the cash, the General enjoyed Madam," quipped one Loyalist.[8]

Howe did indeed enjoy this arrangement immensely. Although he had a wife back in England, he was emboldened by the expanse of the Atlantic and openly pursued his adulterous infatuation.[9] He had "found his Cleopatra in an illustrious courtesan" and indulged in her along with plentiful helpings of rum.[10] Together they gambled, danced, and drank into the nights. They lived in a three-story Turtle Bay estate boasting views of the East River and fashionable decor imported from England.[11] Howe had quite the love nest. Charles Lee, never one to mince his words, crudely summed up the British general: "Howe shut his eyes, fought his battles, drank his bottle, had his little whore."[12]

Meanwhile, American Loyalists criticized Mrs. Loring as a distraction. They wanted Howe to end the war and they despised his mistress for diverting his attention from the effort. The Loyalists sang:

Awake, arouse, Sir Billy,
There's forage on the plain.
Ah, leave your little filly,
And open the campaign.[13]

But Billy slept. And in a way, that "courtesan" helped save the Continental Army, as Howe's dalliance provided Washington with time to lick his wounds.

The United States were at rock bottom. The Revolution had turned into a disaster and the fight for liberty seemed lost. "Trembling for the fate of America," Washington feared that Howe might seize Philadelphia, where he would surely hang any congressman he caught.[14] And, to his shame, his own army was in no position to stop another Howe onslaught. In fact, without coats to warm them or even shoes to protect their feet, Washington's battered and decaying army struggled just to survive the elements. Thomas Paine, the so-called mouthpiece of the Revolution whose patriotic pamphlets helped to rouse public opinion, famously wrote, "These are the times that try men's souls."[15]

In suffering solidarity, Washington rode on horseback alongside his withering troops as they retreated that miserable autumn of 1776. Although he hid his anxiety behind the strong face that he presented to his men, Washington privately confided, "I never was in such an unhappy, divided state since I was born. . . . I am wearied to Death."[16] He predicted, "I think the game is pretty near up."[17]

The commander was not the only one distraught over the American army's poor performance. As people looked for someone to blame for the crushing defeats in New York, General Washington stood out as the most obvious responsible party. Some of his own officers quietly questioned his competency as a military commander.

Eager for Washington's job, the conniving General Lee was quick to impugn Washington for America's defeats. Going behind his commander's back, Lee tattled to Washington's bosses in Congress about Washington's "fatal indecision of mind," calling it "a much greater disqualification than stupidity or even want of personal courage."[18] Not one for self-restraint, Lee did not stop there. He also wrote to another officer, "Entre nous, a certain great man is most damnably deficient. He has thrown me into a situation where I have my choice of difficulties."[19] With Lee's name on the short list of contenders, whispers about replacing Washington crept through the country.

Even as a growing chorus was questioning his capability, Washington retained the ardent loyalty of his troops and the majority in Congress. Although their confidence in the cause was wavering, his troops still believed in him and held out hope for victory. By behaving so heroically yet humbly during the first phases of the war, Washington had built up a deep reservoir of goodwill. And he needed every last drop.

"My neck does not feel as though it was made for a halter [noose]," Washington declared.[20] His persistence was unsinkable. He was determined to outlast the British and knew it would require decisive action. And so he began to voice his exasperation with Congress's ineptitude—although in his typical polite and subtle manner. "Give me leave to say . . . our Affairs are in a more unpromising way than you seem to apprehend," he told Congress. The Continental Army, he warned, "is upon the eve of its political dissolution."[21] The simmering tension between the commander and Congress began to bubble.

Washington went further, expressing some frustration with his own lack of power. Unable even to create a permanent army since it was seen as a stepping stone to tyranny, he was forced to plead with his freezing, starving, unpaid soldiers to reenlist time and again. Under this arrangement, he risked losing most of the remnants of his army when their terms expired at the end of the year. The longer they delayed in raising a standing army, he warned Congress, "the more difficult and chargeable would they find it to get one."[22] Although the commander's neck was not fit for a noose, it certainly sported a figurative leash that was beginning to chafe. Then a funny thing happened.

17

Reevaluation

Whether it was desperation that brought clarity or panic that brought action, Congress decided to remove the leash it had kept around Washington's neck.

With Howe able to seize Philadelphia at just about any time he wished, the elegant Independence Hall was no longer the safe haven it had been. Unbeknownst to Congress, Howe had actually made no preparations to invade Philadelphia that winter of 1776–1777. He was, after all, content to enjoy his winter quarters in Manhattan, partying with Mrs. Loring.[1] But the proximity of the British forces "seized the nerves of some members of Congress."[2] And when a local newspaper announced good intelligence that the British intended to push for Philadelphia, "much alarm" spread throughout the city.[3] With "massacre and starvation chill[ing] the blood in every vein," there was panic all around: "Where shall we go; how shall we get out of town? Was the universal cry."[4] The national government was paralyzed.

If captured by the British, the members of the Continental Congress would surely be hanged as traitors. So they began to scatter: John Adams and Thomas Jefferson returned to their homes, while Franklin was off lobbying the French for more assistance. In fact, so many congressmen were absent, on account of flight or illness or sheer exhaustion, that there were often not enough members for a quorum. The bold Continental Congress that had issued the Declaration of Independence only months earlier was now just a nervous shadow of itself, as the last holdouts anxiously milled within Independence Hall.

This rump Congress became more erratic. They ordered Washington to publicly refute the "false and malicious" report that they were about to flee Philadelphia.[5] Washington, however, realized that his controlling mother was acting a bit batty and thus disobeyed. He politely responded that following Congress's order would "not lead to any good end" and that he would "take the liberty to decline." As if already asserting his growing power as commander, he instead recommended that Congress would be wise to evacuate.[6] Little did Washington know, they already had.

Congress resolved to reconvene in Baltimore, approximately one hundred miles farther from Howe's men. The fact that they transferred to this backwater was itself another sign of desperation. At the time, Baltimore was a rough, dirty boomtown that was known more as a smelly haven for pirates than as a political center. The intellectual John Adams was appalled by what he described as the population's crude quest for profit by any means. Another delegate described Baltimore as "the damnedest hole on earth."[7] But the brutal realities of war had morphed from a far-off, virtuous battle for liberty in Boston and New York, into a very real and very near threat.

Fearing for their own lives, as well as for the American cause, the congressmen realized that their experiment with a weak commander had failed. The limits placed on Washington's control over his own army's tactics were hampering the war effort and endangering Congress itself. It had become painfully obvious that they needed their commander to protect them.

They had jealously clung to power and nervously watched Washington's every move, but now Congress changed course. The attempt to conduct the war by congressional committee—rather than granting full military authority to the commander—had reduced the civilian leadership to this desperate state. And so, while in flight to Baltimore, Congress temporarily ceded its military authority to Washington.

In a groundbreaking resolution, the congressmen voted that "General Washington be possessed of full power to order and direct all things relative to the department, and to the operations of war," until they reconvened a week later.[8] Finally, the commander in chief had full command of his own army, if only for a brief time. With this resolution, Congress threw out the mold for a weak American commander and launched their first experiment with an empowered one. Even though they gave him only a week, Congress had basically unleashed Washington for a run around the yard. They would never get him back on that tight leash again.

Washington's tone shifted in his writings to the states and Congress.[9] In a circular he wrote to the neighboring states about his shortage of weaponry, his tenor was less suppliant, more commanding. Previously he had pleaded for supplies, but now he insisted, "proper Steps should be immediately taken in your State to Collect all that can be purchased from private People." He reminded the states to make sure they obtained quality equipment rather than "light trash Arms" as he had received before.[10] Left to their own devices, the states had imperiled his army with deficient supplies, so Washington grew more forceful. The emboldened leader next turned to Congress.

Washington had beseeched Congress for more troops and supplies for months, and by December 20, 1776, he had had enough of begging. "I have waited with much Impatience to know the determinations of Congress on the Propositions made some time in October last for augmenting our Corps of Artillery and establishing a Corps of Engineers," he wrote in one of his longest letters to Congress, adding that further delay would cause "greatest injury to the safety of these states."[11] These were strong words for a southern gentleman.

Washington would wait no more. Exercising his new power, he ordered that three artillery battalions be recruited, since cannon, mortars, and howitzers had been proving decisive in battle. While the Americans were mostly firing little musket balls and missing their targets more often than hitting them, the British were tearing holes in the patriot lines with artillery fire. Aim mattered little when you sent large balls of lead hurling towards your foe. Raising battalions had been Congress's prerogative and they had bungled it, leaving the army lacking.[12] But now, Washington could take such matters into his own hands.

He even went further and started to spend Congress's money. Without consulting the politicians, Washington promised pay raises to certain regiments. He wrote that such an unprecedented measure "may appear to Congress premature, and unwarrantable; but . . . the Execution could not be delayed till after their Meeting at Baltimore."[13] And he was not done tugging on Congress's purse strings. Determining that he desperately needed even more cannon in particular, Washington took it upon himself to order that they be cast.[14] Rather than ask Congress, he would see to it himself and inform Congress of his actions afterward.

The American commander in chief was becoming a bold one. Washington admitted, "I am going a good deal out of the line of my duty to adopt these Measures, or advise thus freely," but said that necessity required it. "The Enemy are daily gathering strength from the disaffected [Americans who joined their cause]; this strength like a Snow ball by rolling, will Increase."[15] And so Washington seized the chance to act. He wrote to Congress, "It may be said that this is an application for powers that are too dangerous to be Intrusted. I can only add that desperate diseases require desperate Remedies; and with truth declare, that I have no lust after power . . . ."[16] The commander had to assert his authority if America was going to stand a chance. So he did.

Washington even began to criticize Congress's command structure. Its labyrinth of committees had attempted—largely ineffectually—to micromanage the war. He criticized the actions of "Committees without any kind of Controul," and singled out the committee that oversaw prisoner exchange. Prisoners were being handled in an embarrassingly disorganized fashion; some even wandered around without any one person policing their whereabouts. And Washington blamed Congress's setup, in which the commanding officer was "obliged to attend to the business of so many different departments as to render it impossible to conduct that of his own with the attention necessary." Revealing his frustration, he added, "nothing can be more Injurious."[17] In contrast to his timidity in the beginning of the war, Washington was now ready to take control from Congress and work to fix such inefficiencies. It had become painfully clear that the politicians would not do so on their own.

When it came time for Congress to rescind Washington's temporary war powers just days after they had bestowed them, the delegates reconsidered. It was at this opportune time that Washington's officer and confidant, Nathanael Greene, made a direct appeal to Congress on his commander's behalf.

Greene was a thoughtful and intelligent young Quaker who had become one of Washington's most trusted officers and closest friends. He was a handsome man whose long, thin nose pointed down to a bow mouth that contrasted with the sharp angles of his rectangular face. This was fitting, since he indeed was a man of contrasts. Bucking his religion's pacifist doctrine, Greene had taught himself military history and strategy—much to the chagrin of his fellow Quakers. But Greene, unrepentant, jumped to join the patriot cause. A likable, dependable, down-to-earth man, Greene did not always offer the best military advice, but Washington knew he could always count on Greene to be trustworthy and courageous.[18]

Like many in America, and especially in the military, Greene was fed up with Congress's inefficacy. He wrote to Washington, "There is so much deliberation and waste of time in the execution of business before this assembly, that my patience is almost exhausted."[19] He took matters into his own hands, requesting that the politicians relinquish military control to Washington. In his typical commonsense way, Greene urged, "Greater Powers must be lodged in the Hands of the General than he has ever yet exercised," reasoning that the commander could not "be in Readiness so early as General Howe" unless the congressmen would "delegate to him full Power to take such Measures as he may find Necessary to promote the Establishment of the New Army. Time will not admit nor Circumstance allow of a reference to Congress."[20]

Congress listened. The new concept of an "American commander in chief" was an experiment, and its initial phases had failed miserably. New York had been lost along with most of the Continental Army. The American cause was on the brink of destruction. Practical men, they realized that the American commander in chief needed sweeping military control in order to protect the United States from her foes.

By late December 1776, Congress had concluded that the rule-by-committee approach did not work. They not only extended the duration of Washington's power, but also expanded its scope:

This Congress, having maturely considered the present crisis; and having perfect reliance on the wisdom, vigour, and uprightness of General Washington, do, hereby,

Resolve, That General Washington shall be, and he is hereby, vested with full, ample, and complete powers to raise and collect together, in the most speedy and effectual manner, from any or all of these United States, 16 battalions of infantry . . . ; to appoint officers for the said battalions; to raise, officer, and equip three . . . and to establish their pay; to apply to any of the states for such aid of the militia as he shall judge necessary; to form such magazines of provisions, and in such places, as he shall think proper; to displace and appoint all officers under the rank of brigadier general, and to fill up all vacancies in every other department in the American armies; to take, wherever he may be, whatever he may want for the use of the army, if the inhabitants will not sell it, allowing a reasonable price for the same; to arrest and confine persons who refuse to take the continental currency, or are otherwise disaffected to the American cause; and return to the states of which they are citizens, their names, and the nature of their offences, together with the witnesses to prove them . . .[21]

While initially limited to six months, these plenary powers would be renewed again and again as the war raged on, since it was abundantly clear that the American commander needed full authority over the nation's war machine. Washington was empowered to raise new regiments, set their pay, call for the states' militia, take private property, arrest Loyalists, and appoint and dismiss officers.

Congress viewed control over officer rankings as a particularly dangerous power. They relinquished it grudgingly, retaining appointment authority for the highest positions—brigadier general and above. For the rest, soldiers would no longer be obliged to curry favor with the civilians in Congress for promotion. Now their military careers were dependent on pleasing their general. This was especially alarming to Congress since many soldiers scorned Congress's inefficacy and would no longer need to feign loyalty to them. Their general already held the troops' admiration and now he also controlled their careers and future. His power over his soldiers was complete, and some feared he could use this power to destroy the republic.

For all intents and purposes, Washington was able to make whatever military decisions were necessary to fight the war. To reinforce this sweeping authority, Congress sent a circular letter to the states explaining why General Washington's powers had been expanded and asking them to "give him all the aid in their power."[22] Many believed that those expanded powers "constituted him in all respects a military Dictator."[23] In fact, Washington's new mandate was seen as so sweeping that one enemy leader, in a speech at the British House of Commons, claimed that the Continental Congress had made Washington the "dictator of America."[24]

Originally derived from the Latin "dictare," which meant "to prescribe" or "to command," the term "dictator" was rooted in ancient Rome. And dictatorship was not always seen as negative.

Many of the American leaders were well versed in the classics and, unsurprisingly, looked to history as they experimented with the new American republic. Prior to the establishment of the Roman emperors, beginning with Augustus in the first century B.C., Rome had been a republic for nearly five centuries. Although the aristocratic class dominated this ancient republic, free Roman men at least had the opportunity to vote for their leaders. In turn, these leaders followed a largely unwritten, complex constitution based on separation of powers, with checks and balances, among three branches of government. In times of emergency, however, they dissolved their republican government and replaced it with a dictatorship. Their dictator held virtually absolute power over the state, albeit for just six months, after which his powers would lapse and the republic would be reinstated.[25] During his tenure as dictator, he could do just about anything necessary to save the nation from military defeat.[26]

With the present crisis upon them, the American congressmen recalled the saga of Lucius Quinctius Cincinnatus. A humble farmer who lived in the Italian countryside during the early Roman Republic, in the fifth century B.C., Cincinnatus famously served his country during a time of military crisis. A mountain people known as the Aequians had attacked, and the Romans were on the verge of defeat. The Roman senate was thrown into a panic by the thought of enemy hordes soon descending upon Rome. In this desperate situation, they suspended their republic and granted Cincinnatus dictatorial powers for six months. He used that time to defeat the Aequians and save Rome. Afterward, the people sought to crown Cincinnatus king. Instead, the great hero relinquished his dictatorial powers and simply returned to his farm. For his selfless devotion to his people, he was hailed as a paragon of simplicity and virtue. Washington would forever be compared to him.

Washington was really a new type of dictator. Unlike the Romans, Congress did not dissolve the republic and transfer the sovereign power of the nation from the people to Washington. His powers were vast, but they were largely confined to military matters. The supreme authority of the nation remained with the people, while the American commander had full military power to defend them. While perhaps seemingly subtle in the practical sense, this was an important philosophical distinction to the Americans.

In defending Congress's grant of authority to Washington, John Adams argued that "Congress never thought of making him [a true] dictator or of giving him a sovereignty."[27] The United States was not suspending civilian rule. Americans retained their rights, and their commander was still subject to Congress in civilian matters. But by making Washington a *military* dictator, Congress established the precedent of a strong commander in chief who possessed broad military authority to defend the United States without congressional meddling during wartime.

Washington instantly understood the ramifications of his new authority. The country's experimentation with the concept of "American commander in chief" had just reached a turning point. In his response to Congress, Washington wrote,

> they have done me the honor to intrust me with powers, in my Military Capacity, of the highest nature and almost unlimited in extent. Instead of thinking myself free'd from all civil Obligations, by this mark of their Confidence, I shall constantly bear in mind, that as the Sword was the last Resort for the preservation of our Liberties, so it ought to be the first thing laid aside, when those Liberties are firmly established.[28]

He was assuring Congress that a strong commander could nevertheless be a republican one. Washington was very aware of Congress's fears about military rule. He was eager to show them otherwise. He would prove that the American commander could be a powerful one who used his military authority to defend liberty rather than destroy it.

Washington promptly put his military supremacy to good use: the newly empowered commander made a daring bid to turn the tide of battle.

18

Victory or Death

Everyone expected Washington to use the winter of 1776–1777 to gather his army's strength. The British assumed he had no other choice. One British commander wrote, "The fact is their army is broken all to pieces and the spirit of their leaders and abettors is all broken."[1] But Washington's spirit would never be broken.

He did not have time to waste the winter rebuilding. With morale so low and pay so absent, Washington's soldiers were unlikely to reenlist when their terms expired on December 31. The commander faced the very real possibility of his army evaporating. As he met with a member of Congress, he "appeared much depressed, and lamented the ragged and dissolving state of his army in affecting terms." While the congressman "gave him assurance of the disposition of Congress to support him," Washington knew he could expect little help. Only half paying attention to the congressman, he continued "to play with his pen and ink upon several small pieces of paper." Almost like a madman, he was writing over and over: "Victory or Death."[2] This would be the secret code for his stunning surprise attack.

Washington took a risk. He reasoned, "as nothing but necessity obliged me to retire before the Enemy . . . I conceive it to be my duty, and it corrisponds with my Inclination, to make against them so soon as there shall be the least probability of doing it with propriety."[3] In his usual style, Washington concocted an overly complicated plan to attack the Hessians in Trenton, New Jersey. This time, however, his elaborate scheme actually succeeded.

The newly empowered commander was a cunning one. Washington had been defeated time and time again when he attempted to rely on brute force. This time, he would launch a daring surprise attack, as he had done long ago in the Jumonville massacre. Even if it risked what was left of his fading force, he did not hesitate to try now that Congress was in disarray and he was in full control of his army.

The Hessians in Trenton underestimated the American fighting spirit. They believed that Washington's beaten-down force was "almost naked, dying of cold, without blankets, and very ill supplied with provisions." And they were correct on all counts—the Americans were indeed "dying and cold."[4] But as the German mercenaries nested comfortably for the winter in the warm homes, inns, and shops of Trenton, they misjudged Washington's daring. Little did they know, he was poised for a yuletide attack.

On Christmas Day, Washington and his men faced another nor'easter. The same type of nasty storm that had enabled his escape from Brooklyn that summer now pelted his face with sleet. One of the worst storms in years, "it rained, hailed, snowed, and froze, and at the same time blew a perfect hurricane . . . ."[5] But much like before, this nor'easter also masked Washington's movements from his adversaries. He quickly organized a small flotilla of barges and packed them with his troops. Under the cover of wintry darkness, he and his makeshift fleet nervously rowed through the jagged chunks of ice on the Delaware River. The men stood together shaking—due to cold and fear—as they carefully navigated the treacherous currents.[6]

Then Washington ordered his men to march through the night, dead set on reaching the Hessians before the first light. But in the 28-degree weather with violent winds, the exhausted troops slowed to a crawl. The men "were nearly half dead from cold for the want of clothing," and many of them "had not a shoe to their feet and their clothes were ragged as those of a beggar." Washington rode alongside them, his squared nose flaming red in the wind,[7] and warned in his deep, breathy voice, "Keep up with your officers." If they stopped, they would likely freeze to death, as two of them did.[8] But Washington was not just looking out for them. He was running out of time. They were late and each additional ray of sun that shone on the horizon further derailed his plan.

The Americans finally arrived at Trenton in the early morning of December 26, 1776, hours behind schedule. Although they had lost the cover of darkness, they had acquired a camouflage of snow that literally covered them. And luckily, the German guards had skipped their patrols. While popular narrative blamed this lapse on hangovers from their Christmas binge, it was more likely that they were in fighting form but merely "unwilling to emerge into the teeth of a bad snowstorm."[9] Trenton's snowy streets were largely deserted—despite his troops' tardiness, Washington had not lost the element of surprise after all.

In the light of morning, however, he realized that only a fraction of his men were in position. Just one section of his multipronged assault plan had made it across the river and to Trenton by then. So Washington took another risk. Like a desperate gambler, he went for broke and decided to attack the force of one thousand Hessians anyway.

At just after eight in the morning, he launched the assault. Upon his order, the American cannon and muskets sprayed the little town with lead, catching the Germans by surprise. The soundly sleeping Hessian commander needed to be summoned three times before he put on his clothes and ran out into the storm. The bewildered Hessians grabbed their muskets and attempted to resist, but with the howling winds and horrendous visibility they were unsure of which direction to fire! Adding to the chaos, the civilian townsfolk ran screaming in terror through the once-quaint town's icy roads, making it even more difficult for the Hessians to hear their officers' commands.[10]

In the confused hour-long fight, many of the Americans' frozen guns malfunctioned. But the patriots were undaunted. They resorted to running towards their enemies brandishing their swords and yelling at the top of their lungs—and it worked.[11] The Hessians "ran like frightened devils" or surrendered in droves.[12] As the Hessians laid down their guns, the weapons were covered in snow. Not realizing that their enemies had capitulated, the Americans almost shot them. But right before the massacre, a few of the Americans' young eyes drew close enough to notice that they were unarmed.[13] When the Hessians surrendered, Washington secured a treasure trove of prisoners and munitions. The Americans killed or wounded one hundred Hessians and captured over nine hundred, while suffering amazingly few casualties themselves.

Patriots everywhere were overjoyed. Washington proclaimed, "it is a glorious day for our country,"[14] as news of the victory spread quickly and soon filled the newspapers throughout the states.[15] Reports circulated that "Congress untied the General, and then he instantly fought and conquered at Trenton."[16] Capitalizing on the boost in morale, Washington tried to persuade his men to continue fighting after their commissions expired on the 31st. While he had once disdained the crude manners and antihierarchical tendencies of the northern soldiers, he had grown to respect them deeply. And so, the regal Washington humbled himself before these farmers and craftsmen who filled his ranks, pleading with them as brothers in arms.[17]

As they stood in a line on the frozen battleground listening to their commander, the soldiers were moved by his call. Despite their appreciation for their general, however, many were eager to escape the horrendous winter conditions and return home. When he asked those reenlisting to step forward, his men hesitated. So Washington then sweetened the pot. Reaching beyond his traditional powers, he promised his men a 67 percent pay raise over the next month should they remain.[18] He informed Congress after the fact, adding, "I thought it no time to stand upon trifles."[19]

Washington's patriotic and monetary appeal saved the army. Many of the soldiers reenlisted. In a letter explaining to his fiancée why he could not yet return to her, one soldier summed up the growing sentiment among the troops: "I cannot desert a man (and it would certainly be deserting in a court of honor) who has deserted everything to defend his country."[20] Plus, he would enjoy the pay raise.

From their Baltimore hideout, Congress expressed the "highest satisfaction" with this victory and hoped that it would "prove the fore runner of future success." They praised their (now dictatorial) commander, writing, "it is entirely to your wisdom and conduct the United States are indebted for the late success of their arms." Reaffirming their faith in him, they added, "May you still proceed in the same manner to acquire that glory, which, by your disinterested and magnanimous behaviour, you so highly merit."[21] As Washington continued to flex his military muscles, his behavior was not always seen as so magnanimous, however.

But now, he needed to contend with the British backlash. When General Howe received word of the defeat at Trenton, he was furious. No longer willing to wait until spring to crush Washington, he ordered thousands of new troops into New Jersey. And he knew just the man to lead the mission: the decorated general Lord Cornwallis.

At the time, Cornwallis was about to walk the gangplank to sail back to England for a visit with his sick wife, Jemima. But to his dismay, his winter leave was abruptly canceled and he was instead sent to "bag the fox" in New Jersey. Of noble blood, Cornwallis was a highly educated and skilled military leader. Like Howe, he sympathized with the Americans. In fact, Cornwallis was one of the few members of the British House of Lords who called for Britain to stop taxing the colonies before the war. When the war arrived, however, he was ready to defend Britain's interests ruthlessly against the rebels. He had helped to crush the Americans in the Battle of New York and was now ready to finish off Washington's army.

Having just celebrated his thirty-ninth birthday, Cornwallis was a short, well-fed gentleman, whose round, dour face and drooping eyes masked a cunning intellect. He was known as an affable man, but not above occasional fits of rage. Respected by his countrymen for his military service in the Seven Years' War, he was feared by the American side as a tremendously shrewd "madman."[22] Cornwallis displayed a particularly aggressive countenance that winter, having been kept away from his adored wife.

Gathering additional forces along the way, Cornwallis swept through the cold, slushy roads of New Jersey towards Trenton. He was prepared to destroy Washington's force of approximately 5,000 exhausted men with his 8,000 well-trained and well-fed troops. But the foxy Washington still had some more tricks up his painstakingly tailored sleeve.

Slowed by the muddy roads, Cornwallis's main force did not arrive at the outskirts of Trenton until January 2, 1777. Washington knew he could not stop a prolonged assault, but because night battles were treacherous and therefore rare at the time, he needed only to hold back Cornwallis's superior force until darkness fell.

As soon as the mass of redcoats was spotted five miles outside the town at ten o'clock in the morning, Washington unleashed a small team of sharpshooting riflemen to harass them. Firing unexpectedly from behind trees and walls, the Americans slowed down Cornwallis's troops for five precious hours with their guerilla tactics. But the British forces were unstoppable. For Washington, the early January sunset could not come soon enough.

Cornwallis arrived in Trenton late that afternoon. Washington urgently sought a defensible position and came upon a scenic stone bridge over a creek. While the Assunpink Creek would normally be too shallow to provide a defense, it was now swollen from the storm, making it treacherous to ford. Besides, Washington did not have time to be too picky. Dusk settled in, and Washington's forces stood nervously in position along the raging creek. As the drumbeats of the red hordes neared, they braced for the attack.

Amid the ensuing battle, Washington was like a one-man fortress. Sitting stoically on his horse on the American-held side of the bridge, he was a symbol of American resolve. When one soldier accidentally bumped into his commander during the battle, he was astonished to find that "the horse stood as firm as the rider and seemed to understand that he was not to quit his post and station."[23] Unlike his defeat in New York, Washington would see to it that his men did not retreat this time. He would personally make sure they stood and fought. And as usual, he led by example.

Washington's "firm, composed, and majestic countenance . . . inspired confidence and assurance."[24] Amazingly, the Americans held their ground. The patriots fired mercilessly across the creek with their guns and eighteen artillery pieces as Cornwallis sent his men in suicidal droves towards the bridge.[25] Between the descending darkness and the choking smoke, the British found themselves charging blindly into unfamiliar terrain.[26] The darkness was pierced only by terrifying flashes of fire from muskets and cannon. The Americans drove back three attacks.

When the formerly picturesque bridge ran red with the "killed and wounded and red coats," Cornwallis decided to wait for morning to try again.[27] He knew he could readily overwhelm Washington's beleaguered troops then. With the dawn's light, his men would be able to see their targets and also wade through the waist-deep creek as it calmed. And so Cornwallis told his officers, "We've got the old fox safe now. We'll go over and bag him in the morning."[28]

But the fox was not about to wait around for that. Wary of being encircled by Cornwallis's larger force, Washington had no intention of lingering to see what happened in the morning. Instead, he only waited until midnight's darkness again came to his aid. Then he began another daring maneuver, using the same trick he had employed in his stealthy escape from Brooklyn. He left some men behind to tend fires and make noise, thus deceiving Cornwallis into believing the whole army remained just across the bridge, while the bulk of the force slipped away into the night.

Washington did not want just another retreat, however. He lusted for further victory. Emboldened by his new commander-in-chief powers, he was eager to use them to turn the tide. He could take quick, decisive action without getting approval from Congress. So instead of retreating again to safety across the Delaware River, he chose to drive deeper into enemy-held New Jersey.

Drawing upon his spy network, Washington obtained detailed maps of the region. From these, he learned of largely unknown backwoods roads that had recently been cut through the pine forests. His goal was to use these secret paths to slip past Cornwallis's main force towards an unsuspecting British rearguard of just one thousand men. As he had done in Trenton, he wanted to conduct a surprise attack on an isolated inferior force; but first he had to get to them.

Washington ordered his exhausted men to march for twelve miles that night against the stinging winter winds.[29] It was now January 3, and they had been running on adrenaline since their all-night march and their victory in Trenton a little over a week earlier. While their jubilance had buoyed them, the wear was starting to show.

The cold had returned, freezing the muddy roads and the Americans along with them. With starlight as a guide, they marched in utter silence, huddling together and struggling to survive in their scant clothing. Hungry and fatigued, many fell asleep standing up when their column stopped.[30] Some perished along the way, falling into icy ponds or simply collapsing on the road. Like marching zombies, the Americans had become so accustomed to hardship that they were seemingly numbed to the misery.

As daylight arrived, Washington and his men were approaching the sprawling farms and orchards of Princeton. The morning was "bright, serene, and extremely cold, with a hoarfrost that bespangled every object."[31] But the wearied Americans had little time to enjoy the sparkling scenery. Washington's plan had worked beautifully: they stunned the enemy yet again. But the British quickly spotted the ragged Americans and fired on them. The battle was on.

"Parade with us, my brave fellows!" Washington shouted as he led the charge. With his hat in hand, he rode ahead on his horse, yelling "There is but a handful of the enemy, and we will have them directly."[32]

His men were awe-struck by their commander. One admiring soldier marveled at seeing him "brave all the dangers of the field and his important life hanging as it were by a single hair with a thousand deaths flying around him. Believe me, I thought not of myself."[33] The Americans charged!

But the attack almost led to disaster. Perhaps too brave, Washington was caught directly in the crossfire as he led the charge. The British and the Americans were a mere thirty yards apart, and Washington in between, when both lines unleashed a barrage of bullets. An American officer, assuming that Washington had to have been hit, covered his eyes with his hat. But, miraculously, Washington appeared to be bulletproof. Again.

According to one popular tale, back during the Seven Years' War, Washington's Native American foes attempted to kill him in a particularly bloody battle. Their sharpshooters fired shot after shot right at him, with no effect. They were shocked. A brave recalled, "I had seventeen clear shots at him . . . and after all could not bring him to the ground. This man was not born to be killed by a bullet." The chief ordered that they stop firing and declared, "This one is under the special protection of the Great Spirit." Washington too chalked up his survival to a higher power, writing to his younger brother, "I now exist and appear in the land of the living by the miraculous care of Providence, that protected me beyond all human expectation; I had 4 Bullets through my Coat, and two Horses shot under me, and yet escaped unhurt."[34] He survived similar close calls in Brooklyn and during his retreat from Manhattan. And now during this battle at Princeton, he was again miraculously unscathed.

When the "most horrible music" of musketry subsided, Washington's baritone voice emerged, ordering his men to continue their charge.[35] His dashing figure pierced through the smoke like a supernatural force. Reveling in the battle, the commander shouted, "It's a fine fox chase boys!"[36]

He inspired the selflessness the Americans needed to overcome their fears. Despite being outnumbered approximately five to one, the British resisted fiercely, but it was of no use. The Americans overwhelmed their foes, and, in doing so, achieved another stunning victory. The patriots had exacted more than 500 enemy casualties and captured over 200 prisoners while losing just a few dozen men.[37] Washington had turned the psychological tide of the war.

When Cornwallis received word of the rout, he raced towards Princeton with his force "in a most infernal sweat, running, puffing and lowing and swearing at being so outwitted."[38] But he arrived an hour too late. Washington had already evacuated to the north, deeper into New Jersey. The patriots briskly marched another fifteen miles before collapsing in exhaustion.[39] After some searching, Washington decided to hunker down for the winter in Morristown, New Jersey, for some much-needed rest. Just twenty-five miles from Howe's stronghold in New York City, Morristown afforded the Continental Army protection by its surrounding hills as well as food from its ample farmland.

19

Idolatry

News of the American victories spread rapidly around the globe. Frederick the Great, the king of Prussia, described Washington's back-to-back triumphs as "the most brilliant of any recorded in the annals of military accomplishments."[1] This was extremely high praise from a man of such great military acclaim—and the praise was justified. For the first time, it appeared to America and the world that the ragtag American forces might actually be able to humble the British Empire.

For his part, General Howe saw his recent defeats as little more than embarrassing skirmishes, but he did not care to suffer any more of them. He decided to abandon New Jersey for the winter. As usual, he was in no hurry. Happily partying with Mrs. Loring in New York, he assumed he would simply finish off Washington in the spring.

The Americans' empowered commander had retaken most of New Jersey. And with it, Washington's reputation reached new heights. "Had he lived in the days of idolatry," the *Pennsylvania Journal* remarked, Washington would have been "worshipped as a god."[2] With his strong popular backing, the commander gained even more authority.

Previously, the war council appointed by Congress had shot down Washington's ideas time and again, contributing to the disastrous delay in escaping Manhattan. Now Congress informed Washington that he was "not bound by their opinion, but ought finally to direct every measure according to his own judgment."[3] Washington had grown accustomed to the frank debate in the war council meetings, and he would continue to hold these meetings, but now he felt free to reject the council's conclusions. And he would.[4] He had the power to lead his troops as he saw fit.

At this stage, Washington was less concerned about public opinion than he was about protecting his frazzled and fatigued army. In order to do so, he would have to assert his authority more forcefully vis-à-vis the politicians. For one thing, he began to criticize the congressmen more openly. In one letter, he vented his frustration over Congress's "superficial view of the [war] and circumstances of things in general and their Own Troops in particular." According to Washington, Congress was "not sufficiently acquainted with the state and strength of the army."[5]

When he obtained reports that Congress had ordered up troops without informing him, he wrote, "I heartily wish Congress would inform me of the dispositions they make of the troops. Their not doing it, disconcerts my arrangements and involves me in difficulties."[6] Washington had grown impatient with Congress's military incompetency and did not want them attempting to lead troops behind his back. The American army could no longer function as a many-headed beast; it needed to be united under Washington's decisive command. Congress largely agreed and acknowledged that their commander was better equipped to make the military decisions.

In another letter, Washington blasted congressmen for leaking reports to the public. To Washington, proper public disclosure was imperative, and he ran his army accordingly. He had little patience with blabbing congressmen. He blasted Congress as "impolitic" and behaving "injuriously to the common cause." He called it "still more impolitic . . . for individual members to detail matters to the public without Stamping them with the authority of their body."[7] He was now the master of the war effort, and Congress was hampering it. Washington wanted Congress to "shape up" and he let them know it.

Throwing his weight around, Washington bluntly told Congress, "we can no longer drudge on in the old way."[8] He was frustrated that Congress had granted him the power to fight but he still lacked the resources to do so. He faulted Congress for "ill-timing the adoption of measures," explaining, "by delay in the execution of them, or by unwarranted jealousies, we incur enormous expenses and derive not benefit from them."[9] The young nation's scarce resources were precious and Washington, who had honed his penny-pinching skill as he shrewdly built up Mount Vernon in Virginia, had some ardent opinions on the matter. He urged Congress to assert its political authority in relation to the states so that he might better obtain the means to pay, feed, clothe, and arm his troops. This was a far cry from the servile Washington who had edited his letters to make them sound more deferential early in the war.

Like earlier in the war, Washington's actions reinforced his words. But now, he began standing up to Congress rather than obligingly following its militarily imprudent commands. For example, when some congressmen called for another foolhardy attempt to invade Canada, he objected. "I am always happy to concur in sentiment with Congress," he wrote, "and I view the emancipation of Canada as an Object very interesting to the future prosperity and tranquility of these States; but I am sorry to say, the plan proposed for the purpose does not appear to me to be eligible."[10] Ethan Allen's invasion of Canada and subsequent attempts had been disasters, and Washington did not want to repeat them. While many in Congress likewise saw an invasion of Canada as impractical, other members continued to press the matter. When the issue came up again a month later, Washington repeated his opposition and declined to proceed with the invasion.[11] He was now the master of war tactics, not Congress, since he was far better versed in military strategy and more familiar with the strength of his own forces. Barely keeping his army together, he knew that an offensive against Canada would be a ludicrous military decision.

The commander risked exceeding the limits of his vast military authority by objecting to the invasion on political grounds as well. He reasoned that ousting the British from Quebec would leave the country vulnerable to a French attack down the road.[12] While the Americans were courting the French as allies, Washington still did not trust his old adversaries. Luckily for the American cause, Congress acquiesced to their commander's opposition and abandoned the invasion.

Washington had grown bold. In one episode he may have gone too far. He asserted too much authority, and some politicians began to question their benevolent military dictator.

In an effort to turn more of the patriots' American brothers against them, General Howe offered amnesty to defectors. He proposed that any American who swore allegiance to the Crown would be pardoned. This was a very appealing proposition for many Americans—especially since it appeared that the British were winning. The patriotic exuberance that characterized the beginning of the war had faded. And now many Americans saw Howe's offer as a great opportunity to return to their homes and farms in peace, and to escape punishment for their transgressions against the mother country. If Washington was going to lose anyway, they might as well save themselves.

This was a tremendous predicament for Washington, as Howe's amnesty proposal threatened to spur mass defection from the American cause. Washington wrote with alarm that many Americans were being "Influenced By Inimical Motives, [and] Intimidated By The Threats Of The Enemy."[13] Many were beginning to swear allegiance back to the Crown. Washington already faced Loyalist Americans who were working against him, but now Howe's plot threatened to turn the moderates and even some patriots against him as well—or at least keep them from fighting on his side.

Washington no longer knew whom he could count on to fight for him, and thus he drew the proverbial line in the sand.

Washington declared that "it had become necessary to distinguish between the friends of America and those of Great-Britain." So he ordered an oath of his own. In early 1777, to pressure his countrymen to "stand ready to defend the [nation] against every hostile invasion," Washington presented an ultimatum:

> . . . I do therefore, in behalf of the United States, by virtue of the powers committed to me by Congress, hereby strictly command and require every person having subscribed such declaration, taken such oath, and accepted such protection and certificates from Lord and General Howe, or any person acting under their authority, forthwith to repair to Head-Quarters, or to the quarters of the nearest general officer of the Continental Army or Militia (until farther provision can be made by the civil authority) and there deliver up such protections, certificates, and passports, and take the oath of allegiance to the United States of America.[14]

This was an uncharacteristically draconian order. But if Howe's oath was persuading moderate Americans to abandon the patriot cause, Washington would take drastic measures to reverse that trend. He required this "counter-oath" from his countrymen if they wanted to remain in their homes. If they had pledged their allegiance to Britain and now refused to pledge to the United States, then they'd better run. Washington was "hereby granting full liberty to all such as prefer the interest and protection of Great-Britain to the freedom and happiness of their country, forthwith to withdraw themselves and families within the enemy's lines." Adding a thinly veiled threat, Washington concluded, "And I do hereby declare that all and every person, who may neglect or refuse to comply with this order, within thirty days from the date hereof, will be deemed adherents to the King of Great-Britain, and treated as common enemies of the American States."[15]

Washington's order elicited a firestorm of criticism. It was condemned as undemocratic and possibly a sign that Americans had invested their commander with too much power. While many states adopted comparable measures, some Americans saw it as a power too dangerous to entrust to any military leader, however beloved. It was one thing for Washington to command his own troops or punish the enemy, but it was another when he started to order American civilians around. Many of those civilians declared that their empowered commander had grown insensitive to personal liberties and was morphing from a *military* dictator into an *absolute* one. One congressman believed that Washington had "assumed the Legislative and Executive powers of Government in all the states."[16]

A proud republican who deeply believed in the ideals of his budding country, Washington did not intend to use his broad military powers to trample the civilian leadership's nonmilitary laws. John Adams defended America's commander, stating that "General Washington's proclamation . . . does not interfere with the laws of Civil Government of any State; but considering the Army was prudent and necessary."[17] Washington felt wounded by assertions otherwise, and he never actually enforced the order. However, he never recanted it either.[18] As the master of the military, he was not one to back down.

In stark contrast to his defense of New York City, Washington next informed Congress that he did not intend to protect their capital city at all costs.[19] Political pressure had compelled him to take, and linger in, indefensible positions in New York; he would not repeat that mistake in Philadelphia. After Washington drove back the enemy forces at Trenton and Princeton, Congress had returned from Baltimore in March 1777. But Washington did not make them feel particularly welcome.

Even though Philadelphia was the political heart of the nation and the politicians expected him to defend it with the full might of the Continental Army, Washington declined. He knew he could not risk his fragile army against another major British naval and land assault. His main focus was to defend his army, even if it meant ceding cities to the British war machine. Thus, he needed the flexibility of a quick retreat, and so he sent Nathanael Greene to inform Congress of his new defensive strategy.

Greene reported back to Washington, "I explained to the House your Excellency's Ideas of the next Campaign [and] it appear'd new to them."[20] Put less delicately, Congress was shocked. They had expected their commander to defend their capital to the bitter end.[21]

Many of the remaining patriots fled Philadelphia. John Adams colorfully described the largely abandoned city to his wife: "This City is a dull place, in comparison of what it was. More than half the Inhabitants removed into the country as it was their Wisdom to do—the remainder are chiefly Quakers as dull as Beetles."[22] Whatever his dislike for the current populace, however, Adams and other congressmen had not expected Washington to run from any threat to their seat of government. But Washington had adopted a "Fabian Strategy."[23]

20

Dictator Perpetuo

Washington, the "American Cincinnatus," again borrowed from the wisdom of the Roman Republic. His new defensive strategy was based on that of Quintus Fabius Maximus, the fabled Roman general who successfully wore down the stronger Carthaginian forces during the First Punic War, in the third century B.C. Like the army of Fabius Maximus, Washington's forces were relatively weak, so rather than risk his army in the all-out defense of Philadelphia or any other location, he would wear down the British by engaging them in smaller battles much as Fabius had done. Washington's main goal was to preserve his troops, even if that meant ceding land.

Howe indeed had his sights set on Philadelphia, just as Congress feared. Having failed to break the Americans' will, he was growing less sure of his ability to suppress the rebellion. In December 1776 he had been confident of a speedy end to the war, but by April the next year he concluded, "my hopes of terminating the war this year are vanquished."[1] By retaking much of New Jersey, Washington had thwarted Howe's plan to conquer the states one by one. In doing so, he made it very clear to Howe that the patriotic fervor was surprisingly durable; thus, Howe decided to strike at its heart. He saw the conquest of their political capital and largest city as a way to break the Americans' unsinkable spirit. And so the indecisive Howe finally resolved to attack the American political leadership in Philadelphia.

Howe sailed with his armada of a staggering 228 ships from New York, around Washington's army in New Jersey, and landed near the not-so-bustling capital city. No longer dealing with a subservient commander who obediently followed Congress's commands, John Adams now wondered, "Will W. attack him? I hope so . . . ."[2]

While he knew he could not risk his army in a "winner takes all" battle, Washington did resist before ceding Philadelphia to Howe. "Public and Congressional opinion clamored for its defense," and Washington so obliged.[3] He was a deferential dictator, after all. Plus, to avoid battle completely would be disadvantageous, since it would surely breed discontent among his troops and potential recruits.[4] As he showed repeatedly, Washington was as idealistic as he was practical.

The commander also had a theatrical side, which he displayed by leading his troops on a choreographed public relations parade through Philadelphia. The townspeople arose at seven o'clock one rainy August morning in 1777 to the sounds of fife and drum, and saw droves of American soldiers marching through their streets. Washington rode his horse in grand ceremonial style, followed by thousands of soldiers. In fact, they had been threatened with thirty-nine lashes should they abandon the parade, so they marched obediently before the admiring crowds who leaned out of Philadelphia's windows and waved from the rooftops.[5] Washington warned the soldiers to follow the drumbeat "without dancing along or totally disregarding the music."[6] Despite their "motley assortment of dress and occasional undress," the troops "offered an amazing display."[7] Washington sought to exhibit a powerful, trained army that would intimidate the city's Loyalists and inspire men to join the cause.[8]

Due to troop reorganization as well as the surging "patriotism" that not-so-magically accompanied the warmer weather each year, Washington's force had swelled to approximately 11,000 men. But he was still at a great disadvantage. With much of his ill-equipped force composed of unruly militiamen, Washington faced 13,000 well-fed professional soldiers under Howe's command. Therefore, he resorted to his Fabian hit-and-run campaign, to Congress's dismay.

Washington confronted Howe at Brandywine Creek on September 11, 1777. In a hard-fought battle, Howe and Cornwallis outgeneraled Washington. Suffering a disastrous 1,000 casualties versus Howe's 500, the Americans were forced to retreat. But Washington's focus was to protect his army, not Congress's capital.

Eager for another victory like those at Trenton and Princeton, Washington attacked Howe yet again at Germantown on October 4, 1777. His overly complicated assault did not go well, however. One early historian vividly captured the scene:

> the air grew darker as the smoke of the guns, and the still denser smoke of stubble and hay, which the enemy had set fire to, to increase the confusion, mingled with the fog; all hanging over the battle-field in sulphurous folds, which there was no wind to blow aside. And from it came shouts and huzzas, and shrieks and groans, and reverberations of cannon, and the crackling of musketry; and under it the fierce work still went on, the deadly thrust and clash of bayonet, the deadly struggle hand to hand, eyes glaring mortal hate into eyes they had never seen before, and foot sternly pressed on palpitating limbs and bespattering human blood. Look well to it, King George! think well of it under the gilded canopy of your royal closet![9]

Rather than risk the rest of his men in further attempts at defending Philadelphia, Washington fled with his battered army twenty miles back to Valley Forge for the winter. He had allowed the British to take the capital.

Howe was delighted with his new prize. He, Mrs. Loring, and his troops eagerly set up camp for the winter in the elegant homes that had been abandoned by the fleeing patriots. Just as he did in New York, he would enjoy the city's pleasures with parties and rum. But foremost, he was happy in knowing that he had dealt a psychological blow to the patriots.

Many Americans were indeed gravely disheartened by the loss. Cuttingly, Adams criticized Washington's "injudicious Maneuvre" and denounced "timorous, defensive [action], which has involved us in so many Disasters."[10] But Washington was unrepentant. He reasoned that "while we have an Army in the field," Britain's conquest of the cities "will avail them little. It involves us in difficulty, but does not, by any means, insure them conquest. They will know, that it is our Arms, not defenceless Towns, they have to Subdue, before they can arrive at the haven of their Wishes."[11]

While Congress realized that empowering the American commander was necessary to wage war effectively, many remained nervous. Some of the politicians believed that Washington's "influence was already too great; that even his virtues afforded motives for alarm; that the enthusiasm of the army, joined to the kind of dictatorship already confided to him, put Congress and the United States at his mercy."[12]

Some feared that Washington would act less like Cincinnatus than like Julius Caesar, who became *dictator perpetuo*, or "dictator in perpetuity," after gaining control of Rome in the first century B.C. Even Adams, who had nominated Washington for the post and defended him, feared that the "Idolatry and Adulation" for Washington might grow "so excessive as to endanger our liberties" and pave the way for monarchy. In fact, Adams went as far as to applaud Washington's dearth of great victories because it meant the nation could "allow a certain citizen to be wise, virtuous and good without thinking him a deity or a savior."[13]

Regardless of their fear, Congress had little choice—a weak American commander would spell defeat. Washington needed to be powerful to fight the return of the British monarchy and so Congress reaffirmed his authority again and again. The states followed suit.

The New York legislature wrote to Congress concerning the fact that they had "invested a military officer with dictatorial powers."[14] Such a declaration would have stirred outrage at the start of the war, but now the Americans were more comfortable with it. New York was acknowledging Washington's authority rather than criticizing it, and added, "no objection has, that we know of, been made by any State to [this] measure. Hence we venture to conclude, that other States are in sentiment with this."[15] Thus far, Washington had demonstrated that the experimental republican commander could wield expansive military power without undermining civilian rule. And he would continue to do so.

Although he had certainly become more forceful, Washington remained largely respectful of Congress and the other civil authorities. The American commander was a powerful one, but still a republican one. Although he had extensive powers, he need not always use them.

When the army's chief surgeon recommended establishing military hospitals, Washington responded, "altho' the Congress have vested me with full powers . . . and I dare say would ratify whatever appointments and Salaries I should fix; yet I do not think myself at liberty to establish Hospitals, upon such extensive plans and at so great an expense, without their concurrence."[16] Washington was being careful not to extend his powers further into matters that were arguably tangential to warfare. He believed that the politicians retained authority over the nation's purse and was therefore deferential when it came to pecuniary concerns.

Although he had previously promised the soldiers pay raises and had ordered cannon, he generally did not feel that he should spend the states' and Congress's money without their approval. "Money matters are not within the Line of my duty," he wrote, even when they were "intimately connected with all Military Operations."[17] Intent on protecting the republic, this dictator purposefully confined his powers to the military.

Even regarding issues explicitly delegated to him, Washington still acted respectfully. One such issue was AWOL soldiers. Suffering defeat after defeat, Washington faced mass desertion as his exhausted, starving troops grew eager to return to their homes. When a large number of soldiers fled to eastern Pennsylvania, he refused to impose martial law and directly punish them. Congress had granted him power to try deserters, but he did not want to get into the business of hunting down Americans in their own towns.[18] Instead, he left the matter to the civil authorities, whether those authorities were fully functioning or not.

He deferred to local government even if it was "extremely weak" and chaotic, saying, "I am not fully satisfied of the legality of trying an inhabitant of any State by Military Law, when the Civil authority of that State has made provision for the punishment of persons taking Arms with the Enemy."[19] As will be addressed further in Parts IV and V, Washington's powers over enemies and military tactics were plenary, but he did not see the American commander in chief—even the empowered one that developed over the course of the war—as having authority over American citizens.

Washington also continued to convey his demands with respect for the civil authorities. For example, when he was empowered to call forth militiamen directly from the states, he did so delicately. Demanding soldiers from the states was a worrisome power, and at the beginning of the war it would likely have been perceived as an appalling encroachment on state sovereignty. Now, the states had become more obliging, but Washington was nevertheless sensitive to their concerns. "I would not wish to distress the States, but when there is an absolute necessity," he wrote almost apologetically; "but from the present poor prospect of an early reinforcement to the Continental Army, I fear I shall be obliged to make the demand. If I do, I am confident that your State, notwithstanding their former exertions will contribute their quota."[20]

After Washington's initial six-month "dictator" term expired, Congress reaffirmed his extensive powers repeatedly throughout the war.[21] For example, when Congress contemplated perilous battles in the southern and mid-Atlantic states, they made it clear that they expected their commander to wield great authority and trusted him to do what was best to defend the nation. Specifically, Congress resolved that Washington "consider himself at liberty so to direct the military operations of these states as shall appear to him most expedient."[22] This was indeed a recurring theme.

Confident in their decision to make the American commander into a powerful one, Congress granted Washington additional powers as the war progressed. For example, while Washington had already taken the lead in dealing with captured enemy combatants, Congress explicitly gave him the power to negotiate the exchange of prisoners. Congress also removed a restriction that confined his fighting to the United States theater.[23] Washington was finally the master of his troops in conducting an international war.

Whether fighting in the United States or in a foreign nation, the commander in chief had the ultimate say over war tactics. The president of Congress explained to Washington:

> Congress confide fully in your Excellency's Prudence and Abilities; and I am directed to signify to you their wish, that neither an undue Degree of Delicacy or Diffidence may lead you to place too little Reliance on your own Judgment, or pursuade you to make any further Communications of your Designs than necessity or high Expedience may dictate.[24]

And America's empowered commander in chief used that judgment to make the nation proud.

⚜

The founding generation's understanding of "commander in chief" developed gradually. At the outset of the war, in addition to appointing officers, Congress retained the "sole and exclusive right and power" to direct military operations.[25] They feared that the army would crush the fragile new republic, so they experimented with a weak commander in chief who was essentially a congressional puppet. But their experiment failed. Congress's attempts to micromanage Washington were a disaster. The limited commander they had envisioned was simply incapable of defending the country. They learned from their mistakes.

The restrictions on Washington's control over military tactics evaporated as the war progressed and Washington proved that a strong commander could still be a republican one. Congress acquiesced to his exercise of greater power and formally granted him more military authority. The shift away from congressional control was made anxiously. But if the American war effort was to overcome its schizophrenia, it needed one master. And that master was Washington.

From this tug of war over military power emerged a strong American commander with broad discretion over military decisions. Congress and the states controlled the military's purse strings,[26] oversaw all civil matters, and expected to be consulted and informed by their commander whenever feasible. For his part, the American commander possessed authority over military tactics and enemy treatment.[27] And Washington used this authority to defend his nation fiercely—and virtuously.

Washington lived up to the challenge of being America's first republican commander. He promised, "whatever Military Powers shall be intrusted to me, shall ever be exerted first to establish and then protect the Civil."[28] And he lived true to his word, exercising his military powers with great restraint and respect for the civil authorities. "While acting in my Military capacity," he wrote, "I am sensible of the impropriety of stepping into the line of civil Polity."[29] As will be discussed in greater detail in Parts IV and V, Washington used his expansive mandate to guard the rights of his people rather than trample them. The nation's worries about a powerful commander subsided.

The Framers revisited the issue of commander-in-chief authority after the war. When drafting the Constitution, they drew upon their vivid memories of the Revolution, recalling, "Such was the situation of our affairs then, that the power of dictator was given to the commander-in-chief, to save us from destruction. This shows the situation of the country to have been such as to make it ready to embrace an actual dictator."[30] And that dictator had saved the United States from destruction. The founding generation had learned the hard way that the American commander in chief needed to be a powerful one if he was to defend his nation, and that "war powers needed to be fixed to guarantee effective common defense."[31]

So when they designated the president as "Commander in Chief of the Army and the Navy of the United States" in 1787, it was clear to the American people what this meant: the role that General Washington had forged amidst battle. The wartime American commander was to be a new kind of deferential republican dictator—he had broad authority to lead the military in defending the nation, while Congress and the states held authority over the American people.

"The task of facing and fighting the enemy was enough for the ablest of men," observed one early biographer, "but Washington was obliged also to combat and overcome the inertness and dullness born of ignorance, and to teach Congress how to govern a nation at war."[32] He defined the role of the American commander in chief not only for Congress but also for posterity.

Back on Wall Street in New York City, Washington is honored for his bravery in forging the nation. The grand statue in front of Federal Hall reminds New Yorkers and throngs of passing tourists that the nation's Constitution and prosperity can be attributed in great part to his heroism as the first American commander in chief. Ironically, had he been granted his dictatorial powers initially, the great man depicted by the statue may have used them to torch all of Manhattan.

IV

TRIBUNALS & TRIBULATIONS

"Resolved, That General Washington shall be, and he is hereby vested with full, ample, and complete powers to . . . arrest and confine persons . . . who are disaffected to the American cause."

—RESOLUTION OF THE CONTINENTAL CONGRESS, DECEMBER 27, 1776

Many have heard of Washington's bout with America's most famous traitor, Benedict Arnold. Less known, however, are the trials and tribulations of Arnold's British co-conspirator, Major John André. The tragic tale unfolded on a scenic bend of a slow-moving river in upstate New York. There, amidst the forest-covered hills that plunge into the Hudson, today sits a famous American landmark: the United States Military Academy at West Point.

The preeminent source of commissioning officers for the army of the world's lone superpower, this institution feeds a thousand new cadets each year into leadership posts in the United States Army. Rigorously trained in academics, military leadership, combat, and physical fitness, these young men and women are well prepared to defend their country from any threat. But before these patriotic souls commence their service to their country, they enjoy four years on the beautiful, hallowed grounds of the historic Military Academy. Nestled within the serenity of the rolling hills that dominate the region, the campus brims with a youthful vitality. Here, on tree-lined paths that cross the manicured lawns, the nation's future military elite proceed to their intense academic and physical exercises. Some, dressed in crisp uniforms, chat casually as they stroll while others in jogging suits run together in groups. Whether they are heading to weapons training or applied quantum physics, they go proudly. The objective of the Military Academy is to foster excellence. Boasting two American presidents, seventy-four Medal of Honor recipients, seventy Rhodes Scholars, and eighteen astronauts as alumni, the institution has clearly succeeded.[1]

Unsurprisingly, this time-honored symbol of American military prowess pays homage to George Washington as the country's father and first commander in chief. In fact, Washington Hall is one of the more popular places on the campus. Just as the general breathed life into his nation, Washington Hall energizes the cadets: it houses their mess hall. Before the entrance stands the striking, larger-than-life effigy of the general. While the bronze is weathered blue-green with age, the statue still clearly depicts a strong military leader on horseback. With his hat in his hand and a sword by his side, the gallant hero towers over all who walk by. His right hand stretches outward as if reaching towards the future that he would shape so dramatically. With this tribute to General Washington at its heart, the handsome Collegiate Gothic campus exudes a stately permanence.

West Point today is the epitome of safety and security. It was not always this way. Once called "Fort Arnold," this post was nearly betrayed to the British—a betrayal that would have doomed the American cause. Washington retaliated against the treachery with deadly military justice, the ramifications of which can still be felt today.

The chapters in this part scrutinize the United States' Revolutionary War precedents for military tribunals. In his fierce defense of the nation, Washington forged the American way of meting out justice.

21

Gentleman Johnny vs. Granny Gates

When the military post was hastily constructed at West Point, its success was so vital to the revolutionary cause that it became known as "the key to the American Continent."[1] After the British invaded New York City, Washington feared they were going to seize the opportunity to sever New England from her sister states. The rebellious New England states not only constituted the heart of the young nation's patriotic fervor, but also were a vital source of rations, supplies, weapons, and soldiers for Washington's army. Barely holding the battered Continental Army together, Washington desperately needed all of these. It was imperative that he retain access to the region. General Howe had other designs.

After conquering New York City, Howe placed the "utmost importance" on securing "free communication between Canada and New York, by means of the Lake Champlain and Hudson's River, . . . in order to facilitate the operations of the British arms in the mediate plan of subjugating the Colonies."[2] If the British were to gain control over the Hudson, it would enable them to utilize their naval assets to funnel massive quantities of troops and weapons through Montreal and down into New York City, leaving Washington with little means to attack. In the process, Howe would cut the heart out of the rebellion by isolating New England.

Consequently, Americans were equally interested in sparsely populated upstate New York "from every sound principle of policy," in order to counteract the British actions and "to preserve the communication between eastern and southern states, for the conveyance of supplies of provisions, and for the marching and counter-marching of troops . . . ."[3]

Still without a navy to match Britain's, the Americans had little choice but to rely on a land-based defense. Congress determined that "a fort should be erected . . . to check any naval force"[4] and resolved that "a post be . . . taken in the Highlands on each side of Hudson's River and batteries erected in such a manner as will most effectually prevent any vessels passing that may be sent to harass the inhabitants on the borders of said river . . . ."[5]

Prior to deciding on the West Point location, the patriots first attempted to build a fort downriver. About fifty miles outside of New York City, they threw together a somewhat crude defense: They created a chain of floating logs across the river to obstruct ships attempting to pass, and guarded their barrier with six cannons housed in an ill-conceived fort. Built on a low-lying position, Fort Montgomery was vulnerable to Britain's tall gunships and lacked adequate munitions to repel an intense assault.

Determined to destroy this and all obstacles to British domination of the region, Sir Henry Clinton, a British Army lieutenant general serving under Howe, led a raiding party from his New York City stronghold up the Hudson riverbank. The son of the former colonial governor of New York, Clinton knew these parts and was hell-bent on returning them to British rule. Towards this end, his immediate objective was to crush the rebel installations and clear the way for British support from Canada.

Of noble blood, Clinton had quickly risen through the ranks of the British Army by purchasing higher commissions and capitalizing on familial connections. He possessed a long nose, softly cleft chin, and gentle eyes. His prominent arching eyebrows defined the lower boundary of a high forehead that added to his aristocratic air. Clinton was described by his staff as "[v]ain, open to flattery; and from a great aversion to all business not military, too often misled by aides and favourites." He was particularly noted for being hot-tempered, jealous, and wary of perceived slights.[6] A self-described "shy bitch," he tended to be excessively cautious and inordinately touchy.[7] Upon obtaining command of New York City from Howe after the British commander and Mrs. Loring relocated to Philadelphia, this insecure underling was eager to prove his military prowess to his scornful British superiors. He resented being Howe's subordinate and embraced the chance to display his superiority over his master.

Clinton's raiding party took a treacherously steep, winding path over a mountain in order to catch the Americans at Fort Montgomery by surprise on October 6, 1777. As night closed in, they pounced on the undermanned fort, while the cannon of their fearsome naval support lit up the darkening sky. "[T]he Gallies with their Oars approaching, firing, and even striking the Fort; the Men of War that Moment appearing, crouding all Sail to support [Clinton's troops]; the extreme Ardor of the Troops" all added up to a lethal blow that slaughtered the American forces.[8] The defending patriots, outnumbered three to one, fought valiantly until they were driven out at the points of enemy bayonets. By the time darkness had fallen, more than half of the patriot fighters were killed, wounded, or captured.

Once the Americans were crushed, the British force advanced up the Hudson, "carrying fire and devastation before them." The town of Kingston, seat of the rebel government, "beautifully situated near the West bank of the Hudson river," was "laid to ashes."[9] Clinton's men destroyed approximately four hundred structures—homes, barns, and mills.[10] This British victory proved to be a pyrrhic one, however. The American forces were trounced, but Clinton's campaign was ineffective in helping the British hold the Hudson Valley. His destructive little campaign was intended to divert American ire from a larger British force that was besieged to the north; but the patriots refused to take the bait. If anything, Clinton's brutality hastened the British defeat in the region: the local populace was enraged.

Britain's dominion over the Hudson Valley was cut short, ironically, by the military genius of none other than the duplicitous Benedict Arnold. Upriver from Clinton's troops, the American Northern Army, led by Horatio Gates and his brilliant officer, Arnold, confronted a British force that was marching south from Canada.

This force of 7,000 well-trained soldiers was a fearsome one, led by "Gentleman Johnny" Burgoyne. A dashing man with a strong jaw and a prominent widow's peak, Burgoyne was known for his stylish clothes and lavish spending. He was rumored to be a heavy gambler, and he certainly gambled with his force: he underestimated the journey to New York City. With cooks, smiths, officers' wives, servants, and a herd of cattle in tow, Burgoyne's army resembled a "lumbering baggage train" more than a nimble fighting force.[11] And that train became dangerously bogged down in the dense forests above Albany, New York.[12]

As he neared his objective of connecting with the British forces in New York City—and thereby securing the entire Hudson—Burgoyne's unwieldy regiment faced difficulties in transporting equipment and artillery through upstate's primitive dirt pathways. With its supply lines stretched in these backwoods, the British force was also short on food. To make matters even worse, their mere presence roused the local patriot militiamen in substantial numbers. The Americans were enraged by over reports that Britain's Native American allies had shot, scalped, and stripped an American teenage girl.[13]

Despite the growing peril, the brash Burgoyne was eager to obtain a quick victory about which he might boast. "The Messengers of Justice and of Wrath await them in the Field," he exclaimed, "and Devastation, Famine, and every concomitant Horror that a reluctant but indispensible Prosecution of Military Duty must occasion, will bar the way to their return."[14] Overconfident as ever, Burgoyne "spent half the nights in singing and drinking, and amusing himself with the wife of a commissary, who was his mistress, and who, as well as he, loves champaign."[15] But the strength of his bravado exceeded that of his military position. Gentleman Johnny was perilously isolated from supplies and reinforcements—Howe was distracted fighting Washington in Pennsylvania and Clinton was reluctant to divert troops from defending New York City. The floundering force was on its own.

The Americans took full advantage and pounced. The patriot force swelling to 14,000 as incensed farmers flocked to the cause, the Americans clawed at Burgoyne's army. But when the fog lifted one late summer morning in 1777, the tricky Burgoyne struck back. His goal was to outsmart Washington's third-in-command, "Granny Gates."

Horatio Gates was an ambitious forty-nine-year-old English immigrant. He was a well-mannered, courteous man who exhibited no great bravery.[16] In fact, his subordinates called him "Granny Gates" due to his avoidance of direct attacks as well as his relatively advanced age and sagging spectacles. His large, hooked nose and drooping, sleepy eyes made for a homely man who lacked looks as well as any particular military aptitude. His father a minor government official and his mother a housekeeper, Gates was determined to surpass the modest circumstances into which he was born. And he saw the military as a means of doing so.

Gates entered the British Army as a teenager and garnered quite respectable, albeit not particularly illustrious, military experience over the next two and a half decades. He fought alongside Washington in the Seven Years' War, so his old friend as commander in chief urged Congress to grant Gates a high position in the new American army. Gates was not content with his commission, however. He wanted more, and he possessed the means to get it. He had many prattling friends in Congress as well as a knack for political intrigue.[17]

Gates first set his sights on the job of his immediate superior, General Philip Schuyler. Washington's third-in-command when the war began in 1775, Schuyler was a generous and courteous gentleman who treated Gates with the utmost respect. With a kind face, narrow-set dark eyes, and a bulbous nose, he resembled the "puppy-dog" that he was in temperament. Schuyler once stumbled upon a wounded enemy soldier who had just attacked his party. Moved by the soldier's cries, he carried him to a doctor, thereby saving his life.[18] But Gates and his friends were more than willing to kick this puppy.

Like a high school election campaign, the congressional cliques' rumor mills began to churn. The New England faction was particularly vocal. Typical of the regional clashes between the states, New Englanders generally disdained New Yorkers as the two regions competed for power and influence. As a legislator, Schuyler had defended New York's claims to Vermont lands against those of the bombastic Ethan Allen and his New England brethren. "For this crime the men of New England were never able to forgive him, and he was pursued with vindictive hatred until his career as general was ruined."[19] Gates's New England allies in Congress spread rumors of Schuyler's military mismanagement and even indirectly accused him of treason.[20] While Gates did not possess the brashness to lead this slander coup, "his nature was thoroughly weak and petty, and he never shrank from falsehood when it seemed to suit his purpose."[21]

The rumors worked. The majority in Congress slowly turned against Schuyler. Just as the New Englanders in Congress had planned, Gates took Schuyler's spot as Washington's third-in-command. Now he finally had a chance for greatness as he confronted Burgoyne in the woods of upstate New York.

Referring to Gates as the "old midwife," Burgoyne struck back at the American forces.[22] The inert Gates was nearly outflanked, but Arnold foresaw their opponent's strategy and argued vehemently for dispatching troops to counter the maneuver. Gates, a man often "influenced by spite," disliked his brash underling's know-it-all demeanor.[23] He did not like being second-guessed or having his newly won authority questioned. But he held his rage in check and finally came to agree with Arnold.

For his part, Arnold was "maddened" by Gates's incompetency and "seemed inspired with the fury of a demon." In a bold frontal attack that sent the British troops recoiling, he "proved his courage and ability."[24] In the fierce battle, the ill-trained, ragtag American troops swarmed against the British regiment. Both sides suffered disastrous casualties in the intense fighting, but by the time the Americans retreated, they had inflicted far more casualties than they sustained. One American officer wrote, "I trust we have convinced the British butchers that the 'cowardly' Yankees can, and when there is a call for it, will fight."[25]

Mere weeks later, a second battle erupted between Gentleman Johnny and Granny Gates. The American forces now outnumbered the British 11,000 to 5,000.[26] Still confident he could win, Burgoyne struck the Americans on the afternoon of October 7, 1777. After yet another quarrel over tactics, Gates angrily relieved Arnold of his field command and told him, "I have nothing for you to do; you have no business here."[27] Not one to be dismissed, Arnold nevertheless charged into the battle. He bravely led his men, quite literally risking life and limb—he was shot in the leg during the firefight and nearly crushed by his horse.[28] When the gunpowder and cannon smoke dissipated, the Americans emerged triumphant. After a horrific day of fighting, dusk settled upon the battered men.

The British sat awake that early autumn night, listening to the groans of their comrades dying in the battlefield that separated the two opposing camps. However well trained they were, Burgoyne's ranks were thinning while the American side was continually refueled with fresh militiamen from around the countryside. His supplies of food and munitions dwindling along with his hopes, Burgoyne frantically attempted to formulate a plan of escape.

Meanwhile, Howe was so fixated on Philadelphia that he never ordered Clinton to provide reinforcements from New York. While Burgoyne assumed that Clinton was bound by orders to join him "at all risks," Clinton never received such a command.[29] Leaving much to Clinton's discretion, Howe had merely said, "if you can make any diversion in favor of General Burgoyne's [army], I need not point out the utility of such a measure."[30] And Clinton did not exactly jump to Burgoyne's rescue of his own accord.

Instead, ever cautious, Clinton feared that Washington would launch a renewed attack on New York City and decided to retain the bulk of his forces there. Like Howe before him, he was thoroughly enjoying the New York high life, as evidenced by his tremendously high liquor bill. Not only did he have four houses, but he also took a liking to an officer's wife, Mrs. Mary Baddeley.[31] He had little desire to venture out of the city.

When Clinton received Burgoyne's plea that "an attack on Fort Montgomery must be of great use," he dispatched just that small force for its quick assault on the fort and rampage up the Hudson.[32] Not fully grasping his comrade's desperation, Clinton failed to do more, writing merely, "I hope this little success of ours may facilitate your operations . . . . I heartily wish you success."[33]

Clinton's diversionary effort was too little, too late. Refusing to divert troops south towards Clinton, the Americans proved unrelenting in their pressure on Burgoyne.

After days of hesitation, Burgoyne was surrounded by the Americans, who "swarmed around the little adverse army like birds of prey."[34] Retreat became impossible. As a chilly rain began to fall, he knew his beleaguered force was doomed. Burgoyne surrendered on October 17, 1777, at what came to be called the "Battle of Saratoga." His ego finally checked, he would return to Britain in disgrace. The Americans took thousands of prisoners in a victory that stunned the world.

This was not just a military victory, but also a hugely symbolic one, since it demonstrated the Americans' ability to defeat the British in large-scale European-style warfare. If the sneak attacks at Trenton and Princeton had been the psychological turning point in the war, Saratoga was the political one. It prompted the French, eager to prey on their old rival's weakness, to enter the war on the United States' side. Washington was overjoyed. Although suspicious of the French, he adhered to the ancient Chinese proverb "the enemy of my enemy is my friend," since he badly needed the help of this "friend." He looked forward to France's money, ammunition, clothing, and troops. Perhaps most of all, he wanted the aid of her powerful navy. His efforts had repeatedly been hobbled by his lack of a naval force, and France was his only hope to counter Britain's maritime supremacy. When France then prompted Spain to declare war on Britain also in an attempt to settle old scores, Washington exclaimed that these new allies brought "universal joy" to the patriots.

This joy was not so universal, however. Little did Washington know, the great victory at Saratoga would lead to treachery that nearly ended the Revolution. Ironically, Arnold's great triumph also led to his betrayal of the American cause.

22

A Traitor Lurks

Benedict Arnold was born into a wealthy and socially prominent Connecticut family. After two of his sisters died during a yellow fever epidemic that swept New England during his childhood, Benedict's grieving father began paying more attention to rum than the family finances. He eventually squandered the family fortune and was thrown into a debtors' prison, thereby forcing his family out of the Arnold ancestral home in a humiliating public spectacle. These hardships instilled in Benedict a tremendous drive for both financial success and public recognition. As a headstrong, ambitious teenager, he sought to prove his worth through military service and enlisted in the provincial militia to fight in the Seven Years' War in 1757. Although he served for very short stints and saw no combat before returning to his family, his service in the war instilled in him a taste for battle and a hatred for the French.[1]

Back home in Connecticut, he grew into a courageous man, though haughty and vain. Reaching five foot nine, he was of average height for the era but powerfully built. He was stern-featured, with a sharp chin, high cheekbones, a prominent nose, and intense blue eyes that quickly transformed from cordial to cold when his temper flared. As quarrelsome as he was bold, Arnold had a knack for making enemies. He once attempted to kill an English sea captain in a duel over a perceived slight, and he fired a pistol at a Frenchman he caught alone with his only surviving sister.

When he was not busy fighting, he worked furiously to rebuild the family's estate. With the funds he could scrape together, he founded a small trading company in New Haven, Connecticut. He married the sheriff's daughter and benefitted financially from her family's investments in his business. Protected from creditors by his father-in-law, Arnold's trading house thrived. Enterprising, he eventually became one of the most successful merchants in New England, trading wares all along the eastern seaboard. It was in this role as a prosperous merchant that Arnold became disenchanted with British rule.

Angered by the Crown's rising taxes in the lead-up to the Revolution, Arnold turned to smuggling to avoid the new duties. He came to see the Crown's actions as a threat to his enterprise and to Americans' personal liberty. As usual, Arnold was eager to fight. Thus, upon hearing of the outbreak of war, he swiftly organized a small group of New Haven militiamen to join the fight, declaring that Britain's actions had rendered him "obliged to have recourse to arms in defense of our lives and liberties."[2]

Despite his patriotic fervor, however, Arnold did not fit in well with his revolutionary compatriots. To many Americans, Arnold's mannerisms, powdered wig, and fashionable dress made him seem more a Brit than a patriot. No matter how many times he proved himself in the early battles of the war, he was disliked on a personal level by the Revolution's political and military leaders. This fact crystallized for Arnold following his great victory at Saratoga.

"Granny Gates," ever eager for more power after ousting Schuyler, claimed credit for the Americans' triumph at the Battle of Saratoga, even though it was due in large part to Arnold's tactics and bravery. Adding injury to insult, he even accused Arnold of insubordination. This infuriated the prideful man. The serious leg wound he suffered during the battle was far less vexing to him than the fact that Gates took credit for routing the British. When asked about his injuries, Arnold—

dejected from all the ill-treatment—whispered in a wavering voice that he had been shot in the leg and added, "I wish it had been my heart."[3]

After Arnold's victory at Saratoga, General Howe's days enjoying the Philadelphia highlife ended abruptly. He resigned as commander of the British forces in 1778 so that he might return to Britain to defend his honor. He was anxious to explain his failure to end the American uprising before his vocal detractors in the British Parliament, and to make them understand the difficulty of subduing such a large nation's rebellious populace. He was unsuccessful. Fiercely condemned for his indecisive leadership, he lost the seat in Parliament that he had held for two decades. He had lost his command along with Mrs. Loring. And to add insult, his smug underling benefitted from Howe's fall from grace.

Sir Henry Clinton, much to his delight, was selected as the new British commander in chief. He had arrived with Howe and Burgoyne in 1775, and, as the last man standing, he held seniority. Taking a less conciliatory approach to the rebels than his predecessor, Clinton was eager to show that his leadership could crush the American rebellion.

During the transition of command in the spring of 1778, London ordered Clinton to abandon Philadelphia. With the French navy looming, the British feared that the city was under threat, and they chose to employ their overextended resources elsewhere. Clinton sent some of the troops to the Caribbean to protect British interests there and ordered the others to bolster his New York City stronghold. With a supply train twelve miles long, 10,000 redcoats set out across New Jersey back towards the island.[4] Believing them to be more vulnerable as they traveled, Washington seized this opportunity to keep the British off-guard, and in the process, he settled some old political scores.

When the British withdrew from Philadelphia, Washington received intelligence that the redcoats were on the move across New Jersey. He convened a war council to seek advice on how best to disrupt Clinton's plans. Meanwhile, the ever-insubordinate Charles Lee had returned to the scene.

Washington had negotiated Lee's release in a prisoner exchange following his humiliating capture at Widow White's, but Lee was far from appreciative. Greeting Lee "as if he has been his brother," Washington brought him back to his headquarters, held a dinner in his honor, and provided him with Martha's sitting room to sleep. The next morning, however, Lee missed breakfast and, when he finally awoke, he appeared "as dirty as if he had been in the street all night." It turned out he had snuck a "miserable dirty hussy" into his room that night.[5] Martha was not pleased.

Resuming his old antics, Lee was ever ready to criticize Washington. At the war council, he lambasted Washington's plan of attack as "criminal" and convinced the council to reject it.[6] But Washington, now effectively a military dictator, ignored them. He prepared to pounce on Clinton's rearguard at Monmouth, New Jersey.

Washington had used the winter of 1777–1778 to drill his unruly troops into a lethal fighting force. Much of the credit for this transformation falls to Friedrich Wilhelm August Heinrich Ferdinand von Steuben. A veteran of the Prussian army, he claimed the title of Baron, although it was a sham based on a falsified lineage invented by his father. Due to "alleged homosexuality and accusations of his having taken improper liberties with young boys" in 1776, Steuben had resigned his post in Europe and sought work far away.[7] Agreeing to aid the American army gratis, he was soon on a ship sailing across the Atlantic.

Regardless of his questionable background, Baron von Steuben was welcomed by the Americans with open arms. What was most important to Washington was that Steuben was schooled in the cutting-edge fighting tactics of Frederick the Great, whose machine-like style Washington aspired to emulate.[8] With his beady eyes and drooping jowls, Steuben looked like a bulldog as he barked orders in his English-French-German mix. Throughout the winter, he mercilessly drilled the troops in the ways of European warfare. A gruff and short-tempered man, he unwittingly amused the American soldiers when he would exhaust his vocabulary and demand of his aide, "Come and swear for me in English; these fellows will not do what I bid them!"[9] The Americans respected his efforts and tenacity—Washington included. The troops learned to march more efficiently, fire their guns more accurately, and use their bayonets more lethally. So when the warm weather arrived, Washington was eager to put his newly trained force to the test.

On the scorching hot morning of June 28, 1778, Washington sent Lee to lead the initial assault on the British force at Monmouth. It was a natural assignment for Lee as second-in-command, but Washington kept a close eye on his perpetual detractor since he was dubious of Lee's loyalties after his yearlong captivity. The British had treated him a little too well, showering him with wine and even allowing him to dine with officers, thus fueling suspicion that Lee had leaked intelligence to them. Washington could not count on him to fight.

With temperatures climbing to over 100°F before the sun even reached its zenith, the well-clothed British were finally at a disadvantage—the Americans' rags breathed far better than the redcoats' red-hot wool uniforms. One British soldier wrote,

> We proceed for miles on a road composed of nothing but sand which scorched through our shoes with intolerable heat. The sun beating on our head with a force scarcely to be conceived in Europe and not a drop of water to assuage parching thirst. A number of soldiers were unable to support the fatigue and died on the spot.[10]

Washington was undeterred by the blazing heat and ordered Lee to strike.

Lee, however, still opposed the action and had developed no real battle plan. His troops were in disarray as they approached the British columns on the scorched fields, and they soon began to retreat. Lee followed.

While Washington was a rather sensitive man who was usually quite unforgiving of perceived slights, he had remained surprisingly tolerant of Lee's insubordination. But this time, Lee had gone too far. As Washington rode along to buoy the troops, he came upon a lone fifer. Perplexed, he asked the young man where he was going. The fifer answered that he had been ordered to retreat. As he had been in New York, Washington was "exceedingly surprised" and "exasperated" by this unauthorized withdrawal. He followed the trickle of retreating soldiers back towards Lee.[11] Upon finding him, Washington lost his composure. Quivering with rage, he purportedly called Lee a "damned poltroon" to his face and swore at him "till the leaves shook on the trees."[12]

Putting himself directly into the line of fire yet again, Washington took over command and rallied his troops. With the British artillery "rending up the earth all around him," Washington courageously led another bold attack.[13] The redcoats tried again and again to pick off the American commander, but he proved as indestructible as he seemed to fancy himself—the British missed and the patriots charged.

As the 20,000 soldiers shot and bayoneted one another throughout the blazing afternoon, more men died on both sides from heatstroke than gunfire.[14] In fact, the British reported, "some preferred the shade of the trees in the direct range of shot to the more horrid tortures of thirst."[15] The Americans' aim had improved, however, and one such thirsty gentleman "had his arm shattered to pieces."[16] Clocking in at over five hours of continuous fighting, it was the longest battle in the war.

By sunset, Washington's forces had held their ground. The Battle of Monmouth was technically a draw, but the British suffered higher casualties and withdrew that night towards New York. For the first time in years, Washington was left in possession of the battlefield. He showed the world that his troops had finally gained the skill necessary to stand up to the British, and he further solidified his standing as the unquestionable leader of the American army.

On the other side, Clinton's embarrassment over Monmouth made him ever more eager to punish the Americans. And he would soon have that opportunity presented to him by Arnold. Washington never suspected it, for he was too busy dealing with his other subversive officer, Lee.

Following his shameful retreat, Lee tried to deflect blame. But Washington had had enough. He ordered that Lee be tried before a panel of military judges for his "disgraceful" conduct.[17] The gypsy trial moved along with the Continental Army during New Jersey's hot summer of 1778. After six weeks of often-heated proceedings, the indignant Lee was finally convicted of disobedience of orders, misbehavior before the enemy, and disrespect to the commander in chief.[18] As punishment, he was suspended from command for a year, which effectively ended his military career. Livid, Lee "publicly abused General Washington in the grossest terms," running his mouth off to anyone who would listen.[19] Word quickly traveled back to camp. When he learned of the scurrilous attacks on his beloved leader, Washington's aide John Laurens challenged Lee to a duel.

A relic of the Middle Ages, dueling originally developed as "judicial combat," a means of letting God determine who is in the right by allowing him to win. It was still commonly used to settle serious disputes in the eighteenth century. When one man's honor was grievously offended by another, he might challenge him to a duel. The man so challenged could apologize, thus ending the disagreement, or he could fight. Simply attempting to avoid the fight was seen as cowardly, and word would likely spread throughout the community.

The combatants, typically armed with large-caliber, smoothbore flintlock pistols, stood at a certain distance from one another and fired on cue. Taking more than three seconds to aim their pistols was viewed as dishonorable, so they merely raised their guns and fired rather blindly. Along with the pistols' inherent inaccuracy, this ensured that death for either party was quite unlikely.[20]

Laurens was a young southern gentleman with big eyes and a round nose. The son of a wealthy merchant and landowner, Laurens had quickly made a name for himself as an abolitionist and an ardent patriot who loyally served Washington. The reckless twenty-four-year-old set out with Washington's most trusted aid, Alexander Hamilton, to avenge his general's honor. Although Washington condemned the practice of dueling, it was improbable that these two men would have done this without at least tacit approval.[21] Laurens hit Lee in the side, thereby achieving his objective.

Lee retired home with his pack of dogs and died in a tavern just a few years later, in 1782. In his will, composed mere days before his passing, Lee wrote, "I desire, most earnestly, that I may not be buried in any church or church-yard, or within a mile of any Presbyterian or Anabaptist meeting-house, for, since I have resided in this country, I have kept so much bad company when living, that I do not choose to continue it when dead." His wishes ignored, he was buried with military honors in the churchyard of Christ Church in Philadelphia.[22] Washington paid his respects.

Although his old rival was no longer a threat, Washington faced a far more dangerous and unexpected one. His trusted officer Arnold was beginning to scheme.

When Philadelphia was liberated that hot June of 1778, Arnold became the military supervisor of the capital's reconstruction. During Howe's occupation, the British had destroyed much of the city, looting buildings and burning homes as firewood. The devastation and the inhabitants' suffering had been great, and Washington therefore turned to Arnold to ameliorate their plight. On Washington's suggestion, Arnold was appointed military governor of Philadelphia to reestablish order and rebuild. Still hobbling around on crutches, he used the time to heal from his battle wounds.

Arnold's wife had died three and a half years earlier, and a local socialite caught his eye. Margaret "Peggy" Shippen, age eighteen, was the beautiful youngest daughter of a prominent Philadelphia family. Descended from the founder of the College of New Jersey (Princeton) and other politically powerful men, she had a great pedigree to match her smarts. And with her blond curly locks, small pretty face, and piercing glance, she was a woman of "every engaging attraction."[23] This lady of high society had been courted by many, but being passionate about politics, she favored military men.

Arnold was beguiled by the coquettish and intelligent young woman, two decades his junior, with "gray eyes that stared even as they smiled."[24] Besides, marrying a Shippen would certainly enhance his social standing. While the Shippens' wealth had faded during the war, a misfortune shared by many Tories, their aristocratic prominence had not. So as he enjoyed the extravagances of Philadelphia's high life, he actively courted the young beauty.

Peggy was likewise attracted to the courageous soldier. She had read about his exploits since childhood and was ecstatic to be lavished with attention from such a famous war hero. She also enjoyed "the vitality that irradiated his light-blue eyes and his high-cheekboned face."[25] Soon she was seen with him at parties around town, unable to resist his flamboyance and spendthrift ways.

Peggy's father had misgivings about the match, however. The upper-crust, Loyalist-leaning Edward Shippen IV did not particularly care for a patriot with a money-hungry reputation, and he rejected Arnold's first request for his daughter's hand in marriage. But he came to appreciate Arnold's fair treatment of Philadelphia's Loyalists and to believe that Arnold's apparent wealth would keep his favorite daughter happy. The Shippens eventually gave their approval, and Peggy soon married the dashing officer. Their divergent political views quickly became less of a problem: Arnold adopted her Loyalist tendencies as he grew more disgusted with his fellow patriots.

Despite his pretenses, Arnold was heavily indebted by his lavish lifestyle and by his spending of personal funds to support his military campaigns. To his great insult, Congress had balked when he demanded reimbursement for his contributions to the war effort, and so he took matters into his own hands. Always astute in turning a profit, he was purported to have "established lucrative connexions" with the Continental Army's provision suppliers and their wives, and "made them the instruments of converting into money, his embezzlements of public stores."[26] In one alleged scheme, he made deals with the merchants to protect their wares in exchange for a cut of the profits. In another shady deal, he was said to have used army wagons to transport his own goods for sale.[27]

Even though such profiteering was commonplace among officers during the war and often overlooked, the politicians in Philadelphia seized the opportunity to disgrace Arnold. His brashness had elicited resentment from Pennsylvania's executive council, which went so far as to charge him with "various accounts of extortion on the citizens of Philadelphia, and with peculating funds of the continent."[28]

Humiliated, Arnold stood trial before a panel of military judges for these corruption charges, starting on June 1, 1779.[29] Washington privately sided with Arnold but publicly did little to aid him. This was because the great Virginian was being blackmailed.

The governor of Pennsylvania, determined to flex his political muscle, threatened to withdraw the state's support for the war should Washington come to Arnold's rescue. Desperate for supplies as he was, Washington decided not to interfere in the charged situation. Arnold, unaware of the blackmail, saw Washington's silence as betrayal.

Arnold was acquitted of the serious charges, but the scandal left its disgraceful taint.[30] He wrote his commander a pain-filled letter pleading for help in clearing his name, but Washington's hands were tied.

Arnold snapped.

In a shocking twist, he defected from "the cause he had so gallantly maintained."[31] He came to see the once virtuous revolutionary cause as having been sullied by the people who now led it. While recovering from his injuries, both physical and emotional, Arnold expressed his deep feeling of betrayal by the American leaders. To his friends, he "complained of being ill used by Congress and the executive council of Pennsylvania, which had treated him with injustice."[32]

As far as Arnold was concerned, he had courageously led the American forces to victory on multiple occasions, sacrificing not only his finances but also his health. And in return he was disgraced time and again as his political enemies in Philadelphia charged him with corruption and his military associates took credit for his victories. They had so offended his sense of honor that he came to consider the new American leadership just as suspect as the British government. The ideal of a government run by "educated, fair-minded men" was gone, and in its place was "something dark and venal."[33] The American cause was further degraded in Arnold's mind by the nation's new alliance with the French Crown. He was outraged that his blood and toil at Saratoga had led to an association with the absolute monarch of a "perfidious people."[34]

Arnold perceived the corruption of the American cause as having trickled down into the thinning ranks of the patriot soldiers. The middle-class stock that made up the bulk of the troops at the beginning of the war had mostly returned home, discouraged by poor rations, low pay, harsh discipline, and shattering military defeats. In fact, as Americans grew weary of the struggle, the Continental Army's fluctuating numbers plummeted from 27,500 to as low as 3,000. Those who had been motivated by ideals went back to their farms, while those in desperate need of the military wages stayed on. Arnold looked down on these lower classes, and he feared that the revolutionary spirit was gone.

Having lost the initial patriotic zeal, the American cause had indeed fallen into dire straits. Even Washington began to question the future of the new nation, writing, "unless a system very different from that which has long prevailed be immediately adopted throughout the states, our affairs must soon become desperate, beyond the possibility of recovery. Indeed, I have almost ceased to hope."[35]

After fighting valiantly for the patriotic cause, Arnold now found himself with "a ruined constitution, and this limb (holding up his wounded leg) now rendered useless." He fumed to his friends, "At the termination of this war, where can I seek for compensation for such damages I have sustained?"[36] Enterprising as ever, Arnold devised a diabolical plan to get recompense. He would betray the revolutionary cause for £20,000.

23

Treason of the Blackest Dye

After Arnold helped expel the British from upstate New York, the necessity of building an "insurmountable barrier against the British navy" was clear.[1] The Americans appointed their best military engineer to scout the area and discern the best location to rebuild a land-based defense.[2] They selected a "point of land projecting in the river on the west side" on account of "the natural advantages presented not only from the strength of the circumjacent ground, but from the narrowness of the Hudson, where here takes a short winding circuit east and west." This would force the British ships to tack to a shift in the wind while they drew cannon fire.[3]

At this ideal location, called West Point, the Americans swiftly constructed the "Great Chain" across the Hudson to Constitution Island in the spring of 1778. This large barricade was composed of a 600-yard iron chain floating atop multiple wooden rafts built from forty-foot waterproofed logs.[4] With each two-foot link of the chain weighing 114 pounds, the entire barricade weighed approximately 65 tons and presented a formidable obstacle even to Britain's most powerful vessels. On a natural plateau on an adjacent hill, the Americans built a fortification from which to defend this "Great Chain" from land assault and bombard any foolish ship captain who dared challenge the blockade. Unlike Fort Montgomery, which had been built a short way downstream two years earlier, the fort at West Point was largely "bomb proof and unassailable from its strength and elevated situation, being built on and composed of rocks," and was "abundantly stored with every military means of defence that the country was capable of affording at that stage of the war, and made the grand arsenal of the main army."[5]

Enticed by the value of this "American Gibraltar," Arnold "intimated a great desire to have the command at West Point."[6] Washington was puzzled. He respected Arnold's abilities and was prepared to appoint him to command a large portion of his army. He correctly viewed Arnold as a man of action and a valuable leader in battle. But Arnold turned down a prestigious command in favor of a relatively sleepy defensive role guarding the Great Chain. It was difficult for Washington to refuse Arnold's request since the officer's "prowess and gallantry" during his rapid rise through the ranks had "justified his appointment."[7] So he appointed Arnold to the command of West Point. Washington wondered why he wanted this particular station. He never fathomed the actual reason.

After slowly cultivating a relationship with Clinton's command in New York City, Arnold began negotiating his defection as early as 1778. In order to build trust with the British and prove the value of his services, he transmitted bits of sensitive American military intelligence: he divulged Washington's troop movements, details regarding the French alliance, and information about the Americans' inability to defend Charleston, South Carolina. This was all groundwork for wringing top dollar from the British when he sold America's crown jewel, West Point.

Arnold knew that such a sale would inflict a "deadly wound if not a fatal stab" on the American cause, and he therefore expected the British to pay dearly.[8] His quarrelsome ways reemerging, he began to argue with the British over compensation and became offended when Clinton refused to treat him as an equal. After haggling like a street urchin, Arnold finally settled on the £20,000 figure that would scar the history books—roughly the equivalent of 25.7 million in modern U.S. dollars, which he considered "a cheap purchase for an object of so much importance."[9] Because Clinton refused to meet with him directly, Arnold had to orchestrate the plot through a young British major named John André.

John André was an unusually well-educated young man known more for courtesy than for cunning. "To an excellent understanding, well improved by education and travel, he united a peculiar elegance of mind and manners, and the advantage of a pleasing person."[10] With his soft manners, he seemed to be "fraught with the milk of human kindness" rather than suited to warfare.[11]

Born in 1750 to a prosperous mercantile family in London, he grew into a handsome man with soft features and mannerisms. His large eyes, small mouth, and gently cleft chin gave him a kind and youthful appearance. His long, thick head of hair hung down his back, tied fashionably with a black ribbon.[12] André was adept at painting, writing lyric and comic verse, and playing the flute. Educated in Switzerland, he was noted for an "inquiring mind" and an aptitude in mathematics and drawing.[13] With a knack for language, he attained fluency in English, French, German, and Italian. But his father was unimpressed by his academic accomplishments.

When André was seventeen years old, his father demanded that he return home to work in the family's counting house. André obeyed, albeit unhappily. Always a romantic, he looked for a means of escape from the family business, which he despised. Toiling as an accountant in a "gloomy" room warmed by a small coal fire, the teenager longed to join in the adventurous British Army battles he had read about at school.[14] The glamour of military life would have to wait, however, for duty and love delayed his enlistment.

Two years after André returned home, his father died. André felt obligated to assume leadership of the family business in order to support his mother and siblings. He trudged through the days, but, as with many young men, his sense of duty was handily overwhelmed by his sense of attraction: André's attention shifted to a wilting seventeen-year-old named Honora Sneyd.

A blonde "sickly angel" who had survived a bout of tuberculosis, Honora welcomed André into her literary coterie.[15] André was warmly received into the group, and together they enjoyed poetry, song, and philosophical debate. In what became a magical time in his life, he joined Honora at her scenic family estate in Lichfield, England.[16] Here, "where the shadows of the spires darkened the well-clipped lawn," Honora and her elite group of romanticists talked of poetry, and André "played his flute as they sang to their reflections in the minster pool."[17] Anna Seward, Honora's sister, described the beloved young gentleman:[18]

> Belov'd Companion of the fairest hours
> That rose for her in Joy's resplendent bow'rs,
> How gaily shore on thy bright Morn of Youth
> The Start of Pleasure, and the Sun of Truth!
> Full from their source descended on thy mind
> Each gen'rous virtue, and each taste refin'd.
> Young Genius led thee to his varied fane.
> Bade thee ask all his gifts, nor ask in vain;
> Hence novel thoughts, in ev'ry lustre drest
> Of pointed wit, that diamond of the breast.[19]

But despite André's intelligence, charm, and heart of gold, Honora's affections proved fleeting. She fell out of love with him just as quickly as she had fallen into it. She came to feel that he was a frivolous dreamer who "did not possess the reasoning mind that she required."[20] Nevertheless, she followed the era's rules of high romance and kept up the pretense: she "agreed to be in love with him."[21] To the love-struck André's delight, the beautiful Honora soon accepted his marriage proposal. However, her powerful family intervened to quell the teenage romance's rapid progression.

They demanded that André accumulate significant wealth before marrying their daughter. So he returned home and made an effort to "win Honora by making his fortune in the family business." He was ultimately unsuccessful at amassing enough money to please Honora's famously wealthy parents, and they broke off the engagement. "His love affair shattered," André "revived an older ambition. Fame, honor, glory called him to the profession of arms."[22] Finding it too painful to remain in Britain, André would run.

He joined the British Army in March 1771, hoping to "dissipate the memory of his sorrows in the turmoil and dangers of war."[23] After training in Germany, he was transferred to Canada by the time the Revolution erupted in 1775. He fought bravely against the Americans and was even held captive for a short time. Writing of his imprisonment, he said, "[I] was stripped of everything except [my] picture of Honora, which I concealed in my mouth. Preserving that, I yet think myself fortunate."[24]

After his release from American custody in a prisoner exchange, André spent nine months enjoying Philadelphia during Howe's occupation. He lived in Benjamin Franklin's abandoned home and quickly became a favorite of the city's high society. As such, he spent much time with the family of Edward Shippen IV, whose lively young daughter Peggy caught his attention. He invited her to a military masquerade ball and even sketched a portrait of her—just as he had done as he was falling for Honora. But any budding romance was promptly cut short by the winds of war. When France entered the war and the British withdrew from Philadelphia in order to defend more vital locations, André departed with them. The American forces rolled in to retake the city, and Benedict Arnold replaced André as Peggy's suitor.

The overachieving André continued to impress his British superiors with his intellect and writing ability. In recognition, he was appointed adjunct general on Clinton's staff in New York City, where he won "friendship and even fondness" from his "solitary, resentful, and stubborn" superior.[25] Clinton respected the charming, young André's discretion and placed him in charge of the army's secret intelligence activities. It was in this role that André eventually came into contact with his old friend's new husband, Arnold.

Having successfully lobbied Washington for command of the West Point garrison, Arnold took over the post in July 1780 and proceeded to prepare his "treason of the blackest dye."[26] Eager to gain the maximum profit from his subterfuge, he had the audacity to request funds and horses from New York's state government on the pretext that he needed them to fix his soldiers' barracks.[27] This could get him some quick cash, though the real money would come from the British when they took over.

The fox in charge of the henhouse, Arnold began sending large groups of soldiers off on trivial assignments like chopping wood in order to diminish the fort's defenses.[28] Hoping to offer the British much more, he lobbied to remove the Great Chain across the Hudson, pretending that it required repairs, though the real purpose was to open the river to British warships.[29] He even toured the fortresses to analyze their vulnerabilities. Exploiting the help of American engineers, he identified the exact angles by which the British might take advantage of weaknesses in the fortifications. For example, walls facing in the directions from which the British would most naturally attack were nearly impenetrable, but the Americans had neglected areas with rougher terrain from which they did not expect an assault.

While Arnold was unsuccessful in removing the Great Chain, he whetted Clinton's appetite by informing him that a well-loaded ship could break it. He also offered to provide detailed plans of the fortifications.[30] These plans were the reason why Arnold met with André.

As summer set in 1780, Arnold requested to meet with the British in order to finalize the arrangements for the surrender of West Point and to coordinate the plan of assault. Even though Washington had an uncanny ability to read people, he was clueless about Arnold's scheming. He never suspected that the man who had fought so valiantly for his army would ever consider such duplicity. Arnold enjoyed free rein, and he turned to his friend Joshua Hett Smith to facilitate a final meeting with the British.

From a prosperous family of British-sympathizers, Smith was a lawyer of relatively low abilities yet high self-regard.[31] He was described as a "timorous, prying, bustling sort of character" who wanted to "have a hand in weighty affairs" and who tried, in particular, to stay "on good terms with whomsoever was uppermost."[32] Since the British still appeared to be winning, it was unsurprising that Smith himself was suspected of sympathizing with them.[33] He was rather homely with his sleepy eyes above a prominent nose and somewhat wild gray hair, but his small, feminine mouth would come in handy as part of a transvestite disguise.

Smith lived with his wife and children in a stately two-story home. Located about eighteen miles south of West Point, on the main route "where all communications passed from the eastern and southern states," this house was ideally situated for Arnold's purposes.[34] From its elevated position, it offered a sweeping view of the ships passing on the Hudson. So the Smith home became the central location for Arnold's plot.

Arnold and Smith had grown close during the time since the traitor's transfer to West Point. A social climber who was eager to cultivate a relationship with someone of Arnold's power, Smith had frequently entertained Benedict and Peggy with elaborate meals.[35] While the Arnolds appeared to enjoy the friendship, the other Americans did not take as kindly to Smith. In fact, one of Arnold's aides called him "a damned rascal, a scoundrel, and a spy."[36] In late September 1780, Arnold approached this scoundrel to arrange his meeting with André.

Adhering to strict orders from Arnold, Smith and his servants rowed under the cover of darkness, in a "silent manner," to rendezvous with Arnold's British contact.[37] Their oars were muffled so as not to alert the American boats guarding the shores of the river. With the sky dimly lit by the bright stars, the crew cruised along the tranquil river, the waters of which were "unruffled except by the gentle current."[38]

Although "[t]he night was serene and the tide favourable," Smith was apprehensive about the clandestine mission.[39]

They approached a small British sloop-of-war called the *Vulture*.[40] Smith presented a letter from Arnold to André, uncreatively code-named "John Anderson," and together they returned to shore at approximately one o'clock that night. Arnold was waiting on the western shore of the river, hiding among the fir trees near the foot of Long Clove Mountain.[41] There, in the pitch-black woods, Peggy's dear old friend and her current husband finally met. Arnold did not extend him a warm welcome. Instead, they went right to work.

With only their discreet lanterns to shed light as they schemed, Arnold and André plotted the final preparations for the surrender of West Point. They orchestrated the moves of the attacking British forces and determined what orders Arnold would give to his American troops so he would appear loyal to the United States but nevertheless quickly surrender with minimal British bloodshed.[42]

The rendezvous lasted through the night, ending only when Smith interrupted to warn of the approaching dawn. Arnold handed André the fortification plans along with other intelligence, which the young man hid in his boots. They hurried back to the river, but it was too late to return André to the *Vulture* "without being discovered from either shore by the inhabitants, whose eyes were constantly watching the movements on the river, not only from the forts, but the surrounding shores."[43] As the sun's first rays lit the sky, nearby American troops fired on the *Vulture*. Set partially ablaze in the rude awakening, the wounded boat limped downriver as flashes of fire pierced through the billowing smoke. The plan was botched. With his ship gone, André was trapped deep within hostile American territory. Arnold reluctantly decided to fall back to Smith's house three miles away.

Back at Smith's house that morning, Arnold, ever the astute tactician, quickly adapted his plan. He ordered André to remove his British officer uniform and put on a civilian coat provided by Smith, who was approximately the same size. Nervous about being caught as a disguised spy, "André, who had been undesignedly brought within [American] posts in the first instance, remonstrated warmly against this new and dangerous expedient."[44] Arnold insisted, and André had little choice but to go along.

Furnishing André with a passport, Arnold sent him to take a land route through American territory back to British-occupied New York City. Smith provided André with a horse and agreed to accompany him through the first and most dangerous part of the passage. This stretch in Westchester, New York, was a treacherous civil war zone fraught with "plunder, outrage, inhuman barbarity, and even murder" as patriots and Loyalists clashed.[45] Many on both sides seized the lawlessness of war as an opportunity to exact revenge for old insults or merely to indulge in looting. This was not a safe neighborhood, to put it mildly.

With trepidation, Smith and André rode side by side along the dirt pathways. Soon into their journey, they were stopped and questioned by American patrols searching for enemy spies. Smith took the lead, and, presenting the passports that Arnold had provided, he explained to their inquisitors "that they were on the public services, on business of the highest import" to the American cause.[46] Smith then had the nerve to threaten these interrogators that they "would be answerable for [André's] detention one moment."[47] His brashness paid off. In fact, Smith was so successful in assuaging the Americans' suspicions that one American colonel invited them to dine at his house. Unsurprisingly, André "seemed desirous to decline," and they did.[48]

After days of riding and partaking in friendly conversation about books, music, and their desire to see an end to the war, Smith and André arrived at Pines Bridge. Smith expected that André would encounter fewer American forces past this point. As they ate breakfast porridge at a wayside cottage, Smith provided André with directions for the remainder of his journey back to Clinton's post in New York City. Smith jovially paid the bill and they parted amicably, unaware that they would soon see each other again in far less cheerful circumstances—as prisoners at West Point.

24

Commissions & Courts-Martial

At nine o'clock on the morning of Saturday, September 23, John André was riding down a wooded path towards safety behind British lines. At a narrowing in the road in Tarrytown, New York, just six miles from where he parted ways with Smith, three American militiamen suddenly leapt from the woods and seized his horse's bridle.[1] The three men had been playing cards by the road, hoping for such an opportunity to ride by. "The law of the state gave to the captors of any British subject, all his property," according to Joshua Hett Smith's account, "and of course, his horse, saddle, and bridle, were in the first instance a temptation to stop him on the least ground of suspicion, while he being alone, they were the more bold against an unarmed man."[2]

André panicked. Since his captors were not in proper uniforms—they were a ragged bunch, with one wearing a faded Hessian jacket likely "borrowed" from a dead man—he did not know whether they were Loyalists or patriots. "At this critical moment, his presence of mind forsook him" and instead of producing his papers from Arnold and pretending to be an American on official military business, he asked the men whose side they were on. The wily men lied, stating that they were Loyalists.[3] Fooled, André then divulged his true identity as a British officer and demanded that he be freed. This is precisely what the militiamen wanted to hear. They dragged him into the bushes.

André tried bribing the men with his gold watch and promises of cash, but this only made them more suspicious.[4] The Americans stripped and searched him. In his stockings they found "a plan of the fortifications of West Point; a memorial from the engineer on the attack and defense of the place, returns of the garrison, cannon and stores; [and a] copy of the minutes of a council of war held by General Washington a few weeks before."[5] Only one of the men was literate, but they quickly surmised that they had stumbled upon something big. What they did not realize was just how far-reaching the conspiracy was. Even though the documents were in Arnold's handwriting and pointed directly to his complicity, Arnold's involvement in such treachery was so unfathomable that the commander of the New York militia stupidly reported André's capture right back to the treasonous mastermind.

When Arnold received the news at West Point, he bounded into action. Desperate to escape before word of his involvement reached the garrison, he immediately ordered his horse to be saddled and a boat readied. Telling his wide-eyed wife Peggy that he "must fly to save his life without having time to explain," Arnold bolted from the house and leapt onto his horse. Four of his light horsemen, unaware of what was transpiring, met him outside. They announced to their hurried superior that Washington, who had received intelligence of André's capture, was approaching. Washington's forces closing in, Arnold ordered the soldiers to stable their horses in order to slow their pursuit of him once they received word of his treachery. He then took a risky shortcut down to his boat, where, like a wild man, he threw his pistols onto the deck, jumped aboard, and commanded the boatmen to set off.[6]

He had not yet escaped Washington's tightening noose. His boat was quickly stopped by an armed boat that Washington had dispatched. In the confusion, the ship's crew had yet to receive their orders to detain Arnold, however. He told them to "go up to the house to get refreshment," and when Washington arrived, to say that he would return before dinner. They fell for the ploy. Arnold got away from the wharf, but soon the armed vessel was in pursuit.[7] With the Americans closing in on his small, unarmed boat, Arnold turned to his crew and promised them two gallons of rum if they hurried. The bewildered men raced to the *Vulture*. Once safely on the British gunboat, Arnold took his own boatmen prisoner. His daring flight had succeeded. America's greatest traitor had escaped.

General Washington "was thrown into the greatest distress from the failure of so well concerted a plan, so near ending the rebellion, as it would have given [the British] all of the forts, half the army, and cut off all communication with the Southern and Eastern Provinces as also the French."[8] He was so shaken that he began to question who else from among his trusted officers might be involved. As he was pondering his next move, Washington was duped by Arnold's cunning wife.

Peggy was in grave danger on account of her knowledge about the conspiracy, so she relied on her feminine wiles. When Washington's men found her in the house, she put on a "most affecting scene," masterfully acting as though Arnold's treachery were such a shock that it had thrown her into a state of delirium.[9] Not above showing some skin, Peggy opened her dress in feigned hysterics. She wailed and convulsed as she held her baby to her bosom. "One moment she raved, another she melted into tears," lamenting Arnold's supposed deception. "All the sweetness of beauty, all the loveliness of innocence, all the tenderness of a wife and all the fondness of a mother" worked to hoodwink Washington and his officers.[10] The chivalrous general could not believe that such a beautiful, well-bred woman could be complicit in so nefarious a plot. Besides, her seemingly fragile mind made her appear to be an unlikely accomplice in so complicated a conspiracy.

Washington did not know whom he could trust. But despite his fear, he kept a cool head as he tried to gauge the extent of the treason. First, though, he had to defend West Point from the impending attack. He ordered up more troops to reinforce the fort. An American regiment, receiving the call at 1:00 A.M., marched sixteen miles through driving rain to secure West Point by sunrise.[11] Then Washington turned to the matter of exacting justice. And he was out for blood.

At midnight on Monday, September 25, Joshua Smith lay in bed with his wife. He was exhausted, having gotten little rest since he had become embroiled in Arnold's plot a few days earlier: he had been up all night keeping a lookout while Arnold and André conspired, and then shared a bed with the restless British officer as they traveled. But after he parted ways with his young charge, Smith returned to the confines of his stately home for some much-needed recuperation. As he lay surrounded by the comforts of his British fineries, his bedroom door was violently opened and the room filled with American soldiers.

The adrenaline-fueled young men immediately drove Smith out of bed by fixed bayonet and angrily ordered him to dress. His disorientation exceeded only by his terror, Smith obeyed. The household was "thrown into great confusion; the female part especially were in the deepest distress."[12] Once he was dressed, Smith was forced out the door without any explanation and marched for eighteen miles through the warm night. As dawn's first rays shone on the horizon, the party arrived at a wealthy Tory's home that Washington had commandeered. Smith was thrown into the guarded back room where irate soldiers questioned him intensely. For hours, Smith adamantly denied aiding the British. After a rough night and morning, he was hungry and exhausted. The soldiers placed him in a room with biscuits, but warned him—rather inhospitably—that he would be shot if he touched them.

Washington then entered to interrogate Smith regarding his involvement in the conspiracy. He demanded answers and coldly threatened to hang Smith if he did not open up. Smith was terrified by this enraged demigod fuming before him. Cowering in his chair, he contended that he was ignorant of the scheme to betray the American cause and was merely helping General Arnold on diplomatic business.

Washington did not believe him. The commander declared that he had evidence against Smith that was sufficient to impose a death sentence.[13] Whether this was a bluff or merely his rage speaking is unclear, but on further reflection he decided to remand Smith to a court-martial proceeding. For although Washington was incensed, he was not one to act rashly. Since Smith was an American, Washington deferred to Congress's authority in deciding how he should be brought to justice. As will be further discussed in Part V, American citizens were under the civil authorities' control.[14] But those politicians were not always forgiving—while he had escaped the gallows for the time being, Smith still faced a trial for his life.

Under the Articles of War passed in 1775, Congress made no provisions for trying spies.[15] This was remedied on August 21, 1776, when Congress resolved:

> All persons, not members of, nor owing allegiance to any of the United States of America . . . who shall be found lurking as spies in or about the fortifications or encampments of the armies of the United States . . . shall suffer death, according to the law and usage of nations . . . by sentence of a court-martial, or such other punishment as such court-martial shall direct.[16]

This resolution directed Washington to try foreign spies according to the rules of courts-martial.[17] Congress followed this up with a resolution aimed at Loyalists, "authorizing the commander in chief of the army, to hear and try by courtmartial, any of the citizens of the United States who should harbour or [abet] any of the subjects or soldiers of the King of Great Britain."[18]

The court-martial was a type of military court with origins dating back to thirteenth-century England, where King Edward I was striving to restore royal authority over the feudal barons. As part of this effort, he issued a royal prerogative asserting the power of the Crown to regulate and discipline the army. Military courts called courts-martial emerged to enable the military to carry out justice when soldiers violated the monarch's orders. The republican Americans inherited this tradition but substituted congressional resolution for royal edict. In the new United States, court-martial trials were a legislative enactment governed by Congress.

The American courts-martial provided the accused person with "due process," which is the legal term for the principles of fundamental fairness and justice used in hearing a prisoner's case. Courts-martial sought to respect the rights of the defendant since these courts were meant to determine justice rather than merely dole out swift punishment.[19] In order to provide due process, Congress employed certain procedures to promote a fair trial.

First, Congress required that court-martial proceedings be conducted before a panel of thirteen commissioned officers, to decrease the likelihood of a skewed sample of biased jurors that may occur with a smaller group. Second, Congress placed special limitations on the panel's composition based on the ranking of the accused. This was to ensure that jurors had the necessary seniority and insight to judge the defendant properly. Third, in order to promote impartiality, Congress forbade the officer convening the court-martial—in Smith's case, General Washington—from sitting on the panel of jurors as president.[20] This twist from the traditional British system helped to prevent the commander in chief from influencing the other officers to convict the accused. Finally, the members of the court typically swore an oath to "duly administer justice . . . without partiality, favor, or affection," and to use their "conscience, the best of [their] understanding, and the custom of war in like cases."[21]

Although courts-martial historically granted no right to counsel,[22] they often involved thorough inquiries with many witnesses called, and provided the accused with opportunity to defend himself. When a man fell within the realm of court-martial proceedings, he was tried according to Congress's rules and the accompanying guarantees of a fair trial. He had a fighting chance of acquittal. This was not always the case for those unfortunate enough to be brought instead before so-called "military commissions."

A military commission was similar to a court-martial in the sense that it was likewise a military proceeding to dispense punishment for offenses. But while these commissions often mimicked some of the procedures of courts-martial, they did not need to provide the accused with the same protections for a fair trial.[23] A military commission traditionally served as a "quick and dirty" way to eliminate the due process protections used in courts-martial and criminal trials.[24] According to a nineteenth-century treatise, "Its proceedings are not a trial, nor, is its opinion, (when it expresses one,) a judgment."[25] Indeed, such war courts were more summary in their proceedings and they would not be deemed illegal even if they left out details required by courts-martial.[26] Military commissions involved a relatively superficial inquiry, which usually resulted in a swift hanging of the accused.

While courts-martial were held under rules passed by Congress, military commissions were held according to the commander in chief's discretion and did not necessarily provide the accused with any protections whatsoever.[27] These tribunals were often more like investigative bodies than formal courts, with procedures largely left to the whims of the commander. They were not bound by Congress's court-martial rules since the commander made up his own, adapting them to the occasion. And his decision was final.[28]

Washington's actions in the fall of 1780 suggest that whether the commander was obligated to try a prisoner by a congressional court-martial or had the option to convene a special military commission depended on whether the accused was American or British. Nationality could thus mean the difference between life and death.

From the beginning of the war, Washington ordered that prisoners' cases be examined to determine "who of them were subject to Military Jurisdiction and who came properly under the cognizance of civil power."[29] He was in the awkward position of having to juggle congressional and state laws as well as international customs, since the relatively new national legislature did not yet possess the legal foundation to trump laws derived from other sources.[30] So while he took care to respect civilian control over military tribunals where appropriate, Washington admitted that he was operating in a confused state of affairs. The process of examining individual cases, he confessed, was "somewhat irregular, and out of the common order to things" due to the chaos of war. He recognized, and Congress agreed, that "the distinction between Civilian and Military power" could not, in the circumstances, be maintained "with that exactness which every friend to Society must wish."[31] Nevertheless, Washington conscientiously did his best to protect the rights of his fellow Americans. As Hamilton wrote, "His Excellency desires to avoid nothing more, than . . . the least Encroachment either upon the rights of the Citizens, or of the Magistrate."[32]

"His Excellency" was unique among the great revolutionary leaders of history in that he never declared martial law. He demonstrated that "a republican government could fight effectively in the face of overwhelming odds without resorting to the suspension of civil liberties."[33] Martial law, dating back as far as the fourteenth century in England, was in reality "not a law, but something rather indulged than allowed as a law," and only in times of crisis.[34] Basically, martial law enabled the military to create its own expedient rules, suppressing any legal rights so chosen. It was "not necessarily consistent with the law of the land, but rather provided for a rough, summary justice . . . on the grounds that 'neither the time nor place suffer the tariance of pleading.'"[35] But even while he was losing the war on various fronts, Washington was so committed to defending the rights of Americans that he made time for "the tariance of pleading."

Washington was intent on showing that a republican commander could effectively fight a war without trampling on civil authority.[36] Rather than rule by military decree, he deferred to Congress and the state governments on civil matters. He had attained broad authority over the enemy and war tactics, but not over his fellow Americans. Although there certainly were some deplorable irregularities in the way his officers tried and even executed American civilians outside the direction of civil authorities, Washington opposed such actions, believing that the "temper of the Americans and the principles on which the present contest turns, will not countenance proceedings of this nature."[37]

For most crimes, Americans were to be tried in civilian courts, with fair trials and representation as decided by Congress and the states.[38] Washington supported this policy, stating that civil authorities "best know the Charge and Merit of the Case, consequently should ultimately determine it."[39] When it came to the crime of spying, Congress ordered military trials for Americans and Brits alike. Specifically, Congress ordered Washington to try the accused by a court-martial.[40] Showing great deference to Congress and the states, he wrote, "it is not my desire, neither indeed is it within my power" to interfere with the determinations of the civil authority.[41]

25

American Military Justice

Joshua Hett Smith, being an American, fell within Congress's purview. Therefore, despite Washington's knee-jerk urge to hang him "on yonder tree," Smith was afforded a trial.[1] Upon his capture, adhering to their resolution of August 21, 1776, Congress swiftly passed a specific resolution that called for Smith to be tried in a court-martial. This meant his case would receive a thorough inquiry rather than the quick summary judgment of a military commission.[2] Thus, even though he faced a military trial for his crimes, he would still receive the protections that Congress set up.

Smith was soon brought before a panel of military officers. The sensational trial was held at the Old Dutch Church in the hamlet of Tappan, New York. In this dusty little room, Smith stood terrified as the court-martial commenced. He was formally charged with ten counts, which, upon his request, were consolidated into one: "You stand charged with aiding and abetting Benedict Arnold, late major general in our service, in a combination with the enemy, for the purpose of taking, seizing, and killing, such of the loyal soldiers of these United States, as were garrisoned in West Point."[3] He was in deep trouble.

During the initial proceedings, Smith was allowed to make his case for citizens being amenable only to the nonmilitary courts. He sought a civilian court because it would provide additional protections and trial by jury, thereby giving him a better chance of acquittal. He argued that Congress and General Washington, by bringing him before this court-martial, were effectively making "the military paramount to the civil authority."[4]

After deliberation, the court-martial ultimately rejected this argument. Refusing him a civilian trial, they stated that Smith would be tried by the resolve of Congress, "authorizing the commander in chief of the army, to hear and try by court-martial, any of the citizens of the United States, who should harbor or secret any of the subjects or soldiers of the King of Great Britain . . . ." Over Smith's objection that they were establishing "a precedent dangerous to the liberties" of Americans, the court-martial began with hearing testimony.[5]

In what turned out to be a rather thorough inquiry lasting six weeks,[6] Smith had a chance to question the many witnesses called by the court.[7] He did his best to discredit them, but their evidence against him seemed damning. Some of the Continental Army's top brass provided their accounts of the events surrounding Smith's arrest and described him as a knowledgeable conspirator in Arnold's plot. One such officer presented his evidence "with acrimonious severity, and malignant bitterness."[8] The odds were stacked against Smith. Like Washington, these officers dearly wanted a conviction—not only for the sake of justice but also to dissuade future American traitors. Despite their desires, however, Smith was given the opportunity to rebut their accusations. He maintained that he was ignorant of the broader plot and believed he was aiding the American cause by following Arnold's orders.

Testifying subsequently to the top brass were the two boatmen, Samuel and Joseph Colquhoun, who had rowed Smith out to the *Vulture* to pick up André mere days before. They were poor, hardworking men who spoke with "plainness, perspicuity, and firmness."[9] These simple boatmen were plunged right into the middle of a sensational trial. In fact, the night before he was to testify, Samuel was purportedly "taken into a field by some of General Washington's officers," who offered him a purse of gold if he would testify against Smith.

He allegedly replied that "although he was a poor man, he could not swear falsely for money . . . and, if made rich by such means, . . . that he should be miserable for life."[10]

Both Samuel and Joseph testified to all they knew and nothing more: that they had rowed Smith out to the *Vulture*, returned to shore with André, and then were unable to bring André back to the *Vulture* due to the approaching dawn and their own fatigue. They explained that they understood the mission to be "irregular and hazardous" but were assured it was well known to the American side.[11] Their testimony did not further condemn Smith, but it did not exonerate him either. Washington's strong case against him remained on track.

The prosecution next sought to refute Smith's contention that he was ignorant of the plot. The court introduced witnesses who had observed him interacting with André as they traveled back towards New York City. These witnesses testified to what "appeared to them an intimacy between Major André and [Smith], that was of a very long standing."[12] This was damning to Smith since it suggested that he had long been in cahoots with André and Arnold, rather than being a pawn who unwittingly aided in one small task. To further demonstrate the absurdity of Smith's plea of ignorance, the prosecution finally brought forth the coat that he had lent André to cover his British uniform. However Smith tried to argue it, this coat showed that he had helped disguise an enemy officer. In all, this case against Smith was a formidable one.

Smith, mustering his modest lawyering skills, presented his own defense for forty-eight hours. Standing alone in the small, dusty chamber, he reiterated that he was merely a private citizen obeying the commands of an American military leader, Arnold. He adamantly contended that he never knew he was partaking in any treachery. In the face of testimony against him by top military officials and other witnesses, as well as physical evidence implicating him, Smith argued that no one could definitively prove that he knew of Arnold's plot. However, "[t]he reasons he assigned were improbable and his attempts at an explanation only drew a deeper shade over his candor."[13]

Desperate to place a high burden of proof on the prosecution, he next argued that he should be presumed innocent until proven guilty, for "it was better ninety-nine criminals should pass unpunished, than that one innocent man should unjustly suffer."[14]

Seemingly, the court-martial agreed with his contention that "the law demanded" his conviction to be "supported by the strongest testimony."[15] After a fortnight of deliberation, the court-martial determined that the evidence presented was not enough to prove definitively that Smith knew of Arnold's treacherous plot.[16] Even though Washington had "anxiously meditated [his] destruction," Smith was "favoured by the Law."[17]

To the shock of many, Smith was acquitted. But he was not released. He was taken into custody by civil authorities on additional charges of aiding Loyalists. He did not remain behind bars for long, however. A slippery character, he soon escaped from prison disguised as a woman—perhaps the ugliest ever to walk the streets of New York—and fled to Manhattan, where he was protected by the Loyalist population.[18] Smith's co-conspirator did not enjoy such a colorful ending to the saga. André, though accused in the same plot, was not afforded such a thorough inquiry because he was a foreigner. And so he met with a far less fortunate fate.

Days after André's capture, Washington wrote, "Major André was taken under such circumstances as would have justified the most summary proceedings against him. I determined however to refer his case to the examination and decision of a Board of General Officers."[19] Despite the congressional resolution calling for spies to be tried by court-martial, Washington viewed it as his prerogative instead to try a foreign enemy combatant without "the formality of a regular trial."[20] André was accused in the very same plot as Smith, but Washington felt no obligation to provide him with any of the same legal protections. Although Washington's thirst for vengeance was foiled by Smith's court-martial, he need not worry about due process or such a high level of proof in his case against André, and "the general was determined to hang him."[21]

Major André's military commission was worlds apart from Smith's court-martial. Whereas Smith enjoyed a systematic inquiry, the format of André's commission and the rights allotted to him were left to Washington's whim.[22] His "board of inquiry" was not sworn to administer justice, but was simply meant to "examine and inquire."[23] Always meticulous about proper procedure, Washington charged the board with reviewing the evidence of André's conspiracy with Arnold and his subsequent capture within American lines "in a disguised habit, with a pass under a feigned name."[24] He appointed a board of fourteen military officers to dictate the young man's fate.

"The Board was a virtual who's who of revolutionary figures" and news of the trial quickly found its way into headlines on both sides of the Atlantic.[25] The gripping story of the villainous Arnold's treachery and the dashing young André's capture was disseminated widely through the cities, towns, villages, and farms, from the backwoods of America to metropolitan London. At the epicenter of the shockwaves was the hapless André, who stood before America's top military brass inside the same stone church where Smith was tried.

In this makeshift courtroom, André's life hung in the balance as he faced the "glowing and prosecuting enmity of General Greene."[26] Washington ordered the board "as speedily as possible, to report a precise state of his case, together with [their] opinion on the light in which he ought to be considered, and the punishment that ought to be inflicted."[27] Although "no precise charge was exhibited against him," the investigation quickly went ahead.[28]

The United States' case was based almost entirely on hearsay,[29] as no witnesses were brought forward, "nor could any be brought who had the slightest knowledge of the secret part of [the Arnold] transaction." Instead, the board relied on the written "statements of some facts" from André's captors regarding his disguise and the documents found in his possession.[30] To his dismay and frustration, André had no opportunity to confront these witnesses against him.[31] He just stood, choking back his fear and resolutely believing in his own innocence.

When the board questioned him directly, André spoke passionately but was ultimately "defenseless, friendless."[32] Though he had no legal training, he was offered no assistance in defending himself.[33] He badly needed it. The only counsel he did receive was the mere suggestion that he "not hasten his replies to the interrogatories . . . and if the questions appear to him to be worded with ambiguity, to demand a fair explanation of them, which would be granted."[34]

The board primarily delved into the transcripts of André's answers to previous interrogatories during his captivity, in which he argued that he could not be treated as a spy since he had disembarked from the British gunship "in discharge of his duty, acting in obedience to his sovereign's proclamation . . . to receive the terms and conditions of a returning rebel," Arnold.[35] He argued that once he was trapped ashore by the *Vulture*'s retreat downriver, he had become a "prisoner of war subject to Arnold's orders."[36] He claimed that he merely complied with Arnold's command to disguise his clothing because he was a prisoner attempting to escape from hostile territory.

Clinton and Arnold wrote letters on André's behalf, pleading that he could not be considered a spy since he had come ashore "under the sanction of a passport of flag of truce" given to him by Arnold, who at the time had as much authority to extend the invitation "as General Washington himself."[37]

After reviewing the evidence, such as it was, the board of officers entered into debate. The "amiable, virtuous, and humane" Baron von Steuben argued that André ought not be condemned.[38] He reasoned that according to historical and contemporary writers on the subject, "an enemy, having once entered the lines of an enemy . . . under the sanction of the flag, . . . his personal safety becomes guaranteed from violation . . . ."[39] The other officers were less interested in historical precedents, and less moved by "feelings of humanity, and sentiments of justice." Steuben was overruled by a majority of the board.[40]

Although Washington and his officers knew that the real villain was the elusive Arnold, they sought to exact vengeance where they could.[41] Within days of his capture, the board ruled that "Major John André, adjunct general of the British Army, ought to be considered as a spy from the enemy, and that, agreeably to the law and usage of nations, it is their opinion that he ought to suffer death."[42]

André had little chance to mount a defense in this ad hoc system. Without a formal charge, a unanimous vote, representation, a thorough investigation of the background evidence, a right to confrontation, or even direct questioning of pertinent witnesses, he was sentenced to the gallows.[43] And with that, the young officer was quickly readied for execution.

Meanwhile, André's friends "were incessant in their efforts to rescue him from his impending fate."[44] Clinton and Arnold both wrote letters to Washington urging him to refrain from taking his rage out on André when Arnold was his real target. They implored Washington to trade André for American prisoners they held. Arnold even threatened that although "Clinton had never put to death any person for the breach of the rules of war," he held many American prisoners whom he could execute in retaliation. Washington, however, was unwavering in his resolve. He would only trade André for Arnold.

Clinton despised the traitorous Arnold and desperately wished to save André, but he could not renege on his agreement to protect Arnold lest he discourage other American defectors and appear treacherous himself. Arnold was safe. Though the Americans hoped he would "undergo a punishment comparatively more severe" than André's in "the permanent, increasing torment of a mental hell," Arnold instead lived out the rest of his life after the war in England.[45] André did not.

André approached his impending doom with "the manly firmness, and complacency of countenance, which spoke the serene composure of his mind."[46] He merely requested that he be shot rather than hanged, since the latter method of execution was perceived as more disgraceful. Washington, though he pitied the young man, refused this request since "the practice and usage of war . . . were against the indulgence."[47] Washington was not being cruel, but pragmatic: he needed to present a strong front against such treachery in order to win the war. He felt sorry for the young man, but had to execute him for the good of the nation. At no other time did he obey "the stern mandates of duty and policy" more reluctantly.[48]

André's execution was held at midday on October 2. Less than two weeks after he had disembarked from the *Vulture* with Smith that late summer night, he prepared himself for a swift death behind the old church in which he was convicted.[49] Dressed in full crimson British uniform, he marched to his death, "the gland of his throat sinking and swelling as though he choked with emotion."[50] The American soldiers lining his path were "astonished at the dignity of his deportment." As he passed along, "a glow of sympathy pervaded the breasts of the soldiers, and the tears of sensibility were present in every eye."[51] Like Washington, "they deemed him a victim of Arnold's treachery."[52]

When André climbed a small hill and spotted the gallows, he stopped cold. He had held out hope that he would instead be executed in a more honorable fashion: by gunshot. He asked, "What! Must I die in this manner?"[53] He quickly regained his composure and, though visibly disgusted by the lowly means of his execution, bowed to the American officers as he stepped up onto his own black coffin.

When the clumsy hangman approached to place the noose around his neck, André vehemently swatted the man's hands away, took the noose, unpinned his collar, and placed the rope around his own neck. Pacing back and forth on top of his coffin, the young man looked up at the pole and then took in "the whole scenery by which he was surrounded."[54] Through welling eyes, he peered over the heads of the crowd, out to where the leaves on the trees were inching towards the explosion of color that arrived each fall and sparrows busily braced their nests for the coming cold. This was the last sight he would ever see, for he then tied the blindfold over his own eyes and implored the crowd to bear witness to the world that he "died like a brave man!"[55] With that, the commanding officer gave the signal and the cart bearing André's coffin violently jerked out from underneath him.

Due to the height of the gallows, André fell, his neck cracked, and he quickly perished. The crowd watched in morbid fascination as his body silently swung in the early autumn breeze.

After cutting his corpse down for burial, an American soldier found a poem in André's breast pocket that he had written just days before, as he contemplated his own demise:

> Hail, sovereign love that first began
> The scheme to rescue fallen man!
> Hail, matchless free, eternal grace
> That gave my soul a hiding place.
>
> . . . .
>
> A few more rolling suns at most
> Will land me on fair Canaan's coast;
> Where I shall sing the song of grace,
> And see my glorious Hiding Place.[56]

After his hanging, Congress demonstrated its approval of the seemingly unauthorized military commission by cheering Washington's decision and the fact that "insidious designs of the enemy [had been] baffled, and the United States rescued from impending danger."[57] But while Americans were overjoyed that Arnold's plot had been foiled and justice served upon one of the conspirators, they nevertheless mourned the young man. Hamilton captured the sentiment when he wrote, "never, perhaps, did any man suffer death with more justice or deserve it less." John André "perished universally esteemed and lamented; indeed, a general sorrow at his fate pervaded all ranks of people through the continent of America."[58]

Washington was among those who mourned André, writing, "When youth, adorned with such rare accomplishments, is consigned prematurely to the grave, all our sensibilities are roused, and for a moment human society seems to sustain a deprivation by the melancholy stroke."[59] The British Army's sense of loss was coupled with rage, as "mingled sensations of horror, grief, sympathy, and revenge" ran throughout the forces.[60] A wave of anguish swept from the United States across the Atlantic, where Anna Seward, André's dear friend and the sister of his long-lost beloved Honora, powerfully captured the spirit:

> Remorseless Washington! The day shall come
> Of deep repentance for this barbarous doom;
> When injured André's mem'ry shall inspire
> A kindling army of reistless fire . . . .

Washington's military commission had spoken. John André was dead. Benedict Arnold's plot was unraveled. The revolutionary cause had survived to fight another day. And the commander had defined American military justice.[61]

The Military Academy at West Point exists today as a testament to America's life-and-death struggle. What is now perhaps one of the safest place on earth was once the place where the future of the nation teetered in the balance. As far as Washington was concerned, the military post at West Point was the most important one in the United States during the Revolutionary War.[62] In a tale of treachery and tragedy, the crucial fort was nearly sold out to the enemy, and the traitor escaped, but a military commission dispensed swift justice on a co-conspirator. Washington's response to the crisis was ad hoc. It was merciless. It was condemned by many. Nevertheless, the patriotic security and serenity that now pervade the campus of the United States Military Academy stem directly from the actions of the gallant man depicted on a horse in front of the dining hall.

V

HIS EXCELLENCY'S LOYAL SUBJECTS

"The immediate objects are the total distruction and devastation of their settlements and the capture of as many prisoners of every age and sex as possible. . . . [L]ay waste all the settlements around [so] that the country may not be merely overrun but destroyed. I need not urge the necessity of using every method in your power to gain intelligence of the enemy's strength motions and designs."[1]

—GEORGE WASHINGTON, 1779

For over two centuries, a majestic bur oak has stood sentinel to a forgotten past. Much like the memories of the ground it marks, this old tree's vitality has faded with time. The giant hangs on to life amidst the stumps of fallen kin, its gnarly gray bark regally hovering above a green panorama of rolling grass. The old oak's leaves seem to let out a whisper as a May breeze interrupts the silence of the little park. So quiet and abandoned, this tree is a place where excitement comes to die.

It was not always this way. Quite to the contrary, the oak guards a secret history of incredible depravity and raging vengeance. Called the "Torture Tree," this old giant marks the location where Native Americans brutalized American soldiers and Washington retaliated with "total destruction and devastation."[2]

The Torture Tree's history illustrates Washington's ardent defense of his countrymen's rights, even if it meant wreaking devastation on his enemies. The following chapters present the gory details.

26

Total Ruin

Washington demanded annihilation. Finally living up to his old Native American name, "Devourer of Villages," he ordered the "total ruin" of the Native American settlements in northwest New York. This was not Washington's first time dealing with the Seneca tribe that dominated the region. Ironically, these were the people of the late Half King Tanacharison—the ax-happy warrior who had ensnared Washington in the Jumonville debacle so many years earlier. The commander certainly displayed no affection for his former ally's tribe. To the contrary, he ordered that their entire nation "not be merely overrun but destroyed."[1]

Known as the Onöndowága' or "great hill people," the Seneca lived off their fields' grain and forests' game. As the primary keepers of the homes and farms, women played a prominent role in their society: they chose the tribe's (male) chief. While the women looked after the home front, the men hunted, developed new settlements, traded, and made war. Unfortunately for these women, the Seneca men decided to make war against Washington.

Along with their Loyalist allies, the Seneca and five allied tribes launched attacks on American patriots throughout the region. The British, of course, were behind this plot. King George III promised the Native Americans their old lands in exchange for support against the

American rebels. Eager to seize this opportunity, the six tribes ended their neutrality and began slaughtering patriots, taking their livestock, and burning their homes.

On a hot July day in 1778, the Native Americans and Loyalists moved south into a gorgeous valley in eastern Pennsylvania. Between two mountain ranges, the Wyoming Valley was kept lush by the Susquehanna River. Here, the American settlers, along with their cattle and farmlands, flourished on the river's fresh waters. Isolated from the horrible war to the east, these patriots enjoyed bountiful harvests and nature's tranquility. But their visitors would put a swift end to their happy existence.

When the Americans learned that their "paradise of beauty and fertility" had been invaded, they were quick to defend their homes: "the whole population flew to arms. Grandfathers and their aged sons, boys, and even women, seized such weapons as were at hand, and joined the soldiery."[2] This untrained mob advanced towards the trespassers, intent on repelling them. But the invaders had devised a deadly plan.

As the Native Americans lay unseen amid the riverbank's tall marsh grasses, the Loyalists coaxed the Americans into a frontal assault. Seeing their traitorous countrymen before them, the irate patriots took the bait and charged. But suddenly, the Native Americans "sprang forward like wounded tigers" from the grass.[3] With their darker skin, flowing black hair, and foreign clothing that displayed limbs toned and tanned by a lifetime of hunting, they appeared almost otherworldly to the terrified patriots. Providing "no quarter," the tribes mowed down the patriots in close, gruesome combat.[4] The bloody forty-five-minute clash was described in the following poem:

> Scarce had he utter'd—when Heaven's virge extreme
> Reverberates the bomb's descending star,
> And sounds that mingled laugh,—and shout,—and scream,—
> To freeze the blood in once discordant jar
> Rung to the pealing thunderbolts of war.

Whoop after whoop with rack the ear assail'd;
As if unearthly fiends had burst their bar;
While rapidly the marksman's shot prevail'd:—
And aye, as if for death, some lonely trumpet wail'd.[5]

By nightfall on that horrible day, the fighting had ceased and the patriots were utterly defeated. But while "[d]arkness put an end to the conflict," it only "increased the horrors": according to patriot sources, the American prisoners "were tortured and murdered. At midnight sixteen of them were arranged around a rock, and strongly held by the savages, when a half-breed woman, called Queen Esther, using a tomahawk and club alternately, murdered the whole band."[6]

The victorious Native Americans and Loyalists then "spread over the plains, and with torch, tomahawk, and scalping-knife made it an absolute desolation. Scarcely a dwelling or an outbuilding was left unconsumed; not a field of corn was left standing; not a life was spared that the weapons of the savages could reach."[7] Tales of torture, barbarity, and even cannibalism quickly spread throughout the region.[8] The area's remaining patriots deserted their homes in a panic. One eyewitness wrote, "I never in my life saw such scenes of distress. The river and the roads leading down it were covered with men, women and children, flying for their lives . . . ."[9] The Loyalists and Native Americans spread terror and murder, turning the whole region into a "dark and bloody ground."[10]

This atrocity would not go unanswered. Washington saw the defense of his countrymen's lives and liberty as so crucial that he diverted a quarter of his sorely needed troops to this frontier mission. And to lead this operation, he turned to his quarrelsome underling, Major General John Sullivan.

A vain and ambitious lawyer, Sullivan was not a popular man. The hardworking son of Irish immigrants, he had set up the only law practice in the rural town of Durham, New Hampshire, at the tender age of twenty-four. This did not make him friends, however. He soon became the town pariah on account of his penchant for suing his neighbors.[11]

The brash young man became embroiled in multiple foreclosure disputes, making a small fortune at the expense of the townsfolk. Needless to say, he was rather detested around this agrarian community. Fed up with this obnoxious attorney, his neighbors eventually sued him for "Oppressive Extortive Behavior." But the crafty Sullivan defeated their lawsuits and even dared to countersue for libel. Despite suffering multiple mob attacks, he pressed on and won over thirty-five legal actions. And in doing so, he attained financial success while still in his twenties.[12] But this was not enough. Beneath a black mane and a high brow, his dark eyes were fixated on personal advancement.

The never-satisfied Sullivan next sought power. He slowly rehabilitated his reputation in the region and managed to curry favor with the political elite of New Hampshire. On the eve of the Revolution, Sullivan renounced his support for the Crown and emerged as an ardent patriot. Harnessing New Hampshire's patriotic fervor, he convinced the New Hampshire legislature to appoint him to the Continental Congress. There he sided with the radical Massachusetts representatives' calls for liberty and made known his eagerness for armed resistance. For his ardent patriotism and militant background, he was awarded an officer's commission in the new Continental Army. The young lawyer relished the fight.

Washington acknowledged that Sullivan was "active, spirited, and Zealously attach'd to the Cause," but noted that his performance in leading troops was mixed.[13] Sullivan's dearth of military accomplishment would not temper his ambition, however. Ever the argumentative attorney, he quarreled with Washington and Congress over promotions. Notwithstanding his mediocre performance, he took great umbrage at the fact that he was not granted a higher rank. At one point, Washington became so exasperated with Sullivan's "unjustifiable Suspicions" of being wronged that he told him, "No other officer of rank in the whole army has so often conceived himself neglected, slighted and ill-treated as you have done, and none I am sure has had less cause than yourself to entertain such ideas."[14] So when it came time for Washington to send one of his officers far out into the wilderness, he sent the pesky Sullivan.

Eager to prove himself and win a promotion, Sullivan led 5,000 men on Washington's scorched-earth campaign against the tribes. Washington had ordered him, "you will not by any means, listen to any overture of peace before the total ruin of their settlements is effected."[15] Thus, the fighting Irishman began his march, beating back the tribes and destroying their villages throughout the summer of 1779. At first, Sullivan's mission went swimmingly—he soon boasted to Washington that he had destroyed forty towns and burned their surrounding farmlands.[16] But, as usual, Sullivan eventually ran into trouble. More precisely, he got lost.

Sullivan was seeking the Seneca capital, Genesee Castle. Located in a remote region in northwestern New York State, Genesee was a "beautifully situated" village of 128 homes, "mostly large and elegant." It was "encircled with a clear flat, which extended for a number of miles, where the most extensive fields of corn waving, and every kind of vegetable that can be conceived."[17] Washington wanted this bountiful haven wiped off the map, but Sullivan had to find it first.

Arguing with his guides over Genesee Castle's location, Sullivan dispatched a scouting party. They eventually found the capital, but it was six miles farther away than Sullivan's team realized, resulting in a delay that the scouts could not afford. As the sun rose through the clouds on that raw September morning, they found themselves deep in hostile territory without the cover of darkness. Proceeding anxiously back towards Sullivan's camp, the thirty American scouts were intercepted by a force of four hundred Native Americans and Loyalists.[18] The vastly outnumbered patriots fired valiantly from a grove of trees, but were quickly overwhelmed.

The two leading American scouts were taken prisoner, stripped naked, and tied to a hardy young oak.

In a vengeful rage, the Native Americans inflicted on them gruesome "malice & savage barbarity," some of it "too shocking to relate."[19] According to multiple patriot accounts (which did tend to demonize the tribes), the captors were careful to keep the men alive "in order to heighten [their] misery & satisfy their revenge," as they whipped them, tore off their fingernails, stabbed them with spears, cut out their tongues, and plucked out their eyes.[20] They then allegedly took special care to skin one man's genitals, partially detach them, and leave them hanging from his body. After suffering "other tortures which decency will not permit . . . mention," the captives finally found relief only in their beheadings.[21] Sullivan's troops arrived later that day to find pieces of their fellow patriots scattered around the "Torture Tree."

Horrified and outraged, they razed Genesee Castle. Although the oak survived, little else did—the Americans burned down the whole village and all the surrounding farms they could find. Then they pressed on with their mission of annihilation, leaving a trail of "devastation, destruction, flames and death."[22] They searched the whole region for Native American settlements, tracing "[e]very creek and river," to ensure that there was "not a single town left."[23] After his force had destroyed an estimated fifty towns, including 1,200 homes,[24] Sullivan reported back to the Continental Army that he had completed Washington's "extermination of the original lords of this vast empire."[25]

Washington had effectively answered the Native American threat. This episode seemingly shows him as a ruthless commander who would do anything to win the war, but that was not the case. To the contrary, he highly valued individuals' rights—as long as those individuals were American. The "Native American" peoples were not viewed as "American." (Indeed, the term "Native American" would not be coined until centuries later.) Washington saw these tribes as a "cruel and bloodthirsty enemy" that brutally massacred American settlers and destroyed their property.[26] And so Washington annihilated them.

To Washington, the Native American attacks were not just another horror of war; they were a grave affront, and as commander in chief, he had a duty to counter it. Ardent in his belief in the sanctity of American rights, he would defend his countrymen with a vengeance.

27

Band of Brethren

As commander, Washington saw himself as the guardian of American liberty; but, on the flip side of the coin, he had far less respect for his enemies' liberty. Washington treated men quite differently depending on their nationality.

During the Revolutionary War, nationality was a tricky and somewhat fluid notion. For the first year of the war—from the Battle of Lexington to the start of the disastrous New York campaign—the "Americans" were technically British subjects. It was not until the Continental Congress issued the Declaration of Independence on July 4, 1776, that the Americans formally renounced their place within the British Empire. At that point, Americans would no longer be royal "subjects"; instead, they became "citizens."

The notion of citizenship was still a developing one, but it had a long history. The concept harks back to the ancient Greek city-states, particularly democratic Athens. In the fourth century B.C., Aristotle defined a citizen as "he who has the power to take part in the deliberative or judicial administration of any state."[1] Of course, this privilege was restricted to Greek male property owners.

Such men had the right to vote and to hold office, but with these rights came duties: to pay taxes, serve in the military, and participate in their own self-governance. This meant not merely voting, typically conducted by a show of arms "naked to the shoulder,"[2] but also being present, active, and vocal in the life of the city. In fact, the Greeks had a term for those who did not actively participate in their democracy: *idiotai*.[3]

The Romans adopted a similar concept of citizenship, calling it *civitas*. Under the Roman Empire, citizenship grew more expansive, guaranteeing rights and protections of law. But many of these notions were lost as Rome disintegrated.

During Europe's medieval era from the fifth to the fifteenth century, a sense of citizenship existed in some free cities, but the concept of national citizenship was practically nonexistent.[4] Instead, society revolved more around individuals' feudal obligations to the nobles who controlled the land on which they worked. Ordinary people were "subjects" of a ruler and had few rights.[5]

In the eighteenth century, the Western political world still clung to trappings of a sovereign-subject relationship. The members of the English king's community were regarded as dependents who were afforded defense against outside aggressors in return for unwavering loyalty to the Crown. Under this tradition inherited by the American colonists, there was a general sense that there should be a distinction between outsiders, to whom the king owed nothing, and the king's subjects, who had a right to protection.

Analogized to the bond between parent and child, this king-subject relationship was one in which the subject held a "natural" allegiance to the king. This relationship was deemed immutable: the subject owed "lasting obedience to his natural superior, the king."[6] The Americans, however, bristled against this notion of perpetual allegiance.[7] They rejected the perception of the king as a father figure to whom they owed a natural, unending loyalty. Instead, they developed the idea that the community owed allegiance only insofar as the government protected their rights. And King George III, along with Parliament, was not protecting theirs.

Inspired by the revival of classical political philosophy that began in the Renaissance, the Americans embraced the relatively radical idea of citizenship. They sought to emulate ancient Greek democracy and the Roman Republic and likewise empower the people to participate in all aspects of government. However, just as in ancient Greece, not all types of people were considered citizens. The backbone of the new American republic was to be white men, while slaves and Native Americans were excluded. Moreover, white women were disfranchised citizens who could not vote or hold office.[8] Instead, their role was to raise sons with the civic virtue required to govern the nation.

The white, male American citizens owed their allegiance not to some monarch, as "subjects" did, but to each other.[9] The citizens of the United States were to be their own masters and, together, to strive for the betterment of their country. A land of *idiotai* was to be avoided at all costs. Thus, American citizens were expected to fulfill their civic duties, which included remaining informed and actively improving their republic. Self-government meant hard work, but along with these duties came privileges.

In some respects, American citizenship was a club. One congressman characterized the American citizenry as a "band of brethren, united to each other by the strongest ties, . . . attached to the same principles of government, very similar in their manners and customs."[10] Being a part of this band provided certain perks: citizens were guaranteed their natural right to "life, liberty, and property."[11] It was the government's duty to protect these rights, and Washington, as commander in chief, served as the defender of citizens' rights in wartime.

This club of citizenship was so unaccustomed at the time that Thomas Jefferson, in an early draft of the Declaration of Independence, referred to the American people as "subjects." But he remedied this mistake with zeal. While he simply crossed out other errors in the draft, "subjects" was the only word that he obliterated with the furious strokes of his pen.[12] He was so intent on removing that word because it signaled loyalty to King George III. The Americans wished to renounce their allegiance to the British Crown and declare themselves citizens of the new United States of America. With the Declaration of Independence, the American people collectively naturalized everyone living in the states (except those of African descent and Native Americans) and automatically made them United States citizens.[13]

The Declaration basically formalized the prevailing notion that "Americans" were those who had lived in the colonies prior to the outbreak of war. In keeping with the general xenophobia common at the time, those who had recently emigrated from Britain were often viewed with suspicion, however. For example, Charles Lee was an Englishman who had moved to America only three years before the war. Even though his military qualifications were superior to those of the Virginia-born Washington, his relatively recent arrival—along with his many other faults—made Lee a less desirable candidate for commander in chief.[14] But while newcomers were often distrusted, they were still generally considered Americans. Surprisingly, the same largely held true for Loyalists.

Not even a clear majority of white males living in the United States actively supported the Revolution at the time. About 40 to 45 percent of them were active patriots, while approximately the same numbers where indifferent or uncommitted. The final 15 to 20 percent supported the British as Loyalists.[15] This posed a dilemma for the Americans: quashing their fellow Americans' rights ran afoul of their republican principles, but suppressing opposition to the Revolution was vital to the very survival of the new nation. With an estimated 50,000 Loyalists joining the British to fight against the patriots, these Tories were a serious threat.[16]

They were hated. Likening them to "Spiders, Toads, [and] Snakes," John Adams colorfully described them as "the most despicable Animal in Creation."[17] But at the same time, abusing them would violate the Americans' own republican principles. While there was disagreement on the point, many Americans believed that Congress and the state governments acted on behalf of *all* the American people, including the unpatriotic ones. To many patriots, the Loyalists were indeed Americans.[18] Rather than treat them as British subjects, as many of them desired to remain, such patriots instead considered them a dissenting minority within the larger American society.[19] And that minority was expected to obey the patriotic will of their neighbors. When they did not, they would be punished.[20]

Some patriots certainly made life difficult for Loyalists—for while Washington saw American rights as sacrosanct, others were not as principled. Though the "American revolutionists were [typically] not bloody-minded men" and the country never suffered a reign of terror on par with the mass murders perpetrated during other wars, there was nevertheless much violence and destruction. Patriot mobs looted Tory homes, taking valuables and burning other possessions. As discussed in Part II, patriotic mobs forced Loyalists to "ride the rails," endure gruesome spickettings, and face tar and featherings.[21] They whipped Loyalists, or forced them to sit on hot coals and cut off ears.[22] They stripped many Loyalists of their freedom and even their lives. This was also a civil war, after all.

"The division among the people is much greater than I imagined," wrote Nathanael Greene, "and the Whigs [patriots] and Tories persecute each other, with little less than savage fury. There is nothing but murders and devastation in every quarter."[23] The threat of violence and destruction was so palpable that even many of the bravest Loyalists backed down or fled from patriot wrath. One such man, ironically, was rather friendly with Washington.

Reverend Jonathan Boucher was a gifted orator and outspoken critic of the Revolution. Although he had served as Washington's stepson's teacher and enjoyed cordial relations with the great patriot, his loyalties remained with Britain. Cutting an imposing figure, this argumentative gentleman possessed a prominent widow's peak and confident eyes that blazed from his pulpit. From his strong jaw spewed fiery sermons that condemned the revolutionaries. This made Boucher some powerful enemies, and he took to preaching with loaded pistols under the cushions on his chair in church.

This unfinished—and unflattering—portrait by Gilbert Stuart ironically came to be the most famous depiction of Washington. Martha Washington criticized it as not a "true resemblance." *Photograph © 2013 Museum of Fine Arts, Boston; National Portrait Gallery, Smithsonian Institution / Art Resource, NY*

Martha and George Washington entertained a great many visitors at their grand Mount Vernon estate beside the Potomac. In fact, the visitors became so frequent that George resorted to removing signage in order to confuse would-be houseguests. *Library of Congress, Prints & Photographs Division, LC-DIG-pga-01228*

This print depicts Independence Hall at the time of the signing of the Declaration of Independence in 1776. This building served as the principle seat of government, except for periods when Congress was forced by the advancing British forces to evacuate. With the postwar government failing, Washington and other patriot leaders returned in 1787 for the Constitutional Convention. *Library of Congress, Prints & Photographs Division, LC-DIG-pga-04142*

With the help of his assistants, Washington produced an amazing 140,000 documents during the Revolutionary War. Foreseeing his letters' value to posterity, he checked virtually all of the scribes' work and held each letter to exacting standards. He spent his nights documenting his actions and explaining to Congress what was needed to conduct the war. This image of his inaugural address depicts Washington's own fine penmanship. *National Archives (Records of the U.S. Senate)*

Washington was born into a family of relatively modest means but worked (and married) his way into wealth. This depiction of Washington as a child is titled "Father, I cannot tell a lie: I cut the tree," and perpetuates the cherry tree myth. Washington indeed told a great many lies, and his knack for deception enabled the United States to outwit the British and win the war. *Library of Congress, Prints & Photographs Division, LC-DIG-pga-02152*

The Sons of Liberty punish a Loyalist for his opposition to the Revolution. The practice of "tarring and feathering" had originated in 1189 with Richard the Lionheart during the Crusades, but was not used extensively until the colonists revived it during their revolt against Britain. *National Archives photo no. 148-GW-436 (The George Washington Bicentennial Commission)*

Throwing caution to the wind, Ethan Allen launches a daring surprise attack on Fort Ticonderoga in May 1775. The sleeping British did not even have time to dress, let alone put up a fight. *National Archives photo no. 111-SC-94758 (Signal Corps Photographs of American Military Activity)*

This portrait depicts Benjamin Franklin, John Adams, and Thomas Jefferson poring over a draft of the Declaration of Independence at Jefferson's lodgings in Philadelphia in June 1776. In an early draft, Jefferson referred to the American people as "subjects." While he simply crossed out other errors in the draft, this was the only word that he obliterated with furious strokes of his pen. The American people were no longer "subjects" of any king. *Library of Congress, Prints & Photographs Division, LC-USZC4-9904*

George Washington organizes a masterful secret retreat from Long Island during a violent storm in August 1776. According to one soldier's diary, the troops, "strictly enjoined not to speak, or even cough," silently filed into the boats, and New England fishermen used their unique skill set to ferry them to safety in Manhattan. *National Archives photo no. 148-GW-174 (The George Washington Bicentennial Commission)*

During that winter of 1777–1778 at Valley Forge, Washington pleaded with Congress for food, clothing, and supplies, writing, "I am now convinced, beyond a Doubt that unless some great and capital change suddenly takes place in that line, this Army must inevitably be reduced to one or other of these three things. Starve, dissolve, or disperse, in order to obtain subsistence." *National Archives photo no. 148-GW-436 (The George Washington Bicentennial Commission)*

Sloppy in appearance and crude in manner, Charles Lee was reputed to have a romantic life "of the transient kind." A military genius who resented serving under Washington, he got along better with his pack of dogs than he did with most people. *Library of Congress, Prints & Photographs Division, LC-USZ62-3617*

"Parade with us, my brave fellows!" Washington shouts as he leads the charge at Princeton in January 1777. With his hat in hand, he rode ahead on his horse, yelling, "There is but a handful of the enemy, and we will have them directly." Despite being caught in the crossfire, Washington emerged unscathed as he had done time and again. He believed that a divine Providence protected him. *National Archives photo no. 148-GW-335 (The George Washington Bicentennial Commission)*

American women were crucial to winning the Revolutionary War, with some even jumping into battle. When John Adams wrote his wife of the Continental Army's defeats, Abigail confidently declared that if Washington's troops were overrun, the British forces would then be compelled to fight "a race of Amazons in America." *National Archives photo no. 148-GW-436 (The George Washington Bicentennial Commission)*

Alexander Hamilton served as Washington's shrewd right-hand man and one of his closest confidants during the war. After the United States' victory, he ardently advocated a more centralized nation. *National Archives photo no. 148-GW-436 (The George Washington Bicentennial Commission)*

A mere five feet tall and 120 pounds, James Madison was an intellectual giant and a driving force behind the drafting of the Constitution. He declared that creating even a "limited monarchy . . . was out of the question" and used his masterful political skills to help form the new republican government. *Library of Congress, Prints & Photographs Division, LC-DIG-ppmsca-19166*

The wily Benjamin Franklin used his guile to charm the French court—particularly the female contingent. Through parties and chess games, he persuaded the French to send aid to the American cause and eventually declare war on Britain. As the war wound down, he then infuriated the French by working with John Adams and John Jay to outmaneuver them in the peace process. *Library of Congress, Prints & Photographs Division, LC-DIG-pga-01591*

One Sunday, Boucher faced a mob of two hundred patriots blocking his way to the pulpit. The mob's leader forbade him to give his sermon, but to the dauntless reverend "there was but one way by which they could keep me out of it, and that was by taking away my life." With his sermon in one hand and a pistol in the other, Boucher obstinately pressed on towards the altar. He was saved only because a friend threw his arms around him and warned that twenty men were under orders to fire the moment he reached the pulpit.[24] Like many Loyalists, Boucher fled the country.

Many patriots in Congress and among state authorities regarded such "lawless mobs" as an effective means of suppressing the Loyalists. In fact, the New York Provincial Congress even ordered that the pitch and tar "necessary for the public use and public safety" be made available.[25] While mob action lacked any strict legal backing, it was often met with a wink and a nod from the authorities. And Washington often did not see it as his place to stop the mobs, since he did not want the military to interfere in matters sanctioned by the civil authorities, if only implicitly. For example, as related in Part II, Washington scolded Old Put for interrupting the New York City patriots' abuse of the Tories.

Congress was slow to develop a formal system for suppressing the Loyalists. They began gingerly by striking at the citizens' wallets. Couching their actions in moral terms, Congress held that anyone "so lost in virtue and regard for his country" that he refused to accept the (quickly devaluing) bills of credit that Congress used to finance the war would be treated as an enemy and therefore "precluded from all trade or intercourse" with other Americans.[26] This was akin to imposing an embargo on their own people. When this relatively gentle action did not seem effective in quelling the Loyalist threat, Congress gradually invented harsher measures.

Next, Congress recommended that local authorities disarm all those who were "notoriously disaffected to the cause of America, or who have not associated, and shall refuse to associate, to defend, by arms, these United Colonies, against the hostile attempts of the British fleets and armies; . . . ."[27] This was another attack on property, but the patriots could not allow the Tories to keep their weapons. Guns in the hands of Loyalists had proven to be too great a danger to the revolutionary cause. And when Washington uncovered a potentially disastrous Loyalist plot, Congress realized that its legal weaponry against the Loyalists needed even more bite.

28

Poison & Peas

One Loyalist scheme was feared to be such an elaborate conspiracy that it "would have made America tremble, and been as fatal a stroke" to the Revolution had it been carried out. As one patriot reported, the plan was "to have murdered, with trembling heart I say it, the best man on earth, Gen. Washington."[1] Although the facts were never fully uncovered, shocking rumors implicated high-ranking New York politicians, musicians in the Continental Army, and even Washington's own bodyguards.

Like any good story, this tale of intrigue began with a mysterious woman. One warm June afternoon in 1776, she insisted on speaking privately with the commander. Taking her aside, the general learned of an "infernal plot": the woman claimed to have witnessed one of Washington's bodyguards poisoning his peas for that evening's dinner![2]

According to one account, the unflappable Washington reacted calmly and decisively: he threw the peas into the yard, where some unlucky hungry chickens swiftly met their demise.[3] Convinced that the woman's revelation was true, he then pondered his next move. A master of espionage, Washington knew it was imperative that he act with secrecy so as not to lose the element of surprise. He quietly called a meeting among his trusted friends and members of the New York Provincial Congress. They set up a twenty-four-hour guard, secured civilian approval to strike against the Loyalist suspects, and then patiently prepared to act.

On a night soon thereafter, Washington went to bed at his usual hour, but then arose at two in the morning. He soothingly told Martha—who was visiting him at his headquarters, as she often did—to "make herself easy, and go to sleep." He told her that he was merely "a going, with some of the Provincial Congress, to order some Tories seized."[4] But he was really going on an all-night raid to unravel a plot against his life.

Carrying lanterns and "proper instruments to break open houses," Washington and a few select men set out to apprehend the conspirators. By sunrise, they had arrested forty men, including several merchants, five of Washington's bodyguards, and even the mayor of New York City. Washington soon gained confessions from various members of this motley crew and discovered that they had planned to "assassinate the General, and as many of the superior officers as they could, and to blow up the [Americans' ammunition] upon appearance of the enemy's fleet, and to go off in boats prepared for that purpose to join the enemy."[5] Had such a plot been accomplished, it would very likely have ended the Revolution.

As Washington dug deeper, the backstory unfolded. The mastermind of the plot was the royal governor of New York, William Tryon. With a double chin to match his ill-defined cheeks, Tryon was "haughty and unfeeling in temper, fond of show and of absolute power."[6] And he astutely used his military and aristocratic social connections to gain that power. Securing a royal appointment as governor of New York, he reveled in the role. He lavished tax dollars on ostentatious displays of wealth and grandeur as he entertained New York's elite. But when war broke out, the patriots became rather unruly constituents. It was "very probable," wrote Tryon, that he might be "taken prisoner, as a state Hostage, or obliged to retire on board one of His Majesty's Ships of War to avoid the insolence of an inflamed mob."[7] This proved prophetic.

Soon after the outbreak of war, the Continental Congress had recommended that the states arrest all royal officers bold enough to remain in the colonies. The New York Provincial Congress was not yet willing to follow through on that suggestion, but Tryon considered it wise to sneak off to the safety of the British gunships sitting around New York City. Though exiled in effect, this shrewd and cunning man was still dangerous.

Washington feared that Tryon might use his considerable influence to encourage more Loyalist New Yorkers to fight against the patriots. The commander ordered one of his officers to "Keep a watchful Eye upon Governor Tryon, and if you find him directly or indirectly, attempting any Measures inimical to the common Cause, use every Means in your Power to frustrate his Designs [and] if forcible Measures are judged necessary, . . . I should have no Difficulty in ordering of it, if the Continental Congress was not sitting."[8] And Washington's wariness was well founded. Tryon indeed was eager to suppress the patriots and regain his seat of power. To do his bidding, he soon called upon the Loyalist whom he had appointed as mayor of New York City, David Mathews.

The "obnoxious" Mathews was a money-hungry attorney who seized the chance to cash in on Tryon's scheme.[9] With a wife and ten children, he certainly had many mouths to feed. And he boldly remained with them in his home within American lines around New York City, even as Washington's forces swarmed around it.[10] Although Washington and others suspected his Loyalist leanings, they respected Mathews's rights as an American. He used this respect against them and began to employ his sanctuary within the American lines to liaise with other undercover agents. Mathews readily recruited Loyalists and even convinced some patriots to defect with the lure of Tryon's British pounds—of which he would presumably take a cut, of course. Mathews and his henchmen were rumored to have persuaded an astonishing seven hundred patriots to defect to the British side.[11] One such defector was Washington's bodyguard Thomas Hickey.

Hickey was a rascal who had previously deserted the British Army. At five foot six, he was sturdily built and had a complexion that was rather dark for an Irishman.[12] Having cultivated a good reputation while residing in Wethersfield, Connecticut, he was selected to join Washington's newly formed personal guard. Although this trusted position was quite honorable, Hickey was looking for something more lucrative. He decided to moonlight for a counterfeiting ring.

The currency of the era employed few security measures. The bills did not have especially complicated designs or colors nor did they use special ink. In fact, all a counterfeiter needed was an ordinary printing press and a certain kind of paper, which was not too difficult to come by. One just needed to know the right press operators.[13]

Unsurprisingly, counterfeiting was somewhat common. But as the war sparked inflation, the patriots made a concerted effort to capture the "unpatriotic" counterfeiting rings. The authorities kept a watchful eye out for people asking the wrong questions or passing inordinate quantities of bills. The not-so-bright Hickey drew such attention.[14] He was caught passing counterfeit bills and thrown into jail. For this relatively minor offense, he would likely have received only a mild punishment, but Hickey's wretched fate would be sealed by his big mouth.

While in prison, Hickey bragged to another inmate about his involvement in the Loyalist conspiracy. He boasted of the plot against Washington and additional plans to have moles within American forces turn their guns against their compatriots in the middle of battle.[15] Upon overhearing this, a fellow prisoner ran to the authorities in hopes of securing his own release. Hickey was interrogated at once and the plot unraveled. The conspirators swiftly divulged the names of others in the ring as well as incriminating details. One conspirator swore he had received 100 British pounds towards the plot from Mathews.[16] This information corroborated the patriots' other intelligence and set in motion the events that led to Washington's late-night raid.

That night, Washington rounded up Mathews and Hickey's other co-conspirators from both inside and outside the army's ranks. Next he turned to exacting justice. But he trod carefully, since he was dealing with American citizens. While he held great authority to decide the fate of foreigners, Americans were a different story. Here, he deferred to the civil authorities' mandates, which instructed him to deal with the conspirators differently based upon whether they were soldiers or not.

Congress had provided for the military to deal with its own men through the congressionally authorized procedures of courts-martial. And so with congressional backing, Washington put Hickey on trial in front of his fellow soldiers, on charges of "exciting and joining in a mutiny and sedition, and of treacherously corresponding with, inlisting among, and receiving pay from the enemies of the United American Colonies."[17] He was prosecuted not merely for being a Loyalist, but for violating his obligations as a soldier.

In his own defense, the rascal argued that he merely pretended to be part of the plot in order to collect the money. But the American soldiers deciding his fate were unconvinced, to say the least. After hearing multiple witnesses condemn him, they found him guilty of treason.

Washington and the patriots were intent on making an example of this treacherous scoundrel with a public hanging. Thus, they quickly sentenced Hickey to death and Washington ordered that every brigade witness his fate as "a warning to every soldier in the army."[18] Hickey walked unrepentantly to the gallows and refused any clergy "on the grounds that all of them were cut-throats."[19] In addition to the army, virtually all of New York City, around 20,000 people, turned out to watch the spectacle in an open field in southern Manhattan at eleven in the morning on June 28, 1776.[20] For many people, this was prime—if morbid—entertainment.

Hickey attempted to remain stoic and not give the heckling crowds much of a show. But as the scratching noose tightened around his trembling neck, he momentarily lost his nerve and a "torrent of tears flowed over his face."[21] Then he promptly regained his composure and his defiant bearing.

A dour Washington strangely seized this occasion to give a moral lecture to his troops, telling them, "in order to avoid these crimes, the most certain method is to keep out of the temptation of them and particularly to avoid lewd women who, by the dying breath of the poor criminal, first led him into practices which ended in an untimely and ignominious death."[22] Whether New York City's prostitutes led to Hickey's money problems or a more general degradation of character is unclear. In any case, Hickey had become the first American to be hanged in the name of the Revolution.[23]

His nonmilitary co-conspirators met with a happier fate. As commander in chief, Washington did not see himself as having the right to punish private citizens. Instead, he left the fates of the civilian conspirators largely to the discretion of the civil authorities.[24]

While Tryon sat smugly aboard a British ship just outside the Americans' grasp, his underlings did not enjoy the benefits of Britain's naval supremacy. After Washington arrested David Mathews by order of a committee of the New York Provincial Congress, he then scoured the mayor's house for evidence. Washington did not ransack the American's property by virtue of his broad military powers, but rather as a servant of the civilian who was executing the Provincial Congress's order. This was important to Washington because he firmly believed that the military lacked the right to molest Americans or their property. He was fighting for the American citizens' liberty, and he was not about to allow the military to trample it. Citizens had rights, which should be stripped only by the civil authorities. Those authorities threw Mathews in jail.

As a civilian American, Mathews was a problem for the patriots, however. While the early congressional resolution had deemed it appropriate for Washington to drag the soldier, Hickey, before a court-martial and hang him for violating his duties as a soldier, the Americans were still grappling over the appropriate treatment of someone such as Mathews. He was not a soldier and could therefore not be tried for violating military duties as Hickey was.

News of the plot—in its various incarnations—helped to rally public opinion against the Loyalists. No longer would the patriots merely preclude Loyalists from trade or confiscate their guns. In June 1776, Congress passed a resolution that would transform disaffection from the patriot cause into treason. Recommending that the colonial legislatures pass measures against treason, Congress resolved:

> That all persons residing within any of the United Colonies, and deriving protection from the laws of the same, owe allegiance to the said laws . . . .
>
> That all persons, members of, or owing allegiance to any of the United Colonies, as before described, who shall levy war against any of the said colonies within the same, or be adherent to the king of Great Britain, or other enemies of the said colonies, or any of them, within the same, giving to him or them aid and comfort, are guilty of treason against such colony.[25]

As the colonies followed up with their own legislation, it became a crime for civilians to resist the Revolution. Although Congress would make exceptions later in the war for spies such as Joshua Hett Smith, as discussed in Part IV, civilians were generally referred to civilian trials.[26]

The Americans had to sort this all out before they could properly deal with Mathews. As a civilian citizen, he deserved a high burden of proof. But since Washington found nothing incriminating in his house, the Americans lacked direct evidence of his complicity. Doubting that the witnesses alone would be enough to condemn Mathews, as in the case of Hickey, the cautious American authorities held him in jail while they mulled their next step. But the wily Mathews would not rot for too long.

Mathews spent his months in prison complaining about his treatment and plotting his escape. Not about to leave his fate to the American "Insurgents," he bribed his Connecticut guards with 150 pounds sterling.

They let him go, and he raced back to British-occupied New York City.[27] He was frustratingly outside the patriots' grasp, but they took some solace when the New York Provincial Congress labeled him a traitor and seized his two homes and 26,000 acres of land.

This episode is illustrative of Washington's approach to American lives and property: he did what he was told by the civil authorities. While he possessed authority over war tactics, the treatment of foreign prisoners, and even foreigners' trials, the same was not true for American citizens. He served as their protector and, as such, he would not deprive them of due process or seize property without the consent of civil authorities. The legislatures and civil courts referred their fellow Americans to courts-martial, confiscated their property, executed them, and did a host of other nasty things to them. But Washington let the civilian leaders make those decisions.

Neither Mathews nor Tryon was ever captured, and both lived out the rest of their lives in Britain. The accounts of their plot mutated as the stories spread throughout the colonies. Some believed that there were no poisoned peas and that the Loyalists wanted instead to take Washington alive. This kidnapping rumor was bolstered by Mathews's later admission that he had "formed a Plan for the taking Mr Washington & his Guard Prisoners."[28] Other gossips denied that there was ever a plot against Washington at all, pointing to the fact that the plot was not included in Hickey's official trial documentation. But still others saw this absence merely as proof of a patriot cover-up meant to prevent widespread alarm.[29] There was much debate about the specifics as the tales of treachery swirled through America's camps and towns. While the true facts about the peas or the kidnapping were never definitively known, the talk was more crucial than the specifics. Whatever form the rumors took, they helped to harden the patriots' resolve against their Loyalist neighbors.

29

America's Defender

A merican courts were soon flooded with prosecutions for treason as hundreds of Loyalists were indicted for the new crime. They were imprisoned or forcibly relocated and stripped of their property.[1] The British denounced these actions as

> Arbitrary Imprisonments, Confiscation of Property, Persecu-
> tion and Torture, unprecedented in the Inquisitions of the
> Romish Church . . . inflicted by Assemblies and Committees,
> who dare to profess themselves Friends of Liberty, upon the
> most quiet Subject without Distinction of Age or Sex, for the
> sole Crime, often the sole Suspicion, of having adhered in
> Principle to the [British] Government under which they were
> born, and to which, by every Tie divine and human, they owe
> Allegiance.[2]

The Loyalists who were tried in civil courts generally fared better than those left to the whims of mobs, however, since they escaped with their lives—usually.

Following the liberation of Philadelphia in 1778, for example, mobs exacted revenge upon those who had supported the brutal occupation of their capital city. Among these Loyalists, 490 were formally prosecuted in court. Nearly all of their property was confiscated and several were hanged for aiding the British.[3] But this ratio is telling: relatively few Loyalists throughout the colonies were executed under official sentence. The revolutionaries generally kept their bloodlust in check and reserved the ultimate punishment for the most egregious cases. Court-ordered executions were the exception rather than the rule.[4]

The American courts took "great pains to observe procedural safeguards once the formal machinery of justice was called into play."[5] While treasonous, the Loyalists were often viewed as citizens, after all. Thus many patriots adopted the philosophy that the "Law should be strictly adhered to, severity exercised, but the doors of mercy should never be shut."[6] As a result, convictions were somewhat rare and pardons for those few convicted were surprisingly common. Rather than serve time or face the gallows, many Loyalists were given the option of joining Washington's army—a sentence which Washington did not particularly care for due to its obvious impact on morale and discipline.[7] But when it came to his fellow Americans, he abided by the politicians' and judges' directives, however irksome they might be.

Punishing Americans was the civil authorities' prerogative, as Congress made very clear. At the outset of the war, they resolved that "no man in these colonies, charged with being a tory, or unfriendly to the cause of American liberty, be injured in his person or property, or in any manner whatever disturbed," except by authorization from civilian politicians.[8] While the civil authorities could sanction Loyalists and strip them of rights, Washington did not see himself as having the power to do so. As in the cases of Joshua Hett Smith, David Mathews, and Thomas Hickey, he referred Americans to the civil courts whenever possible and tried citizens by congressionally defined courts-martial when explicitly authorized to do so. Throughout the war, he repeatedly said that he "would rather have them punished agreeable to the Civil than by military law."[9] This included all Americans—even the traitorous ones.

Washington "strenuously discouraged patriot groups from taking the law into their own hands and avoiding the judicial process" against the Tories.[10] He had many Loyalist friends and understood that Americans could not all be forced to have the same viewpoint. Since his youth, he had maintained a close relationship with the Fairfax family, one of the most powerful British noble families in Virginia, and many of its members were ardent Loyalists. Washington exchanged "heated, although polite" letters with them, debating the patriotic cause but exhibiting his tolerance of deep political disagreement among Americans.[11] Militant as he was, Washington was not one to bring a sword to a civilized debate.

In another example of his respect for Tories' safety, Washington received a request from a Loyalist, Judge Andrew Elliot. An avowed enemy of Washington's cause, accused of being a "rapacious, dissolute, overbearing fraud," Elliot nevertheless had the nerve to ask that the commander check in on his daughter, herself married to a Loyalist.[12] Washington graciously obliged, writing, "I shall be happy in occasions of rendering her any service which may be in my power."[13] Nonmilitant Loyalists deserved the same protection that Washington attempted to provide all Americans. He assured Elliot "that the most perfect regularity and good Order prevail in this City, and that every description of People find themselves under the protection of the Laws of the State."[14]

Washington's tolerance was particularly notable when he faced Loyalists taking up arms against him. Rather than quickly crushing them, he asked the governor of Connecticut, "Would it not be prudent to seize those tories who have been, are and we know will be active against us? Why should persons who are preying upon the vitals of their country be suffered to stalk about while we know they will do us every mischief in their power?"[15] After consulting with Connecticut authorities, he ordered his men "to seize upon such persons as held commissions under the crown and were acting as . . . enemies to their country and hold them hostage."[16] This was yet another sign of restraint—he limited his arrests to royally commissioned officials. He made sure to exclude private individuals, no matter how rabidly pro-Britain they might be, since he did not see it as part of the military commander's role to seize them. He was not a complete saint, however, for he warned, "the day is not far off when they will meet with this or a worse fate if there is not a considerable reformation in their conduct."[17] And on one occasion, Washington may have violated his own principles.

Thomas Shanks was a sticky-fingered ensign of Pennsylvania's 10th Regiment.[18] This rascal attempted to steal two pairs of shoes from his lieutenant, perhaps to protect his feet from the autumn chill of 1777.[19] He proved a lousy thief, however. He was caught and promptly cashiered from the army, since Washington would brook no thievery in his ranks. But Shanks would not merely go home after his disgraceful discharge. Instead, he went over to the enemy. Unfortunately for him, he proved to be as lousy a spy as he had been a thief.

In the late spring of 1778, the British devised a plan to smuggle Shanks back inside American lines to spy on Washington. The plot quickly unraveled when a redcoat deserter informed the Americans of Shanks's intelligence activities. This British grenadier, Sergeant William Sutherland, testified that he was meant to lead Shanks through the British lines so he could return to the American base. After they got past the British defenses and parted ways, however, Sutherland took a shortcut to beat Shanks to the Americans' camp and informed them of the conspiracy.[20] For his trouble, Washington gave Sutherland 60 pounds—blood money.[21]

When the obtuse spy arrived at the camp, the Americans confronted him with the grenadier's testimony. It was apparently enough to make him crack: under intense interrogation, Shanks confessed to spying. And with that, Washington decided to "avoid the formality of a regular trial," reasoning that it "ought to be dispensed with" in a case like this one. Instead, he would have a military commission examine Shanks, "and if his guilt is clear, his punishment will be very summary."[22] Washington had previously reserved this kind of summary treatment for noncitizens.

Even though Washington was careful to protect Americans' right to due process, this time he strayed. A seemingly illegal military commission was assembled to try a citizen. The panel of soldiers heard from the British grenadier as well as Shanks's apprehenders. Taking Shanks's own admission into account, they deemed him a spy by a vote of 10 to 4. Per Washington's request, his officers—by a slim 8 to 6 margin—voted to make Shanks "a proper subject for an example" and ordered that he be hanged.[23]

On Washington's terse instruction that Shanks "be hanged tomorrow morning at Guard mounting at some convenient Place," the soldier was brought to the gallows the next day.[24] "Muffled drums beat, fifes wailed the death march," and excited spectators looked on as Shanks solemnly neared his wretched fate.[25] He was unceremoniously hanged, and his name would fade back into obscurity.

Washington had denied due process to an American. It was quite possible that he skipped a congressionally mandated court-martial because he categorized Shanks as a mutinous soldier, or he believed that the traitor's confession made a full trial superfluous, or perhaps Washington received undocumented authorization from Congress to employ the military commission. In any case, this was the exception rather than the rule.[26] Washington generally remained a staunch defender of Americans' right to be prosecuted according to the procedures established by civil authorities. He was careful to protect the lives and liberty of Americans, however treacherous they may have been.

30

License to Plunder

While Washington and the courts largely defended Americans' lives and liberty, they were less respectful of the Tories' property. As congressional and state coffers were rapidly depleted, many patriots eyed the Loyalists' vast wealth as a means to pay for the war, which had driven the nation to the brink of bankruptcy.

Lacking taxation powers, Congress attempted to print more currency to satisfy its obligations. As a result, the Continental became nearly worthless and the populace became unable to afford even the basic necessities. "America has much more to fear from the effects of the large quantities of paper money than from the operations of [the British]," wrote one patriot in a letter to his father. He recounted the privation suffered by the people due to what he estimated to be a 200 percent increase in prices over a short time. A pair of boots cost him $21 ($444 current dollars), a hat went for $18 ($381), a quart of rum for $20 ($423), and a quart of whiskey for $10 ($211).[1] These prices were crushing the American home front.

Even Washington's mother was clamoring for supplies. At approximately seventy years old, Mary Ball Washington was an unstable character who lacked her son's finesse. She carried the emotional scars of childhood tragedy and revealed them with her flair for the dramatic. Mary's father died when she was three, and she was rendered an orphan when her mother passed on nine years later. The girl was graciously taken in by a family friend, George Eskridge.[2] A prominent lawyer and member of the Virginia House of Burgesses, Eskridge was a part of the burgeoning colonial gentry. Fortunately for Mary, he was also a compassionate and down-to-earth man who made sure the young orphan was well cared for. He attempted to ensure that she had proper breeding and even introduced her to her future husband, Augustine Washington.

While Mary shunned the high society in which she was raised, she was thankful to Eskridge. Out of appreciation, she named her firstborn (and surprisingly sturdy) son after him. And she came to expect this new George to care for her as well, because she had grown into an anxious and needy woman.[3]

Her neediness was aggravated by the loss of her husband when George Washington was eleven years old. A slovenly woman with little regard for social conventions, she never remarried. Instead, Mary viewed her strapping eldest son as her husband's replacement around the farm and in raising her four other children. Washington grew into the role and complied with her many demands. As he matured into an adventurous young man, however, he became eager to escape.

As self-centered as she was willful, Mary perceived George's opportunities as competition for his devotion, and she thwarted his attempts to leave as a teen. When he eventually broke away to become a surveyor and then a soldier, Mary never completely forgave him. She sent him letters incessantly complaining of his abandonment and even boycotted his wedding to Martha when he was twenty-seven.[4]

A devoted son, Washington attempted to care for his mother even in his absence. He purchased for her a darling white house situated near those of his two brothers and his sister. Because she was not pleased, he built on a large porch overlooking a garden, but Mary remained unsatisfied and asked for an additional home on the other side of the mountains. Washington apparently received not an ounce of appreciation but plenty of grief.[5] His mother excelled at doling that out.

Mary seemed never to acknowledge Washington's amazing accomplishments as commander, either. Instead, she was known to say, "Ah George, had better have stayed at home and cultivated his farm."[6] She neither congratulated him on his military victories nor consoled him after his defeats. In fact, to add insult to injury, she was even rumored to be "one of the most rabid Tories"![7]

Ignoring the fact that her son was battling for his life as well as the fate of the Revolution, Mary acted as though he had neglected her. Like much of America, she suffered from the wartime shortages of food and medicine. However, unlike most of America, she had a son who was the commander in chief. Mary did not care. While her eldest was desperately trying to feed and clothe his army, she went behind his back to petition the Virginia General Assembly for a government stipend. The speaker of the assembly, fearful of insulting Washington, timidly asked him how he would like the legislature to proceed.

Washington was mortified. He wrote his brother saying that their mother was "upon all occasions, and in all Companies complaining of the hardness of the times, of her wants and distresses; and if not in direct terms, at least by strong innuendos inviting favors which not only makes her appear in an unfavourable point of view but those also who are connected with her"—especially her eldest son, a man who worked assiduously to craft his public persona.[8] Deeming her requests to be for "imaginary wants" that were "oftentimes insatiable," he sent his brother on a mission to ascertain her real needs and ask that she cease embarrassing him.[9] He also took the time to write the Virginia Assembly to explain his mother's irrationality and instruct them to ignore her.[10] He knew she was relatively well off compared with his troops starving around him. The country was suffering and he urged the assembly to deal with bigger problems.

As the costly war raged, Congress soon owed great debts to the nation's own soldiers and civilians, as well as to France. The nation was on the verge of bankruptcy, but Congress was unwilling to default on its debts, seeing those obligations as sacrosanct. The congressmen did not feel the same way about the value of the currency, however.

By the winter of 1780, the financial situation was so bleak that Congress repudiated the Continental in order to stave off bankruptcy. Although Congress refused to default on the debt owed to its own citizens and foreign governments, it saw this devaluation as an alternative solution. Therefore, the national government retired the circulating Continentals by accepting them at just one-fortieth of their face value.[11]

The result was near chaos. American troops watched in dismay as the value of their pay virtually evaporated. Bartenders stopped accepting Continental bills to purchase rum. Merchants barred their doors, unwilling to sell their wares for anything but gold or silver. Protesters marched through the streets of Philadelphia, parading as their unhappy mascot a tarred dog that was "feathered" with Continentals.[12]

Meanwhile, Benjamin Franklin was in Paris vigorously lobbying for more monetary aid. French loans and subsidies kept the United States financially afloat, but just barely. Even Franklin's unmatched shrewdness could not get enough money to alleviate America's suffering. And as the costly war drained even Louis XVI's deep coffers, France's patience waned.

The Americans were so desperate for funds that many turned to seizing the riches of their neighbors—the hated Loyalists. While the courts and politicians showed the Loyalists clemency when it came to their lives, the civilian authorities were less merciful to their wallets. Congress and the states launched an "attack on their personal fortunes which gradually impoverished them." They began their monetary assault with a "nibbling system of fines and special taxation."[13] In addition to the double and treble taxes commonly imposed by the states, Loyalists also faced fines for refusing to fight for the patriots, for the misdeeds of the substitutes they hired to fight in their stead, and for almost any showing of support for the British.[14] A Loyalist convicted of entering the British lines could be fined a whopping 2,000 pounds, roughly worth $350,000 in modern U.S. dollars![15]

If the Loyalist could not—or would not—pay such fines, his property could be sold from under him.[16] And the wretch whose property did not cover the fine risked a whipping, branding, or even the loss of an ear.[17] This hardship was heightened by the fact that in some states, a Loyalist who refused to swear allegiance to the patriots' cause could neither buy nor sell land, sue his neighbor for amounts owed, or even practice as an attorney if that was his profession.[18]

When Congress and the states were still not collecting enough from these Tory outlaws, they resorted to outright confiscation. Congress resolved "it be earnestly recommended to the several states, as soon as may be, to confiscate and make sale of all the real and personal estate therein, of such of their inhabitants and other persons who have forfeited the same, and the right to the protection of their respective states, and to invest the money arising from the sales in continental loan office certificates."[19] The states readily heeded this recommendation. New York alone confiscated 3.6 million pounds worth of property from its Loyalist population.[20]

While the civil authorities were seizing property like a drunken kleptomaniac, Washington was far more restrained. As a corollary to his defense of Americans' lives, the commander also defended their property.

It was the American commander's role to protect Americans' rights and employ the proper procedures determined by the republic. In fact, it was the Continental Congress and the state legislatures that often trampled on Americans' property rights, while the commander in chief sought to protect them. For example, after Congress evicted Loyalists throughout Philadelphia from their own homes in 1778, Washington fired off a letter of protest, criticizing the move as "impolitic," contending that "to exile many of its Inhabitants cannot be the interest of any State."[21] But even though he disagreed with some of the legislators' actions, he understood such measures to be their prerogative.

The American commander refused to be a plundering one, and his men suffered for it. He had matured since those days leading up to the Jumonville Affair decades earlier, when he played loose with the rules on confiscation. Now, rather than permit his troops to ravage the countryside like ravenous hyenas, Washington believed his only lawful option was to obtain supplies via the proper congressional channels. And Congress had proven utterly inept at obtaining supplies for his army. Early in the war, they attempted to collect assessments from the states and supplement the shortfall by printing Continentals. But when the states were not paying enough and the Continentals plummeted in value, Congress then attempted a republican experiment in "direct supply."[22]

Under this plan, the states were expected to supply guns, shoes, pork, etc. on request. Like a starving man shouting into the wind, these requests fell on deaf ears—the states were usually unable (and often unwilling) to supply Washington's army. The states were concerned about defending themselves and reluctant to divert their resources for the protection of their sister states. New York even went so far as to take clothing meant for the Continental Army and keep it for the state militia. With his troops "perishing for want of it," Washington lambasted this appropriation of the clothing as "a most extraordinary piece of Conduct"[23]

"People are starving," Washington lamented; "the Cry of want of Provisions comes to me from every Quarter."[24] His army had been fighting for years without adequate pay or supplies. During the winter months especially, his men perished for want of food and clothing. The supply shortage became particularly acute at Valley Forge during the bitter winter of 1778.

Upon the arrival of Washington's troops, the farming community of Valley Forge quickly transformed into a military city of death. Like locusts, the 14,000 soldiers culled trees for miles in every direction to use for construction material and firewood. They worked furiously to erect thousands of crude wooden huts before the frigid winds could pierce their ragged clothing. They built defensive fortifications, and raced against the freezing ground to dig miles of trenches designed by Washington to repel attacks. But the smell of the trenches was probably repulsive enough—they also came to serve as the army's latrines. Within a few days, the pastoral valley turned into a field of putrid misery.

One patriot reported, "It is certain that half the army are half naked, and almost the whole army go barefoot."[25] Washington's officers recommended that to keep the army in good fighting condition, each soldier needed daily rations of a pound of beef, pork or salted fish, a pound of flour or hard bread, a half gill of rum or whiskey (liquid courage), and a half pint of rice.[26] But Congress could not keep up with this demand at a cost of three shillings and four pence per ration,[27] and the soldiers were lucky to receive just a fraction of that amount, or any at all.

Washington pleaded for more. "I am now convinced, beyond a doubt," he wrote to Congress, "that unless some great and capital change suddenly takes place in that line, this Army must inevitably be reduced to one or other of these three things. Starve, dissolve, or disperse, in order to obtain subsistence." Bemoaning the lack of food and clothing, one of his officers summarized, "All things seem to contribute to the ruin of our cause."[28]

A staggering 2,500 of Washington's men were estimated to have perished that winter. His principled opposition to plunder was certainly put to the test; there must have been tremendous emotional and political pressure to allow his men to run carte blanche through the countryside seizing supplies for mere self-preservation. But Washington was determined to "crush in its earliest stage every attempt to plunder even those who are known to be Enemies to our Cause."[29] It was his role to protect the Americans. Only the civil authorities, he believed, had a right to strip Americans of their property.

Washington was fighting to create a democratic republic, not a military dictatorship, after all. And while his powers over war tactics were sweeping, even dictatorial, these did not extend to the American citizens themselves. And so he declared:

> The General prohibits both in Militia and Continental Troops, in the most positive terms, the infamous practice of plundering the Inhabitants, under the specious pretence of their being Tories—Let the persons who are known to be enemies to their Country, be seized and confin'd, and their Property disposed of, as the Law of the State directs—It is our business to give protection, and support, to the poor, distressed Inhabitants; not to multiply and increase their calamities. After the publication of this order, any officer, either Militia or Continental, found attempting to conceal the public Stores; plundering the Inhabitants under the notion of their being Tories, or venduing of Plunder taken from the Enemy, in any other manner than these Orders direct, may expect to be punished in the severest manner; and be obliged to account for every thing taken, or sold.[30]

There was also a practical side to Washington's principled stance, because he believed that "no plundering Army was ever a successful one."[31] Cognizant of the fact that he was also fighting for the hearts and minds of the war-weary American people, he reasoned that plundering would "create dreadful Apprehensions in our Friends, and when it is once begun, none can tell where it will stop."[32] Confiscating property without authorization would "embitter the minds of the People, and excite perhaps hurtful jealousy against the Army."[33] Washington aimed to distinguish his army from the plundering British and Hessian forces that had terrorized the countryside. In this way, Washington was acting virtuously not just because he was a "good guy" but also because it was crucial to be seen as such.

Washington was so "resolved to put a stop to plundering, and converting either public, or private property" to military use that he reacted swiftly and severely when his troops violated his orders.[34] Any soldier found to have plundered American property was to be "immediately confined" and "most rigidly punished."[35] Surprisingly, the prohibition on plunder by the army even extended, for the most part, to the property of civilian Loyalists—much to his ravenous troops' dismay. While he detested the Loyalists as "abominable pests," Washington was astonishingly protective of their rights.[36] Though he viewed them as traitorous Americans, the key was that he still generally considered them to be Americans. And he believed this afforded them protection from his military. Many of his starving soldiers, as well as many congressmen, saw his refusal to confiscate Loyalist property as outrageous.

When some troops inevitably disobeyed his strict rules, Washington was not surprised—to his unending frustration, the Continental Army was not the paragon of American virtue that he wished it to be. Exasperated, he explained to Congress, "I have with some others, used my utmost endeavours to stop this horrid practice, but under the present lust after plunder, and want of Laws to punish Offenders, I might almost as well attempt to remove Mount Atlas. I have ordered instant corporal Punishment upon every Man who passes our Lines, or is seen with Plunder . . . ."[37] The commander vigilantly strove to keep his unruly men in line.

On one occasion, a whole regiment was accused of "the infamous practice of Plundering."[38] Along with a party of twenty men, the colonel of the regiment had purportedly robbed a house on the outskirts of the American encampment. A bemused Washington wrote that the young man was found with "large Pier looking Glasses, Women's Cloaths, and other Articles which one would think, could be of no Earthly use to him."[39] But this was no laughing matter. Washington promptly tried the soldier by court-martial, and when the court acquitted him and called for him merely to apologize, Washington rejected such leniency. He "ordered a Reconsideration of the matter, upon which, . . . they made Shift to Cashier him."[40] Then Washington proceeded to have the regiment expelled along with the colonel. For a man who needed all the troops he could get, this was true conviction.

Washington even went so far as to execute a member of his personal guard for taking supplies from an obstinate Tory. He had entrusted this guard, John Herring, with obtaining supplies from the countryside. With a horse and a pass, Herring set out and arrived at the home of Mr. Prince Howland.[41] A known Loyalist living in Fishkill, New York, Howland owned a collection of fine garments, which Herring spotted during his visit.[42] Following Washington's protocol, Herring asked to purchase the clothes, but Howland refused to sell them; he was not one to aid the patriot cause.

Herring was not willing to take no for an answer. He gathered other members of Washington's guard and organized a heist. They knew the policy under Washington: the penalty for such thievery was hanging. Therefore, they donned disguises. While careful to blacken their faces with burnt cork, these not-so-stealthy burglars foolishly wore the round bearskin hats that clearly identified them as Washington's guard. The bumbling burglars broke into Howland's house and stole the fine clothing along with some silver spoons and cash.[43] Then they proceeded to loot his neighbor before returning to Washington's camp. Howland promptly reported the theft, complete with a damning description of the burglars' telltale hats.

Washington was livid. "Shocked at the frequent horrible Villainies of this nature committed by the troops of late," he was "determined to make Examples which will deter the boldest and most harden'd offenders."[44] He had Herring and his cat burglars tried by courts-martial. When they were found guilty and Herring condemned to death, Washington upheld this harsh punishment. He wrote in his general orders for the day, "Men who are called out by their Country to defend the Rights and Property of their fellow Citizens, who are abandoned enough to violate those Rights and plunder that Property deserve and shall receive no Mercy."[45] The commander had made a strong statement in defense of a Tory's property.

Realizing their inability to supply Washington's army, Congress soon granted him license "to take, wherever he may be, all such provisions and other articles as may be necessary for the comfortable subsistence of the army under his command, paying or giving certificates for the same; to remove and secure for the benefit of the owners, all goods and effects, which may be serviceable to the enemy."[46] Washington was reluctant to take advantage of this authorization, however. During the winter of 1778 he wrote, "I shall use every exertion . . . for subsisting the Army and keeping it together; But I must observe, that this never can be done by coercive means. Supplying of Provisions and Cloathing must be had in another way, or it cannot exist."[47] He believed it was Congress's place to confiscate supplies, not his. But with his men in such dire need, he eventually did seize American property—albeit in the least coercive way possible.

Washington acted as a tool of Congress, and a delicate one at that. He reasoned that he must proceed gently, since the military's exercise of power was always viewed "with a jealous and suspicious eye."[48] Thus, when he did order his men to confiscate supplies, he provided careful instructions.

In order to requisition supplies in the most democratic way possible, Washington set up a sort of confiscation checklist. His soldiers were required to: 1) have a compelling reason for the taking; 2) work with local authorities as closely as possible in carrying out the seizures; 3) take only small amounts so as not to harm the citizens; and 4) arrange for some type of repayment or, more likely, a promise thereof.

The first criterion was easy to fulfill. By the winter of 1780, Washington had shifted north from his previous quarters at Valley Forge to the area around the tiny village of Morristown, New Jersey. He and his 9,000 men settled into this little hollow nestled in a tranquil region of rolling farms and pasture in northern New Jersey. The land was dotted by picturesque cottages built in the so-called "ancient Dutch form," with signature sloping dormitories that projected from a dramatically pitched wooden roof. Almost uniformly painted white, these houses varied in size but were typically encircled by "verdant lawns, shrubbery, and well-cultivated gardens."[49] The Continental Army, however, did not find their stay so idyllic.

Far from a rural utopia, this was a warzone. Adjacent to New York City, the county had been scarred by gruesome battles and had witnessed Washington's disastrous defeats following his loss of New York. By 1780, Washington had retaken New Jersey and was determined to remain in the mid-Atlantic in hopes of retaking New York. He set up camp at Morristown so that he might keep pressure on Clinton's troops holed up in the city. The two commanders still assumed there would be a climactic battle between them after so many grueling years of bloodshed. But for now, Washington just worked to survive.

His contest with Clinton had devolved into a war of attrition. And he was losing. In fact, Parliament kept the British troops so well fed and clothed—albeit to the British taxpayers' growing dismay—that Clinton began putting on a great deal of weight from all the dinner parties he enjoyed in New York. The Americans were unable to keep pace.[50] Washington, for his part, was living comfortably with Martha, five of his officers and eighteen servants in the white Georgian mansion that served as his headquarters. The grand house had been owned by a late patriot, and Washington respectfully paid rent to the widow.[51] But despite his comfort, he was not one to grow detached from the condition of his soldiers, who were shivering and hungry in the less genteel lodgings in the surrounding areas.

The Revolution had already robbed northern New Jersey of its tranquility, and now Washington wanted its food. At the same time, he was aware of the civilian population's fears. The 250 residents of Morristown locked up their chickens and daughters as they watched the hungry-looking patriots warily.[52] With the coldest winter of the century hitting in 1780, the region was a powder keg of trouble. Before things turned ugly, Washington dispatched his troops to collect 200 head of cattle and 800 bushels of grain from the neighboring farms.[53] He demanded that his men act cautiously and respectfully in doing so, telling them:

> I have reposed this trust in you from a perfect confidence in
> your prudence, zeal and respect for the rights of Citizens. While
> your measures are adapted to the emergency, and you consult
> what you owe to the service, I am persuaded you will not forget,
> that as we are compelled by necessity to take the property of
> Citizens for the support of the Army on whom their safety
> depends, we should be careful to manifest that we have a rever-
> ence for their rights, and wish not to do any thing which that
> necessity and even their own good do not absolutely require.[54]

This was a clear expression of Washington's stance: the military should remain subservient to the civilians they protect.

Even when authorized by Congress to take citizens' property, the army should work alongside local civilian authorities,[55] and "with as much tenderness as possible to the Inhabitants, having regard to the Stock of each Individual, that no family may be deprived of its neces-sary subsistence."[56] He warned his men, "Nothing is to be taken by way of plunder under any pretence whatever."[57] Washington would rather his troops starve than trample Americans' rights.

Though the country was verging on bankruptcy, Washington even took measures to repay citizens for the property taken from them. "The Commissary is either to pay or give proper Certificates for whatever he takes," he directed.[58] While this was somewhat wishful thinking since repayment seemed unlikely, the principle was clear: Citizens had a right to their property, and the government could seize it only in extreme circumstances. Even then, the citizens were owed compensation.[59]

Washington was so delicate in carrying out these authorized con-fiscations, in fact, that he was ridiculed in Congress for being weak. But he considered his restraint to be a form of strength—the strength of American liberty. He wrote to Congress, "I confess, I have felt myself greatly embarrassed with respect to the vigorous exercise of Military power. An Ill placed humanity perhaps and a reluctance to give distress may have restrained me too far."[60]

31

Not-So-Civil War

As Washington struggled to hold his army together while also defending Americans' rights from his ravenous troops, the British shifted their focus to conquering the southern states. Lord George Germain, the British secretary of state for the American Department, hatched an aggressive strategy that relied on aid from the Loyalists who pervaded the South. With his large, pointed nose, gaping almond eyes, and sharp chin, he appeared almost gremlin-like as he sent his many directives from London to Clinton, Cornwallis, and other officers in the warzone.[1] More gifted as an orator than as a strategist, Germain was a distinguished aristocrat with a fine educational and military pedigree, but little understanding of the American continent. For one thing, he sorely overestimated the Loyalists.

According to Germain's southern strategy, the British could easily conquer Georgia and the Carolinas, leaving the Loyalists to occupy in their wake. He assumed that once the Tories were placed in charge, the British would not need to expend precious forces policing and holding their conquests, as they had been compelled to do in the highly rebellious northern states. In effect, Germain envisioned a southern conquest as more like a liberation effort. The British forces just needed to throw off the chains of the patriot oppressors and install the loyal subjects back into power—or so Germain believed.

General Howe knew better. Back in London, the disgraced former commander warned against this simplistic view of America. But he was ignored, and the British invaded Savannah in late December 1778.

From 1778 to 1780, it appeared that Germain was correct. As Washington remained with the main force in the north outside New York City, the British racked up victories in Georgia and South Carolina. By the spring of 1780 it looked as if the American southern forces were defeated. At the Battle of Charleston, the combined might of the British naval and land forces trapped the patriots on a peninsula. With no means of retreat, the haggard troops were besieged on all sides for many blood-soaked weeks. In May, 5,500 tattered Americans finally emerged from the smoky rubble to surrender. They had just handed Clinton his biggest prize of the war: the American Southern Army.

Clinton's delight was premature, however. A wave of patriotism swept the region and the Americans hastily raised a second Southern Army. At its helm, Congress placed Granny Gates.

Riding high on his victory at Saratoga, the ambitious Gates had become the stalking horse for Washington's position as commander in chief. The thrill of the great victories at Trenton and Princeton in 1777 had long since subsided, and Washington was now perceived by many politicians as the man defeated by the British around Philadelphia. Congressmen even began to criticize his deference to Americans' rights as a sign of weakness. Gates, on the other hand, was enjoying renewed admiration in Congress after taking credit from Arnold for defeating Burgoyne. Of course, the cunning "Granny" leveraged this esteem to seek more power.

Gates was soon confronting an old foe in the South. But Cornwallis had reentered the war a changed man. Following his embarrassing defeat at Princeton, he had finally obtained leave to return to his sick wife. He was able to tend to his wilting love for just a few months before she died on Valentine's Day 1779. The man was devastated. After burying her, Cornwallis threw himself into his work: warfare.

Cornwallis returned to America "not with views of conquest and ambition" but because he could not stand to remain in England. His wife's death, he said, had "destroyed all my hopes of happiness in this world."[2] There was nothing left for him to do but crush the Americans. For a man with nothing to lose, Cornwallis certainly grew accustomed to winning: by the spring of 1780, he was well on his way to conquering the South. Fearing all was lost, Congress turned to Granny Gates to stop him.

Washington recommended his trusted friend Nathanael Greene for the job of stopping Cornwallis, but Congress astonishingly handed command of the Southern Army to their darling Gates. Washington was livid and Gates smug. Gates hoped to stage a repeat of Saratoga and thereby topple Washington's reign as leader of the entire Continental Army.

With 3,700 troops versus Cornwallis's 2,100, Gates had the numbers on his side.[3] But quality would trump quantity: Gates's army was dominated by untested militiamen, while Cornwallis led battle-hardened veterans. Further, while Gates would never admit it, Cornwallis was simply a superior military leader. Even Charles Lee had smugly warned Gates, "Take care lest your Northern laurels turn to Southern willows."[4] But the proud Gates did not heed this advice. Overestimating the battle readiness of the Americans, as well as his own prowess, he chose to make a stand.

Gates's and Cornwallis's armies unexpectedly collided at Camden, South Carolina. As the sun rose over the quaint town on the hot, summer morning of August 16, 1780, both sides were surprised when musket fire interrupted the birds' serenade. Although neither side was prepared, this was especially inopportune timing for the patriots. Short on food and rum, Gates had served his troops half-cooked meat and molasses for dinner the night before. Thus, not only were they lacking their usual liquid courage, they were also suffering from gastrointestinal problems as they faced a terrifying mass of British red and metal. It was not a great morning to be sober and sick.

Within minutes, the patriots' exuberant calls for battle were quickly replaced by yelps of pain and terror. When Cornwallis's highly trained regiments fired on Gates's militia, panic spread through the sickly American ranks. As their compatriots fell and the British bayonets neared, many of the terrified Americans ran without even firing a shot. Cornwallis seized this weakness and effectively used his cavalry to shred the American lines.

Gates was among the first to flee. As his army crumbled behind him, he galloped northward on the army's swiftest horse.[5] In fact, by the time the Americans were defeated after just one hour of combat, Gates was already many miles away. His abandoned army suffered over 2,000 casualties. Lord Germain wrote from London, "The Glorious success of Lord Cornwallis at Camden . . . will have removed all apprehensions of further disturbance from the rebel troops and must crush every hope in the secret abettors of rebellion of again subverting the King's authority . . . ."[6] It appeared to the patriots that the South was lost.

Washington was not pleased. While he remained politely silent on the matter, Hamilton and his other aides ridiculed Gates mercilessly. For his devastating miscalculation, Congress relieved Granny Gates of his command and resolved "that the Commander-in-Chief be and is hereby directed to appoint an officer to command the southern army, in the room of Major General Gates."[7] They had gone against Washington's counsel in appointing Gates and had now learned their lesson. This time, the choice was left to the commander. Washington gave the position to his old friend who had lobbied Congress to grant him sweeping powers a couple of years earlier: Nathanael Greene. In selecting this "man of abilities, bravery, and coolness," Washington had chosen wisely.[8]

Despite their catastrophic losses, the Americans proved scrappy. As Howe predicted, Germain's southern strategy underestimated the difficulty of occupation. The British had crushed the Americans' two southern armies, but they had inflamed the patriotic sentiments of the local populace. Cornwallis had kicked a hornets' nest.

The patriots rose up against Loyalist dominance. Old rivalries and land disputes sent the region spiraling into civil war. Like a fire feeding on itself, the region erupted into a vengeful bloodbath when patriots and Tories plundered one another's homes and massacred each other in retaliation for atrocities. There were over one hundred battles and skirmishes in South Carolina alone in which not one Brit even participated. It was American vs. American.

The British were taken aback by the mayhem. "The houses of desolate widows have been laid waste [and] innocent and neutral persons murdered," said one officer.[9] Washington would likely not have approved of the carnage, but he was far away in New Jersey, with little means of stopping it.

One massacre occurred when patriots tricked a Loyalist regiment with their snappy uniforms. With short green jackets and plumed helmets, resembling the uniforms of a nearby British regiment, the patriots fooled the Tories into believing they were friendly forces.[10] As the patriot leader was shaking hands with his duped Loyalist counterpart, the South Carolina militia emerged from the trees and mowed down ninety Tories.[11]

With patriots gaining the upper hand and Loyalists running scared, it became very clear that Germain's southern strategy was flawed. Cornwallis realized he could not count on the Loyalists to hold the South, as small bands of angry frontiersmen began attacking his forces from behind trees and rocks in guerilla warfare. Never camping in the same place for more than two nights in a row, the Americans confounded their hulking British pursuers. One American named Frances Marion particularly angered Cornwallis.

A Carolinian of French Huguenot descent, Marion was called the "Swamp Fox" due to his penchant for hiding his forces in the Carolinas' abundant marshlands. His cunning and bravery were complemented by an almost supernatural ability to discern the redcoats' next move. As his ambush attacks on Cornwallis's men kept succeeding, the patriots throughout the region began to look upon his thin face and intense gaze with admiration and hope. He was an inspiration. One patriot gushed, "His genuine love of country and liberty, and his unwearied vigilance and invincible fortitude, coupled with the eminent success which attended him through his brilliant career, has endeared him to the hearts of his countrymen, and the memory of his deeds of valor shall never slumber so long as there is a Carolinian to speak his panegyric."[12] Eluding Cornwallis's determined efforts to kill him, the Swamp Fox was able to "keep alive the expiring hopes of an oppressed militia."[13] Thanks in part to Marion, the American forces were growing and Cornwallis's were shrinking.

Still, Cornwallis had the superior force. When Nathanael Greene took command of the resurrected Southern Army, he described it as something like a zombie army, "wretched beyond description . . . living upon charity and subsist[ing] by daily collections" and having "not a drop of spirits." Without ameliorative measures, Greene added, "I foresee we must starve."[14] He predicted, "An army naked and subsisted in this manner, and not more than one-third the size of the enemies' army, will make but a poor fight."[15] But Greene proved himself wrong. He transformed those wretched men into an agile yet lethal fighting force.

In order to prevent his unseasoned militiamen from retreating, Greene placed men behind them with orders to "shoot down the first man that runs."[16] As draconian as this sounds, it was a common and effective method of getting men to fight. But Greene was careful not to expect too much from the frightened farmers who dominated his ranks. After his militiamen fired two volleys, he allowed them to resume their usual flight "like a flock of sheep frightened by dogs."[17] He reasoned that the British would advance anyway, but with those two barrages of lead flying towards them.

Greene also shrewdly adopted Marion's guerilla tactics against Cornwallis's larger force. Outnumbered and inexperienced, Greene's small regiment was still no match for Cornwallis. Avoiding an all-out battle (in stark contrast to Gates's disastrous approach), Greene instead pestered the British force with a hit-and-run campaign. Utilizing the Americans' knack for fast retreat, he adroitly picked side skirmishes that he could win and then slipped away before Cornwallis could squash his army. Hamilton marveled at Greene's ingenuity with his "destitute" troops, praising his ability to strike and quickly retreat as "a masterpiece of military skill and exertion."[18]

In an attempt to keep up with his nimble foe as he chased the patriots throughout 1780 and into 1781, the infuriated Cornwallis destroyed all of his own heavy tents, most of his wagons, and even all provisions in excess of what his men could carry.[19] Determined to decimate the Americans, he even resorted to grapeshot, a messy technique in which cannons were loaded with items ranging from metal slugs to rocks and glass. Unlike a single large cannonball, these pieces scattered throughout the field, ripping through soldiers' flesh. Grapeshot was tactically costly, however; it was impossible to control, and the British therefore lost many to friendly fire. In one battle, between grapeshot and Greene's relentless barrage, Cornwallis lost a quarter of his men.

Although Greene retreated repeatedly into 1781, leaving Cornwallis with technical triumphs, one British politician quipped from London, "Another such victory would destroy the British Army."[20] Cornwallis, still emotionally numb from the loss of his beloved wife, seemed to care little about the inhumanity of it all as his army disintegrated.

The American forces gradually wore down the once-superior British forces with masterful maneuvers. Washington monitored the southern campaign from New Jersey, where he was pinning Clinton down in the Northeast to prevent him from reinforcing Cornwallis's beleaguered army. Washington and Greene were proving to be a dynamic tag team.

Though they did not realize it at the time, the Americans were drawing near to their great victory. And Washington would make sure that victory did not come at the expense of his fellow citizens' liberties.

●

Washington defined the American commander in chief as the people's defender. Fighting to establish a new republic in which the (white) American people enjoyed the right to "life, liberty, and the pursuit of happiness," he saw it as his duty to protect them from all threats— whether foreign or domestic.

On this principle, he ordered his troops "to preserve tranquility and order . . . and give security to individuals of every class and description [from] every species of persecution, insult or abuse, either from the soldiery to the inhabitants or among each other."[21] Even the Loyalists, he wrote, "those execrable Parricides, whose Counsels and Aid have deluged their Country with Blood, have been protected from the Fury of a justly-enraged People."[22]

Washington strove to ensure that no American's life or freedom would be torn away without a proper trial, as defined by the civil authorities. Thus, he routinely referred citizens to the courts that they prescribed.[23] While these courts were typically lenient, they did occasionally apply severe penalties: they locked up Loyalists indefinitely, inflicted bizarre corporal punishment, and executed many. But Washington saw it as their prerogative to do so. He would reinforce the procedures determined by the civilian government, and let the cards fall where they may.

He was similarly careful of American property rights. Even though supplying his forces was a vexing problem,[24] he confiscated property only with congressional approval and a plan for repayment.[25] He took special care to avoid "greatly distressing the families" and to employ the proper procedures that citizens deserved.[26] Washington would rather risk the lives of his troops than permit the military to violate citizens' liberty. While the American commander in chief had vast powers in dealing with enemy combatants, he was conscious of his limitations when it came to impinging on the rights of fellow citizens.[27] Americans were to be protected and their liberty cherished.

The old bur oak that stands in Boyd-Parker Memorial Park in western New York may be viewed in two different lights. As the "Torture Tree," it serves as a dark symbol of the horrors of war. Each side inflicted death and destruction upon the other. On this very ground, the Seneca mutilated patriots in the most horrendous manner imaginable. In turn, Americans under Washington's command obliterated the thriving village that encircled the oak.

The tree may also be viewed as a beacon. Washington's destructive response did not stem from cruelty, but from an ardent desire to defend Americans. In describing the character of the United States, Washington wrote, "Liberty is the Basis, and whoever would dare to sap the foundation, or overturn the Structure, under whatever specious pretexts he may attempt it, will merit the bitterest execration, and the severest punishment which can be inflicted by his injured Country."[28] Liberty was the battle cry of the Revolution, and Washington guarded it, ruthlessly.

Washington was intent on guarding against precedents by which the military might later subjugate freedom. He preached for the new nation to "avoid the necessity of those overgrown military establishments, which, under any form of government, are inauspicious to liberty, and which are to be regarded as particularly hostile to Republican Liberty."[29]

Thomas Jefferson famously wrote, "The Tree of Liberty must be watered from time to time with the blood of patriots and tyrants."[30] He was not thinking of this bur oak, but in a way the Torture Tree is like the tree of liberty. Patriot blood watered that tree during Washington's battle to protect his new nation. Those scouts' sacrifice helped create the United States and define its principles. It is because of great American patriots like them and the many service men and women of subsequent generations that the oak stands in the peaceful little park today. The 250-year-old tree has withstood the ages as an enduring reminder of the ongoing struggle to preserve American liberty.

VI

COULD HAVE
BEEN KING

"If he does that, he will be the greatest man in the world."
—KING GEORGE III, 1783

America has lost a crucial piece of her history. But unlike the metaphorical sense in which time robs us of our memories, this piece was literally stolen. It was a pair of reading glasses, with surprisingly heavy frames made of solid silver, artfully hinged and elaborately hand engraved. The small, circular lenses were designed with +3.50 magnification to correct the presbyopia that afflicts all people as they age.[1] Aside from being old, these tarnished glasses were seemingly ordinary. What made them priceless was the person whose vision they were believed to have corrected—George Washington.

In Washington's time, eyeglasses were considered a sign of weakness. They displayed a vulnerability of which most men were deeply ashamed. Glasses were seen as a "humiliating disfigurement," akin to a clubfoot or hunchback, but early America made an exception for this specific pair.[2] These spectacles were cherished as a great relic of national history. They were enshrined at Independence Hall, which came to be a temple to the nation's founding after the Constitutional Convention.

Prominently featured on the "New York" table near the bar in the Assembly Room, the glasses drew the fascination of Americans from all walks of life.[3] Washington's figurative vision had helped to forge the nation, and this simple device had helped to make his literal vision 20/20. The symbolism was likely not lost on the many proud men, women, and children who viewed them; these eyeglasses were treasured as a precious piece of Americana.

In fact, the spectacles proved to be all too precious. They were reported stolen at 9:35 A.M. on Saturday, August 19, 1967, in a mysterious heist that remains unsolved to this day.[4] And with them, a tangible link to our past was lost. Without it, many more Americans are sure to forget that Washington's eyeglasses quite literally saved the republic.[5]

The chapters in this part examine America's approval of Washington's wartime actions as detailed in Parts II through V. Washington saved the new nation from near destruction and led the way to victory. For doing so, he was revered to the point of near deification and became the model for all future American commanders in chief. Returning full circle back to Part I, this section explains how Washington's wartime precedents defined the powers granted in the new Constitution to all future presidents.

32

O God! It Is All Over!

Washington was beloved. As victory neared, his celebrity intensified. From soldiers to politicians to the general citizenry, the American people praised his military leadership. They had scrutinized Washington's actions for years, avidly following the letters, newspaper reports, pamphlets, and (most often) word-of-mouth accounts that chronicled his exploits. Whether he was explaining the justification for torture, dictating military strategy, convening military tribunals, or defending citizens' liberty, Americans watched intently as the nation hung in the balance. They liked what they saw.

By 1781, it had been years since Washington had won any great victory on the battlefield, but he was still adulated. As he orbited around New York City, hoping in vain to recapture it, he fought only small skirmishes. But his esteem was deeper and more subtle than that of a coach with a winning scorecard: he was the personification of the revolutionary struggle. Washington did not have many victories, but after nearly six years of battle, he still held the hearts of the people.

Americans credited his "good destiny and consummate prudence [for having] prevented want of success from producing want of confidence on the part of the public."[1] They praised not only his bravery and leadership, but also his impeccable character and astute handling of the messy war. "He was received with that heart felt exultation, which superior merit alone can inspire, after having, in his progress through the states, been honoured with every mark of affection and esteem which they conceived were due the man, the whole continent looked up to for safety and freedom."[2] And he soon won that freedom for them.

Nothing catapulted Washington's popularity higher than winning the war. And thanks to Nathanael Greene's southern campaign, he was on the verge. The American Southern Army had driven Cornwallis to Yorktown, Virginia, an unremarkable piece of southeastern Virginia that jutted into the York River. Inhabited by fewer than a couple thousand citizens nestled around its harbor, Yorktown was a diminutive port village that Cornwallis fancied a prime location from which to exploit Britain's sea power. But the British could no longer count on their naval supremacy—the French fleet was finally on its way.

In a strange twist of fate, a failure of communication between Washington and his Southern Army proved crucial to winning the war. The Southern Army sent a message to Washington requesting that he support their Yorktown assault, while Washington simultaneously sent a message outlining his objective of retaking New York City. Only one reached its intended recipient. Fortuitously, Washington's plan was intercepted, putting Clinton on high alert for an attack on New York and thus unwilling to divert troops to reinforce Cornwallis. But while Clinton was fretting over the north, Washington had received the Southern Army's request for support. Having grown highly adaptable, he quickly devised another sneak attack back in his home state.[3]

Before he left his perch outside New York, Washington concocted a "judiciously concerted stratagem" to throw Clinton into alarm and prompt him to call back part of his forces from Virginia in order to defend his New York garrison.[4] Washington—this time intentionally—began cultivating false information about a fake plan to attack Manhattan via Staten Island. He left a small skeleton army behind in order to create the illusion of an invasion force, ordering his men to pitch tents, keep the fires burning, and lay pontoons so that Clinton might believe they were preparing for an amphibious assault.[5] His ruse set, Washington then ordered as many men as he could spare to march southward.

His designs were so secret that his own army was flummoxed. A doctor attending to the Continental Army described the situation as being like "some theatrical exhibition, where the interest and expectations of the spectators are continually increasing, and where curiosity is wrought to the highest point. Our destination has been for some time a matter of perplexing doubt and uncertainty."[6] That is exactly what Washington wanted.

However confused they were by his intentions, the troops held Washington in such high esteem that they placed "the fullest confidence" in his "capacious mind, full of resources." The soldiers marching south had no idea where they were going or where they would fight, but they would follow their commander unquestioningly, trusting in the plans he held "under an impenetrable veil of secrecy."[7] Many of them believed they were preparing for an amphibious assault on New York rather than a 550-mile march down to Virginia—and so did Clinton.

Soon, Washington's caravan of men, weapons, wagons, and camp wives and children streamed through New Jersey. Keeping step to the unusually swift beat of the fife and drum on those dry summer days, the soldiers kicked up a cloud of blinding dust into the hot air. His men were happy to follow their esteemed leader blindly (at times literally so, due to the dust) in order to fulfill his secret plan. As they raced, the ragged soldiers were "cheered with enthusiasm by the populace, who hailed them as the war-torn defenders of the country."[8]

Clinton had no idea of Washington's true intentions until the Continental Army had already marched all the way through New Jersey and crossed the Delaware River. He had duped his old adversary, but Washington worried that his plan would still fall apart. He was very much dependent on French naval support to block both Clinton's reinforcements and Cornwallis's retreat. Therefore, he and his officers had lobbied hard to get the French ships to leave their posts defending France's interests in the Caribbean and come to assist in the American siege. The American Revolution had become a world war, with the French forces harassing the British from the Caribbean to Egypt to India. While such far-flung warfare indirectly aided the Americans by diverting British power, the Americans viewed the situation more myopically: they wanted the French to be directly involved in *their* fight. With only a small window of opportunity, the French agreed to make a detour to the waters surrounding Yorktown. Washington could only hope they would hold true to their word.

As the days ticked by without any sign of the French, Washington grew increasingly nervous that Cornwallis would slip away before his forces were positioned. He was "distressed beyond expression," questioning whether the French warships would arrive before the British fleet could "frustrate all our flattering prospects."[9] When masts were spotted out over the water, both sides watched in great suspense to see which flags they flew. To the Americans' jubilation—and Cornwallis's dread—the summer horizon filled with fleurs-de-lis.

Winning the race, twenty-four French ships took up defensive positions in time to repel the nineteen British rescue warships that had finally been sent from New York City.[10] "So unexpected a naval superiority on the side of the enemy—which far exceeded everything we had in prospect—was not a little alarming," wrote a stunned Clinton, "and seemed to call for more than common exertion to evade the impending ruin."[11]

When the aggressive French cannon sent the British ships recoiling back to New York, the Americans knew they finally had the upper hand. An officer informed Greene that they had gotten Cornwallis "handsomely in a pudding bag."[12] Another said, "Cornwallis may now tremble for his fate, for nothing but some extraordinary interposition of his guardian angels seems capable of saving him and his whole army from captivity."[13]

Washington began pounding Cornwallis with a terrifying artillery barrage. He sent his French troops and a contingent of Americans under his trusty protégé Hamilton to confront British defensive positions. The allied forces trounced the British, and Cornwallis grew desperate to escape with what was left of his men. His guardian angels did not save him after all. Once again, the elements came to the Americans' aid, as a sudden storm prevented Cornwallis from fleeing northward into the night.[14] The allied American and French forces had sealed him in.

Riding to the front line, Washington appeared almost godlike as he fearlessly dismounted his horse amidst the British fire. One of his aides, "solicitous for his safety," suggested nervously, "Sir you are exposed here. Had you not better step a little back?" To which Washington replied, "if you are afraid, you have liberty to step back."[15] Washington struck a few ceremonial blows into the ground with a pickax and the Americans dug in for a siege. Finally, they were the ones attacking.

As Cornwallis and his men hunkered down within the city praying for Clinton to rescue them, the American and French forces rained metal upon their prostrate bodies. One patriot described the ships as "enwrapped in a torrent of fire . . . spreading with vivid brightness among the combustible rigging" against the night sky, "while all around was thunder and lightning from our numerous cannon and mortars." In his eyes, it was "one of the most sublime and magnificent spectacles which can be imagined." The Americans marveled at the magnitude of the cannon fire hitting the town and the river beyond, sending up "columns of water like the spouting of monsters of the deep."[16]

Cornwallis found the spectacle far less entertaining. He realized that reinforcements would not arrive in time, and "thus expired the last hope of the British army."[17] Thinking it "wanton and inhuman to the last degree to sacrifice the lives of [his] small body of gallant soldiers," Cornwallis drafted his surrender in October 1781.[18] Washington, expressing his "Ardent Desire to spare the further Effusion of Blood," accepted the surrender on generous terms: Britain's army at Yorktown would surrender to Washington and its navy to the French.[19] The Americans would take the common soldiers prisoner, but allow Cornwallis and his officers to retain their private property and return home. Washington thus came off as not only triumphant, but magnanimous.

The surrendering British, on the other hand, were not viewed so positively. One New Jersey officer wrote that "the British officers in general behaved like boys who had been whipped at school. Some bit their lips; some pouted; others cried. Their round, broad-brimmed hats were well-adapted to the occasion, hiding those faces they were ashamed to show."[20] Cornwallis, who had so often "appeared in splendid triumph at the head of his army," now sailed in disgrace back to England, where only his wife's grave was awaiting him.[21]

When news of Yorktown reached Congress, they did not even have enough money to pay the messenger. But, after taking up a collection from among themselves to settle the tab, the congressmen—and the rest of America—could rejoice. Washington had finally humbled the British Empire.

Word of America's great victory took over a month to sail across the Atlantic. When news arrived on the British Isles in late November 1781, it was met with shock and humiliation. The prime minister of the British Parliament, Lord North, took the news like "a ball in his breast." He "opened his arms, exclaiming wildly, as he paced up and down[,] 'O God! it is all over!'"[22] And it was. After suffering 25,000 military deaths and losing more battles than they had won, the American forces had humbled the mightiest empire on earth.

33

Winning the Peace

The British people sued for peace. Anticlimactically for him, Clinton lost his post as British commander in a whimper rather than a grand battle with Washington. His legacy was mixed: some described him as "an honourable and respectable officer" and others as "fool enough to command an army when he is incapable of commanding a troop of horse."[1] In his own defense, Clinton attempted to pin the blame on Cornwallis, who shot back by publicly reciting the strategic blunders of his former commander. Clinton would continue to serve his country as a soldier and a politician. But when he departed New York for London in the spring of 1782 and resumed his seat in Parliament, this body was much different from the one he had left at the beginning of the war.

The British Parliament was deeply shaken by the loss at Yorktown. Antiwar factions took over, and Lord North, saying that "the fatal day has come," resigned as prime minister.[2] King George III accepted his resignation with dread. While he had previously enjoyed control over Parliament, he now faced a legislature that not only wanted to end his war, but also declared that "the power of the Crown has increased, is increasing, and ought to be diminished."[3] Now even his throne was in question.

The king had closely identified his own honor with winning the war. He was said to have aspired to "keep the rebels harassed, anxious, and poor, until the day when, by a natural and inevitable process, discontent and disappointment were converted into penitence and remorse."[4] But the will of his people had changed, thus making his continued crusade impossible. And so he drafted his abdication.

George III was convinced that the shift in Parliament had "totally incapacitated Him from either conducting the War with effect, or from obtaining any Peace but on conditions which would prove destructive" to Britain. Therefore, he felt obliged to take "the painful step of quitting . . . for ever."[5] Although he never submitted the abdication and even managed to fend off major changes to the monarchy, he suffered emotionally and endured bouts of insanity.[6] He nevertheless retained the thrown until his death in 1820, becoming the longest-ruling British monarch up to that time.[7] But he spent the rest of his days knowing that he would go down in history as the king who lost the American colonies.

After Yorktown, the Americans had not won yet, however. They still needed to navigate the treacherous peace process, which proved to be an international diplomatic struggle of colossal magnitude and deep intrigue. As former allies secretly turned against one another and bitter foes joined forces, it appeared probable that the American novices would be diplomatically outmaneuvered by the shrewd old European powers. They were rabbits in a fox den. But as they had shown throughout the war, the wily Americans could outfox just about anyone.

The peace talks would fundamentally shape the future of the new nation, but America's great leader was not at the table. Instead, Washington held down the home front while Benjamin Franklin, John Adams, and John Jay, a thirty-five-year-old congressman, took the helm in Europe.[8] These three men, all brilliant, could not have been any more different in temperament. Franklin was cunning and reserved, while Adams was direct and irascible, and Jay suspicious and isolationist.[9] Together they made a formidable team.

And all their skills would be needed to navigate the tangled web of old alliances and grudges. The European powers were prepared to step all over the United States in pursuit of their own interests. In fact, America's closest ally, France, intended to hijack the peace process in order to obtain the spoils for its Crown. After all, the French had entered the war more out of hatred for the British than any grand love of liberty. And the American peace delegation was not under any illusions otherwise. John Jay was particularly distrustful of French motives. "They are interested in separating us from Great Britain," he surmised, "and on that point we may, I believe, depend upon them; but it is not their interest that we should become a great and formidable people, and therefore they will not help us to become so."[10]

Jay was correct. As long as it meant more leverage for their Crown, the French were willing to allow Britain to hold on to the Midwest, Savannah, Charleston, Maine, and even New York City, thus leaving the United States a not-so-peaceful piece of Swiss cheese.[11] To add to their treachery, the French conspired with the Spanish to block the United States' territorial expansion. For a time, they were even willing to permit the British to deny recognition of the United States' independence at the outset of the talks![12]

It appeared likely that the duplicitous French would succeed in their plans. They not only possessed money, power, and diplomatic expertise, but had influence in the American Congress. "I can do what I please with them," wrote one French agent in the United States.[13] There was even speculation that the French had bribed General Sullivan, who was a congressman at the time. Whether this was true or not, they successfully lobbied Congress to grant them the lead in the peace talks.[14] The hoodwinked congressmen decided to place the French court "in possession of sufficient power to make a peace"[15] and instructed Franklin, Adams, and Jay to make "no step without the approbation of His Majesty," the king of France.[16] However, Franklin, Adams, and Jay were not men to follow another's lead.

In a stunning turn of events, the three American peace commissioners ignored this congressional directive and began separate talks with the British. Adams felt, "amidst all these doublings and windings of European politics," that the Americans should "have opinions, principles, and systems of [their] own."[17] In a coded letter, Jay explained, "Had I not violated the instructions of Congress their dignity would have been in the dust," for the French were not seeking America's best interests.[18] Suspecting that the French were trying to stall the talks until they captured British territory in Europe, the Americans ignored French opposition to the move and demanded that the British acknowledge American independence as a preliminary to any discussions.

The British proved surprisingly compliant. Because Britain was now engaged in a world war with their arch enemies, the "rebellious colonies" were no longer as high a priority as they had been just a few years prior. In fact, the British were most anxious to drive a wedge between the Americans and the French, fearing that a lasting alliance between them would effectively counter their power for as long as it endured. And so they looked for cracks in the "friendship of convenience." Those cracks were easy to find—a rift between the allies became readily apparent to the British when the French sent a secret envoy to Britain in an attempt to block the Americans' demands for fishing rights off Nova Scotia. John Jay intercepted a ciphered French letter on the matter and likewise wrote to the British requesting that they not allow the French and Spanish to wield too much influence in the peace talks. The British smelled blood. They needed only to take advantage of the "profound feud [that] had sprung up between the Americans and their European allies."[19] Luckily for the Americans, the British saw a quick peace with the United States as the best means of doing so.

Leveraging the British agenda, Franklin, Adams, and Jay negotiated a sweetheart deal. They won recognition of American independence, doubled the nation's landmass by extending it west to the Mississippi River, and gained fishing "liberties" off the coasts of New England and Canada. While the British pushed for the Americans to restore the Loyalists' confiscated property, Congress agreed only to *recommend* that the states do so—a recommendation they were very likely to ignore. Instead, the United States would stick the British with the bill. If they wanted those Americans who supported their cause to be compensated, the Parliament would have to dig into its own coffers.

Franklin informed the French of America's separate peace. They were not pleased. "The English buy peace rather than make it," one Frenchman seethed, adding, "Their concessions exceed all that I could have thought possible." The French saw this "dream" treaty as a blatant ploy by the British for "the defection of the Americans."[20] A breach between the allies seemed inevitable.

Like a stern father, the French diplomat Charles Gravier, comte de Vergennes, scolded Franklin, "I am at a loss, sir, to explain your conduct and that of your colleagues on this occasion. You have concluded your preliminary articles without any communication between us, although the instructions from Congress prescribe that nothing shall be done without the participation of the King."[21] A sixty-five-year-old member of the French aristocracy, Vergennes had been instrumental in convincing France to aid the Americans. He had helped persuade the Crown to throw its army and navy into the battle and even loan the Americans $31 million. Now it was becoming clear that the French had been duped out of their chance to obtain territory and other spoils. Instead, Americans reaped the rewards of the French investment.

The cunning Franklin delicately replied that the Americans, as novices, had blundered and had not intended to cut out the French.[22] "But as this was not from want of respect to the King, whom we all love and honor, we hope it will be excused," he wrote, and he hoped that what the two nations had accomplished together would "not be ruined by a single indiscretion of ours."[23] Franklin dissembled, of course. Appealing to France's self-interest, he aimed to close the public breach by concluding with a wily suggestion: "The English, I just now learn, flatter themselves they have already divided us. I hope this little misunderstanding will therefore be kept a secret, and that they will find themselves totally mistaken."[24] The befuddled French could do little to fix the situation. Making the most of bad circumstances, they decided to mend the rift in order to avoid handing the British their objective of splitting their enemies.

Jefferson summed up America's reception of the treaty when he wrote to Jay, "The terms obtained for us are indeed great, and are so deemed by your country."[25] Washington's protégé, Hamilton, remarked that the peace terms exceeded "the expectations of the most sanguine."[26] But despite this grand diplomatic victory, all was not well for America. While Franklin was outsmarting Europe, Washington was busy trying to stop a brewing insurrection.

34

Spectacles & Speculation

Even as the Americans were nearing "the greatest achievement in the history of American diplomacy" by scoring such a favorable peace treaty, their republic was far from safe.[1] Its own military nearly toppled it. From Washington's perspective, the war was still on until the treaty was signed and the British were removed. Because of "their former infatuation with duplicity and [the] perverse system of British policy," he said, he was "induced to doubt everything, to suspect every-thing."[2] He even suspected that the peace talks were a ruse and was certain that "the King will push the war as long as the nation will find men or money."[3] Thus, after his victory over Cornwallis at Yorktown in October 1781, he returned with his wearied army to corner the British troops holed up in New York City. Many saw this move as a power play.

Some Americans believed that Washington would take control of the country after the war. His insistence on maintaining the army at full strength despite the looming peace appeared to signal that he was unwilling—or perhaps unable, considering Congress's ineptitude—to relinquish his quasi-monarchical power.[4] Adding credence to this theory, reports abounded that Hamilton, possibly while intoxicated, expressed his belief that the nation would be far better off if Washington marched with his troops into Philadelphia and disbanded Congress.[5] In fact, Washington's leadership during the war was so highly regarded by the American people that many welcomed the idea—especially his troops.

"Great discontents prevailed" in the Continental Army, even as the end of the war was in sight. By the spring of 1782, Washington's men had been rendered nearly destitute, and on some days "they were absolutely in want of provisions." Congress and the states could barely feed the troops, let alone keep up with their salaries. Many soldiers doubted they would ever see even half the pay they had been promised, and "fears began to be expressed that, in the event of peace, they would all be disbanded with their claims unliquidated and themselves cast upon the community penniless, and unfitted, by long military habitudes, for gainful pursuits of peace."[6] Such fears were justified, as some state legislatures indeed discussed abolishing the Continental Army so that they might void their responsibility to pay the troops.[7]

The soldiers turned to their commander for help. One who directly approached Washington was Colonel Lewis Nicola. Born to a British officer in Ireland, Nicola had followed his father's footsteps into the British Army. He served for decades in Irish garrisons before leaving the army and emigrating to Philadelphia, where he ran a dry goods store and founded a library. Some saw him as "feather-headed and irresponsible," a claim that may be supported by his avid job-hopping: he also tried his hand as an author, pub owner, and teacher before returning to military life as an American soldier. Having developed a professional, but not particularly friendly, relationship with Washington, he wrote his commander in May 1782 to convey his ideas for the future of the country.[8]

In his carefully crafted letter, Nicola reminded Washington that the soldiers were growing restless and resentful of the government, which they saw as inefficient and ineffective. In fact, the troops were so desperate to obtain their rightful pay that they were willing to fight for their "pecuniary rights." Nicola explained, "God forbid we should ever think of involving that country we have, under your conduct & auspices, rescued from oppression, into a new scene of blood &

confusion; but it cannot be expected we should forego claims on which our future subsistance & that of our families depend."[9] Even more alarming was Nicola's proposed solution.

Admitting that he did not favor "a republican form of government," Nicola suggested that the country experiment with a constitutional monarchy in the image of Great Britain. He outlined a "scheme" in which Congress would compensate the soldiers and then delineate a "tract in some of the best of those fruitful & extensive countries to the west of our frontiers" that might be "formed into a distinct State under such mode of government as those military who choose to remove to it may agree on." Since the wartime experience "must have shown to all, but to military men in particular the weakness of republics," he predicted that this new state would adopt a monarchical government.[10]

Nicola pointed to the Continental Army's successes "under a proper head," meaning Washington himself. It was "uncontroverted," he believed, that "the same abilities which have lead us [*sic*], through difficulties apparently insurmountable by human power, to victory and glory, those qualities that have merited and obtained the universal esteem and veneration of an army, would be most likely to conduct and direct us in the smoother paths of peace."[11] Many inferred from this letter that Nicola, and possibly a growing chorus in the army, wished for Washington to be king.[12]

Whatever the letter's precise intent, Washington was appalled. He shot back that very same day, "you could not have found a person to whom your schemes are more disagreeable." Viewing Nicola's proposals "with abhorrence," Washington remonstrated, "no occurrence in the course of the War, has given me more painful sensations than your information of there being such ideas existing in the Army as you have expressed." He was offended by the suggestion that he might participate in such a scheme, saying, "I am much at a loss to conceive what part of my conduct could have given encouragement to an address which to me seems big with the greatest mischiefs that can befall my Country."[13]

Washington was willing to help alleviate the plight of the soldiers, but only via the existing republican system. Although he himself had criticized Congress, he staunchly opposed the establishment of a monarchy in the likeness of the one he had fought against for so many years. He would play no part in ending the republic that he played a pivotal role in creating. Sounding like the strict stepfather that he was, Washington ordered Nicola "to banish these thoughts from your Mind, and never communicate, as from yourself, or any one else, a sentiment of the like Nature."[14] He considered this response to Nicola so momentous that he demanded—for the only time during the war—that his aides provide proof that it had been sealed and posted.[15]

Nicola indeed received the scathing rebuke and promptly replied with three repentant letters. Despite Nicola's mea culpa, discontent continued to seethe within the army, however. If the soldiers were compensated, wrote one officer, they would be "the lambs and bees of the community," but if not, they were likely to become "its tigers and wolves."[16] By the start of 1783, those wolves began to growl.

As the war wound down, Washington settled with his troops in winter quarters near West Point, in the town of Newburgh, New York. No longer burdened by battles, marches, or fear of attack, the troops milled about, anxiously contemplating their future. And if idle hands do the devil's work, here in Newburgh the devil was using them to foment a military coup.

The intrigue began to unfold when the destitute army readied "to procure justice to itself," just as Nicola had foretold.[17] On March 10, 1783, two anonymous tracts circulated, calling on the soldiers to "assume a bolder tone" with Congress and "never sheath your swords . . . until they had obtained justice."[18] The troops were exhorted to do something about a "country that tramples upon your rights, disdains your cries and insults your distresses." Declaring that the army would not "Go, starve and be forgotten," the mysterious author—signing the tracts only as "a fellow soldier"—urged the troops "to oppose tyranny, under whatever garb it may assume; whether it be the plain coat of republicanism, or the splendid robe of royalty."[19]

When his officers planned an unauthorized meeting to discuss the situation, Washington saw a grave threat brewing: it appeared that the army was sliding down a slippery slope towards mutiny and even armed conflict with Congress. He foresaw the possibility of the army marching to Philadelphia to demand their pay at gunpoint. Trembling with anger and shock, he intervened.[20]

Washington blasted the unapproved meeting and vowed "to arrest, on the spot, the foot that stood wavering on a tremendous precipice, to prevent the Officers from being taken by surprise while the passions were all inflamed, and to rescue them from plunging themselves into a gulph of Civil horror from which there might be no receding."[21] Although he sympathized with his men and even admitted that the anonymous call to action was an elegant "force of expression," he needed to nip the uprising in the bud.[22] It could send the country spiraling into civil war, perhaps lead to military rule, or even invite the British to resume hostilities.[23] Washington forbade the unauthorized meeting and proposed, instead, his own meeting of officers for March 15 so that they might air their grievance via ordinary channels.[24] Plus, this would give them a few days to cool off.

Since the commander was not expected to attend this meeting, his old rival Horatio Gates would chair it. This was ironic, because circumstantial evidence pointed to his involvement in the plot: the two anonymous tracts were believed to have been written by his former aide and his current aide, thus leading some to pin the culpability squarely on "Gates and those around him."[25] Although his military ascent may have been halted, his political ambitions remained active. But with little direct proof linking Granny Gates to the scheme, it was unclear whether he had been pulling the strings or merely lending a sympathetic ear. Regardless, with the tract exhorting the troops to "suspect the man who would advise to more moderation," namely Washington, the commander was in danger.[26]

On the day of the meeting, the officers anxiously milled within a building called the "Temple of Virtue" due to its use as a church, dance hall, and Masonic lodge.[27] But at noon on that Saturday, the Temple was far from sanctified. A palpable anger permeated the hall along with the aroma of its freshly milled wood. The murmur of complaints was abruptly cut off by an unexpected attendee—Washington had entered.

Washington's solid steps echoed through the cavernous room. He strode to the front and stood before his surprised officers. Although a man of astonishing control over his emotions, Washington was "sensibly agitated."[28] It being the first and only time that he stood in opposition to his men, he began by reading a lengthy address from a script, uncharacteristically replete with exclamation points.[29] Washington reminded the stone-faced officers of his own devotion to them as their "constant companion and witness of [their] distress." He pledged to use his power to champion their cause and entreated them to "place full confidence in the purity of intentions of Congress."[30] He next turned to castigating the "insidious foe" who had penned the anonymous letters, decrying:

> this dreadful alternative of either deserting our country in the extremest hour of her distress, or turning our arms against it, which is the apparent object, unless Congress can be compelled into instant compliance. My God! what can this writer have in view, by recommending such measures? Can he be a friend to the army? Can he be a friend to this country?[31]

He ordered his men to join with him in suppressing this movement to "overturn the liberties of our country and deluge our rising empire in blood." Attempting to rouse their "sacred honor," he implored them to "give one more distinguished proof of unexampled patriotism and patient virtue, rising superior to the pressure of the most complicated sufferings."[32]

Washington's men were mostly unmoved—hunger trumped words. For all his political genius, he was proving ineffective in maneuvering the country from the verge of a military coup. Looking at the faces of the men before him, Washington sighed. He had failed. But, as had happened so many times throughout his life, a twist of fate would save him—and the republic.

In a last-ditch effort, Washington reached into his coat pocket and pulled out a letter illustrating "the good disposition in Congress towards the army."[33] But he began to stumble through the closely written words of the congressman's scribble. His officers leaned forward, "their hearts contracting with anxiety" as they observed their gallant commander suddenly appear confused and helpless.[34] Then he reached into his pocket again and withdrew something they had never seen: his spectacles.

By April 1783, Washington was fifty-one years old and had aged noticeably since attaining his commission as commander in chief eight years earlier. Violent bloodshed, crushing defeat, stinging sleet, and untold hardships had turned the youthful farmer into a haggard veteran. As inevitably happens, his eyesight eroded along with his youth. During the last part of the war, he had begun borrowing eyeglasses from his officers. Increasingly dependent on them to keep up with his voluminous correspondence, he contacted David Rittenhouse, a renowned mathematician, astronomer, inventor, and optical expert. Washington asked him to craft a pair of spectacles, sending him the borrowed lenses that best met his needs so that Rittenhouse would "know how to grind his Christals."[35] Honored, Rittenhouse promptly began the task at his workshop in Philadelphia. After less than a month, Washington received two pairs of eyeglasses, one with ornate silver frames, and was pleased at how they "shew those letters very distinctly which at first appear like a mist blended together and confused."[36]

Rittenhouse had donated his own time and expertise, but asked reimbursement from Washington for the silversmith's charge. Had he known how prominently the glasses would be featured in the annals of history, he may have absorbed the extra cost and portrayed himself for posterity as even more generous.

As he brought the spectacles to his eyes in the Temple of Virtue, Washington self-consciously told his officers, "Gentlemen, you must pardon me. I have grown gray in the service of my country and now find myself growing blind."[37] They had never seen him exhibit vulnerability before. This was the man who refused to flinch as musket and cannon fire whizzed past his face. Ignoring the words coming from his mouth, they instead fixated on the imagery. This display, "so natural, so unaffected," was "superior to the most studied oratory," reported one witness, adding that "it forced its way into the heart, and you might see sensibility moisten every eye." As Washington spoke, "every doubt was dispelled, and the tide of patriotism rolled again in its wonted course. Illustrious man!"[38] With one unplanned gesture, Washington had melted their anger and possibly saved the republic. He departed the hall, and his officers reaffirmed their support for him and for the United States government. Eventually, the soldiers did receive much of the pay owed them.

The Continental Congress approved the peace treaty on April 15, 1783, and it was officially signed on September 3. Thanks to Washington's leadership, America had won the war. The fight was bloody. It was messy. The nation had fumbled time and again. But America did what it took to win and the United States emerged triumphant as a democratic republic. Now the world wondered: what would happen next?

35

The Greatest Man in the World

While sitting for a portrait, King George III questioned the American-born painter Benjamin West about General Washington's plans for the future. Although he was now the royal court painter, living in London, West retained friendships in America and kept abreast of happenings across the Atlantic. In fact, he so fiercely clung to his roots that he bravely confessed to the king his desire to paint a portrait of Washington.[1] The king thus viewed West as a window into the American psyche and was said to have asked him whether he thought Washington would retain control of the army or immediately become the head of state. West replied, "They say he will return to his farm." According to the legend, the king let out a huff of disbelief and said, "If he does that, he will be the greatest man in the world."[2] He would.

The British evacuated New York City on November 25, 1783. Not above petty antics, the redcoats nailed a British flag to a sixty-foot flagpole at the Battery, greasing the pole to make the Americans look foolish when they struggled to remove it. They also went about removing any Stars and Stripes prematurely raised. According to lore, when a drunken Bloody Bill Cunningham spotted one such flag outside Day's Tavern in Harlem, he went to tear it down. To his great surprise, the "robust" Mrs. Day burst from the tavern, fist and broom flying. Beaten until "the powder flew from his wig," Cunningham retreated with a bloody nose.[3] He would live out his last few years in Britain before he was convicted for forgery and hanged. Poetic justice was served.

Once all the troops and fleeing Loyalists were aboard, the majestic warships' sails filled with the wind and they slowly set off for the British Isles. Throngs of gloating patriots lined the wharves to jeer the humiliated redcoats and the thousands of Loyalists who accompanied them. In anger, the British responded with a boom, firing a cannon towards their hecklers. The lead ball splashed harmlessly into the river, and as it sank into the dark gray waters, the last vestige of British rule in the United States disappeared along with it.

Having secured the nation's independence at last, Washington marched into New York City to a jubilant racket of fife, drum, and fanfare. Like returning home after much time away, even the intact neighborhoods of the bustling island appeared intangibly altered despite the familiar facades. Whether it was the city that changed or the viewer, Washington cared little. He had yearned to retake Manhattan for so long, but now he cared most about getting home to Mount Vernon.

He ordered his officers to Fraunces Tavern for a meeting on December 4, 1783. The stately brick inn had served as a meeting place for the Sons of Liberty at the outbreak of war, and then, during the British occupation, the Freemason who ran the tavern served as an American spy. Considering the central role it played throughout the Revolution, Washington viewed the handsome corner tavern as the perfect place for an impromptu goodbye.

Raising a glass of Madeira, Washington stood to address the three dozen officers gathered in the long banquet hall. With sidelong rays of the weak December sun pouring in through the tall windows of the elegant room, he took a moment of "almost breathless silence" to gaze upon the men in their blue and gold uniforms. "His emotions were too strong to be concealed which seemed to be reciprocated by every officer present," recounted one of those officers.[4] Together they had fought, shivered, and suffered for so many years, but it was over at last. Washington could finally say, "With a heart full of love and gratitude I now take leave of you. I most devoutly wish that your latter days may be as prosperous and happy as your former ones have been glorious and honorable."[5]

The aloof general—a man who normally was not to be touched—then surprised everyone: he began doling out kisses. His deep voice announced, "I cannot come to each of you but shall feel obliged if each of you will come and take me by the hand."[6] The first officer to approach him received more than he expected. Washington, "suffused in tears, was incapable of utterance but grasped his hand when they embraced each other in silence. In the same affectionate manner every officer in the room marched up to, kissed, and parted with this General-in-Chief."[7] The speechless room turned into a "scene of sorrow and weeping." After embracing the last man, Washington raised his arm to wave farewell to "his grieving children" and departed without looking back.[8] He was ready to go home.

Washington boarded a barge and set out to visit Congress. This conduct elicited "astonishment and amazement," for it was "so novel, so inconceivable to People, who, far from giving up powers they possess, are willing to convulse the Empire to acquire more."[9] As he headed south from New York City, Washington was *worshipped*. "I saw the greatest man who has ever appeared on the surface of the earth," boasted a Dutch businessman who witnessed his passage through Philadelphia. ". . . We all waved our hats three times over our heads . . . . I don't know if, in our delight at seeing the Hero, we were more surprised by his simple but grand air or by the kindness of the greatest and best of hero."[10] A French army chaplain, though not a huge fan of Americans, likewise reported,

> Through all the land, he appears like a benevolent god; old men, women, and children—they all flock eagerly to catch a glimpse of him when he travels and congratulate themselves because they have seen him. People carry[ing] torches follow him through the cities; his arrival is marked by public illumi-

nations; the Americans, though a cold people . . . have waxed enthusiastic about him and their first songs inspired by spontaneous sentiments have been consecrated to the glorification of Washington.[11]

While Washington was uncomfortable with such extravagant praise, he had little choice but to accept it. America was more than pleased with her first commander in chief. Stories of his grand exploits were on the tip of every tongue. Scrutinized throughout the war, Washington was accustomed to being the focus of public attention, but this most recent wave of admiration reached new heights. One observer found it amusing that, "in a place so crowded with the fair sex, everybody had eyes only for this Hero. Indeed, we only now and then stole a glance at our girls. His Excellency drew everyone's attention."[12] Now *that* was celebrity.

For the last eight years, Washington's actions as commander in chief had been under intense scrutiny by Congress, the state legislatures, and the American people. His wartime record had "been often detailed" and was "familiar to almost every person."[13] From the highest politician to the humblest everyman, they loved what they heard. The "public mind pointed to him as the most proper person for presiding over the military arrangements of America. Not only Congress, but the inhabitants in the east and west, in the north and south . . . were in great degree unanimous in his favor."[14] One admirer quoted scripture to liken him to Moses: "he was beloved of God and men . . . . The Lord magnified him so that his enemies stood in fear of him, and he made him glorious in the fight of kings."[15] And Washington's reputation only grew with his next move: he resigned.

Washington paid Congress a special visit. The transient assembly had since transferred to Annapolis, Maryland, in hopes that the city's balls and theaters might coax the chronically absent delegates to actually attend its sessions.[16] Approaching the lively city on December 19, 1783, Washington waded through the welcoming dignitaries and fawning citizens. On the 22nd, America threw a grand ball in his honor. Here, he toasted to "competent powers to Congress" and danced all evening with the star-struck young belles as he bathed in America's gratitude.[17] Ready to take his place in history, he awoke the next morning and prepared himself for what he thought would be his final public act.

Wearing his commander-in-chief uniform for the last time, he walked into the Maryland statehouse at noon on December 23. A sense of almost mythic magnitude pervaded the elegant classical chamber as Washington stood before the doting congressmen, while a crowd of gushing spectators in the back of the room peered over a balcony supported by bright Ionic columns. Like a scene out of the *Iliad*, Washington was viewed as a demigod. Feeling the momentousness of the occasion, he was overcome with emotion. His right hand, holding his prepared speech, shook so violently that he needed to steady it with his left.[18]

Deeply affected, Washington humbly offered his "sincere Congratulations to Congress" and requested "the indulgence of retiring from the Service of my Country."[19] His voice "faltered and sank and the house felt his agitations"[20] as he choked out the words, "I consider it an indispensable duty to close this last solemn act of my Official life, by commending the Interests of our dearest Country to the protection of Almighty God." In dramatic yet genuine fashion, he composed himself and concluded with a flourish: "Having now finished the work assigned me, I retire from the great theatre of Action; and . . . take my leave of all the employments of public life."[21] His horses waiting out front, Washington nobly departed amidst the audience's cries of admiration.

An admirer remarked that from the time Washington entered New York in triumph until he resigned his commission, "festive crowds impeded his passage through all the populous towns, the devotion of a whole people pursued him with prayers to Heaven for blessings on his head, while their gratitude fought the most expressive language of manifesting itself to him as their common father and benefactor."[22] But this demigod just wanted to go back to his farm.

After sleeping in over two hundred different locations through the previous nine years, he finally returned to Mount Vernon on December 24, 1783. This Christmas he could finally look forward to surprising not Hessians, but his loving family. As a heavy snow blanketed the estate, he settled back into a peaceful existence. Reflecting on where his path had taken him, he wrote,

> I feel now, however, as I conceive a wearied Traveller must do, who, after treading many a painful step, with a heavy burden on his shoulders, is eased of the latter, having reached the Goal to which all the former were directed; and from his House top is looking back, and tracing with a grateful eye the Meanders by which he escaped the quicksands and Mires which lay in his way; and into which none but the All-powerful guide, and great disposer of human Events could have prevented his falling.[23]

He would live happily as a gentleman farmer for a precious few years—until called upon to oversee the creation of the United States Constitution.[24]

⚜

George Washington's actions throughout the Revolutionary War reveal much about what powers the founding generation meant to bestow on the president. With the Revolution, they established a new and radical republic. They consciously sought to break away not only from British dominance but also from the monarchical mold. They needed to develop their own alternative. In forming their understanding of the appropriate powers for the United States president and commander in chief, the Founders had before them the example of George Washington, their original commander in chief.

Washington had carefully defined the commander-in-chief powers through his actions, as he strove to defend the nation without trampling its republican principles. This was quite a balancing act and America watched intently, with many expecting him to stumble. Newspapers circulated accounts of Washington's treatment of prisoners. Politicians wrote letters detailing the commander's war powers. Soldiers gossiped about his military commissions. Citizens witnessed his defense of their rights. Washington's precedents were known. And they were loved.

He was hailed as "the great soldier of liberty—a man whose exceptional virtue and patriotism assured final triumph."[25] In fact, so great was the public approval of his wartime conduct that few debate whether Washington could have made himself king.[26] But instead, he became a legend.

When it came time to vote on the new Constitution, the states all elected delegates to their individual ratifying conventions. When these delegates saw the words naming the president "Commander in Chief of the Army and Navy of the United States," they knew exactly what that meant: the powers that the great soldier of liberty had shaped in the crucible of war. These war powers became officially fixed in the presidency once the states approved the Constitution one by one, and it went into operation on September 13, 1788.[27]

When they set about to fill this new executive office, Americans could imagine no one else but Washington in it. So his adoring countrymen promptly elected him the first president of the United States, with votes from 100 percent of the electors.[28] In doing so, they placed him right back into the role that he had already defined for all future presidents: America's commander in chief.

In the same way that eyes are the window to the soul, Washington is the window to presidential war powers. Washington's eyes faced horrible prisoner abuse. They witnessed the emergence of dictatorial military might. They oversaw military commissions and swift executions of enemies of the state. They also carefully watched over American citizens' lives and livelihoods. In fact, they had seen so much that they were deteriorating by the end of the war. But that would not impede the great man from defining the new nation.

With his spectacles, the "Father of Our Country" not only saved the republic from an incipient military coup but also wrote hundreds of letters to instruct posterity on how the American republic should defend itself from a perilous world. As always, he led by example, expressing what the new nation should—and should not—do in the name of liberty. We need his direction still.

Washington confronted issues similar to those we face today. And he triumphed. "Held in the highest veneration over the whole continent," he epitomized to America what it meant to lead a United States at war.[29] And when our Founders adopted the Constitution with him in mind, he became the model for all subsequent commanders in chief.[30] It is about time we looked to that model for guidance.

In a gripping eulogy delivered upon Washington's death in 1799, Pastor Jedidiah Morse said, "Washington was the directing spirit without which there would have been no independence, no Union, no Constitution and no Republic. His ways were the ways of truth. His influence grows. In wisdom of action, in purity of character he stands alone." He "hoped posterity will be taught" how Washington transformed the nation, for stories of his deeds will undoubtedly be "instructive to future generations."[31]

I hope so too. We still have much to learn from him.

EPILOGUE

GOVERNING FROM THE GRAVE

"No matter how ingenious, imaginative or artfully put, unless interpretive methodologies are tied to the original intent of the framers, they have no more basis in the Constitution than the latest football scores. To be sure, even the most conscientious effort to adhere to the original intent of the framers of our Constitution is flawed, as all methodologies and human institutions are; but at least originalism has the advantage of being legitimate and, I might add, impartial."[1]
—Clarence Thomas, Associate Justice of the Supreme Court of the United States, 2008

Epilogue

In some fundamental respects, America's current challenges in the ongoing War on Terror mirror those that General Washington faced well over two centuries ago. We have fierce debates today concerning war tactics, drone strikes on Americans, torture, military tribunals, citizens' rights during wartime, and how to reconcile the needs of national defense with liberty and self-rule. It is not too late to learn from Washington's leadership as we navigate our nation towards a better future.

We are lucky to have such a tremendous exemplar to help guide us through troubled times. We can study Washington himself and the founding generation's writings for object lessons in leadership that were developed in the heat of battle and internal strife. To this day, the Founders illustrate how a republic may effectively confront and defeat mortal dangers while retaining its core values. But just in case we are not enlightened enough to learn from them volitionally, there is another important reason to study the founding generation: our legal system calls for it.

More precisely, the legal theory of originalism requires attention to the past. According to this theory of interpretation, the Constitution's provisions have a fixed and discernible meaning that was established at the time of enactment. In order to determine what war powers are granted to today's president, originalism bids us to study the founding era to explain what it meant to be "Commander in Chief of the Army and Navy of the United States" when the Constitution was enacted.

Originalists contend that because our democratic republic's laws emanate from "we the people," it is important to understand what the people who enacted these laws had in mind. Originalism calls for modern interpreters of the Constitution to ascertain what was meant by "commander in chief" to the people when they enshrined their will in that document. Originalists reason that to do otherwise would subjugate the will of the people who created the law to the will of the unelected judges interpreting it.

314

This theory has some powerful adherents. In the 2008 *District of Columbia v. Heller* opinion, ruling on the meaning of the "right to bear arms," the justices of the Supreme Court clearly displayed their originalist stripes. In fact, the *Heller* opinion has been described as "the most detailed display of originalist jurisprudence by a majority opinion in the Court's history."[2] Led by Justice Antonin Scalia, an avowed originalist, the majority analyzed what the language of the Constitution meant to Americans of the founding era. Scalia's opinion—which was joined by Chief Justice John Roberts and Justices Samuel Alito, Anthony Kennedy, and Clarence Thomas—reasoned that the Second Amendment, at the time it was enacted, was understood to allow citizens to possess firearms, even if not serving in a militia. With this opinion, the majority of the United States' final arbiters of justice displayed their belief that history directly shapes modern law. And they are not alone.

Originalists come in many forms. Broadly speaking, liberal jurists and scholars tend to place less weight on original understanding than conservatives do, not least because originalist methodology tends to produce conservative results. But conservative judges are not alone in according at least some authority to history. It is notable, for example, that Justice John Paul Stevens's dissent in *Heller* likewise focused on originalist arguments. The rest of the Supreme Court's more liberal wing, which then consisted of Justices Stephen Breyer, Ruth Bader Ginsburg, and David Souter,[3] joined Stevens in looking at the history of the Constitution's drafting in order to elucidate its meaning. While they arrived at different conclusions based upon their specific analyses, what is most important to this discussion is that both sides relied on the history of the founding. The *Heller* opinion and dissent both reflect the common notion among judges and legal scholars that "triangulating from the wisdom of the past to the . . . circumstances of the present is at least the default point of departure," as William Galston put it. He added, "The alternative to that is chaos."[4]

There certainly are many scholars and jurists who are skeptical of originalism or even reject it altogether. Some of these critics claim that it is ridiculous to allow antiquated—and arguably unascertainable—notions from centuries past to govern modern society. They see the Constitution as a living document whose meaning should be adapted to the realities of our day. For example, what constituted "cruel and unusual" punishment in the eighteenth century may not be the same as how it is understood today. Proponents of a "living Constitution" argue that as times change, judges should reinterpret the words of the text in order to keep the document relevant, even if the new reading does not fit the original meaning or even the clear sense of the words.

Justice Scalia rejects this approach, arguing, "Every time you insert into the Constitution—by speculation—new rights that aren't really there you are impoverishing democracy. You are pushing one issue after another off the democratic stage."[5] Rather than permit the voters and their legislators to decide issues, inserting new rules into the Constitution largely takes those choices out of their hands and into the courts. Scalia admits that originalism can serve to maintain antiquated laws that are no longer useful or beneficial. But our democratic republic has a solution for outdated laws, as Scalia points out: a law "may well be stupid, but if it's stupid, pass a law" to replace it.[6] The republic needs to pass new laws that better reflect the will of modern society, instead of allowing judges to discover new *meanings* in old law, thus aggrandizing their own role at the expense of the political process. In the case of a "stupid" or outdated constitutional provision, the people can amend the Constitution using the mechanisms that the forward-thinking Founders provided.

The interpretation of a law based on its meaning hundreds of years ago may sometimes yield results that appear to be absurd. For example, the Constitution names the president as "Commander in Chief of the Army and Navy." The Framers did not anticipate airplanes, so does this mean that the president should not also command the Air Force? Many originalists consider this a straw-man argument because the phrase "Army and Navy" in the eighteenth century encompassed *all* the armed forces—and all their weaponry. Only the most comically hyper-literal originalist would believe it excludes the Air Force. Even so, this example illustrates how the meaning of the eighteenth-century text may conflict with contemporary common sense. But even if there were a genuine concern over this issue, there is a way to clarify that the president is the commander in chief of the Air Force: pass a constitutional amendment.

It is not the purpose of this book to advocate for a particular level of deference to originalism, or to contend that the history of the Constitution's enactment should be the ending point of an inquiry into its meaning. Rather, I argue that historical understanding should at least be a starting point for interpreting the Constitution.[7] People will have varying subjective convictions as to the merits of originalism in constitutional analysis, but even those who are intellectually opposed to it must agree that this mode of interpretation is objectively important if only because *major players believe it is important*.[8] It is undeniable that history directly affects law and policy today.

There are various angles of history to look at, however, and thus there are different approaches to originalism, as the result in *Heller* suggests. Some scholars and jurists seek the "original intent" of those who wrote the Constitution. To interpret the Commander in Chief clause, they would aim to discern what the delegates to the Constitutional Convention intended that phrase to mean when they wrote it. They would examine the delegates' diaries, the *Federalist Papers*, and other documents of the Framers to determine what war powers those men intended the Constitution to grant the president. Many academics and judges prefer to cast a broader net.

The more prominent branch of originalism seeks to determine the "original meaning" rather than the "original intent" of the Constitution. In this line of inquiry, one must look at history to determine how the constitutional text was understood by the "original readers—the citizens, polemicists, and convention delegates who participated in one way or another in ratification."[9] The idea is to ascertain the will of the entire people rather than just the elite few who drafted the document. The full "intent" of the Framers at the Constitutional Convention may not have been conveyed to the delegates at the state ratifying conventions, or the farmers in the field, through the Constitution's brief words. Those seeking the "original meaning" of the Constitution's Commander in Chief text would be interested not only in the delegates' documents, but also in speeches, debates, newspapers, and even dictionaries of the time.[10] This book, by drawing upon all of these sources, incorporates both major branches of originalism.

When the Founders adopted the Constitution, Washington's precedents were no secret.[11] His frequent letters communicated his views to Congress and the state legislatures, many of whose members became Framers of the Constitution.[12] But his precedents were much more widely disseminated than that. His practices were likewise known by the soldiers who witnessed them, the townsfolk who talked about them, and the farmers who read the newspaper reports. The episodes recounted in this book were on the tips of the everyday tongue during the revolutionary years. The American people loved what they heard and exalted Washington for his military leadership.

To Americans of the time, the plain meaning of the phrase "Commander in Chief" was cast by their recent memories of the only commander in chief that the new nation had ever had. When they created the presidency, Washington personified what it meant to be commander in chief specifically, as well as the president more broadly. In fact, he was so fully identified with the role that when it came time to elect their first president, he received a vote from every single elector. When the American people ratified the Constitution, they envisaged their Revolutionary War commander as the legal model for all subsequent presidents.

While we can certainly derive personal enrichment from our founding generation's struggles, the direct impact of those struggles on modern law provides a practical reason to study the revolutionary era. I am not attempting to oversimplify the weighty issues addressed in this book by arguing that "Washington did X, therefore the modern presidents can also do X under the powers granted them by the Commander in Chief clause." Instead, I more humbly assert that the precedents set by Washington in wartime should be taken into consideration when we interpret the presidential powers established by the Constitution. Does the president have a constitutional power to torture foreign enemy combatants? Overrule Congress on war tactics? Deny formal trials to enemies? Trample on the rights of American citizens? At least consider our first commander in chief's principles when searching for an answer.

George Washington's actions as a leader in wartime demonstrate the moral and practical truths on which the nation was founded. In this way, the story of America's first commander in chief both constrains and empowers contemporary occupants of the Oval Office. Luckily, General Washington set a good example. He still governs from the grave.

"The foundation of our Empire was not laid in the gloomy age of Ignorance and Superstition, but at an Epocha when the rights of mankind were better understood and more clearly defined, than at any former period . . . . At this auspicious period, the United States came into existence as a Nation, and if their Citizens should not be completely free and happy, the fault will be intirely their own."[13]

—GEORGE WASHINGTON, 1783

ACKNOWLEDGMENTS

When we were growing up, my father took us to a reenactment of the Battle of Lexington every year. My mother (a true force of nature who inexplicably looked impeccable even at 4 A.M.), sister, brothers, and I would wake up before dawn and wait in the freezing cold around the little town green. Men in costume would eventually march in, conduct a brief, exciting battle, and then run off just in time for us to head to a nice, warm breakfast. We went to a delightfully hokey restaurant where the waiters pretended to be patriots from 1775. My father, with his boundless wit and humor, would have us laughing around the table as he attempted to trick the man impersonating George Washington into breaking character.

This was on my mind many years later as I sat in Bill Eskridge's Constitutional Law class at Yale Law School. Bill was explaining how presidents have long pointed to the Commander in Chief clause in the Constitution as the source of a whole host of powers, yet many debate what that clause even means. He said, "too bad we cannot ask the Founders what they meant." I instantly thought of the waiter my father tormented. This idea stuck in my head as I started digging with the saintly Teresa Miguel through Yale Law Library's extensive primary source collections. And with Bill Eskridge's tremendous help, encouragement, and wisdom, I wrote the academic paper that would eventually evolve into this book—and that evolution came with an enthusiastic push from Amy Chua. The paper came up in conversation the next year while I was speaking with Amy at her office hours. She had read it and said, "Logan, you need to make this into a book!" It had never occurred to me that I could write anything, let alone a book. But with Professors Eskridge and Chua's amazing help, I was able to work with the unstoppable Glen Hartley at Writers Reps to do just that.

I would like to thank the incredible Encounter team. The dedication of Roger Kimball, Sam Schneider, Lauren Miklos, Carol Staswick, Heather Ohle, and Nola Tully made this book possible. I greatly appreciate Dean Draznin, who is the best and most entertaining publicist anyone could ever dream of.

I am deeply grateful to the incredible Jon Macey, Lee Otis, and Gene Meyer, whose help and support were vital in making this book a reality. I am indebted to Professors Akhil Amar, Hadley Arkes, Patrick Weil, John Witt, Gene Fidel, Richard Bernstein, Richard Meyer, and John Dehn for sharing their many insights with me as I wrote. I am also grateful for the excellent research assistance I received from Yale doctoral candidate Carolee Klimchock, Yale PhD student Michael Hattem, and Yale's Courtney Grafton.

I would like to express my tremendous appreciation for the editing, research, and advice from my amazing friends from Yale Law School: Kory Langhofer, Noelle Grohmann, Katie Schettig, Jason Green, Mark Fitzgerald, Faisal Rashid, Alexandra Roberts, Dara Purvis, Gabe Rosenberg, Steve Winter, Alicyn Cooley, Stephanie Lee, Hayley Fink, Michael Love, Andrew Giering, Patrick Moroney, Jayme Herschkopf, Alan Hurst, Chris Hurtado, Jane Diecker, Jamie Hodari, and Jake Gardener.

A special thank you to Sean Beirne, Thomas Beirne III, Colleen Beirne, Tommy and Collin, Timmy Fitzmaurice, Anta Cisse-Green, Nelle Jennings, Joseph White, Paula Yavru, Jim McFarlane, Abby Beal,

Acknowledgments

Mary Dulko, Michael Brunson, Cathy McLean, Victoria Pugliesi, Natalie Raitano, Alycia Stevenin, Joey Gonzalez, Jonathan Rollo, Cait Levin, Ariana Green, Julie Silverbrook, Ryan Williams, Bob Ford, and Stacey Phelan. It takes an army.

And I would like to thank my partner in crime, the indomitable Deirdre Nora Beirne.

NOTES

FREQUENTLY CITED SOURCES
Document Collections and Primary Narratives

American Archives: Documents of the American Revolution, 1774–1776. Edited by Peter Force et al. Northern Illinois University Libraries, 2001– .

Journals of the Continental Congress, 1774–1789. Edited by Worthington Chauncey Ford et al. Washington, D.C.: U.S. Government Printing Office, 1904–1937.

The Papers of George Washington, Diaries. Edited by Donald Jackson et al. Charlottesville: University of Virginia Press, 1976–1979.

The Papers of George Washington (Chronological Series). Edited by W. W. Abbot et al. University of Virginia Press, 1987– .

The Records of the Federal Convention of 1787. Edited by Max Farrand. New Haven: Yale University Press, 1911; revised 1966.

Smith, Joshua Hett. *An Authentic Narrative of the Causes Which Led to the Death of Major André.* London: Matthews & Leigh, 1808.

The Spirit of Seventy-Six: The Story of the American Revolution as Told by Participants. Edited by Henry Steele Commager and Richard B. Morris. 1958; Cambridge, Mass.: Da Capo Press, 1995.

Thacher, James. *Military Journal of the American Revolution*. 1823; Hartford, Conn.: Hurlbut, Williams & Co., 1862.

The Writings of George Washington from the Original Manuscript Sources, 1745–1799. Edited by John Clement Fitzpatrick. George Washington Bicentennial Commission. Washington, D.C.: U.S. Government Printing Office, 1931–1944.

Modern Works

Chernow, Ron. *Washington: A Life*. New York: Penguin, 2010.

Fischer, David Hackett. *Washington's Crossing*. New York: Oxford University Press, 2004.

McCullough, David. *1776*. New York: Simon & Schuster, 2005.

Preface to the Paperback Edition

1.   Scott Shane, "Assessing the Trade-Offs between Security and Civil Liberties," The Caucus, *New York Times*, July 24, 2012; Jill Kelley, "How the Government Spied on Me," Opinion, *Wall Street Journal*, November 5, 2013; Jess Bravin, "POW Swap Took Place in a Legal Gray Area," *Wall Street Journal*, June 5, 2014.

2.   Charles M. Blow, "Dangerous Divisiveness: Politics Grows More Partisan," Opinion, *New York Times*, June 15, 2104.

3.   Washington's Farewell Address, September 17, 1796, in *The Papers of George Washington, Presidential Series*, available at http://gwpapers.virginia.edu/documents_gw/farewell/transcript.html.

4.   George Washington to Sir Edward Newenham, July 20, 1788, The Constitutional Sources Project, http://consource.org/document/george-washington-to-sir-edward-newenham-1788-7-20/. Thanks to ConSource for their many excellent resources.

5.   George Washington to the Boston Selectmen (Ezekiel Price, Thomas Walley, William Bordman, Ebenezer Seaver, Thomas Crafts, Thomas Edwards, William Little, William Scollay, and Jesse Putnam), July 28, 1795, in *The Writings of George Washington*, 34:253. I greatly appreciate Tara Helfman's brilliant insights.

Introduction

1.   As translated from "Conotocarious," which is the name given to him by the Seneca Native Americans, who had called his grandfather by the same. George Washington, "To his Excellency Horatio Sharp, Governor of Maryland," April 28, 1754, in *The Journal of Colonel George Washington*, ed. Albany J. Munsell (1893), 51.

2.   Fred Anderson, *Crucible of War: The Seven Years' War and the Fate of Empire in British North America, 1754–1766* (New York: Knopf, 2000), 35–36.

3.   Ron Chernow, *Washington: A Life*, 30.

4.   James Thomas Flexner, *Washington: The Indispensable Man* (Boston: Little, Brown, 1974), 8. Washington's exact height is unknown. He measured in at six foot three after his death, but it is unclear whether the doctor pointed his feet upwards to gauge his flat-footed height or allowed them to point downwards as he lay. The latter would gauge his height on his tippy-toes, so to speak. Washington told his tailor that he was six feet tall, which may have been his true standing height. But since he also complained about ill-fitting clothes, it is unclear. I am grateful to Ron Chernow for bringing this to my attention. He has provided many insights and suggested great sources.

5.   Ibid.

6.   *The Papers of George Washington, Diaries*, 1:144.

7.   *The Papers of George Washington, Colonial Series*, 1:73. His men were clamoring about their lack of pay and supplies before they even left Virginia. See also Governor Dinwiddie to Matthew Rowan, March 23, 1754, in *The Official Records of Robert Dinwiddie: Lieutenant-Governor of the Colony of Virginia, 1751–1758*, ed. R. A. Brock (Richmond: Virginia Historical Society, 1883), 122.

8.   Washington to Governor Dinwiddie, Will's Creek, April 25, 1754, in *The Papers of George Washington, Colonial Series*, 1:87–90.

9.   "Speech to Indians at Logstown," November 26, 1753, in *The Writings of George Washington*, 1:25.

10. Based on sculptural rendering by Bryan Rapp.

11. Joseph J. Ellis, *His Excellency: George Washington* (New York: Knopf, 2004), 14. Ellis's introduction offers a vivid account of this episode.

12. Father Bruyas, qtd. in *Handbook of American Indians North of Mexico*, ed. Frederick Hodge (1912), 124.

13. Washington Irving, *Life of George Washington* (1856–1859; repr. New York: G. P. Putnam, 1876), 1:48. Nineteenth-century historians often lacked access to the primary sources now available. Thus, they wrote based on an incomplete understanding of the events. However, in tangential descriptions, I include them as lively color to nonessential points.

14. Qtd. in Donald H. Kent, "Contrecoeur's Copy of George Washington's Journal," *Pennsylvania History* 19 no. 1 (1952): 23.

15. Washington to Robert Dinwiddie, May 29, 1754, in *The Papers of George Washington, Colonial Series*, 1:111.

16. Claude Pierre Pecaudy de Contrecoeur, "Sommation de Jumonville," in *Papiers Contrecoeur et autres documents concernant le conflit anglo-français sur l'Ohio de 1745 à 1756*, ed. Fernand Grenier (Quebec: Les Presses Universitaires Laval, 1952), 130. See also Jacob Blosser, "Getting Away with Murder: The Tragic Story of George Washington at Jumonville Glen," James Madison University (2000).

17. Robert Dinwiddie, "Instruct's to be observ'd by Maj'r Geo. Washington, on the Expedit'n to the Ohio," in *The Official Records of Robert Dinwiddie*, 1:59.

18. Washington to Dinwiddie, 108.

19. Irving, *Life of George Washington*, 1:41.

20. George Washington, "Journal Entry 28 May 1754," in Kent, "Contrecoeur's Copy of George Washington's Journal," 21.

21. René Chartrand, *Monongahela 1754–55: Washington's Defeat, Braddock's Disaster* (Oxford: Osprey Publishing, 2004), 27.

22. Blosser, "Getting Away with Murder," provides an excellent discussion of the Jumonville Affair and brought additional sources to my attention.

23. "We carried out our arrangements to surround them, and we began to march in Indian fashion [until we] . . . had advanced quite near them according to plan, when they discovered us. Then I gave my men orders to fire." Washington, "Journal Entry 28 May 1754," in Kent, "Contrecoeur's Copy of George Washington's Journal," 21.

24. Washington to Dinwiddie, 116.

25. Ibid., 1:107. See also Ellis, *His Excellency*, 13. I am grateful to Deirdre Beirne for her insight on this point.

26. *The Papers of George Washington, Diaries*, 1:195–96.

27. For a summary of the French perspective, see Ian Steele, "Hostage-taking 1754: Virginians vs Canadians," *Journal of the Canadian Historical Association* 16:1 (2005), 49–73.

28. Irving says that Jumonville was shot at the start of the battle. Irving, *Life of George Washington*, 1:42.

29. Tanaghrisson to Joseph Coulon de Villiers de Jumonville, May 28, 1754, qtd. in Fred Anderson, *The War That Made America: A Short History of the French and Indian War* (New York: Viking, 2005), 47.

30. Washington to Dinwiddie, 111–12.

31. Anderson, *Crucible of War*, 6.

32. Ibid.

33. Washington to John Augustine Washington, May 31, 1754, in *The Papers of George Washington, Colonial Series*, 1:118.

34. Laura Wolff Scanlan, "Clash of the Empires," *Humanities* 26 (2005): 3, quoting British MP Horace Walpole.

35. C. C. Felton, qtd. in Paul F. Boller, *Presidential Anecdotes* (New York: Oxford University Press, 1996), 4.

36. Ibid.

37. "Nathanael Hawthorne," *The Spectator: A Weekly Review of Politics, Literature, Theology, and Art*, March 23, 1871, 371.

38. U.S. Constitution, art. 2, sec. 2, cl. 1.

39. The unabashed presentism of this book is sure to make many academic historians cringe. However, when it comes to historical constitutional interpretation, this is an unavoidable nature of the inquiry.

40. The University of Virginia's Papers of George Washington Project has brought to light many documents previously inaccessible. I am extremely grateful to Professor William M. Ferraro and the whole team for their tremendous help with this book.

41. Marcus Cunliffe, *George Washington, Man and Monument* (New York: Mentor, 1960), 5.

Part I: The King of America

1. Pierce Butler to Weedon Butler, May 5, 1778, in *The Records of the Federal Convention of 1787*, 3:308.

Chapter 1: The Not-So-United States

1. For a succinct summary of republican ideology in eighteenth-century Anglo-America, see Gordon S. Wood, *The American Revolution: A History* (New York: Modern Library, 2002), 89–109. Stacey Phelan was instrumental in researching this opening.

2. Prior to the adoption of the Articles of Confederation in 1781, Congress was called the "Continental Congress."

3. Warren E. Burger, "Obstacles to the Constitution," *The Supreme Court Historical Society Yearbook 1987*, 28.

4. *Outline of U.S. Government*, ed. Rosalie Targonski, InfoUSA, U.S. Department of State (2000), 18.

5. Tax Analysts, Tax History Museum: 1777–1815, The Revolutionary War to the War of 1812.

6. Carl Van Doren, *The Great Rehearsal: The Story of the Making and Ratifying of the Constitution of the United States* (1948; New York: Praeger, 1982), 7.

7. John W. Daniel's oration, "George Washington" (1885), in *Library of Southern Literature*, ed. Edwin Anderson Alderman et al., 14:6239. Oration at the dedication of the Washington Monument, February 21, 1885.

8. Ibid.

9.   General Washington, Speech before the Senate Chamber of the State House in Annapolis, December 23, 1783.

10.   Washington to Robert Morris, April 12, 1786, in *The Papers of George Washington, Confederation Series*, 4:15.

11.   Henry Wiencek, *An Imperfect God: George Washington, His Slaves, and the Creation of America* (New York: Farrar, Straus & Giroux, 2003), 4. He also provided for his former slaves' care and education following their emancipation.

12.   John Pickell, *A New Chapter in the Early Life of Washington: In Connection With the Narrative History of the Potomac Company* (New York: Appleton, 1856).

13.   Glenn A. Phelps, "The Republican General," in *George Washington Reconsidered*, ed. Don Higginbotham (Charlottesville: University of Virginia Press, 2001). 167. For example, see Thomas Anburey, July 14, 1779, *Travels Through the Interior Parts of America* (1789; Boston, New York: Houghton Mifflin, 1923), 2:232. Anburey wrote about Washington, "of whom, in all my travels through the various provinces, I have never heard anyone speak disrespectfully, as an individual, and whose public character has been the astonishment of all Europe."

14.   "Gilbert Stuart," in *The National Portrait Gallery of Distinguished Americans*, ed. James B. Longacre and James Herring (1834), 1:35.

15.   Ibid., 34.

16.   James Thomas Flexner, *On Desperate Seas: A Biography of Gilbert Stuart* (1955; New York: Fordham University Press, 1995), 124.

17.   Isaac Weld, *Travels Through the States of North America, and the Provinces of Upper and Lower Canada, During the Years 1795, 1796, and 1797*, 2nd ed. (London: John Stockdale, 1799), 105.

18.   Ibid.

19.   Flexner, *On Desperate Seas*, 124.

20.   Paul F. Boller, *Presidential Anecdotes* (New York: Oxford University Press, 1996), 6.

21.   Weld, *Travels Through the States of North America*, 104–9.

22. Gordon S. Wood, "President George Washington, Republican Monarch," James Madison Leadership Conference Paper (Princeton University), 3.

23. Pickell, *A New Chapter*, vii.

24. Ibid.

Chapter 2: Not as Happy in Peace as They Had Been Glorious in War

1. Alexander Hamilton, "Report Relative to a Provision for the Support of Public Credit," January 9, 1790, in *The Papers of Alexander Hamilton*, ed. Harold C. Syrett et al. (New York: Columbia University Press, 1961–87), 6:51–110.

2. "Bill Providing for Delegates to the Convention of 1787," November 6, 1786, in *The Papers of James Madison, Congressional Series* (Chicago: University of Chicago Press, 1975), 9:163.

3. Thomas Jefferson to William Plumer, July 21, 1816, Thomas Jefferson Papers, 1606–1943 (bulk 1775–1826), Manuscripts Division, Library of Congress. Jefferson made this statement years after the time discussed here, but it expresses the fears of the crushing public debt that gripped the nation following the Revolution.

4. Ibid.

5. *National Gazette*, September 11, 1792. Hamilton was, of course, the force behind assuming the states' war debts and creating the national bank to service it.

6. James Madison to Henry Lee, April 13, 1790, in *The Papers of James Madison, Congressional Series*, 13:147.

7. Many of the notes were no longer held by the veterans at this point, but by speculators. For more on the speculation surrounding bonds in the 1780s, see Woody Holton, *Unruly Americans and the Origins of the Constitution* (New York: Hill & Wang, 2007).

8. Circular to the States, June 8, 1783, in *The Writings of George Washington*, 26:289–90.

9. "To the United States Senate and House of Representatives," in *The Papers of George Washington, Presidential Series*, 14:462–67.

10. Washington's Farewell Address, September 19, 1796, in *The Writings of George Washington*, 35:231.

11. "To Form a More Perfect Union: Identifying Defects in the Confederation," The Library of Congress Essay Collection: Documents from the Continental Congress and the Constitutional Convention, 1774–1789.

12. *Journals of the Continental Congress*, 30:366.

13. Diary Entry for June 30, 1785, in *The Papers of George Washington, Diaries*, 4:157. See also Chernow, *Washington: A Life*, 467.

14. *Proceedings of the town of Charlestown, in the county of Middlesex, and Commonwealth of Massachusetts; in Respectful Testimony of the Distinguished Talents and Prominent Virtues of the Late George Washington*, ed. Samuel Etheridge (1800), 18.

15. Thomas E. Woods, Jr., "The Revolutionary War and the Destruction of the Continental," Ludwig von Mises Institute, *Mises Daily* (online), October 11, 2006.

16. Samuel Breck, *Historical Sketch of Continental Paper Money* (1863), 15.

17. Ralph Volney Harlow, "Aspects of Revolutionary Finance, 1775–1783," *American Historical Review* 35 (October 1929): 46–68.

18. Washington to Joseph Reed, December 12, 1778, in *The Papers of George Washington, Revolutionary War Series*, 18:396–98.

19. In light of the economic chaos and diverging currencies, trade among the states plummeted, thereby thinning the economic tether that bound the largely independent states. In a vicious spiral, the not-so-united states competed with one another for their share of diminishing economic resources. Seeking to protect their citizens from this competition, the states imposed tariffs on goods from their sister states. But this ended up hurting citizens on both sides of the border.

For example, New York had long been supplied with firewood from Connecticut's bountiful forests. But in these difficult times, the New Yorkers decided to keep their hard-earned dollars from flowing "into the pockets of detested Yankees." John Fiske, *The Critical Period of American History, 1783–1789* (Boston: Houghton, Mifflin & Co., 1898), 173. And so New York slapped a protective tariff on all ships arriving from Connecticut. These ships from the neighboring state were required to pay entrance fees and clear customs, just like ships from London. "Great and just was the wrath" of the Connecticut lumbermen. In fact, the tariff so damaged the Connecticut economy that the state held a large meeting of businessmen, who decided to suspend all trade with the "hated state" of New York. Ibid. (Fiske exaggerates the level of animosity. There was certainly resentment, but "hate" is strong, although it provides good color.) Both economies wound up worse off, as both lost a market for their goods.

 The trade war hurt not only the producers but also the consumers in both states. The tariffs relieved competition on the local producers, thus allowing them to raise their prices. For example, New York producers, sheltered by tariffs, could raise their prices without having to worry about their customers buying from cheaper Connecticut producers instead. In this way, local consumers often ended up paying more.

 20. "The Federalist No. 9," in *Alexander Hamilton: Writings*, Library of America, ed. Joanne B. Freeman (New York: Penguin, 2001), 196–201.

 21. Alfred P. Thom, "A Right of States' Which Is Often Overlooked," *Railway Age Gazette* 59 (1915), 49.

 22. Washington to James Warren, October 7, 1785. Here I have used the wording from the Fitzpatrick edition of *The Writings of George Washington* because the "shadow" concept holds true. ("In a word, the confederation appears to me to be little more than a shadow without the substance; and Congress a nugatory body, their ordinances being little attended to.") The actual text of that sentence reads: "In a word, the Confederation appears to me to be little more than an empty sound, and Congress a nugatory body; the ordinances of it being very little

attended to." See Washington to James Warren, October 7, 1785, in *The Papers of George Washington, Confederation Series*, 3:299.

Chapter 3: The Shadow Government

1. This description is based on portraits created after his death, since "there is no known image of him except for a crude woodcut in the National Portrait Gallery." "Daniel Shays," Bringing History to Life: The People of Shays' Rebellion, Springfield Technical Community College.

2. James Russell Trumbull, *History of Northampton, Massachusetts, from Its Settlement in 1654* (Northampton: Gazette Printing Company, 1898–1902), 2:491.

3. Gregory Nobles, "Shays and His Neighbors," in *In Debt to Shays: The Bicentennial of an Agrarian Insurrection,* ed. Robert Gross (Charlottesville: University Press of Virginia, 1993), 185–203.

4. Address from the General Court to the People of the Commonwealth of Massachusetts (Boston: Adams & Nourse, 1786), 40.

5. Howard Zinn, *A People's History of the United States: 1492–Present* (New York: HarperCollins, 1999), 94.

6. *Journals of the Continental Congress*, 32:93–95.

7. *Hampshire Gazette*, September 13, 1786.

8. Marion L. Starkey, *A Little Rebellion* (New York: Knopf, 1955), 101.

9. Petersham Monument (1987), qtd. in "Daniel Shays," Bringing History to Life: The People of Shays' Rebellion, Springfield Technical Community College.

10. Washington to David Humphreys, December 26, 1786, in *The Papers of George Washington, Confederation Series*, 4:478.

11. Washington to James Madison, November 5, 1786, in ibid., 4:331.

12. Washington to James Warren, October 7, 1785, in ibid., 3:298–301.

13. Washington to John Jay, August 1, 1786, in ibid., 4:212.

14. Washington to James McHenry, August 22, 1785, in ibid., 3:198.

15. Washington to Jay, 4:212.

Chapter 4: The Phoenix

1. Carl Van Doren, *The Great Rehearsal: The Story of the Making and Ratifying of the Constitution of the United States* (1948; New York: Praeger, 1982), 1.

2. Ibid.

3. Washington to George Steptoe Washington, March 23, 1789, in *The Papers of George Washington, Presidential Series,* 1:438–41.

4. With the exception of Rhode Island, which believed the convention to be illegal.

5. Merrill Jensen, *The Articles of Confederation: An Interpretation of the Social-Constitutional History of the American Revolution, 1774–1781* (Madison: University of Wisconsin Press, 1940), 5n6.

6. Bruce Ackerman, "A United States of Europe?" *Los Angeles Times*, December 14, 2011.

7. Van Doren, *The Great Rehearsal,* 9.

8. For an excellent anecdote regarding the importance Washington placed on punctuality, see Chernow, *Washington: A Life,* 392–93.

9. Stanley Finger and Ian S. Hagemann, "Benjamin Franklin's Risk Factors for Gout and Stones: From Genes and Diet to Possible Lead Poisoning," *Proceedings of the American Philosophical Society* 152 no. 2 (2008): 189.

10. About 75 percent of the delegates had served in the Continental Congress and many had fought in the American Revolution. For short biographical entries for each delegate in the best, most accessible single-volume narrative of the Constitutional Convention, see Carol Berkin, *A Brilliant Solution: Inventing the American Constitution* (New York: Harcourt Brace, 2002), 211–61.

11.   William Pierce stated that "there is an impetuosity in his temper that is injurious to him; but there is an honest rectitude about him that makes him a valuable Member of Society." William Pierce, Character Sketches of Delegates to the Federal Convention (1787).

12.   Gordon Lloyd, "The Constitutional Convention," Teaching American History Project, Ashbrook Center for Public Affairs at Ashland University.

13.   Thomas Jefferson, *The Jefferson Cyclopedia*, ed. John P. Foley (New York: Funk & Wagnalls, 1900), 522.

14.   Ibid.

15.   Richard C. Box, *Public Administration and Society: Critical Issues in American Governance* (Armonk: M. E. Sharpe, 2004), 66.

16.   Lloyd, "The Constitutional Convention."

17.   On the role of clothing in politics, see Kate Haulman, *The Politics of Fashion in Eighteenth-Century America* (Chapel Hill: University of North Carolina Press, 2011).

18.   All except Franklin, who was also world-renowned.

Chapter 5: Wield the Sword

1.   R. D. Rotunda, "Original Intent, the View of the Framers, and the Role of the Ratifiers," *Vanderbilt Law Review* 41 (1988): 510.

2.   Carl Van Doren, *The Great Rehearsal* (Praeger, 1982), 24.

3.   Isaac Weld, *Travels Through the States of North America, and the Provinces of Upper and Lower Canada, During the Years 1795, 1796, and 1797*, 2nd ed. (London: John Stockdale, 1799), 104–9.

4.   Slaves' teeth were far less expensive.

5.   Ibid.

6.   Van Doren, *The Great Rehearsal*, 24.

7.   *The Records of the Federal Convention of 1787*, 3:85.

8.   Virginia T. Elverson and Mary Ann McLanahan, *Cooking Legacy* (New York: St. Martin's, 1975), 14.

9.   Ibid.; Douglas Southall Freeman, *George Washington, A Biography* (New York: Scribner's Sons, 1948–57), 1:104.

10.   Barbara Holland, *The Joy of Drinking* (New York: Bloomsbury, 2007), 64.

11.   Washington to Thomas Green, March 31, 1789, in *The Papers of George Washington, Presidential Series*, 1:467–69.

12.   There is some debate regarding whether Franklin was the first person to create bifocals, but he is popularly credited with doing so.

13.   Richard C. Box, *Public Administration and Society: Critical Issues in American Governance* (Armonk: M. E. Sharpe, 2004), 66.

14.   Benjamin Franklin, *Poor Richard's Almanac*, qtd. in Norman Kolpas, *Practically Useless Information on Food and Drink* (Nashville: Rutledge Hill Press, 2005), 41.

15.   People drank large amounts of alcohol during the eighteenth century because it was often safer than the unclean drinking water available. As a result, they typically had higher tolerances than the average person today.

16.   James McHenry, A Report of Committee, December 23, 1783, Answer of Congress to General Washington, in *Journals of the Continental Congress*, 25:83.

17.   See e.g. *Outline of U.S. Government*, ed. Rosalie Targonski, InfoUSA, U.S. Department of State (2000), 5.

18.   Bennet N. Hollander, "The President and Congress: Operational Control of the Armed Forces," *Military Law Review* 27 (1955): 49. Hollander notes that the "colonists shared a deep fear of the development under the new government of a military branch unchecked by the legislature and susceptible to use by an arbitrary executive power."

19.   *Journal of William Maclay, United States Senator from Pennsylvania, 1789–1791*, ed. Edgar S. Maclay, 1st ed. (1890), 10. See also Martin S. Flaherty, "Historical Perspective: More Apparent Than Real: The Revolutionary Commitment to Constitutional Federalism," Symposium Papers—Federalism in the 21st Century, *Kansas Law Review* 45 (July 1997): 2125. Flaherty writes, "Constitutionally-minded Americans . . . necessarily abandoned, the dominant English mixed-government conceptions."

20. Edmund Randolph, June 1, 1787, in *The Records of the Federal Convention of 1787*, 1:66.

21. *The Records of the Federal Convention of 1787*, 1:86.

22. Ibid., 1:65; see John C. Yoo, "Foreign Affairs and the Jeffersonian Executive: A Defense," *Minnesota Law Review* 89 (2005): 1654.

23. Akhil Reed Amar, *America's Constitution: A Biography* (New York: Random House, 2005), 187.

24. The Declaration of Independence, paras. 13–17.

25. For example, Hugh Williamson of South Carolina expressed his fear of the eventual reemergence of a king and "he wished no precaution to be omitted that might postpone the event as long as possible." James Madison, July 24, 1787, in *The Debates in the Federal Convention of 1787*, ed. Gaillard Hund and James Brown Scott (Oxford University Press, 1920).

26. "The Federalist No. 69," in *Alexander Hamilton: Writings*, Library of America, ed. Joanne B. Freeman (New York: Penguin, 2001), 366–73. Hamilton uses the king as a point of comparison in describing the new commander in chief but is quick to differentiate.

27. Amar, *America's Constitution: A Biography*, 131.

28. Charles C. Thach, Jr., *The Creation of the Presidency, 1775–1789: A Study in Constitutional History* (1969; Indianapolis: Liberty Fund, 2007), 65.

29. The British monarch as well as the state governors.

30. *Journal of William Maclay*, 248.

31. James Madison, *Notes of the Debates in the Federal Convention of 1787*, ed. Adrienne Koch (New York: Norton, 1987), 175.

32. *The Debates in the Several State Conventions on the Adoption of the Federal Constitution*, ed. Jonathan Elliot (1836), 3:107.

33. Ibid., 393.

Chapter 6: Supreme Law of the Land

1. In *Federalist* No. 69, Hamilton indeed states that the Constitution's commander-in-chief powers are in many respects similar

to those of the king of Great Britain and of the governor of New York. However, he signals that this as a simplification and proceeds to ferret out some of the main differences. As the other sources cited in these pages make clear, the Founders and the American people were not trying to duplicate the old system. It was Washington who had most clearly defined the powers of the American commander in chief—recently and right before their eyes.

2. Thach, *The Creation of the Presidency*, 169.

3. Henry Cabot Lodge, *George Washington* (Boston: Houghton, Mifflin & Co., 1898), 170.

4. Madison, *Notes of the Debates in the Federal Convention*, 334.

5. Pierce Butler to Weedon Butler, May 5, 1778, in *The Records of the Federal Convention of 1787*, 3:302.

6. Madison, *Notes of the Debates in the Federal Convention*, 323.

7. Washington to Catherine Sawbridge Macaulay Graham, January 9, 1790, in *The Papers of George Washington, Presidential Series*, 4:552.

8. They also feared Congress and the new judicial branch, but this book primarily focuses on the executive.

9. James Monroe to Thomas Jefferson, July 12, 1788, in *The Writings of James Monroe*, ed. Stanislaus Murray Hamilton (New York: G. P. Putnam's Sons, 1898), 1:186. Monroe was speaking of the Virginia Convention in particular but the sentiment certainly holds true for the rest of the country, where Washington was also beloved.

10. Declaration of Independence.

Part II: Cruel and Usual Punishment

1. Washington to John Hancock, President of Continental Congress, July 15, 1776, in *The Papers of George Washington, Revolutionary War Series*, 5:325.

2. "The American Revolution and the Post-Revolutionary Era: A Historical Legacy," ch. 1 in *A Counterintelligence Reader*, vol. 1,

American Revolution to World War II, ed. Frank J. Rafalko (National Counterintelligence Center), 8.

3. John Bakeless, *Turncoats, Traitors and Heroes* (Philadelphia: Lippincott, 1959), 13.

4. John Warren to John Adams, October 1, 1775, qtd. in ibid., 15.

5. Ibid., 12.

6. Washington to John Hancock, October 5, 1775, in *The Papers of George Washington, Revolutionary War Series*, 2:99.

7. Warren to Adams, October 1, 1775, 15.

8. Washington to Hancock, October 5, 1775, 2:99.

9. Robert C. Doyle, *The Enemy in Our Hands: America's Treatment of Enemy Prisoners of War, from the Revolution to the War on Terror* (Lexington: University Press of Kentucky, 2010), 12.

10. According to the Merriam-Webster Dictionary, "torture" means 1. "to cause intense suffering to" or 2. "to punish or coerce by inflicting excruciating pain." In modern political dialogue, we often refer to torture as a means of extracting information from an uncooperative enemy combatant. In these chapters, the term "torture" refers to the dictionary definition and does not necessarily connote a singular desire to obtain information from the prisoner. The Founders used torture more to halt the British atrocities against American prisoners than as a means of extracting intelligence. But in a sense, the overall goal likewise was to save American lives.

Chapter 7: The Currents of War

1. The Americans used the Anglophone definition of private property, derived from Locke, which asserted that a man who improved previously unused land—whether by cultivating it, building on it, etc.—had a legitimate claim of ownership. Thus, all of this land "unimproved" by the Native Americans was considered ripe for the taking.

2. The Sugar Act, Stamp Act, and Townshend Acts are certainly not to be forgotten as contributing factors.

3. Thomas Fleming, "Introduction," in Joseph Plumb Martin, *A Narrative of a Revolutionary Soldier* (New York: Signet Classics, 2001), vi.

4. Dedham Historical Society, *The Dedham Historical Register*, 7:132.

5. *Connecticut Gazette*, September 22, 1775.

6. Peter Oliver, *Origin and Progress of the American Rebellion: A Tory View* (San Marino: Huntington Library, 1961), 157.

7. *Connecticut Gazette*, September 22, 1775.

8. Ibid.

9. Donald Barr Chidsey, *The Loyalists: The Story of Those Americans Who Fought Against Independence* (New York: Crown, 1973), 38.

10. John D. Steinmetz, "Tarring and Feathering," in *NationMaster Encyclopedia*.

11. Estimated Times/Temperatures Causing a Full Thickness (third degree) Burn, National Burn Victim Foundation, qtd. in "In the Matter of Bonnie Johnson," Could This Happen?, at http://www.cqc.ny.gov.

12. Terry M. Mays, *Historical Dictionary of Revolutionary America* (Lanham, Md.: Scarecrow Press, 2005), 276.

13. *Connecticut Gazette*, September 22, 1775.

14. Sir George Otto Trevelyan, *The American Revolution* (1926), 1:298.

15. David Hackett Fischer, *Paul Revere's Ride* (New York: Oxford University Press, 1994), 190.

16. Estimates of the number of militiamen and redcoats vary; this figure is based on the deposition of British officer Edward Gould, April 25, 1775. There is an in-depth discussion of this question in Fischer, *Paul Revere's Ride*, 400nn18–20.

17. Reverend William Gordon of Roxbury to a gentleman in England, May 17, 1775, in *The Spirit of Seventy-Six*, 80.

18. Fischer, *Paul Revere's Ride*, 190.

19. There are conflicting accounts of what transpired, and each side blamed the other for the initial shot. It is very possible that there were multiple shots from both sides. This is based on the reports of British officers Major John Pitcairn and Lieutenant Will Sutherland. Major John Pitcairn to General Gage, April 25, 1775. David Hackett Fischer provides a good discussion in *Paul Revere's Ride*, 193–94. Many thanks to David Hackett Fischer for his writings and help. His research was very helpful in writing this book.

20. The Americans were armed with muskets, blunderbusses, or any gun they could find. Exactly who fired the first shot and with what kind of firearm has been lost to history, but many suspect that it was an American with a Scottish flintlock pistol.

21. Fischer, *Paul Revere's Ride*, 193.

22. Oliver, *Origin and Progress of the American Rebellion*, 121.

23. Doyle, *The Enemy in Our Hands*, 36.

24. A journal in London in 1776 stated, "It is whispered that the ministry are endeavoring to fix a certainty which party fired first at Lexington, before hostilities commenced, as the Congress declare, if it can be proved that American blood was first shed, it will go a great way toward effecting a reconciliation on the most honorable terms." "Who fired the first shot in the American Revolution?" Benson John Lossing, *Our Country: Household History for All Readers*, 2 (1877), 780.

Chapter 8: *Exitus Acta Probat*

1. Washington to Charles Lawrence, April 26, 1763, in *The Papers of George Washington, Colonial Series*, 7:201.

2. Paul Leicester Ford, *The True George Washington* (1898), 38.

3. *The Spur of Fame: Dialogues of John Adams and Benjamin Rush, 1805–1813*, ed. John A. Schutz and Douglass Adair, 97–98, as qtd. in Chernow, *Washington: A Life*, 185. Washington was noted as a great dancer.

4. Benjamin Rush to Thomas Rushton, October 29, 1775, in *Letters of Benjamin Rush*, ed. L. H. Butterfield (Philadelphia: American Philosophical Society, 1951), 92.

5. *Journals of the Continental Congress*, 1:101. Emphasis added.

6. Ibid.

7. As was typical in eighteenth-century warfare.

8. J. H. Benton, Jr., *Early Census Making in Massachusetts: 1643–1765* (1905), 72–73 (listing population as 15,570 in 1765); Richard Frothingham, *History of the Siege of Boston* (1851), 235.

9. John Wilkes, *The North Briton* (1769), lxvi.

10. Washington to Bryan Fairfax, July 20, 1774, in *The Papers of George Washington, Colonial Series*, 10:130.

11. Declaration of Independence.

12. Stanley Ayling, *George the Third* (New York: Knopf, 1972), 54.

13. King George III is believed to have had the genetic disease porphyria, which may have been exacerbated by arsenic from medications or the products used on his hair. T. M. Cox, N. Jack, S. Lofthouse, J. Watling, J. Haines, M. J. Warren (2005), "King George III and Porphyria: An Elemental Hypothesis and Investigation," *Lancet* 366 (2005): 332–35.

14. Proclamation by the King for Suppressing Rebellion and Sedition (1775), in Thomas Pownall, *The Remembrancer, or Impartial Repository of Public Events*, 1 (1775), 148.

15. Ibid.

16. Washington to Lieutenant General Thomas Gage, August 11, 1775, in *The Papers of George Washington, Revolutionary War Series*, 1:289.

17. For example, the Americans captured twenty-three British troops when they burned the lighthouse in Boston Harbor. *The Lost War: Letters from British Officers during the American Revolution*, ed. Marion Balderston and David Syrett (New York: Horizon, 1975), 38.

18. Ibid., 417.

19.   The Americans attacked and burned the lighthouse twice: on July 20 and again, under Washington's orders, on July 30.

20.   Washington to John Hancock, August 4/5, 1775, in *The Papers of George Washington, Revolutionary War Series*, 1:223–30. Number of British killed based on a letter from Lieutenant William Fielding, August 13, 1775, in *The Lost War*, ed. Balderston and Syrett, 38.

21.   Fielding to Washington, August 13, 1775, 39.

22.   The accuracy of the British intelligence cannot be confirmed. Washington replied to Gage that such intelligence "has not the least Foundation in Truth. Not only your Officers and Soldiers have been treated with a Tenderness, due to Fellow-Citizens, and Brethren, but even those execrable Parricides, whose Counsels and Aid have deluged their Country with Blood, have been protected from the Fury of a justly-enraged People." Washington to Lieutenant General Thomas Gage, August 19, 1775, in *The Papers of George Washington, Revolutionary War Series*, 1:327.

23.   Thomas Gage to Washington, August 13, 1775, in ibid., 1:302.

24.   Washington to John Hancock, August 31, 1775, in ibid., 1:390–93.

25.   Washington to the Massachusetts Legislature, August 14, 1775, in *The Writings of George Washington*, 3:423–24. Such reprisal was consistent with the laws of war at the time. Unless Congress acts to regulate the matter, as it did during the War of 1812, it is fair to consider retaliatory measures to be within the power of battlefield commanders.

Chapter 9: American Fortitude

1.   Martin Ignatius Joseph Griffin, *Catholics and the American Revolution*, 2 (1909), 255.

2.   *Connecticut Courant*, December 30, 1776, as qtd. in Don N. Hagist, *Escape Stories: Major Christopher French, 22nd Regiment*.

3.   Major French to Washington, in *American Archives*, Fourth Series, 3:1545.

4. Washington to Major French, August 31, 1775, in *The Papers of George Washington, Revolutionary War Series*, 1:389.

5. Washington to Major French, September 26, 1775, in *The Papers of George Washington, Revolutionary War Series*, 2:47–48. He did concede, "My Disposition does not allow me, to follow the unworthy Example set me by General Gage, to its fullest Extent . . . ."

6. *Journals of the Continental Congress*, 1:400. Congress again repeats much of this language on May 21, 1776, in *Journals of the Continental Congress*, 4:370.

7. Stephen Moylan to William Watson, November 16, 1775, in *American Archives*, Fourth Series, 3:1568.

8. Washington acted with full cognizance of the resolution. Congress certainly communicated this resolution to Washington since it was directly related to his function and other parts included resolutions "[t]hat the General be directed" to perform other tasks. Ibid.

9. Edwin G. Burrows, *Forgotten Patriots: The Untold Story of American Prisoners during the Revolutionary War* (New York: Basic Books, 2008), 38.

10. Charles A. Jellison, *Ethan Allen: Frontier Rebel* (Syracuse: Syracuse University Press, 1969), 8.

11. Ethan Allen, *A Narrative of Colonel Ethan Allen's Captivity* (1779; Bedford, Mass.: Applewood Books, 1989), 5–6.

12. Willard Sterne Randall, *Benedict Arnold: Patriot and Traitor* (New York: Morrow, 1990), 94. See Kenneth C. Davis, *America's Hidden History: Untold Tales of the First Pilgrims, Fighting Women, and Forgotten Founders Who Shaped a Nation* (New York: Smithsonian Books, 2008), 167–71, for a lively and amusing description, which I found helpful.

13. Allen and Benedict Arnold were fighting for command of the raid.

14. Jellison, *Ethan Allen: Frontier Rebel*, 134.

15. Washington to Philip Schuyler, August 20, 1775, in *The Papers of George Washington, Revolutionary Series*, 1:331–33.

16. Ibid.

17. William Glanville Evelyn, *Memoir and Letters of Captain W. Glanville Evelyn, of the 4th Regiment from North American, 1774–1776*, ed. G. D. Scull (1879), 100.

18. Allen, *A Narrative of Colonel Ethan Allen's Captivity*, 40.

19. Thomas H. Prescott, *An Encyclopedia of History, Biography and Travel, Comprising Ancient and Modern History* (1856), 667.

20. Jellison, *Ethan Allen: Frontier Rebel*, 159–60.

21. Evelyn, *Memoir and Letters of Captain W. Glanville Evelyn*, 100.

22. Washington Irving, *Life of George Washington*, 3:11.

23. Pendennis Castle.

24. Washington to Sir William Howe, December 18, 1775, in *The Papers of George Washington, Revolutionary Series*, 2:576.

Chapter 10: Necessary Evil

1. Thomas J. Fleming, "The Enigma of General Howe," *American Heritage Magazine* 15 (1964): 2.

2. Robert Leckie, *George Washington's War: The Saga of the American Revolution* (New York: HarperCollins, 1992), 146.

3. Sir William Howe, February 21, 1775, qtd. in Benjamin Franklin, *Life of Benjamin Franklin* (1884), 2:367.

4. Washington to Howe, December 18, 1775.

5. *Journals of the Continental Congress*, 1:402.

6. Jellison, *Ethan Allen: Frontier Rebel*, 162–64.

7. Washington to Henry Laurens, President of the Continental Congress, May 12, 1778, in *The Papers of George Washington, Revolutionary War Series*, 15:109.

8. Michael Pearson, *Those Damned Rebels: The American Revolution as Seen through British Eyes* (New York: Putnam, 1972), 318.

9. William Farrand Livingston, *Israel Putnam: Pioneer, Ranger, and Major-General, 1718–1790* (1901), 279.

10. Document 37 in *Memoirs of the Long Island Historical Society*, vol. 3.

11.   Ibid. The Moravian Church was located just steps from where Washington would be sworn in as president thirteen years later.

12.   Mark M. Boatner III, *Encyclopedia of the American Revolution* (New York: D. McKay Co., 1974), 1094.

13.   Charles Lee to Washington, February 19, 1776, in *The Papers of George Washington, Revolutionary War Series*, 3:340. Thank you to Abigail Beal for her insight on this point.

14.   General Orders, July 2, 1776, in *The Papers of George Washington, Revolutionary War Series*, 5:180.

15.   Thomas Paine, *Common Sense*, 1776.

16.   For an example of this, Jefferson, in his autobiography, gave over only a single paragraph at the start to his family's lineage and concluded it by saying, "To which let everyone ascribe the faith & merit he chooses." *Thomas Jefferson: Writings*, ed. Merrill D. Peterson (New York: Library of America, 1984), 3.

17.   Joseph J. Ellis, *American Sphinx: The Character of Thomas Jefferson* (New York: Random House, 1998), 114, 82.

18.   John Torrey Morse, *Thomas Jefferson* (New York: Houghton Mifflin & Co., 1883), 7.

19.   Ibid., 5; Lance Morrow, "18th Century: Thomas Jefferson," *Time*, December 31, 1999.

20.   Morse, *Thomas Jefferson*, 5.

21.   Jefferson to Henry Lee, May 8, 1825, E-Text Center, University of Virginia Library.

22.   John Adams to Abigail Adams, July 3, 1776, in *Adams Family Correspondence*, ed. L. H. Butterfield et al. (Boston: Massachusetts Historical Society, 1963–2011), 2:30.

23.   Qtd. in McCullough, *1776*, 181. Many thanks to David McCullough for providing an excellent account of the Battle of Long Island in his magnificent *1776*, which was very helpful in writing this book.

24. Ibid., 167. *Letters to and from Caesar Rodney*, Historical Society of Delaware (University of Pennsylvania Press, 1933), 109, qtd. in McCullough, *1776*, 202.

25. Joseph Plumb Martin and James Kirby Martin, *Ordinary Courage: The Revolutionary War Adventures of Joseph Plumb Martin* (New York: John Wiley & Sons, 2008), 21.

26. Ibid., 20–21, qtd. in McCullough, *1776*, 188.

27. McCullough, *1776*, 188.

28. Major Tallmadge's Account of the Battles of Long Island and White Plains, in Henry P. Johnston, *The Campaign of 1776 Around New York and Brooklyn* (Project Gutenberg EBook, 2007), Part II, 78; McCullough, *1776*, 191.

29. Qtd. in Danske Dandridge, *American Prisoners of the Revolution* (Charlottesville: The Michie Co., 1911), 25.

30. Ibid., 24.

31. Judge J. B. O'Neal, "Random Recollections of Revolutionary Characters and Incidents," *Southern Literary Journal and Magazine of Arts* 4 (July 1838): 40.

32. Dandridge, *American Prisoners of the Revolution*, 25.

33. Ibid., 24.

34. O'Neal, "Random Recollections of Revolutionary Characters and Incidents," 40.

35. John Adams to Abigail Adams, February 17, 1777, in *Adams Family Correspondence*, 2:163. John Adams wrote to his wife, "I who am always made miserable by the Misery of every sensible being, am obliged to hear continual accounts of the barbarities, the cruel Murders in cold blood . . . committed by our Enemies. . . . These accounts harrow me beyond Description."

36. Dandridge, *American Prisoners of the Revolution*, 25.

37. "Ebenezer Fox, American Prisoner," in Dandridge, *American Prisoners of the Revolution*, 175.

38. *Potter's American Monthly* 2 (1873): 442.

39. Dandridge, *American Prisoners of the Revolution*, 36.

40. Ibid., 34.

41. Qtd. in M. William Phelps, *Nathan Hale: The Life and Death of America's First Spy* (New York: Macmillan, 2008), 186.

42. Benson J. Lossing, *The Pictorial Field-Book of the Revolution*, 2 (New York: Harper & Bros., 1852), 659.

43. Dandridge, *American Prisoners of the Revolution*, 25.

44. Elias Boudinot, *Journal of Events*, as excerpted in ibid., 27.

45. Washington to John Augustine Washington, November 6, 1776, in *The Papers of George Washington, Revolutionary War Series*, 7:105.

46. Washington to Sir William Howe, January 13, 1777, in ibid., 8:60.

Chapter 11: Fully Justifiable

1. While Lee was technically the third-in-command, he was widely considered to rank just under Washington while the true second-in-command played only a relatively minor role in the struggle.

2. John Shy, *A People Numerous and Armed: Reflections on the Military Struggle for American Independence*, rev. ed. (Ann Arbor: University of Michigan Press, 1990), 135.

3. Barbara Z. Marchant, "Charles Lee: A Disobedient Servant," in *The Revolutionary War in Bergen County: The Times That Tried Men's Souls*, ed. Carol Karels (Charleston: The History Press, 2007), 108.

4. Edward Langworthy, *Memoirs of the Life of the Late Charles Lee* (1813), 2.

5. Ibid., vii.

6. Ibid., 8.

7. James Thomas Flexner, *George Washington: The Forge of Experience, 1732–1775* (Boston: Little, Brown, 1965), 333.

8. Shy, *A People Numerous and Armed*, 135.

9. Thomas Amory Lee, *Colonel William Raymond Lee of the Revolution* (1917), 12.

10. McCullough, *1776*, 266.

11. Arthur D. Pierce, *Smugglers' Woods: Jaunts and Journeys in Colonial and Revolutionary New Jersey* (New Brunswick, N.J.: Rutgers University Press, 1960, repr. 1992), 206.

12. William Glanville Evelyn, *Memoir and Letters of Captain W. Glanville Evelyn, of the 4th Regiment from North American, 1774–1776*, ed. G. D. Scull (1879), 104.

13. Washington Irving, *Life of George Washington*, 1:310.

14. Banastre Tarleton to Jane Tarleton, December 14, 1776, qtd. in Robert D. Bass, *The Green Dragoon: The Lives of Banastre Tarleton and Mary Robinson* (New York: Holt, 1957), 20–22.

15. David Lee Russell, *Victory on Sullivan's Island* (Haverford, Penn.: Infinity Publishing, 2002), 254.

16. Evelyn, *Memoir and Letters of Captain W. Glanville Evelyn*, 109.

17. Ibid.

18. *The Lost War: Letters from British Officers during the American Revolution*, ed. Marion Balderston and David Syrett (New York: Horizon, 1975), 130.

19. There is uncertainty as to whether General Lee's treatment was as harsh as the rumors reported in *Scots Magazine* suggested. Nevertheless, these rumors prompted the Americans to seek revenge.

20. Washington to Sir William Howe, January 13, 1777, in *The Papers of George Washington, Revolutionary War Series*, 8:59–60.

21. He said, "your Conduct must and shall mark mine." Washington to William Howe, January 13, 1777, in *The Papers of George Washington, Revolutionary War Series*, 8:60.

22. Washington to the Continental Congress Executive Committee, January 12, 1777, in *The Papers of George Washington, Revolutionary War Series*, 8:45.

23. Washington to the President of Congress, July 15, 1776, in *The Papers of George Washington, Revolutionary War Series*, 5:325.

24. Samuel Blachley Webb, *Correspondence and Journals of Committee to Washington*, 2:62. Many thanks to Professor John Fabian Witt

for bringing this quote to my attention. It may be found in his excellent account in *Lincoln's Code: The Laws of War in American History* (New York: Free Press, 2012), ch. 1.

25. The American Commissioners to Lord Stormont, April 2, 1777, in *The Papers of Benjamin Franklin*, ed. William B. Wilcox (New Haven: Yale University Press, 1983), 23:548.

26. *Journals of the Continental Congress*, 5:457–58.

27. Major General Artemas Ward to Washington, June 20, 1776, in *The Papers of George Washington, Revolutionary War Series*, 5:60.

28. As cited in David Lee Russell, *Oglethorpe and Colonial Georgia: A History, 1733–1783* (Jefferson, N.C.: McFarland & Co., 2006), 98.

29. Charles H. Walcott, *Sir Archibald Campbell of Inverneill; Sometime Prisoner of War in the Jail at Concord, Massachusetts* (1898), 10; *Illustrated Naval and Military Magazine, A monthly journal devoted to all subjects connected with Her Majesty's land and sea forces* 1 (1889): 479.

30. George Washington to John Hancock, June 30, 1776, in *The Papers of George Washington, Revolutionary War Series*, 5:159–60.

31. Robert A. McGeachy, "The American War of Lieutenant Colonel Archibald Campbell of Inverneill," *Early America Review*, Summer/Fall 2001.

32. *Journals of the Continental Congress*, January 6, 1777, 7:16.

33. George Washington to James Bowdoin, February 28, 1777, in *The Papers of George Washington, Revolutionary War Series*, 8:461.

34. *Scots Magazine* 38 (1776).

35. Lieutenant Colonel Campbell to General Sir William Howe, *Scots Magazine* 39 (1777): 249.

36. Based on portraits of the era.

37. C. Stedman, *History of the American War* (1794), 1:169.

38. McGeachy, "The American War of Lieutenant Colonel Archibald Campbell of Inverneill," quoting "Letter from 'Old England,'" *Scots Magazine* 39 (1777): 250–51.

39. Evelyn, *Memoir and Letters of Captain W. Glanville Evelyn*, 108.

40. See John Richard Alden, *General Charles Lee: Traitor or Patriot?* (Baton Rouge: Louisiana State University Press, 1951).

41. Washington to Bowdoin, February 28, 1777.

42. Ibid.

43. Walcott, *Sir Archibald Campbell of Inverneill*, 32.

44. Irving, *Life of George Washington*, 3:20.

45. *Journals of the Continental Congress*, 7:134.

46. Ibid., 135.

47. McGeachy, "The American War of Lieutenant Colonel Archibald Campbell of Inverneill," quoting "Letter from 'Old England,'" *Scots Magazine* 39 (1777): 250–51.

48. Washington to Lieutenant Colonel Archibald Campbell, March 1, 1777, in *The Papers of George Washington, Revolutionary War Series*, 8:469; see Washington to Bowdoin, February 28, 1777.

49. *Journals of the Continental Congress*, 7:179.

50. David Barron and Martin Lederman have disagreed with me on this issue in their excellent article, "The Commander in Chief at the Lowest Ebb—Framing the Problem, Doctrine, and Original Understanding," *Harvard Law Review* 121 no. 3 (2008): 689. They argue that Washington was not contravening Congress's orders, since the January 6, 1777 resolution called for Campbell to be treated the same as Lee. They reason that because Washington believed Lee was not being treated as poorly as the reports suggested, he was therefore still abiding by the congressional resolution. However, this does not fully address the issue since it does not take into account Congress's subsequent order. Congress expanded its justification for mistreatment in the February 28, 1777 order to include Howe's actions regarding his January 23, 1777 letter in response to the Americans' efforts to trade for Lee, alone. Thus, even if Washington believed that Lee was being treated better than the Americans' reports suggested (and therefore, Campbell should be treated the same according to the January 6 resolution), he was acting against Congress's February 28 order that Campbell be mistreated based on Howe's conduct alone.

51. *Journals of the Continental Congress*, June 2, 1777, 8:411.

52. *Journals of the Continental Congress*, March 2, 1781, 19:227.

53. R. Bickerton to Major John Bowater, March 4, 1778, in *The Lost War*, ed. Balderston and Syrett, 158.

54. American Scenic and Historic Preservation Society, *The Old Martyrs' Prison, New York* (1902).

55. See Washington to Howe, January 13, 1777, in *The Papers of George Washington, Revolutionary War Series*, 8:59–60. "I am sorry that I am again under the necessity of remonstrating to you upon the Treatment which our prisoners continue to receive in New York. Those, who have lately been sent out, give the most shocking Accounts of their barbarous usage, which their Miserable, emaciated Countenances confirm . . . . [I]f you are determined to make Captivity as distressing as possible, to those whose Lot it is to fall into it, let me know it, that we may be upon equal terms, for your Conduct must and shall mark mine."

Chapter 12: To Defend the Nation

1. Balfour to the Militia prisoners of war, May 17, 1781, in *The Remembrancer, or Impartial Repository of Public Events*, 13 (1782), 288.

2. Thomas Anburey, *Travels Through the Interior Parts of America* (1789; Boston and New York: Houghton Mifflin, 1923), 2:295.

3. Ibid., 78.

4. Peter Oliver, *Origin and Progress of the American Rebellion: A Tory View* (San Marino: Huntington Library, 1961), 123.

5. Washington to Sir William Howe, September 23, 1776, in *The Papers of George Washington, Revolutionary War Series*, 6:378.

6. Ibid.

7. "Chinese Torture," Medieval Torture, Medieval-Castles.org. Also, see George Henry Mason, The *Punishments of China* (London: Printed for W. Miller by S. Gosnell, 1808); Lu Xixing, *Zhongguo gu dai qi wu da ci dian: bing qi, xing ju juan,* (Shijiazhuang Shi: Hebei jiao yu chu ban she, 2004).

8. Washington to Howe, September 23, 1776.

9. William R. Wilson, "The Sword to Settle," in *Historical Narratives of Early Canada*, http://www.uppercanadahistory.ca/uel/uel5.html.

10. Washington to Howe, September 23, 1776.

11. Angela E. M. Files, *Loyalist Families of the Grand River Branch U.E.L.A.C.*, United Empire Loyalists' Association of Canada (1991).

12. Indeed, on many occasions, especially in the beginning of the war and when the torture served no purpose, Washington forbade torture; see Washington to Hancock, August 29, 1776, in *The Papers of George Washington, Revolutionary War Series*, 6:155–56 (discussing a plan to convert the Hessians by treating those captured kindly); however, in other instances, such as when torture could be used to better the treatment of American prisoners, he does suggest torture to be an abhorrent, yet viable, option.

13. Anburey, *Travels Through the Interior Parts of America*, 2:62, also qtd. in Robert C. Doyle, *The Enemy in Our Hands: America's Treatment of Enemy Prisoners of War, from the Revolution to the War on Terror* (Lexington: University Press of Kentucky, 2010), 26.

14. *Letters of Brunswick and Hessian Officers during the American Revolution*, transl. William Leete Stone (1891), 163.

15. Ibid.

16. Anburey, *Travels Through the Interior Parts of America*, 2:55.

17. Doyle, *The Enemy in Our Hands*, 26.

18. "Rivington's Reflections," *Royal Gazette of New York*, December 14, 1782.

19. This was the intrepid John Paul Jones.

20. Washington Irving, *History of the American Revolution* (1876), 619.

21. Ibid., 618.

22. "Toms River Blockhouse Fight," Patriot Pirates, www.patriotpirates.com.

23. Frank Landon Humphreys, *Life and Times of David Humphreys: soldier–statesman—poet—"Belov'd of Washington"* (1917), 1:252.

24. Irving, *Life of George Washington*, 4:364.

25. Washington to Sir Henry Clinton, April 21, 1782, in *The Writings of George Washington*, 24:146.

26. Ibid., 147.

27. *The Lost War: Letters from British Officers during the American Revolution*, ed. Marion Balderston and David Syrett (New York: Horizon, 1975), 216.

28. Ibid.

29. Francis Bazley Lee, *New Jersey as a Colony and as a State: One of the Original Thirteen* (1902), 251.

30. *The Lost War*, ed. Balderston and Syrett, 216.

31. Irving, *Life of George Washington*, 4:394–97.

32. James Thacher, *Military Journal of the American Revolution*, 304.

33. Friedrich Melchior Freiherr von Grimm et al., *Historical and Literary Memoirs and Anecdotes, selected from the Correspondence of Baron de Grimm and Diderot* (1815), qtd. in Thacher, *Military Journal of the American Revolution*, 308.

34. Thacher, *Military Journal*, 306.

35. Ibid., 308.

36. Ibid.

37. Von Grimm et al., *Historical and Literary Memoirs and Anecdotes*, qtd. by Thacher, *Military Journal of the American Revolution*, 40.

38. Journal of Colonel Elias Boudinot, as qtd. in Simon Schama, *Rough Crossings: Britain, the Slaves, and the American Revolution* (New York: Ecco, 2006), 143.

Part III: Dictator of America

1. Ironically, the statue is positioned with its left foot forward.

Chapter 13: Scorpion on a Leash

1. Washington to Lund Washington, October 6, 1776, in *The Papers of George Washington, Revolutionary War Series*, 6:494.

2. John R. Bumgarner, *The Health of the Presidents: The 41 United States Presidents Through 1993 from a Physician's Point of View* (Jefferson, N.C.: McFarland & Co., 1994), 9.

3. Brian P. Janiskee, *Local Government in Early America: The Colonial Experience and Lessons from the Founders* (Lanham, Md., Rowman & Littlefield, 2010), 94. Adams oscillated from aggressive to puritanical as his inborn temperament vied with his puritanical upbringing for control.

4. John Adams to Horatio Gates, June 18, 1776, in *Letters of Delegates to the Continental Congress*, ed. Edmund C. Burnett (Washington, D.C., 1921–36), 1:497.

5. Resolution of the Continental Congress, June 16, 1775.

6. Qtd. in Don Higginbotham, *War and Society in Revolutionary America* (Columbia: University of South Carolina Press, 1988), 196; *American Archives*, Fifth Series, 2:1066–67.

7. This fable of unknown origin has been around for millennia. Briefly, the scorpion asks the frog to carry him across the river. When the frog says "no, you will sting me," the scorpion responds, "of course I will not, because then I would drown." So the frog lets the scorpion onto his back and they set out across the river. The scorpion stings the frog and the frog cries out in disbelief, "why?!" The scorpion responds, "it is in my nature."

8. "Address to the New York Provincial Congress, June 26, 1775, in *The Papers of George Washington, Revolutionary War Series*, 1:41.

9. Chernow, *Washington: A Life*, 131.

10. Circular to the States, June 8, 1783.

11. Washington to John Augustine Washington, July 18, 1766, in *The Writings of George Washington*, 1:153.

12. General Orders, July 9, 1776, in *The Papers of George Washington, Revolutionary War Series*, 5:246.

13. Colonel Loammi Baldwin to his wife, Mary, of Woburn, Massachusetts, June 12, 1777, in *The Spirit of Seventy-Six*, 420.

14. Carol Berkin, *Revolutionary Mothers: Women in the Struggle for America's Independence* (New York: Knopf, 2005), 62.

15. Qtd. in ibid.

16. Ibid.

17. Chernow, *Washington: A Life*, 293.

18. *The North-British Intelligencer: or Constitutional Miscellany*, ed. Robert Dick (1777), 26.

19. Ibid.; Glenn A. Phelps, *George Washington and American Constitutionalism* (Lawrence: University Press of Kansas, 1993), 26.

20. Ibid., 37.

21. Abraham D. Sofaer, *War, Foreign Affairs and Constitutional Powers: The Origins* 20–21, 388n76 (1976), as cited in Barron and Lederman, "The Commander in Chief at the Lowest Ebb," 774.

22. Henry Cabot Lodge, *George Washington* (Boston: Houghton, Mifflin & Co., 1898), 170.

23. According to the Papers of George Washington Project.

24. Washington to Joseph Reed, March 3, 1776, in *The Papers of George Washington, Revolutionary War Series*, 3:372.

25. John Adams to Washington, January 6, 1776, in ibid., 3:37.

26. Joseph J. Ellis, *His Excellency: George Washington* (New York: Knopf, 2004), 93.

27. John Adams to Abigail Adams, July 7, 1776, in *Adams Family Correspondence*, ed. L. H. Butterfield (Boston, 1963–2011), 2:38.

28. Ibid.

29. Nicholas Cresswell, *The Journal of Nicholas Cresswell, 1774–1777* (Carlisle, Mass.: Applewood Books, 1924), 159.

30. McCullough, *1776*, 205.

31. John Adams to Abigail Adams, June 26, 1776, in *Letters of Delegates to Congress, 1774–1789*, ed. Paul H. Smith et al. (Washington D.C.: Library of Congress, 1976–2000), 4:324.

32. Qtd. in Ann M. Becker, "Smallpox in Washington's Army: Strategic Implications of the Disease During the American Revolutionary War," *Journal of Military History* 68 no. 2 (2004): 400.

33. Ibid., 401. Becker refers to the *Boston Gazette*, February 12, 1776, and adds, "Though the evidence strongly suggests intentional exposure, Cash discounts the idea that General Howe deliberately spread smallpox among the refugees."

34. Washington to John Hancock, December 11, 1775, in *The Papers of George Washington, Revolutionary War Series*, 2:533–34.

35. Washington to John Hancock, President of Congress, December 14, 1775, in ibid., 2:548.

36. General Orders, May 24–26, 1776, in *The Papers of George Washington, Revolutionary War Series*, 4:384–87.

37. Erwin H. Ackerknecht, *A Short History of Medicine* (New York: The Ronald Press Co., 1968), 45.

38. General Orders, December 11, 1775, in *The Papers of George Washington, Revolutionary War Series*, 2:528–29.

39. Benson John Lossing, *Mount Vernon and Its Associations: Historical, Biographical, and Pictorial* (1859), 52.

40. Washington Irving, *Life of George Washington*, 1:92.

41. Lossing, *Mount Vernon and Its Associations*, 52.

42. Helen Bryan, *Martha Washington: First Lady of Liberty* (New York: Wiley, 2002), 192.

43. Washington to John Augustine Washington, April 29, 1776, in *The Papers of George Washington, Revolutionary War Series*, 4:173.

44. He knew of her anxiety when her son had been inoculated and "doubted she would make good on her pledge" to undergo the procedure. Chernow, *Washington: A Life*, 231.

45. Ibid., 205.

46. Jean Edward Smith, *John Marshall: Definer of a Nation* (New York: H. Holt & Co., 1996), 53.

47. Elizabeth Anne Fenn, *Pox Americana: The Great Smallpox Epidemic of 1775–82* (New York: Hill & Wang, 2001), 101.

48. Joseph Hodgkins to Sarah Hodgkins, qtd. in *This Glorious Cause: The Adventures of Two Company Grade Officers in Washington's Army*, ed. Robert Lively (Princeton: Princeton University Press, 1958).

49. Washington to John Hancock, September 2, 1776, in *The Papers of George Washington, Revolutionary War Series*, 6:199.

Chapter 14: Between a Hawk and a Buzzard

1. McCullough, *1776*, 166.
2. Ibid., 167.
3. John Trumbull, "M'Fingal," *The Spirit of Seventy-Six*, 416.
4. Natalie Wolchover, "Why Do Americans and Brits Have Different Accents?" Life's Little Mysteries, citing John Algeo, *The Cambridge History of the English Language* (Cambridge University Press, 2001).
5. Ibid.
6. Ibid.
7. Ibid.
8. Ibid.
9. *London Chronicle*, qtd. in McCullough, *1776*, 167.
10. Lord Rawdon Francis to Francis, tenth Earl of Huntington, August 5, 1776, in *The Spirit of Seventy-Six*, 424.
11. Ibid.
12. Ibid.
13. Ibid.
14. Lord Hugh Percy to Lord George Germain, September 2, 1776, in *Letters of Hugh, Earl Percy, from Boston and New York, 1774–1776*, ed. Charles Knowles Bolton (1902), 71.
15. From the Journals of Sir George Collier, in *Memoirs of the Long Island Historical Society* (1869), 2:413.
16. Resolution of the Continental Congress, June 16, 1775, in *Journals of the Continental Congress*, 2:92–95.
17. Barron and Lederman, "The Commander in Chief at the Lowest Ebb," 776.
18. Washington to John Hancock, September 8, 1776, in *The Papers of George Washington, Revolutionary War Series*, 6:251
19. Ibid.
20. Ibid.

21. It is unclear how strongly Washington felt about conducting a full withdrawal. His letters to Congress express profound uncertainty about his next moves.

22. Ibid.

23. Congress said they did not intend for Washington to be bound by the war council's decisions, but they did not inform him of this until later.

24. Colonel Joseph Reed to Mrs. Reed, September 6, 1776, in *American Archives,* Fourth Series, 2:198.

25. Ibid.

26. Ibid.

27. Ira K. Morris, *Morris's Memorial History of Staten Island, New York* (1898), 1:144.

28. Walter Isaacson, *Benjamin Franklin: An American Life* (New York: Simon & Schuster, 2004), 319.

29. Francis Wharton, *The Revolutionary Diplomatic Correspondence of the United States* (1889), 2:141–42.

30. Gregory T. Edgar, *Campaign of 1776: The Road to Trenton* (Bowie: Heritage Books, 1995), 170.

31. Ira Gruber, *The Howe Brothers and the American Revolution* (New York: Atheneum, 1972), 199.

32. McCullough, *1776*, 208.

33. *Journals of the Continental Congress*, 5:749.

34. McCullough, *1776*, 208.

35. Nathanael Greene to Washington, September 5, 1776, in *The Spirit of Seventy-Six*, 456.

36. *Journals of the Continental Congress*, 5:733.

37. Washington to Lund Washington, October 6, 1776.

Chapter 15: Onslaught

1. Journal of Ambrose Serle, Secretary to Lord Howe, September 15, 1776, in *The Spirit of Seventy-Six,* 464.

2. Ibid.

3. Joseph Plumb Martin, *A Narrative of a Revolutionary Soldier* (New York: Signet Classics, 2001), 31.

4. Journal of Ambrose Serle, Secretary to Lord Howe, September 15, 1776.

5. Ibid.

6. Ibid.

7. Martin, *A Narrative of a Revolutionary Soldier*, 31.

8. Ibid., 32.

9. McCullough, *1776*, 213.

10. General George Weedon to John Page, President of the Virginia Council, September 20, 1776, in *The Spirit of Seventy-Six*, 467.

11. Colonel George Hanger, *To All Sportsmen and Particularly Farmers, and Gamekeepers* (1814), 205, as qtd. in Harold L. Peterson, *The Book of the Continental Soldier* (Harrisburg, Penn.: Stackpole Co., 1968), 27.

12. Ibid.

13. Diary of Captain Frederick Mackenzie, September 20, 1776, in *The Spirit of Seventy-Six*, 473.

14. Eyewitnesses reported that the fire broke out in multiple locations, thus indicating arson. However, it is possible that the fire was indeed accidental and the wind spread it to other buildings, thereby making it appear to originate from multiple places. Barnet Schecter, *The Battle for New York* (New York: Walker & Co., 2002), 206.

15. Sir William Howe to Lord George Germain, September 23, 1776, in *The Spirit of Seventy-Six*, 475. To the contrary, see Schecter, *The Battle for New York*, 207. Some Americans blamed the British and Hessians for starting it as pretext for plunder.

16. *The Spirit of Seventy-Six*, 471.

17. Diary of Captain Frederick Mackenzie, September 20, 1776.

18. Fischer, *Washington's Crossing*, 107.

19. Governor William Tryon to Lord Germain, September 1776, in *The Papers of George Washington, Revolutionary War Series*, 6:370.

20. William Glanville Evelyn, *Memoir and Letters of Captain W. Glanville Evelyn, of the 4th Regiment from North American, 1774–1776*, ed. G. D. Scull (1879), 86.

21. *The Spirit of Seventy-Six*, 471.

22. Ibid., 468.

23. Lieutenant Colonel Tench Tilghman to his father, September 19, 1776, in *The Spirit of Seventy-Six*, 470.

24. *The Spirit of Seventy-Six*, 468.

25. Journal of Dr. James Thacher, September 15, 1776, in *The Spirit of Seventy-Six*, 64. It is likely that the British tarried due to Clinton's orders, but the Americans nevertheless credited Mrs. Murray as their savior. Special thanks to Jonathan Rollo for his insight into this event.

26. *Diary of Frederick Mackenzie* (New York: Arno Press, 1967), 111–12, qtd. in Edwin G. Burrows, *Forgotten Patriots: The Untold Story of American Prisoners during the Revolutionary War* (New York: Basic Books, 2008), 276n8.

27. Abigail Adams to John Adams, July 31, 1776, in *The Book of Abigail and John: Selected Letters of the Adams Family, 1762–1784*, ed. L. H. Butterfield et al. (1975; Boston: Northeastern University Press, 2002), 164.

28. Ibid. Abigail Adams did not believe the spanking rumors, however.

29. Joan N. Burstyn, *Past and Promise: Lives of New Jersey Women* (Metuchen, N.J.: Scarecrow Press, 1990), 32. Mary Hays McCauley's exact age is unknown, but it is estimated that she was born on October 13, 1754. Many historians believe that Mary "became immortalized as the representative, if not the only, 'Molly Pitcher,'" a name given to the various women who took direct action in the war effort. Ibid.

30. Martin, *A Narrative of a Revolutionary Soldier*, 88. Special thanks to Joseph Gonzalez for his excellent insights into this event, which occurred at the Battle of Monmouth, New Jersey.

31. Linda Grant De Pauw, "Women in Combat: The Revolutionary War Experience," *Armed Forces and Society* 7 no. 2 (1981): 218.

32. *Gettysburg Compiler*, March 27, 1822.

33. Washington and Congress initially rejected slaves and free African Americans from the army; but when the British began to enlist free blacks and promise freedom to slaves, Washington changed his mind and allowed free blacks to fight.

34. Fischer, *Washington's Crossing*, 52.

35. Ibid.

36. Robert C. Doyle, *The Enemy in Our Hands: America's Treatment of Enemy Prisoners of War, from the Revolution to the War on Terror* (Lexington: University Press of Kentucky, 2010), 29. Estimation based on MeasuringWorth.com's conversion using average earnings.

37. Fischer, *Washington's Crossing*, 60.

38. The Examination of Witnesses in the House of Commons on the Conduct of Lord Howe and Sir William Howe, 1779: The Examination of General Robertson, in *The Spirit of Seventy-Six*, 529. See also Fischer, *Washington's Crossing*, 64.

39. From Philipp Losch, *Soldatenhandel : mit einem Verzeichnis der Hessen-kasselischen Subsidienverträge und einer Bibliographie* (Kassel: Hamecher, 1974), as translated in Fischer, *Washington's Crossing*, 63.

40. *American Archives*, Fifth Series, 3:1188.

41. Memoirs of Elisha Bostwick of the Seventh Connecticut Regiment, in *The Spirit of Seventy-Six*, 512.

42. Fischer, *Washington's Crossing*, 114.

43. Washington Irving, *Life of George Washington*, 1:297.

Chapter 16: The Times That Try Men's Souls

1. McCullough, *1776*, 249.

2. Geo. Bickham, Council of Safety Report, December 27, 1776, in Clark Kinnaird, *George Washington: The Pictorial Biography* (New York: Hastings House, 1967), 106.

3. Ibid.

4. Chernow, *Washington: A Life*, 263.

5. McCullough, *1776*, 267.

6. Joseph R. Conlin, *The American Past: A Survey of American History* (San Diego: Harcourt Brace Jovanovich, 1984), 147.

7. Ibid.

8. Thomas Jones, *A History of New York During the Revolutionary War*, ed. Edward Floyd de Lancy (1879), 1:351.

9. Carol Berkin, *Revolutionary Mothers: Women in the Struggle for America's Independence* (New York: Random House, 2006), 65.

10. Francis Josiah Hudleston, *Warriors in Undress* (1926), 90.

11. Benson J. Lossing, *The Pictorial Field-Book of the Revolution* (1866), 611.

12. Marvin Olasky, *The American Leadership Tradition* (New York: Free Press, 2000), 9.

13. Ibid. This verse was directed at Howe's inactivity while he was in Philadelphia.

14. George Washington to Fielding Lewis, July 6, 1780, in *The Writings of George Washington*, 154, 157.

15. Thomas Paine, *The Crisis*, December 23, 1776.

16. Washington to Lund Washington, September 30, 1776, in *The Papers of George Washington, Revolutionary War Series*, 6:440–43.

17. Washington to Samuel Washington, December 18, 1776, in *The Papers of George Washington, Revolutionary War Series*, 7:370.

18. Charles Lee to Joseph Reed, November 24, 1776, in *The Papers of George Washington, Revolutionary War Series*, 7:237n1.

19. Charles Lee to Horatio Gates, December 13, 1776, in *American Archives*, Fifth Series, 3:1201.

20. Washington to Colonel Reed, 1776, qtd. in George F. Scheer and Hugh F. Rankin, *Rebels and Redcoats: The American Revolution Through the Eyes of Those Who Fought and Lived It* (Cleveland: World Publishing, 1957), 204.

21. Qtd. in Joseph J. Ellis, *His Excellency: George Washington* (2004), 96.

22.   Washington to Lund Washington, September 30, 1776.

Chapter 17: Reevaluation
1.   McCullough, *1776*, 268.
2.   Papers of the Continental Congress, no. 36, IV, folio 241, Library of Congress Manuscript Division.
3.   McCullough, *1776*, 255.
4.   Journal of Sergeant William Young, *Pennsylvania Magazine of History and Biography* 8 (1884), 255.
5.   *Journals of the Continental Congress*, 6:1022.
6.   Washington to Hancock, December 12, 1776.
7.   Benjamin Harrison V, qtd. in *Maryland: A Guide to the Old Line State*, Writers' Program of the Work Projects Administration in the State of Maryland (1940), 208.
8.   *Journals of the Continental Congress*, December 12, 1776, 6:1027.
9.   His tone remained polite and mostly humble, but there certainly was an authoritative shift.
10.   Circular to the New England States, February 6, 1777, in *The Papers of George Washington, Revolutionary War Series*, 8:257.
11.   Washington to John Hancock, December 20, 1776, in *The Papers of George Washington, Revolutionary War Series*, 7:381.
12.   Ibid.
13.   Ibid.
14.   Ibid., 381–86
15.   Ibid., 382.
16.   Ibid.
17.   Ibid.
18.   Greene was likely complicit in the disastrous Battle of Fort Washington.
19.   Nathanael Greene to Washington, in George Washington Green, *Life of Nathanael Greene* (1871), 1:346.

20. General Greene to John Hancock, the President of Congress, December 21, 1776, in *The Papers of General Nathanael Greene*, 1:370, 372. Emphasis added.

21. *Journals of the Continental Congress*, 6:1045–46.

22. Ibid., 1047.

23. Jared Sparks, *The Life of George Washington* (Boston, 1839), 208.

24. "The Continental Congress Grants Washington Greater Powers, December 27, 1776," The American Revolution, 1763–1783, Library of Congress.

25. Marcus Tullius Cicero, *The Political Works of Marcus Tullius Cicero: Comprising His Treatise on the Commonwealth; and His Treatise on the Laws*, ed. Francis Barham, Esq. (London, 1841–42), 1:237.

26. Glenn A. Phelps, *George Washington and American Constitutionalism* (Lawrence: University Press of Kansas, 1993), 38.

27. John Adams to Abigail Adams, April 6, 1777, as qtd. in Fischer, *Washington's Crossing*, 144.

28. Washington to the Executive Committee of the Continental Congress, January 1, 1777, in *The Papers of George Washington, Revolutionary War Series*, 7:500.

Chapter 18: Victory or Death

1. Qtd. in McCullough, *1776*, 251.

2. Benjamin Rush and Henry J. Williams, *A memorial containing travels through life or sundry incidents in the life of Dr. Benjamin Rush* (1905), 94.

3. Washington to John Hancock, December 5, 1776, in *The Papers of George Washington, Revolutionary War Series*, 7:262.

4. General Grant to Johaan Gottlieb Rall, December 21, 1776, in *The Spirit of Seventy-Six*, 507.

5. Bruce Chadwick, *The First American Army: The Untold Story of George Washington and the Men Behind America's First Fight for Freedom* (Naperville, Ill.: Sourcebooks, 2005), 142.

6. Ibid.
7. Chernow, *Washington: A Life*, 30.
8. Chadwick, *The First American Army*, 142.
9. Ibid., 143.
10. Ibid., 144.
11. Ibid.
12. Ibid., 146.
13. Ibid.
14. Qtd. in Nathaniel Hervey, *The Memory of Washington* (Boston: James Munroe & Co., 1852), 130.
15. McCullough, *1776*, 283.
16. John Adams to Abigail Adams, April 6, 1777. John Adams disagreed with this rumor, writing to his wife that this notion "was without foundation, for as his hands were never tied, so they were not untied."
17. Chernow, *Washington: A Life*, 278.
18. Chadwick, *The First American Army*, 149.
19. Washington to the Executive Committee of the Continental Congress, January 1, 1777, in *The Papers of Geroge Washington, Revolutionary War Series,* 7:500.
20. William Tudor to Della Jarvis, December 24, 1776, qtd. in McCullough, *1776*, 271.
21. John Hancock to Washington, January 1, 1777, in *The Papers of George Washington, Revolutionary War Series*, 7:506.
22. Chernow, *Washington: A Life*, 416.
23. Private John Howland, as qtd. in Fischer, *Washington's Crossing*, 300.
24. Ibid.
25. Fischer, *Washington's Crossing*, 300.
26. Gerald M. Carbone, "Battle of Princeton Exacts a Heavy Toll," *Nathanael Greene*, Image Library, Warwick Historical Society, 31.
27. Sergeant Joseph White, as qtd. in Fischer, *Washington's Crossing*, 307.

28. Cornwallis, as qtd. in Carbone, "Battle of Princeton Exacts a Heavy Toll."

29. Chernow, *Washington: A Life*, 280.

30. Ibid.

31. An unnamed American soldier, qtd. in Carbone, "Battle of Princeton Exacts a Heavy Toll."

32. Qtd. in McCollough, *1776*, 289.

33. Ibid.

34. Washington to John Augustine Washington, July 18, 1755, in *The Writings of George Washington*, 1:152.

35. Captain Olney, qtd. in Carbone, "Battle of Princeton Exacts a Heavy Toll."

36. Qtd. in Richard M. Ketchum, *The Winter Soldiers: The Battles for Trenton and Princeton* (New York: Macmillan, 1999), 308.

37. Chernow, *Washington: A Life*, 282.

38. Washington to John Hancock, January 5, 1777, in *The Papers of George Washington, Revolutionary War Series*, 7:529n10.

39. Chernow, *Washington: A Life*, 284.

Chapter 19: Idolatry

1. As cited in Chernow, *Washington: A Life*, 283.

2. James Thomas Flexner, *George Washington in the American Revolution, 1775–1783* (Boston: Little, Brown, 1968), 189.

3. *Journals of the Continental Congress*, March 24, 1777, 7:197.

4. At the Battle of Monmouth in 1778.

5. Washington to John Armstrong, May 18, 1779, in *The Papers of George Washington, Revolutionary War Series*, 20:518.

6. Washington to Governor Jonathan Trumbull, May 11, 1777, in ibid., 9:392.

7. Washington to John Augustine Washington, May 12, 1779, in ibid., 20:460.

8. Washington to Joseph Jones, May 31, 1780, in *The Writings of George Washington*, 18:453.

9. Ibid.

10. Washington to Henry Laurens, November 11, 1778, in *The Papers of George Washington*, 18:94.

11. Washington to John Jay, December 13, 1778, in *The Papers of George Washington, Revolutionary War Series*, 18:405; H. L. Landers, *The Virginia Campaign and the Blockade and Siege of Yorktown, 1781* (1931), 50.

12. Washington to Henry Laurens, November 11, 1778, in *The Papers of George Washington, Revolutionary War Series*, 18:94–112.

13. "Proclamation concerning Persons Swearing British Allegiance," January 25, 1777, in ibid., 8:152–53.

14. Ibid.

15. Ibid.

16. Abraham Clark to John Hart, February 8, 1777, in *Letters of Delegates to Congress, 1774–1789*, ed. Paul H. Smith et al. (Library of Congress, 1976–2000), 6:241.

17. *Journals of the Continental Congress*, 7:165–66.

18. Glenn A. Phelps, *George Washington and American Constitutionalism* (Lawrence: University Press of Kansas, 1993), 39–40.

19. Joseph J. Ellis, *His Excellency: George Washington* (2004), 101.

20. Nathanael Greene to Washington, March 24, 1777, in *The Papers of George Washington, Revolutionary War Series*, 7:627.

21. Ellis, *His Excellency*, 101.

22. John Adams to Abigail Adams, March 7, 1777, in *Adams Family Correspondence*, ed. L. H. Butterfield et al. (Boston, 1963–2011), 2:169.

23. John Marshall, *The Life of George Washington*, ed. Robert Faulkner and Paul Carrese (1838; Indianapolis: Liberty Fund, 2000), 84.

Chapter 20: *Dictator Perpetuo*

1. Sir William Howe to Lord George Germain, April 22, 1777, in *Documents of the American Revolution*, ed. K. G. Davis (1972–1981), 14:65.

2. John Adams, Diary Entry, September 15, 1777, in *Diary and Autobiography of John Adams*, ed. L. H. Butterfield et al. (1961), 2:262.

3. Marshall, *The Life of George Washington*, 152.

4. Ibid.

5. Chernow, *Washington: A Life*, 302.

6. General Orders, August 23, 1777, in *The Papers of George Washington, Revolutionary War Series*, 11:51.

7. Marquis de Lafayette, August 23, 1777, as qtd. in Carl G. Karsch, "Washington's Army Marches Past the Hall," Carpenters' Hall website, Independence Hall Association, UShistory.org.

8. To look more professional, Washington likewise ordered that "the multitude of women in particular, especially those who are pregnant," be left behind. General Orders, August 4, 1777, in *The Papers of George Washington, Revolutionary War Series*, 10:496.

9. George Washington Greene, *The Life of Nathanael Greene* (New York: Hurd & Houghton, 1867), 1:478.

10. John Adams, Diary Entry, September 21, 1777, in *Diary and Autobiography of John Adams*, 2:265.

11. George Washington to Henry Laurens, October 3, 1778, in *The Papers of George Washington, Revolutionary War Series*, 17:238.

12. Washington Irving, *Life of George Washington*, 3:210.

13. John Adams to Abigail Adams, October 26, 1777, in *Adams Family Correspondence*, 2:360–61. Adams was referring specifically to Horatio Gates leading the victory at the Battle of Saratoga rather than Washington.

14. Paper presented by the Legislature of the State of New York to the Continental Congress, February 1781, in *The Writings of George Washington*, ed. Jared Sparks (1833–37), 7:442n. The Jared Sparks edition contains many known errors and misrepresentations, but this language is included here since it is not unique in descriptions of Washington's powers. For example, Richard Lee wrote to James Lovell, Theodorick Bland, and Joseph Jones of Washington's "dictatorial powers." *The Writings of George Washington* (ed. Fitzpatrick), 22:383n. The

Pennsylvania Supreme Court likewise wrote that Washington had "possessed almost dictatorial powers." Address from the Judge of the Pennsylvania Supreme Court, in *The Papers of George Washington, Presidential Series*, 2:85n1.

15. Ibid.

16. Washington to William Shippen, Jr., January 27, 1777, qtd. in Glenn A. Phelps, *George Washington and American Constitutionalism* (Lawrence: University Press of Kansas, 1993), 39.

17. Circular to the States, May 4, 1782, in *The Writings of George Washington*, 24:236.

18. Phelps, *George Washington and American Constitutionalism*, 39.

19. Washington to William Livingston, April 15, 1778, in *The Papers of George Washington, Revolutionary War Series*, 14:525.

20. Washington to William Livingston, April 11, 1778, in ibid., 14:477.

21. For example, Congress again granted dictatorial powers as they fled Philadelphia on September 17, 1777, but it was to last for only sixty days.

22. *Journals of the Continental Congress*, 14:566–69.

23. Washington to Henry Laurens, August 20, 1780, in *The Writings of George Washington*, 19:402n52.

24. John Jay to Washington, May 10, 1779, in *The Papers of George Washington, Revolutionary War Series*, 20:426.

25. Articles of Confederation (1781), art. IX. See also, Bennet N. Hollander, "The President and Congress—Operational Control of the Armed Forces," *Military Law Review* 27 (1965): 50, noting that the "colonists shared a deep fear of the development under the new government of a military branch unchecked by the legislature and susceptible to use by an arbitrary executive power."

26. Although, as discussed, Washington did infringe upon this power at times.

27. Enemy treatment is detailed in Part II.

28. Washington to the New York Convention, December 16, 1776, in *The Papers of George Washington, Revolutionary War Series*, 7:356.

29. Circular to the States, May 4, 1782, in *The Writings of George Washington*, 24:237.

30. *The Debates in the Several State Conventions on the Adoption of the Federal Constitution*, ed. Jonathan Elliot (1836), 3:79.

31. Ibid.

32. Henry Cabot Lodge, *George Washington* (Boston: Houghton, Mifflin & Co., 1898), 170.

IV. Tribunals & Tribulations

1. The Army Athletic Council's Report, *The Theory and Practice of Athletics at the Military Academy, West Point*, 1927, i; "Notable USMA Graduates," United States Military Academy.

Chapter 21: Gentleman Johnny *vs.* Granny Gates

1. Joshua Hett Smith, *An Authentic Narrative of the Causes Which Led to the Death of Major André* (1808), 12.

2. Ibid., 3.

3. Ibid., 4.

4. Ibid.

5. *Journals of the Continental Congress*, May 25, 1775, 2:60.

6. Manuscript of Major James Wemyss, Sparks Manuscripts in Harvard College Library.

7. Sir Henry Clinton (1775), in *The Spirit of Seventy-Six*, 585.

8. A report from Lieutenant General Sir Henry Clinton to General Sir William Howe , October 9, 1777, *Naval Documents of the American Revolution*, 10, *American Theatre: October 1, 1777–December 31, 1777* (Washington, D.C.: U.S. Government Printing Office, 1996), 98–99.

9. Smith, *An Authentic Narrative*, 8.

10. A report by Major General John Vaughan to Lieutenant General Sir Henry Clinton, undated (likely October 26, 1777), *Naval*

Documents of the American Revolution, 10:300, reporting the destruction of Kingston, New York.

11. *The Spirit of Seventy-Six*, 545.

12. Robert C. Doyle, *The Enemy in Our Hands: America's Treatment of Enemy Prisoners of War, from the Revolution to the War on Terror* (Lexington: University Press of Kentucky, 2010), 14.

13. The girl's name was Jane McCrea. Journal of Lieutenant William Digby of the Shropshire Regiment, in *The Spirit of Seventy-Six*, 559.

14. Proclamation of John Burgoyne, June 23, 1777, in *The Spirit of Seventy-Six*, 548.

15. Journal of General Riedesel's wife, October 1777, in *The Spirit of Seventy-Six*, 600.

16. John Fiske, *The American Revolution* (Boston: Houghton, Mifflin & Co., 1896), 1:255.

17. While Gates did express a desire for higher rank, it is unclear how much of a role he played in the underhanded plot to oust Schuyler. The latter seems to have viewed Gates largely as a puppet of the New England congressmen. See General Philip Schuyler to Gouverneur Morris, September 7, 1777, as cited in Max M. Mintz, *The Generals of Saratoga: John Burgoyne & Horatio Gates* (New Haven: Yale University Press, 1990), 262n9.

18. Benson John Lossing, *The Life and Times of Philip Schuyler* (1883), 1:131.

19. Fiske, *The American Revolution*, 1:254.

20. "General Philip Schuyler," Son of the South website, http://www.sonofthesouth.net/revolutionary-war/general/philip-schuyler.htm.

21. Fiske, *The American Revolution*, 1:254.

22. Proclamation of John Burgoyne, June 23, 1777.

23. Fiske, *The American Revolution*, 1:264.

24. Recollections of Captain E. Wakefield, in *The Spirit of Seventy-Six*, 581.

25. Major Henry Dearborn, in *The Spirit of Seventy-Six*, 577.

26. *The Spirit of Seventy-Six*, 590.

27. Ebenezer Mattoon to General Philip Schuyler, October 7, 1835, in ibid., 594.

28. Major General David Wooster, Military Journal Entry, 1777, qtd. in Barry Wilson, *Benedict Arnold: A Traitor in Our Midst* (Montreal: McGill-Queen's University Press, 2001).

29. Hoffman Nickerson, *The Turning Point of the Revolution, Or Burgoyne in America* (Cambridge, Mass.: Riverside Press, 1928; repr. 2006), 352.

30. Henry Beebee Carrington, *Battles of the American Revolution* (1876), 357.

31. Stanley Weintraub, *Iron Tears: America's Battle for Freedom, Britain's Quagmire: 1775–1783* (New York: Free Press, 2005), 202.

32. John Burgoyne to Henry Clinton, September 23, 1777, qtd. in Nickerson, *The Turning Point of the Revolution*, 343.

33. Ibid., 352.

34. *The Lost War: Letters from British Officers during the American Revolution*, ed. Marion Balderston and David Syrett (New York: Horizon, 1975), 130.

Chapter 22: A Traitor Lurks

1. James Thomas Flexner, *The Traitor and the Spy: Benedict Arnold and John André* (New York: Harcourt Brace, 1953).

2. Captain Benedict Arnold's Connecticut Company's Proclamation, April 24, 1775, qtd. in James Kirby Martin, *Benedict Arnold, Revolutionary Hero: An American Warrior Reconsidered* (New York: New York University Press, 1997), 63.

3. Jim Murphy, *The Real Benedict Arnold* (New York: Clarion Books, 2007), 165.

4. Don Higginbotham, *The War of American Independence: Military Attitudes, Policies, and Practices, 1763–1789* (1978; Northeastern University Press, 1983), 246.

5. Elias Boudinot, *Historical Recollections of American Events During the Revolutionary War, from his original manuscript* (Philadelphia: Bourquin, 1984), 78.

6. *The Spirit of Seventy-Six*, 708.

7. Philander D. Chase, "Friedrich Wilhelm von Steuben," *American National Biography* (February 2000).

8. Ibid.

9. William Cullen Bryant and Sydney Howard Gay, *Scribner's Popular History of the United States* (1879), 597.

10. Qtd. in Walter Harold Wilkin, *Some British Soldiers in America* (London: Hugh Rees, Ltd., 1914), 258.

11. Testimony of Lieutenant Colonel Richard Harrison, in *The Spirit of Seventy-Six*, 712.

12. *The Spirit of Seventy-Six*, 708.

13. Joseph Plumb Martin, *A Narrative of a Revolutionary Soldier* (New York: Signet Classics, 2001), 91–95.

14. Ibid.

15. Wilkin, *Some British Soldiers in America*, 260.

16. Ibid.

17. *The Spirit of Seventy-Six*, 710. This was a court-martial.

18. Francis Vinton Greene, *The Revolutionary War and the Military Policy of the United States* (1911), 148.

19. Qtd. from Colonel Laurens (aide to Washington), in Charles Lee and Edward Langworthy, *The Life and Memoirs of the Late Major General Lee* (1813), 49.

20. *The History of Dueling in America*, PBS Special Feature, http://www.pbs.org/wgbh/amex/duel/sfeature/dueling.html.

21. Chernow, *Washington: A Life*, 346.

22. Benson John Lossing, "General Charles Lee: Traitor of the American Revolution," in *Our Country: Household History for All Readers*, 2 (1877).

23. Smith, *An Authentic Narrative*, 16.

24. Flexner, *The Traitor and the Spy*, 226.

25. Ibid., 234.

26. Major Henry Lee, "Capture of Major André," *Pennsylvania Magazine of History and Biography* 4 (1880), 61.

27. Flexner, *The Traitor and the Spy*, 230.

28. Martin, *Benedict Arnold, Revolutionary Hero*, 443.

29. John Talbot, *History of North America* (1820), 1:338. This was a court-martial.

30. Lee, "Capture of Major André."

31. Smith, *An Authentic Narrative*, 16.

32. Ibid.

33. Murphy, *The Real Benedict Arnold*, 191.

34. Ibid.

35. Washington to Joseph Reed, May 28, 1780, in *The Writings of George Washington*, 18:436.

36. Isaac Q. Leake, *Memoir of the Life and Times of General John Lamb* (1857), 379.

Chapter 23: Treason of the Blackest Dye

1. Smith, *An Authentic Narrative*, 10.

2. Polish General Tadeusz Kościuszko.

3. Smith, *An Authentic Narrative*, 10.

4. Thacher, *Military Journal of the American Revolution*, 215.

5. Smith, *An Authentic Narrative*, 10.

6. Diary of Tobias Lear, Private Secretary to Washington, October 23, 1786.

7. Smith, *An Authentic Narrative*, 10.

8. Orders of Nathanael Greene, September 26, 1780, qtd. in *The Diary of the American Revolution*, ed. Frank Moore (New York: Washington Square Press, 1967), 2:323.

9. Benedict Arnold to John André, July 15, 1780, qtd. in Alex Storozynski, *The Peasant Prince: Thaddeus Kosciuszko and the Age of Revolution* (New York: Thomas Dunne Books, St. Martin's, 2009), 85–92. The modern comparison comes from the MeasuringWorth Project's

average earning index. Many thanks to Samuel H. Williamson for his help on this point. Estimates vary widely, but this is just meant to provide an estimate for the modern reader.

10. Alexander Hamilton to John Laurens, October 15, 1780, in *The Papers of Alexander Hamilton*, ed. Harold C. Syrett et al. (New York: Columbia University Press, 1961–1987), 2:467.

11. Smith, *An Authentic Narrative*, 20.

12. Frank Bertangue Green, *The History of Rockland County* (1889), 94.

13. Winthrop Sargent, *The Life and Career of Major John André* (Boston, 1861), 8.

14. Smith, *An Authentic Narrative*, 9.

15. Flexner, *The Traitor and the Spy*, 26.

16. Letter from John André, October 19, 1769.

17. Flexner, *The Traitor and the Spy*, 26.

18. Smith, *An Authentic Narrative*, 21.

19. Anna Seward, "Monody on Major Andre" (1817).

20. Richard Lovell Edgeworth, *Memoirs of Richard Lovell Edgeworth, Esq.* (1821), 1:109.

21. Flexner, *The Traitor and the Spy*, 25.

22. Ibid., 28.

23. Sargent, *The Life and Career of Major John André*, 39.

24. John Davison Lawson, ed., *American State Trials* (1916), 6:465.

25. "Major John Andre," Revolutionary War 1777: People, Independence Hall Association, UShistory.org.

26. Orders of Nathanael Greene, September 26, 1780.

27. Benedict Arnold to George Clinton, Governor of New York, August 22, 1780, George Washington Papers, Manuscript Division, Library of Congress.

28. Jim Murphy, *The Real Benedict Arnold* (New York: Clarion Books, 2007), 202.

29. Benedict Arnold to George Clinton, Governor of New York, August 22, 1780.

30. "Obstructed the Hudson," *New York Times*, February 16, 1895.

31. Robert McConnell Hatch, *Major John André: A Gallant in Spy's Clothing* (Boston: Houghton Mifflin, 1986), 236.

32. Sargent, *The Life and Career of Major John André*, 280.

33. Major Henry Lee, "Capture of Major André," *Pennsylvania Magazine of History and Biography* 4 (1880), 64.

34. Smith, *An Authentic Narrative*, 15.

35. Ibid.

36. Flexner, *The Traitor and the Spy*, 363.

37. Smith, *An Authentic Narrative*, 15.

38. Jared Sparks, *The Life and Treason of Benedict Arnold* (New York: Harper & Bros., 1848), 198.

39. Smith, *An Authentic Narrative*, 15.

40. Ibid.

41. Intelligence Report of Andrew Elliot of New York, October 4–5, 1780, in *The Spirit of Seventy-Six*, 752.

42. "Major John Andre Trial: 1780," Notable Trials and Court Cases—1637 to 1832, Law Library—American Law and Legal Information, http://law.jrank.org.

43. Smith, *An Authentic Narrative*, 21.

44. Ibid.

45. Ibid., 26.

46. Ibid.

47. Ibid., 25.

48. Ibid.

Chapter 24: Commissions & Courts-Martial

1. There is evidence that these three men were actually mere highway robbers who were honored as militiamen after the fact as a reward for catching André.

2. Smith, *An Authentic Narrative*, 48.

3. Ibid., 49.

4. Ibid.

5. Alexander Hamilton to John Laurens, October 15, 1780, in *The Papers of Alexander Hamilton*, ed. Harold C. Syrett et al. (New York: Columbia University Press, 1961–1987), 2:467.

6. Smith, *An Authentic Narrative*, 46.

7. Intelligence Report of Andrew Elliot of New York, October 4–5, 1780.

8. Ibid.

9. Alexander Hamilton to Elizabeth Schuyler, September 25, 1780, in *The Papers of Alexander Hamilton*, 2:441.

10. Chernow, *Washington: A Life*, 383–84, provides a good description of this scene.

11. General Anthony Wayne to H. A. Sheel, October 2, 1780, in *The Spirit of Seventy-Six*, 753.

12. Smith, *An Authentic Narrative*, 31.

13. Ibid., 32.

14. Although Part V focuses on Washington's treatment of Americans, I include the description of Smith's treatment in Part IV to illustrate the difference between his and André's fate.

15. David Glazier, "Precedents Lost: The Neglected History of the Military Commission," *Virginia Journal of International Law* 46 (2005): 20. Professor Glazier provides an excellent discussion of the André affair.

16. Resolution of the Continental Congress, August 21, 1776, in *Journals of the Continental Congress*, 5:693.

17. Washington was fully cognizant of this resolution, as evidenced by his letter to members of Congress seeking clarification on it. George Washington to Continental Congress Committee to Inquire into the State of the Army, July 19, 1777, in *The Papers of George Washington, Revolutionary War Series*, 10:332–37. "Written after the new Articles of War were adopted in September 1776, it confirms Washington's

understanding that the resolution on spies was not superseded by the new law." Glazier, "Precedents Lost," 8n97.

18.   Smith, *An Authentic Narrative*, 131.

19.   Major Christopher W. Behan, "Don't Tug on Superman's Cape: In Defense of Convening Authority Selection and Appointment of Court-Martial Panel Members," *Military Law Review* 176 (2003): 209.

20.   Ibid.

21.   American Articles of War of 1776, as cited in ibid., 209n118.

22.   *Journals of the Continental Congress*, 15:1277–78.

23.   *Hamdan v. Rumsfeld*, 126 S. Ct. 2749, 2839n15 (2006).

24.   Richard J. Wilson, "Military Commissions in Guantánamo Bay: Giving 'Full and Fair Trial' a Bad Name," *Gonzaga Journal of International Law* 10 (2007): 65.

25.   William Winthrop, *Military Law and Precedents* (1886), 1:731.

26.   United Nations War Crimes Commission, *Law Reports of Trials of War Criminals*, 1 (1997), 116–17.

27.   Captain Brian C. Baldrate, "The Supreme Court's Role in Defining the Jurisdiction of Military Tribunals: A Study, Critique, and Proposal for *Hamdan v. Rumsfeld*," *Military Law Review* 186 (Winter 2005): 11.

28.   *Hamdan v. Rumsfeld*, 126 S. Ct. at 2749 (quoting W. Birkhimer, *Military Government and Martial Law*, 3rd ed. (1914), 537–38).

29.   Alexander Hamilton to William Livingston, April 21, 1777, in *The Papers of Alexander Hamilton*, 1:235.

30.   Glazier, "Precedents Lost," 22.

31.   Washington to Jonathan Trumbull, April 21, 1777, in *The Papers of George Washington, Revolutionary War Series*, 9:232.

32.   Hamilton to Livingston, April 21, 1777.

33.   Christopher A. Chrisman, "Article III Goes to War: A Case for a Separate Federal Circuit for Enemy Combatant Habeas Cases," *Journal of Law and Politics* 21 (2005): 40.

34. J. V. Capua, "The Early History of Martial Law in England from the Fourteenth Century to the Petition of Right," *Cambridge Law Journal* 36 no. 1 (1977): 152.

35. Ibid., 153.

36. Chrisman, "Article III Goes to War," 40.

37. Washington to Brigadier General Preudhomme de Borre, August 3, 1777, in *The Papers of George Washington, Revolutionary War Series*, 10:495.

38. John Ross successfully represented "Loyalists prosecuted by [Congressman Joseph] Reed in the state courts." Willard Sterne Randall, *Benedict Arnold: Patriot and Traitor* (New York: Morrow, 1990), 425–31.

39. Washington to Brigadier General Thomas Mifflin, February 14, 1777, in *The Papers of George Washington, Revolutionary War Series*, 8:337.

40. Hence Washington's fixation on whether "a person who belongs to any of the United States of America . . . can be tried . . . and punished as a spy." Washington to Continental Congress Committee to Inquire into the State of the Army, July 19, 1777.

41. Washington to Mifflin, February 14, 1777.

Chapter 25: American Military Justice

1. Smith, *An Authentic Narrative*, 63.

2. A. Wigfall Green, "The Military Commission," *American Journal of International Law* 42 (1946): 833.

3. Smith, *An Authentic Narrative*, 130.

4. Ibid., 132.

5. Ibid., 73.

6. Ibid., 64.

7. Marquis de Lafayette, General Knox, and Colonels Harrison and Hamilton all gave (somewhat conflicting) accounts of Smith's involvement in the André affair. Next, the testimony of two boatmen, Samuel and Joseph Colquhoun, corroborated Smith's account. Despite "disgraceful means that were used to impeach the integrity of the eldest

Samuel," the two men "seemed to have much weight with the court-martial." Finally, two militiamen testified to finding a paper on André that listed Smith's name, to which Smith did not object since "no man was bound to say that legally which might condemn himself." Ibid., 137.

8. Ibid.

9. Ibid.

10. Ibid., 138.

11. Jared Sparks, *The Life and Treason of Benedict Arnold* (New York: Harper & Bros., 1848), 197.

12. Smith, *An Authentic Narrative*, 139.

13. John D. Lawson, *American State Trials* (1916), 7:487.

14. Smith, *An Authentic Narrative*, 207.

15. Ibid., 206.

16. See Washington to George Clinton, October 29, 1780, in *The Writings of George Washington*, 20:262.

17. Smith, *An Authentic Narrative*, 64.

18. Major Henry Lee, "Capture of Major André," *Pennsylvania Magazine of History and Biography* 4 (1880), 64.

19. Washington to Sir Henry Clinton, September 30, 1780, in *The Writings of George Washington*, 20:103 (emphasis added).

20. Washington to a Board of General Officers, June 2, 1778, in *The Papers of George Washington, Revolutionary War Series*, 15:296.

21. Smith, *An Authentic Narrative*, 63.

22. This tribunal was not even a "trial," per se. "Although Washington himself at least once referred to André as having been 'tried,' the Board was an advisory panel, not a 'court' that legally determined guilt or imposed a sentence." David Glazier, "Precedents Lost: The Neglected History of the Military Commission," *Virginia Journal of International Law* 46 (2005): 19.

23. William Winthrop, *Military Law and Precedents* (1886), 1:731.

24. General George Washington's Orders, September 29, 1780, Early American Imprints, no. 30012.

25. Jonathan Turley, "Tribunals and Tribulations: The Antithetical Elements of Military Governance in a Madisonian Democracy," *George Washington Law Review* 70 (2002): 649.

26. Smith, *An Authentic Narrative*, 92.

27. General George Washington's Orders, September 29, 1780.

28. Smith, *An Authentic Narrative*, 92.

29. Were this in a court-martial proceeding during the present day, virtually all of the government's case would likely constitute a violation of Rule 801 of the Federal Rules of Evidence.

30. Smith, *An Authentic Narrative*, 99.

31. Were this in a court-martial proceeding during the present day, this would likely constitute a violation of the confrontation clause of the Sixth Amendment.

32. Smith, *An Authentic Narrative*, 99.

33. Ibid., 152.

34. Ibid., 92.

35. Ibid., 96.

36. "Major John Andre Trial (1780)," in *Great American Trials*, ed. Edward W. Knappman (Detroit: Gale Research, 1994), 75.

37. Smith, *An Authentic Narrative*, 53–54.

38. Ibid., 99.

39. Ibid., 53.

40. Ibid.

41. Ibid., 55.

42. Ibid., 107.

43. Glazier, "Precedents Lost," 21. Glazier writes, "Washington handled André's case more summarily than the actual court-martial that Congress had called for."

44. Smith, *An Authentic Narrative*, 89.

45. Washington to John Laurens, October 4, 1780, in *The Writings of George Washington*, ed. Worthington C. Ford (New York and London: G. P. Putnam's Sons, 1890), 8:494.

46. Joseph Dennie and Asbury Dickins, *The Port Folio* (1809), 509.

47. Washington to the President of Congress, October 7, 1789, in *The Writings of George Washington* (ed. Fitzpatrick), 20:131.

48. Smith, *An Authentic Narrative*, 96.

49. Major Henry Lee, "Capture of Major André," *Pennsylvania Magazine of History and Biography* 4 (1880), 64.

50. Winthrop Sargent, *The Life and Career of Major John André* (Boston, 1861), 304.

51. Smith, *An Authentic Narrative*, 97–98.

52. "Loan Exhibition at Tappan, NY," *The Churchman* 38 (August 10, 1878), 14.

53. Ibid.

54. Sargent, *The Life and Career of Major John André*, 304.

55. Smith, *An Authentic Narrative*, 167.

56. Sinclair B. Ferguson, *Deserted by God?* (Grand Rapids: Baker Books, 1993), 87–88.

57. *Journals of the Continental Congress*, November 3, 1780, 1009.

58. Dennie and Dickins, *The Port Folio*, 509.

59. John Marshall, *The Life of George Washington*, ed. Robert Faulkner and Paul Carrese (1838; Indianapolis: Liberty Fund, 2000), 5.

60. Sargent, *The Life and Career of Major John André*, 403.

61. Professor Glazier makes a good point when he cautions: "Any residual precedent from Washington's actions must be considered in the context of the Constitution, which repudiates claims of continuing executive authority to ignore statutory enactments. The Supremacy Clause of the Constitution explicitly makes statutes and treaties 'the supreme Law of the Land' but makes no mention of customary international law. Also clearly on point is the constitutional commitment to Congress of the authority to 'define and punish Piracies and Felonies committed on the high Seas, and Offenses against the Law of Nations.' This clause gives the Congress, not the Executive, primary authority in

the field. Taken together, these two clauses suggest that Washington's handling of the André affair was mooted by the Constitution. Ironically, the resolution on spying was not; its language about 'lurking as a spy' remains recognizable in the UCMJ to this day." David Glazier, "Precedents Lost," 23.

62. Journal of Major General Benjamin Lincoln, in Thacher, *Military Journal of the American Revolution*, 215.

Part V: His Excellency's Loyal Subjects

1. Instructions to John Sullivan, May 31, 1779, in *The Writings of George Washington*, 15:190.

2. Ibid.

Chapter 26: Total Ruin

1. Instructions to John Sullivan, May 31, 1779.

2. Benson John Lossing, *Our Country: A History of the United States from the Discovery of America to the Present Time* (New York: Lossing History Co., 1905), 4:998.

3. Ibid.

4. Ibid.

5. Thomas Campbell, "Gertrude of Wyoming," in *Gertrude of Wyoming; a Pennsylvanian Tale. And Other Poems* (London: Longman, Hurst, Rees, & Orme, 1809), 59.

6. Lossing, *Our Country*, 4:999

7. Ibid.

8. Ernest Alexander Cruikshank, *The Story of Butler's Rangers and the Settlement of Niagara* (1893), 47.

9. Ibid., 50.

10. Lossing, *Our Country*, 4:999.

11. Steve Adams, "NH: Years of Revolution," *Profiles Publications and the NH Bicentennial Commission* (1976).

12. Ibid.

13. Washington to the President of Congress, June 17, 1776, in *The Papers of George Washington, Revolutionary War Series*, 5:21.

14. Washington to John Sullivan, March 15, 1777, in *The Writings of George Washington*, 7:290. Steve Adams, "NH: Years of Revolution," brought this statement to my attention.

15. Washington to John Sullivan, May 31, 1779, in *The Papers of George Washington, Revolutionary War Series*, 20:718.

16. John Sullivan to Washington, September 30, 1779, in Thomas Coffin Amory, *The Military Services and Public Life of Major-General John Sullivan* (1868), 137–38.

17. General John Sullivan's Report to Congress, September 30, 1779.

18. Journal of Lieutenant Erkuries Beatty, 4th Pennsylvania Regiment, September 13, 1779, in *Journals of the Military Expedition of Major General John Sullivan*, 31–32.

19. Journal of Lieutenant Robert Parker, of the Second Continental Artillery, September 14, 1779, in Jeremiah Whitaker Newman, *The Lounger's Common-Place Book*, 1 (1796), 170. The two Americans tortured were Lieutenant Thomas Boyd and Sergeant Michael Parker. Since the bodies were so mangled, it became unclear which gruesome act was performed on whom.

20. Journal of Sergeant Moses Fellows, 3rd New Hampshire Regiment, September 14, 1779, in *Journals of the Military Expedition of Major General John Sullivan*, 91.

21. Journal of Lieutenant Rudolphus Van Hovenburgh, 4th New York Regiment, September 14, 1779, in ibid., 275–84; Colonel John Butler's report to Lieutenant Colonel Bolton, September 14, 1779.

22. *Journals of the Military Expedition of Major General John Sullivan*, 530.

23. Except for one town far off, near Alleghany. John Sullivan to Washington, September 30, 1779, in Amory, *The Military Services and Public Life of Major-General John Sullivan*, 137–38.

24. Allan Eckert, *Wilderness War: A Narrative* (Boston: Little, Brown, 1978).

25. Address by Ellis H. Roberts, in *Journals of the Military Expedition of Major General John Sullivan*, 426.

26. James Thomas Flexner, *George Washington: The Forge of Experience, 1732–1775* (Boston: Little, Brown, 1965), 323. The Native Americans were also commonly referred to as "savages."

Chapter 27: Band of Brethren

1. Aristotle, *Politics*, transl. Benjamin Jowett, bk. 3, pts. 1–3, 7.

2. Aristophanes, *Ecclesiazousai*.

3. *Idiotes* meant "layman, person lacking professional skill" in ancient Greece and mutated into Middle English *idiot*, meaning "simple man, uneducated person, layman" by the fourteenth century. Douglas Harper, Online Etymology Dictionary.

4. A notion of citizenship existed in medieval cities, particularly in the commercially advanced cities of Italy and the Low Countries. A medieval text by Galbert of Bruges, *The Murder of Charles the Good* (New York: Harper Torchbooks, 1967), shows a sense of citizenship in tension with feudal ties. Many thanks to Carol Staswick for her insights into this area.

5. Rogers M. Smith, "The Meaning of American Citizenship," in *Constitution: A Bicentennial Chronicle*, published by Project '87 of the American Political Science Association and American Historical Association (1985).

6. While "new conceptions emerged that saw society and government as the product of individual consent and compact, . . . [Sir Edward] Coke's conclusions regarding the character of allegiance—his maxims and definitions to the effect that the subject-king relationship was personal, natural, perpetual, and immutable—remained deeply embedded in the law." James H. Kettner, "The Development of American Citizenship in the Revolutionary Era: The Idea of Volitional Allegiance," *American Journal of Legal History* 18 no. 3 (July 1974): 209.

7. It is important to note that Great Britain was far from a tyrannical government but was actually quite progressive compared with the other world powers. Its main legislative body, the Parliament of Great Britain, was composed of the House of Lords and the popularly elected House of Commons. Nevertheless, the notion of unending loyalty to the Crown persisted.

8. Smith, "The Meaning of American Citizenship," 3.

9. Marc Kaufman, "Jefferson changed 'subjects' to 'citizens' in Declaration of Independence," *Washington Post*, July 3, 2010.

10. John Jay, *Federalist* No. 2 (October 31, 1787). Seemingly ignoring the religious and ethnic diversity already in the states, he also wrote that the citizens were "descended from the same ancestors, speaking the same language, professing the same religion."

11. Declaration of Independence.

12. Kaufman, "Jefferson changed 'subjects' to 'citizens' in Declaration of Independence."

13. United States Naturalization and Citizenship, FamilySearch. org (2011).

14. Samuel Adams to James Warren, June 28, 1775, in *Letters of Delegates to Congress*, ed. Paul H. Smith et al. (Library of Congress), 1:554. See also Donald N. Moran, "Why George Washington?" *The Valley Newsletter* (Sons of the American Revolution), February/March 1996.

15. Robert M. Calhoon, "Loyalism and Neutrality," in *A Companion to the American Revolution*, ed. Jack P. Greene and J. R. Pole (Malden, Mass.: Blackwell, 2000), 235.

16. Claude Halstead Van Tyne, *The Loyalists in the American Revolution* (1902), 182–83.

17. John Adams to Abigail Adams, September 14, 1774, in *Adams Family Correspondence*, ed. L. H. Butterfield et al. (Boston, 1963), 1:155.

18. Kettner, "The Development of American Citizenship in the Revolutionary Era," 213.

19. This notion indeed dissipated somewhat as the war raged— so much so that the Congress eventually referred to them as British

subjects again in the peace treaty—but Washington still displayed respect for their rights.

20.   Kettner, "The Development of American Citizenship in the Revolutionary Era," 213.

21.   W. Stewart Wallace, *The United Empire Loyalists: A Chronicle of the Great Migration* (1914), 10.

22.   Angela E. M. Files, *Loyalist Families of the Grand River Branch U.E.L.A.C.* (United Empire Loyalists' Association of Canada, 1991).

23.   Nathanael Greene to Alexander Hamilton, January 10, 1781, in *The Papers of Alexander Hamilton*, ed. Harold C. Syrett et al. (New York: Columbia University Press, 1961–87), 2:529.

24.   Wallace, *The United Empire Loyalists*, 9.

25.   Ibid., 10.

26.   Qtd. in Kettner, "The Development of American Citizenship in the Revolutionary Era," 213.

27.   Qtd. in ibid., 214.

Chapter 28: Poison & Peas

1.   "Dr. William Eustis, Surgeon in the Continental Army," in David A. Adler, *George Washington: An Illustrated Biography* (New York: Holiday House, 2004), 111. The details of the plot are largely unknown and the story herein reflects the somewhat conflicting reports from contemporaries.

2.   Reverend John Marsh, July 9, 1776, in Washington Irving, *Life of George Washington*, 2:83n. The account of the peas is subject to debate; it was added as a note by antiquarian Benson J. Lossing in 1859 to Washington's step-grandson's memoirs. George Washington Parke Custis et al., *Recollections and Private Memoirs of Washington* (1860), 411.

3.   Adler, *George Washington: An Illustrated Biography*, 111.

4.   Irving, *Life of George Washington*, 2:83n.

5.   Ibid.

6. Cornelia Phillips Spencer, *First Steps in North Carolina History* (1888), 76.

7. Governor William Tryon to Lord Dartmouth, July 7, 1775, in William Walter Legge, 5th Earl of Dartmouth, *The Manuscripts of the Earl of Dartmouth* (1895), 2:329.

8. Washington to Philip Schuyler, June 25, 1775, in *The Papers of George Washington, Revolutionary War Series*, 1:37.

9. Daniel Parker Coke, M.P., *The Royal Commission on the Losses and Services of American Loyalists, 1783 to 1785*, ed. Hugh Edward Egerton (1915), 168. Many thanks to Stephen Davidson for bringing to my attention much of the material on Mathews.

10. His home was in Brooklyn, to be precise.

11. Chernow, *Washington: A Life*, 233.

12. Irving, *Life of George Washington*, 2:81.

13. John Bakeless, *Turncoats, Traitors and Heroes* (Philadelphia: Lippincott, 1959), 97.

14. The records containing the exact details of his capture are largely lost.

15. Bakeless, *Turncoats, Traitors and Heroes*, 98.

16. Ibid., 102.

17. Court Martial for the Trial of Thomas Hickey and Others, June 26, 1776, in *American Archives*, Fourth Series, 6:1084.

18. General Orders, June 28, 1776, in *The Papers of George Washington, Revolutionary War Series*, 5:129.

19. Qtd. in Charles P. Niemeyer, *The Revolutionary War* (Westport, Conn.: Greenwood Press, 2007), 36.

20. Chernow, *Washington: A Life*, 233.

21. "Dr. William Eustis, Surgeon in the Continental Army," in Adler, *George Washington: An Illustrated Biography*, 111.

22. General Orders, June 28, 1776, 129–30.

23. James H. Kettner, "The Development of American Citizenship in the Revolutionary Era: The Idea of Volitional Allegiance," *American Journal of Legal History* 18 no. 3 (July 1974): 215.

24. Irving, *Life of George Washington*, 2:81.

25. *Journals of the Continental Congress*, June 24, 1776, 5:475.

26. Joshua Hett Smith was likewise a civilian. He was tried via court-martial later in the war by a 1777 resolution calling for such, as well as a specific congressional authorization. Generally, civilian Loyalists were tried in nonmilitary criminal courts.

27. Daniel Parker Coke, M.P., *The Royal Commission on the Losses and Services of American Loyalists, 1783 to 1785*, ed. Hugh Edward Egerton (1915), 168.

28. Memorial of David Mathews Esq., Late Mayor of New York (August 25, 1784), in ibid., 168.

29. Bakeless, *Turncoats, Traitors and Heroes*, 98.

Chapter 29: America's Defender

1. Michael Pearson, *Those Damned Rebels: The American Revolution as Seen through British Eyes* (New York: Putnam, 1972), 318.

2. Proclamation of John Burgoyne, June 23, 1777, in *The Spirit of Seventy-Six*, 547.

3. W. Stewart Wallace, *The United Empire Loyalist: A Chronicle of the Great Migration* (1914), 11.

4. After the Battle of King's Mountain, thirty-nine Loyalists were condemned to death. Nine were executed on the spot for being "the most noted horsethieves and Tories" of North Carolina and the rest were pardoned. Robert Stansbury Lambert, *South Carolina Loyalists in the American Revolution* (Columbia: University of South Carolina Press, 1987), 102.

5. Kettner, "The Development of American Citizenship in the Revolutionary Era," 217.

6. North Carolina patriot, qtd. in Wallace, *The United Empire Loyalists*, 11.

7. Kettner, "The Development of American Citizenship in the Revolutionary Era," 217.

8. *Journals of the Continental Congress*, June 18, 1776, 5:464.

9. Washington to Colonel Israel Shreve, April 4, 1778, in *The Papers of George Washington, Revolutionary War Series*, 14:408.

10. Don Higginbotham, *George Washington: Uniting a Nation* (Lanham, Md.: Rowman & Littlefield, 2002), 55–56.

11. Ibid.

12. Judith L. Van Buskirk, *Generous Enemies: Patriots and Loyalists in Revolutionary New York* (Philadelphia: University of Pennsylvania Press, 2002), 114.

13. Washington to Andrew Elliot, December 1, 1783, in *The Writings of George Washington*, 27:253.

14. Ibid.

15. Washington to Jonathan Trumbull, Sr., November 15, 1775, in *The Papers of George Washington, Revolutionary War Series*, 2:379.

16. Washington Irving, *George Washington: A Biography*, ed. and abridged by Charles Neider (1976; Cambridge, Mass.: Da Capo Press, 1994), 201.

17. Ibid.

18. General Orders, October 12, 1777, in *The Papers of George Washington, Revolutionary War Series*, 11:490.

19. Harry S. Blain, "Who Stole the Shoes at Valley Forge: A Tragedy and a Vindication" (1966), 3.

20. John B. Trussell, Jr., *Epic on the Schuylkill: The Valley Forge Encampment* (Harrisburg: Pennsylvania Historical Commission, 1992), 27.

21. Blain, "Who Stole the Shoes at Valley Forge," 5.

22. Washington to a Board of General Officers, June 2, 1778, in *The Papers of George Washington, Revolutionary War Series*, 15:296.

23. Ibid.

24. General Orders, June 3, 1778, ibid., 15:305.

25. "The Hammer of Valley Forge," *Boy's Life Magazine*, March 1950, 52.

26. Washington likewise ordered that Thomas Lewis Woodward be tried by a commission, but he was freed since land records show

him purchasing land from his brother in 1782. Washington to Major General Israel Putnam, February 20, 1777, in *The Papers of George Washington, Revolutionary War Series*, 8:389.

Chapter 30: License to Plunder

1. Joseph Eggleston, Jr., to Joseph Eggleston, September 2, 1777, in *The Spirit of Seventy-Six*, 791. The modern-day prices are calculated using Professor Samuel H. Williamson's MeasuringWorth Consumer Price Index metrics.

2. George Eskridge is the ancestor of William Eskridge, Jr., the John A. Garver Professor of Jurisprudence at Yale Law School. Professor Eskridge was integral in formulating the idea for this book and making it a reality. I am tremendously grateful for his guidance and support.

3. Chernow, *Washington: A Life*, 6.

4. Ibid., 97.

5. Ibid., 158.

6. Washington Irving, *Life of George Washington*, 558, as qtd. in Chernow, *Washington: A Life*, 55.

7. Paula S. Felder, *Fielding Lewis and the Washington Family*, 295, as qtd. in Chernow, *Washington: A Life*, 423.

8. Washington to John Augustine Washington, January 16, 1783, in *The Writings of George Washington*, 26:44.

9. Chernow, *Washington: A Life*, 432.

10. Ibid., 396–97.

11. *The Spirit of Seventy-Six*, 793.

12. *Rivington's Royal Gazette*, May 12, 1781, in *The Spirit of Seventy-Six*, 795.

13. W. Stewart Wallace, *The United Empire Loyalists: A Chronicle of the Great Migration* (1914), 10.

14. Ibid.

15. James H. Stark, *The Loyalists of Massachusetts* (1907), 54. Modern equivalent comes from the MeasuringWorth Project's retail price index. Estimates vary widely.

16. Ibid.

17. Stark, *The Loyalists of Massachusetts*, 54.

18. Wallace, *The United Empire Loyalists*, 10.

19. *Journals of the Continental Congress*, November 27, 1777, 9:971.

20. Ibid.

21. Washington to Henry Laurens, June 2, 1778, in *The Papers of George Washington, Revolutionary War Series*, 15:303.

22. Glenn A. Phelps, "The Republican General," in *George Washington Reconsidered*, ed. Don Higginbotham (Charlottesville: University of Virginia Press, 2001), 185.

23. Washington to William Duer, January 14, 1777, in *The Papers of George Washington, Revolutionary War Series*, 8:63.

24. Washington to Matthew Irwin, February 22, 1777, in ibid, 8:412.

25. Friedrich Kapp, *The Life of John Kalb, Major-General in the Revolutionary Army* (1884), 139.

26. Washington to Henry Laurens, November 11, 1777, in *The Papers of George Washington, Revolutionary War Series*, 12:208–10.

27. Approximately $28 in modern U.S. dollars, according to MeasuringWorth.

28. Washington to Henry Laurens, December 23, 1777, in *The Papers of George Washington, Revolutionary War Series*, 12:683; *The Spirit of Seventy-Six*, 647.

29. Instructions to Colonel Benedict Arnold, September 14, 1775, in *The Papers of George Washington, Revolutionary War Series*, 1:458.

30. General Orders, January 21, 1777, in ibid., 8:119.

31. General Orders, September 6, 1776, in ibid., 6:229.

Notes

32.   Instructions to Colonel Benedict Arnold, September 14, 1775.

33.   Washington to Henry Laurens, November 11, 1777.

34.   General Orders, September 6, 1776. This paragraph is adapted from Logan Beirne, "George vs. George vs. George: Commander-in-Chief Power," *Yale Law and Policy Review* 26 (2007): 303.

35.   General Orders, March 21, 1776, in *The Papers of George Washington, Revolutionary War Series*, 3:501.

36.   Washington to Jonathan Sturges, May 16, 1776, in ibid., 4:321.

37.   Washington to John Hancock, September 25, 1776, in ibid., 6:399.

38.   Ibid.

39.   Ibid.

40.   Ibid.

41.   Chernow, *Washington: A Life*, 287.

42.   Bruce Chadwick, *The First American Army: The Untold Story of George Washington and the Men Behind America's First Fight for Freedom* (Naperville, Ill.: Sourcebooks, 2005), 249.

43.   Ibid.; Chernow, *Washington: A Life*, 287.

44.   General Orders, October 23, 1778, in *The Papers of George Washington, Revolutionary War Series*, 17:539.

45.   Ibid.

46.   *Journals of the Continental Congress*, September 17, 1777, 8:751.

47.   Washington to the Board of War, January 2–3, 1778, in *The Papers of George Washington, Revolutionary War Series*, 13:112.

48.   Washington to Henry Laurens, December 14[–15], 1777, in ibid., 12:606.

49.   Thomas Gordon, *A Gazetteer of the State of New Jersey* (1834), 100.

50.   Washington to Nathanael Greene, February 2, 1781, in *The Writings of George Washington*, 21:171–73.

51.   Joseph Reidy, "Washington Headquarters," Morristown National Historical Park (Morristown, N.J., 2008), 6.

52. John T. Cunningham, "Morristown: Worse Than Valley Forge," Washington Association of New Jersey (1979).

53. Instructions to Officers to Collect Provisions, January 8, 1780, in *The Writings of George Washington*, 17:360.

54. Ibid., 362.

55. Rather than make property seizure a purely military action, Washington was careful to involve the county magistrates, thus meeting the second criterion of his checklist. He reasoned that this would democratize the process and enable him to work with the local authorities to proceed in a manner that was "least inconvenient to the Inhabitants." Ibid. He could add a layer of protection for the citizenry and also diminish the perception that the military was undemocratically suspending their rights. While Washington was sensitive to civilian concerns, he did not leave the matter of requisitions completely to civilian discretion. He already had congressional approval, after all. He added to his order, "but in case the requisition should not be complied with, we must then raise the supplies ourselves in the best manner we can. This I have signified to the Magistrates." Ibid. In 1780, some of those local magistrates were indeed pushing back against the congressionally sanctioned impressment. Washington responded by commanding his men, "In case of [the magistrates'] refusal you will begin to impress till you make up the quantity required." Ibid.

56. Ibid., 360.

57. Washington to Colonel David Henley, November 25, 1778, in *The Papers of George Washington, Revolutionary War Series*, 18:292. In another example (excerpted from Beirne, "George v. George v. George," 308–9), Washington reasoned, "it being represented to me that the Millers, either from an unwillingness to part with their Flour, or the difficulty of obtaining Wheat from the Farmers, do not Imploy their Mills, by which means the Army under my Command is like to suffer for want of Bread." Faced with this crisis, and fighting to save the Continental Army, he handled the millers in a way that is telling: "I do hereby Authorize and Instruct [Carpenter Wharton] to enquire

into the State of this matter; with full powers if it should be found that the default is in the Miller, to Sieze [*sic*] the Mill and grain, and Imploy it for the use of the Public . . . paying the full Value . . . ." Rather than taking the grain to save his troops, he instead used a process that respected the miller's property and allowed for compensation. Orders to Carpenter Wharton, December 20, 1776, in *The Papers of George Washington, Revolutionary War Series*, 7:391. Also, see Washington to Major General John Armstrong, December 28, 1777, ibid., 13:28.

58. Washington to Colonel David Henley, November 25, 1778.

59. On one occasion, Washington's policy was put to the test by some pesky farmers. Washington complained that he was having a difficult time getting wheat from the farmers, which meant that his army was likely to "suffer for want of Bread." Orders to Carpenter Wharton, December 20, 1776. To remedy the infuriating situation, he ordered his troops to approach each farmer and "with full powers . . . to take his Grain for the Public Service." But he also ordered that each farmer be paid in full for any wheat taken. Ibid. Then Congress stepped in, and Washington took a harder line. After Congress directly authorized him to do so, he "issued a Proclamation ordering the Farmers to Thresh out their Wheat and prepare it for Mill, and that in case of Noncompliance within certain Periods, it shall be Siezed upon for the use of the Army and only paid for as Straw." Washington to Major General John Armstrong, December 28, 1777. This order seemingly violated the policy of just compensation, for straw was far less valuable than wheat, but Washington was not merely being a hypocrite, however; he proceeded because he was carrying out Congress's wishes. It was more acceptable for civil authorities to initiate such controversial action than the military.

60. Washington to Henry Laurens, December 14[–15], 1777.

Chapter 31: Not-So-Civil War

1. Based on a sketch from 1780. Benson J. Lossing's sketch likewise depicts Germain in a strange light. Other portraits are more flattering.

2. General Cornwallis to his brother, qtd. in Franklin B. Wickwire and Mary Wickwire, *Cornwallis: The American Adventure* (Boston: Houghton Mifflin, 1970), 115.

3. "The Battle of Camden," The American Revolutionary War, http://www.americanwars101.com/battles/800816.html.

4. Charles Lee to Horatio Gates, in *The Spirit of Seventy-Six*, 1124.

5. *The Spirit of Seventy-Six*, 1126.

6. Lord Germain to Royal Governor Sir James Wright, November 9, 1780.

7. *Journals of the Continental Congress*, October 5, 1780.

8. Washington to George Mason, October 22, 1780.

9. Colonel John Watson of the British Army, in *The Spirit of Seventy-Six*, 1169.

10. William S. Powell, *Dictionary of North Carolina Biography*, 5:160.

11. C. F. William Maurer, *Dragoon Diary: The History of the Third Continental Light Dragoons* (Bloomington: AuthorHouse, 2005), 299.

12. Memoirs of Captain Tarleton Brown, in *The Spirit of Seventy-Six*, 1147.

13. Nathanael Greene to Francis Marion, April 24, 1781, in ibid., 1173.

14. Nathanael Greene to Joseph Reed of Pennsylvania, January 9, 1781, in ibid., 1152.

15. Ibid., 1153.

16. *The Spirit of Seventy-Six*, 1160.

17. Major St. George Tucker of the Virginia militia to his wife, March 18, 1781, in ibid., 1166.

18. Alexander Hamilton, 1781, in ibid., 1160.

19. Ibid.

20. Charles James Fox, in Henry Lee, *Memoirs of the War in the Southern Department of the United States* (1827), 179.

21.   Washington to Major General Benedict Arnold, June 19, 1778, in *The Papers of George Washington, Revolutionary War Series*, 15:472. Although he sought to protect Loyalists, Washington was more inclined to give his troops' discretion the benefit of the doubt, such as when Major Ballard was faced with felony charges in New York for confiscating Loyalist property. Washington wrote to New York's governor that "the good of the service sometimes requires things to be done in the military line, which cannot be supported by the civil law." Washington to Governor George Clinton, December 13, 1779, in *The Writings of George Washington*, 17:252–53. Washington, however, made clear to Clinton that he would nevertheless not tolerate any confiscations where there were "appearances of oppression or fraud" or "spirit of plunder." Ibid., 17:253.

22.   Washington to Lieutenant General Thomas Gage, August 19, 1775, in *The Writings of George Washington, Revolutionary War Series*, 1:327.

23.   But see Thomas Shanks commission.

24.   Glenn A. Phelps, "The Republican General," in *George Washington Reconsidered*, ed. Don Higginbotham (Charlottesville: University of Virginia Press, 2001), 184.

25.   Logan Beirne, "George vs. George vs. George: Commander-in-Chief Power," *Yale Law and Policy Review* 26 (2007), 288.

26.   For example, see *Journals of the Continental Congress*, July 24, 1776, 5:605–6 (discussing congressional actions); Washington to John Hancock, January 30, 1776, in *The Papers of George Washington*, 1:214–21 (referencing confiscation by the state of New York).

27.   For further discussion of Washington's refusal to confiscate property or suspend habeas corpus, see Bruce Chadwick, *George Washington's War* (Naperville, Ill.: Sourcebooks, 2004), 227–30.

28.   Circular to the States, June 8, 1783, in *The Writings of George Washington*, 26:490.

29.   Washington's Farewell Address, September 19, 1796, in *The Writings of George Washington*, 35:222–23.

30. Thomas Jefferson to William Stephens Smith, November 13, 1787, in *The Papers of Thomas Jefferson*, Main Series, ed. Julian P. Boyd et al. (Charlottesville: University of Virginia Press, 1955–), 12:356.

Part VI: Could Have Been King

1. "Washington's Spectacles," *American Optical* (1918), courtesy of the Optical Heritage Museum.

2. Rudolph Marx, M.D., "The Health of the President: George Washington," *Health Guidance*, June 15, 2008.

3. David Fleishman, "Optical Treasures: Missing-Stolen," Antique Spectacles, http://www.antiquespectacles.com/treasures/stolen. htm.Many thanks to David Fleishman for his help in learning more about Washington's elusive spectacles.

4. Ibid.

5. While these glasses were believed to be Washington's, there is no way to verify whether they were definitely his. Nor is there any way to verify whether they were the same ones he wore at Newburgh in 1783, but this passage is more concerned with their symbolism as a reminder of Washington's actions. Ibid.

Chapter 32: O God! It Is All Over!

1. *Proceedings of the town of Charlestown, in the county of Middlesex, and Commonwealth of Massachusetts; in Respectful Testimony of the Distinguished Talents and Prominent Virtues of the Late George Washington*, ed. Samuel Etheridge (1800), 62.

2. Ibid., 61, quoting a letter from John Bell, Esq. to a friend in Europe "during an early period of the American Revolution," from *Massachusetts Magazine*, 1791.

3. The Memoirs of Lafayette, in *The Spirit of Seventy-Six*, 1208.

4. Journal of Dr. James Thacher, August 15, 1781, in ibid., 1215.

5. Chernow, *Washington: A Life*, 407.

6. Ibid.

7. Ibid., 1214.

8. Washington Irving, *Life of George Washington*, 4:843.

9. Washington to Lafayette, September 2, 1781, in *The Spirit of Seventy-Six,* 1217.

10. *The Spirit of Seventy-Six*, 1219.

11. Sir Henry Clinton, *The American Rebellion*, in ibid., 1222.

12. General George Weedon to Nathanael Greene, September 5, 1781, in ibid., 1218.

13. Colonel St. George Tucker to his wife, September 15, 1781, in ibid., 1224.

14. Ibid.

15. Journal of Dr. James Thacher, in ibid., 1233.

16. Ibid., 1232.

17. Lieutenant Colonel Banastre Tarleton, "History of Campaigns in the Southern Provinces," in ibid., 1236.

18. Lord Cornwallis to Sir Henry Clinton, October 20, 1781, in ibid., 1237.

19. Washington to Cornwallis, October 17, 1781, in ibid., 1239.

20. Ibid.

21. Journal of Dr. James Thacher, October 19, 1781, in ibid., 1243.

22. Memoirs of Sir Nathaniel Wraxall, November 1781, in ibid., 1243–44.

Chapter 33: Winning the Peace

1. Piers Mackesy, *The War for America, 1775–1783* (Lincoln: University of Nebraska Press, 1993), 213.

2. *The Spirit of Seventy-Six*, 1276.

3. Ibid.

4. Sir George Otto Trevelyan, *George the Third and Charles Fox: The Concluding Part of the American Revolution* (1912), 1:5.

5. Draft Message from the King, March 1782, in *The Spirit of Seventy-Six*, 1281–82.

6. King George III is believed to have had porphyria, a genetic disease. T. M. Cox, N. Jack, S. Lofthouse, J. Watling, J. Haines, M. J.

Warren, "King George III and Porphyria: An Elemental Hypothesis and Investigation," *Lancet* 366 (2005): 332–35.

7. *The Spirit of Seventy-Six*, 1277.

8. Henry Laurens was named as the fourth commissioner, but he was "strangely dilatory in joining his fellow commissioners" and played less of a role in the main discussions. *The Spirit of Seventy-Six*, 1249.

9. Ibid., 1250.

10. John Jay to Robert R. Livingston, November 17, 1782, in ibid., 1265.

11. Ibid., 1250.

12. Ibid., 1261.

13. Ibid., 1250.

14. Ibid.

15. Thomas Rodney to Caesar Rodney, June 15, 1781, in ibid., 1251.

16. Statement of Chevalier de la Luzern, May 28, 1781, in *Journals of the Continental Congress*, 20:562n.

17. John Adams to Robert R. Livingston, September 6, 1782, in *The Diplomatic Correspondence of the American Revolution*, ed. Jared Sparks (Boston, 1829–1830), 6:401.

18. Decoded letter from John Jay to Gouverneur Morris, October 13, 1782, in *The Spirit of Seventy-Six*, 1263.

19. Edmond Fitzmaurice, *Life of William, Earl of Shelburne* (1876), 267.

20. *The Spirit of Seventy-Six*, 1270.

21. Comte de Vergennes to Benjamin Franklin, December 15, 1782, in *The Papers of Benjamin Franklin*, ed. William B. Wilcox (New Haven: Yale University Press, 1983), 38:405.

22. Benjamin Franklin to Comte de Vergennes, December 17, 1782, in ibid., 38:416–17.

23. Ibid.

24. Ibid.

25. Ibid.
26. Ibid.

Chapter 34: Spectacles & Speculation

1. *The Spirit of Seventy-Six*, 1249.
2. Washington to Nathanael Greene, August 6, 1782, in *The Writings of George Washington*, 24:472.
3. Washington to James McHenry, September 12, 1782, in ibid., 25:152.
4. Joseph J. Ellis, *His Excellency: George Washington* (New York: Knopf, 2004), 138.
5. Ibid., 138–39.
6. Washington Irving, *Life of George Washington*, 4:400.
7. George L. Marshall, Jr., "The Rise and Fall of the Newburgh Conspiracy: How General Washington and His Spectacles Saved the Republic," *Early America Review*, Fall 1997.
8. Robert F. Haggard, "The Nicola Affair: Lewis Nicola, George Washington, and American Military Discontent during the Revolutionary War," *Proceedings of the American Philosophical Society* 146 no. 2 (June 2002): 139–69.
9. Lewis Nicola to Washington, May 22, 1782, in George Washington Papers, Manuscript Division, Library of Congress.
10. Ibid.
11. Ibid.
12. For example, see Irving, *Life of George Washington*, 4:402; Thacher, *Military Journal of the American Revolution*, 509.
13. Washington to Colonel Lewis Nicola, May 22, 1782, in *The Writings of George Washington*, 24:273.
14. Ibid., 274.
15. Chernow, *Washington: A Life*, 428.
16. Henry Knox to Benjamin Lincoln, March 3, 1783, in Francis Samuel Drake, *Life and Correspondence of Henry Knox* (1873), 79–80.

17. Alexander Hamilton to Washington, February 13, 1783, in *The Papers of Alexander Hamilton*, 3:254.

18. *Journals of the Continental Congress*, April 29, 1783, 24:297, 307. The second quotation is based on Washington's address from March 15, 1783.

19. *Journals of the Continental Congress*, April 29, 1783, 24:296.

20. Marshall, "The Rise and Fall of the Newburgh Conspiracy."

21. Washington to Alexander Hamilton, March 12, 1783, in *The Papers of Alexander Hamilton*, 3:287.

22. Washington to Governor Benjamin Harrison, March 19, 1783, in *The Writings of George Washington*, 26:240.

23. Thomas Fleming, "Unlikely Victory," in *What If? The World's Foremost Historians Imagine What Might Have Been*, ed. Robert Cowley (New York: Berkley Books, 2000), 155–88.

24. Washington to Governor Benjamin Harrison, March 19, 1783, 241.

25. Marshall, "The Rise and Fall of the Newburgh Conspiracy."

26. *Journals of the Continental Congress*, April 29, 1783, 24:296.

27. Chernow, *Washington: A Life*, 434. Chernow provides a great depiction of this scene.

28. Washington to Elias Boudinot, March 18, 1783, in *The Writings of George Washington*, 26:229n.

29. Chernow, *Washington: A Life*, 434.

30. *Journals of the Continental Congress*, April 29, 1783, 24:307–8.

31. Ibid.

32. Ibid., 309–10.

33. Irving, *Life of George Washington*, 4:415.

34. James Thomas Flexner, *Washington: The Indispensable Man* (Boston: Little, Brown, 1974), 175.

35. Washington to Tench Tilghman, January 10, 1783, in *The Writings of George Washington*, 16:28.

36. Washington to David Rittenhouse, February 16, 1783, in *The Writings of George Washington*, 25:138.

37. Douglas Southall Freeman, *George Washington: A Biography* (1948–57), 5:435.

38. Samuel Shaw, *The Journals of Major Samuel Shaw* (1847), 104.

Chapter 35: Greatest Man in the World

1. Stanley Weintraub, *General Washington's Christmas Farewell: A Mount Vernon Homecoming* (New York: Free Press, 2003), 107.

2. James R. Gaines, *For Liberty and Glory: Washington, Lafayette, and Their Revolutions* (New York: Norton, 2007), 150.

3. Page Smith, *A New Age Now Begins: A People's History of the American Revolution* (New York: Penguin, 1989), 1788.

4. Memoirs of Colonel Benjamin Tallmadge (1830).

5. Ibid.

6. Ibid.

7. Ibid.

8. Ibid.

9. John Trumbull to his brother, May 10, 1784, qtd. in Gordon S. Wood, *Revolutionary Characters: What Made the Founders Different* (New York: Penguin, 2006), 42.

10. Gerard Vogels to his Wife, in *The Papers of George Washington, Confederation Series*, 1:195n.

11. Qtd. in *George Washington as the French Knew Him*, ed. Gilbert Chinard (New York: Greenwood Press, 1969), 69.

12. Ibid., 196.

13. *Proceedings of the town of Charlestown, in the county of Middlesex, and Commonwealth of Massachusetts; in Respectful Testimony of the Distinguished Talents and Prominent Virtues of the Late George Washington*, ed. Samuel Etheridge (1800), 61.

14. Ibid., 35.

15. Ibid.

16. Chernow, *Washington: A Life*, 453.

17. Ibid., 455.

18. Ibid., 456.

19. Washington's Address to Congress on Resigning His Commission, December 23, 1783, in *The Writings of George Washington*, 27:285.

20. James Thomas Flexner, *George Washington in the American Revolution, 1775–1783* (Boston: Little, Brown, 1968), 526.

21. Washington's Address to Congress on Resigning His Commission, 286.

22. *Proceedings of the town of Charlestown*, 63.

23. Washington to Henry Knox, February 20, 1784, in *The Papers of George Washington, Confederation Series*, 1:138.

24. Which brings us full circle back to Part I.

25. John Marshall, *The Life of George Washington*, ed. Robert Faulkner and Paul Carrese (1838; Indianapolis: Liberty Fund, 2000), 84.

26. Gordon S. Wood, *The Radicalism of the American Revolution* (New York: Knopf, 1991), 206. Wood writes, "Though it was widely thought that Washington could have become king or dictator, he wanted nothing of the kind."

27. This occurred after eleven states ratified, since only nine were required for the Constitution to go into effect. North Carolina and Rhode Island were the last two states to ratify the Constitution, and did so after it went into operation.

28. Virginia utilized direct election, of which Washington received 100 percent, and the other states sent delegates. Each delegate had two votes to cast. Every delegate voted for Washington with his first vote, and then used his second vote to decide among eleven candidates for the vice presidency.

29. Carol Borchert Cadou, *George Washington Collection: Fine and Decorative Arts at Mount Vernon* (Manchester, Vt.: Hudson Hills Press, 2006), 215.

30. Ibid.

31. *Proceedings of the town of Charlestown*, 62.

Epilogue

1. "How to Read the Constitution," Excerpt from Justice Thomas's Wriston Lecture to the Manhattan Institute, *Wall Street Journal*, October 20, 2008, A19.

2. William Eskridge and John Ferejohn, *The Republic of Statutes: The New American Constitution* (New Haven: Yale University Press, 2010), 439.

3. Justices Stevens and Souter have since retired and been replaced by Justices Kagan and Sotomayor.

4. *C-Span Weekend*, C-Span television, March 19, 2006, comments of William Galston, former Deputy Domestic Policy Advisor to President Clinton, 1993–95. "Both the Supreme Court and leading academics have come to accept that evidence of the original understanding of the Constitution is relevant to any discussion of the document's meaning." John Yoo, *The Powers of War and Peace: The Constitution and Foreign Affairs After 9/11* (Chicago: University of Chicago Press, 2005), 25. For example, see Michael Glennon, *Constitutional Diplomacy*, 1st ed. (Princeton: Princeton University Press, 1990); Louis Henkin, *Foreign Affairs and the U.S. Constitution*, 2nd ed. (New York: Oxford University Press, 1996); Harold Koh, *National Security Constitution*, 1st ed. (New Haven: Yale University Press, 1990).

5. Associate Justice Antonin Scalia, in a speech before Princeton University's conference "A Constitution for the Ages: James Madison the Framer," February 23, 2001.

6. Ibid.

7. "Even for non-originalists, the Founders' unparalleled experience in applied constitutional thought, along with their not inconsiderable acumen, gives their views a certain persuasive, perhaps even presumptive, authority." Martin S. Flaherty, "Historical Perspective: More Apparent Than Real: The Revolutionary Commitment to Constitutional Federalism," Symposium Papers—Federalism in the 21st Century, *Kansas Law Review* 45 (July 1997): 1006. See also Wil-

liam M. Treanor, "The Original Understanding of the Takings Clause and the Political Process," *Columbia Law Review* 49 (1995): 859.

8.   It is important to note that this study does not take into account the political, moral or other considerations that may be necessary in fully evaluating some of these controversial issues.

9.   Jack Rakove, *Original Meanings: Politics and Ideas in the Making of the Constitution* (New York: Knopf, 1996), 8.

10.   Yoo, *The Powers of War and Peace*, 28.

11.   As addressed in Part VI.

12.   As addressed in Part I.

13.   Circular to the States, June 8, 1783, in *The Writings of George Washington*, 26:486.

INDEX

Adams, Abigail, 130
Adams, John, 102–3, 130, 140;
    on army's plight, 109;
    on Baltimore, 141; on
    Loyalists, 241; monarchy
    fears, 170; on New York
    defense, 108; at peace
    negotiations, 291–94; on
    Philadelphia, 168, 170; on
    smallpox, 109; at Staten
    Island talks, 119–21; on
    Washington's powers, 148,
    165
Alito, Samuel, 315
Allen, Ethan, 66–70; and Fort
    Ticonderoga, 67–68;
    Montreal attack, 68–69,
    162; as prisoner, 69–70,
    72; and Schuyler, 185; in
    Vermont, 67

André, John, 178, 202–4; and
    Arnold's plot, 205–8;
    capture of, 209–10; and
    Honora Sneyd, 203–4; in
    Philadelphia, 204; and
    Smith trial, 219–20; trial &
    execution of, 221–27
Aristotle, 238
Arnold, Benedict, 178, 183,
    189–91; and André's trial,
    222–27; betrayal plot, 199,
    201–2, 205–8; corruption
    trial, 198–99; escape of,
    210–11; financial schemes
    of, 197–98; and Gates, 185–
    86; grievances of, 190–91,
    198–99; injuries of, 190–91,
    196, 199; as merchant, 190;
    and Peggy Shippen, 196–
    97, 206; in Philadelphia,

Morocco, 132
Morse, Jedidiah, 311
Mount Vernon, 17, 24, 162, 305, 309
Murray, Mary, 129–30
muskets, 125–27

Native Americans: British appeasement of, 51–52; as British / Loyalist allies, 183, 231–33; in Jumonville Affair, 3–6; as noncitizens, 240, 241; torture by, 230, 236, 279; vengeance against, 235–37; on Washington's invulnerability, 158
Netherlands, 15, 95
Newburgh (N.Y.) conspiracy, 299–303
New Hampshire, 233–34
New Jersey, 16, 136, 269; Monmouth battle, 192, 193–95; Morristown, 159, 268–70; Princeton battle, 157–59, 160; Toms River attack, 92–93; Trenton battle, 151–56
New York: and army provisions, 263; civil war in, 208; Hudson Valley, 180–87, 200–1; and Loyalist property, 262; military

conspiracy in, 299–303; plot against Washington, 245–47; and "torture tree," 235–37, 278–79; trade wars in, 331–32; see also New York Provincial Congress
New York City, 284, 296; Brooklyn battle, 74, 76–78, 108, 156–58; Clinton in, 181–82, 186–87, 269, 285, 286; Continental Army in, 104–5; defense efforts, 73–74, 108–14, 117–19, 121; Federal Hall in, 100–1; Hickey hanging in, 249–50; Howe's quarters in, 137–38, 140, 159; Manhattan attack, 121–27; retreat from, 127–29, 133–34, 135–36; September 11 attack, 100–1; victory in, 304–5; Washington's farewell in, 305–6; Washington's ruse on, 285–86; see also Manhattan
New York Provincial Congress: on dictatorial powers, 171; on inoculation, 110, 111; and Mathews arrest, 250, 252; and plot against Washington, 245–47; on tar & feathering, 243
Nicola, Lewis, 297–99